Attention Authors

Manas Publications is fighting a war to tell the world that India can win the battle not only by bullet but also by pen. We are converting fighters into writers since our country is full of intellectuals but their knowledge is only confined to them. No sincere effort has been made by any publisher to give the right direction to their knowledge and the talent of intellectual is still hidden. An author always gives the raw material in the shape of manuscript and it is the sense of publisher to make it a finished product. We are motivating the intellectuals' mind and publishing their manuscripts for more than two decades and would like to publish your manuscript too. If you or your colleagues have any manuscript or are working on, please don't hesitate to contact us with detailed synopsis and contents for its publication. We take utmost care in production and give a wide publicity to the book and its author. We can also suggest you the title for writing related to your subject, since we are the publishers who believe more in quality than in quantity.

Sports, Games and Adventure Sports

(An unique collection of 70 disciplines)

Sports, Games and Adventure Sports

(An unique collection of 70 disciplines)

Air Commodore (Dr) C N Ghosh

Manas Publications
New Delhi-110002 (INDIA)

MANAS PUBLICATIONS
(Publishers, Distributors, Importers & Exporters)
4402/5A, Main Ansari Road
(Adjacent Bank of Baroda)
Darya Ganj, New Delhi-110 002 (INDIA)
Off. ✆ 23260783, 23265523, Res. ✆ 23842660
Fax: 011-23272766
E-mail: manaspublications@vsnl.com

ISBN 978-81-7049-309-9
Rs. 795/-

Typeset by
Manas Publications

Printed in India by
Sri Ganesh Enterprise, Delhi
and Published by Mrs Suman Lata for
Manas Publications, 4402/5A, Main Ansari Road
(Adjacent Bank of Baroda)
Darya Ganj, New Delhi-110 002 (INDIA)

Dedicated to

Tuhin, Surochita

&

Nilabh, Monami

Disclaimer

The author and the publisher assume no responsibility or liability for any injury, loss or damage incurred as a result of any use or reliance upon the information and material contained within the book ***Sports Games and Adventure Sports***.

The author and publisher have taken considerable care in preparing information and materials which are displayed in the entire book ***Sports Games And Adventure Sports***. However, the author and the publisher are unable to provide any warranty concerning the accuracy or completeness of any information contained herein.

Contents

Preface

Information Technology has created a virtual world around us especially related to sports. We can recall any activity on the ground and review it as and when we desire. Technology enables a viewer to gaze into the mindset of the match winner. Thanks to the media explosion the head butt of Zidane, too, could never go unnoticed. You browse the Internet and you get an avalanche of information. Present TV viewers are inundated with past shots, statistics and track records of veteran players as the proceedings on the ground gain momentum. One has to be quick to synthesize the info or you are left behind. But the dilemma—how and at what rate—remains ingrained. Unless of course you are a living, breathing encyclopedia of the sporting world.

No sports book of the current generation has tried to pay attention to this serious anomaly. You watch a game or adventure sports on the television, which is as common as the hip swinging beauties of the Hindi films. But how do we understand the dare devil acts? It looks thrilling but pangs of preparation along a predetermined route are left out clearly for only the specialists to understand and take care of.

No doubt Internet is a good source, but it has its own limitations. Collection, collation and assimilation of cyberspace info is not easy. Reading through multiple electronic pages is painful. That is where the necessity of a sports reference book arose. This kind of book is needed badly for easy reference at least to understand the nuances of the game and to follow the proceedings intimately. Preset knowledge is a must. No televised game will wait for you to appreciate its technicalities as the thrill of the game is over once the result is known.

I conceived the book a long time ago. But unfortunately due to my present illness I could not carry on with the work. It required many hours of hard work for compilation and getting the right kind of illustrations. Internet resources are fairly miserly. You may read them and view them but cannot use them. Every info or a photograph is Copy Righted. One has to pay as you go by. The only alternative is to buy the info from the market as has been done in this book. All illustrations and photographs have been procured from open sources. Long hours of personal guidance were needed for the formatting of the book. The operators like Bhupinder Talan worked on Page Maker or Quark like software incessantly, to give the collected and synthesized info the shape of a book. Diligence won and finally we completed such collation and you are presented with a unique collection. Enjoy the book and refer it as and when needed.

I am grateful to my wife Rupa Ghosh for being with me at my hospital be side or at the computer and for encouraging me to complete this mammoth task. Without her support it would have been almost impossible for a cancer patient to compile a book with fifty-seven Sports and Games disciplines and thirteen Adventure sports.

I would like to express my heartfelt gratitude to my comrade in arms and bosom friend Air Vice Marshall Amal Sen. He has been a constant emotional source of sustenance during my sickness. He has also been a great friend, philosopher and guide and has truly motivated me to undertake and complete this Herculean task.

Last but not the least I will remain forever indebted to Sanjeev Malhotra for providing me with the necessary infrastructural support for days together. Without his help this book would never have seen the light of the day.

Lance Armstrong, a lung cancer patient, championed Tour de France by winning it seven times. I took a clue from this great sports person to carry on.

■

AEROBICS

Chapter - 1

Graceful athletic activity where you dance to the tune and achieve synchronization of body and mind

The word "Aerobics" was coined by Kenneth H. Cooper, a physician at the San Antonio Air Force hospital in Texas. He invented a set of exercises to prevent coronary artery disease. He published his book on Aerobics in 1968. Following this development Jackie Sorenson developed a series of dance routines to improve cardiovascular fitness. The Next two decades saw a rapid acceptance of Aerobics in the USA and in many other countries.

In 1983 Sportaerobics was organized by Howard and Karen Schwasrtz, who established the Sport Fitness International (SFI). The first championship in Aerobics was conducted by SFI in the very next year. In 1989, the International Aerobatics Federation (ICAF) was formed and the first world championships were held at San Diego in March 1990 with athletes from 15 countries. The ICAF has now become the Association of National Aerobics Championship with membership from 38 countries.

Sportaerobics began competitions in four categories: individual male and female, mixed pairs, and trio which include any three athletes. In the year 2002, the competition included groups of six athletes. Competitors are judged on a one minute and 45 seconds routine set to music. They are judged on two basic criteria: artistic merit and technical talents, with a maximum of 10 points each.

The Federation of International Gymnastics held its first world championships in 1995 and formally accepted Sportaerobics as a gymnastics discipline in 1996.

Entry Criteria

- Athletes must be 18 years old and be citizens or permanent residents of a country participating in the championships.
- Athletes must abide by the eligibility rules of the ANAC and those of the athlete's national member affiliate federation.
- Athletes are entered into international and world-class events through the ANAC member affiliate federation. Each national federation is responsible for certifying the eligibility of athletes from its country.

Competition Information

- Competition Floor Size:20 x 20 square feet (6.1m x 6.1m) for local and regional events, 23x23 square feet (7m x 7m) for national and international events.
- Competition Music Length: One minute forty-five seconds (1:45) Grace=+/-5 sec.

Competitor Dress Code-Rules

Medium or long hair must be secured close to the head. Body oil, paint, or glitter is prohibited. Use of props, theatrical hair accessories and jewelry is prohibited. Aerobic shoes and supportive undergarments are required. Private body-parts must be concealed.

Male: Athletic tops, form fitting shorts or unitards. The top may not have an open cut in the front and/or back and armhole not below the ribcage.

Female: One piece leotard and flesh colored tights. The leotard may have an open cut in the front and/or back, however, the top and bottom must come together with material a minimum of two inches in width. The leotard must pass through the crest of the ileum and not be cut higher than the waist. G-string leotards are prohibited.

Compulsory Exercise Requirements

(Compulsory exercises are mandatory within a competitive routine).

- Four consecutive repetitions of high leg kicks performed "side-on" to the Judge.
- A jumping jack phrase consisting of 32 counts of standing, rebound aerobic movements and patterns beginning with the performance of four jumping jacks.

- Four consecutive push-ups performed "side-on" to the Judges (only for Class II and Masters Divisions).

Compulsories may be performed at any time during the routine. All competition divisions may select compulsories listed in value from A=1 through F=6.

Rules and Requirements specific to Alternating High Leg Kicks

- Start/finish position: Both feet on the floor.
- Kicks must be performed in the sagittal plane: Straight forward from the body.
- Kicks must alternate: L,R,L,R or R,L,R,L
- Kicks must be minimum waist height. A variety of arm movements and/or arm positions are acceptable.

Rules and Requirements specific to Push-Ups:

- Start/finish position is with the elbows extended. A minimum 90 degree angle must be formed at the elbow joint.
- Hands must remain in contact with the floor.
- Any variation of leg movement is permitted provided one foot remains in contact with the floor.

Judging and Scoring

- Total Maximum Score 10 points.
- Judging Panel for local/regional events: 3 Technical Merit, 3 Artistic Merit, 1 Difficulty and 1 Head Judge.
- Judging Panel for national/international events: 4 Technical Merit, 4 Artistic Merit, 2 Difficulty, 1 Head Judge and 2 Line Judges.
- Technical Merit Scoring Criteria (45% of Total Score): Execution, Intensity, Balance of Strength and Flexibility, Coordination.
- Artistic Merit Scoring Criteria (45% of Total Score): Choreography, Musicality, Showmanship, and Sports aerobics content.
- Difficulty scoring criteria (10% of Total score): Competitors must select elements from the current Element Pool list. A maximum

of ten elements are allowed. Elements are listed in value as: Free=no difficult value, A=.1, B=.2, C=.3, D=.4, E=.5 and F=.6. A minimum of one element (free or valued) from each of the four (4) families is required. The four families are explained below:

- Dynamic Strength (Push-Ups)
- Static Strength (Supports and Balances)
- Kicks and Splits
- Power (Jumps and Leaps)

a) A maximum of two airborne or standing to push-up landing movements and two airborne to split landing movements are allowed.

b) The compulsories, alternating high leg kicks, jumping jack phrase and push-ups (when applicable) are not included in the maximum of ten elements allowed, and do not satisfy the requirement to perform a minimum of one element from each family. Free elements do not contribute to the difficulty score, or count as one of the maximum ten elements allowed. Use of a free element will satisfy the requirement for a minimum of one element from each skill family.

c) Criteria for receiving difficulty value: "Recognizability" of an element, minimum competency of an element, and satisfying the minimum time required to hold Static Strength and Static Balance elements—two seconds at the top of the move.

d) Prior to the competition, competitors are required to submit a routine documentation form that lists the elements and compulsories contained in their routine by order of appearance. During documentation, competitors are required to perform their routines before the Head Judge and Difficulty Judge at which time the competitor's difficulty score is determined.

e) Start/Finish of a Routine: Competitors may use static strength or static balance elements for beginning and end poses without having them count as one of the maximum number of elements allowed. However, to receive difficulty value for a Static Strength or Static Balance element, competitors must maintain the beginning and/or end pose for two seconds after the music starts or before the music ends.

f) Mixed Pairs and Trios: Execution standards are assessed at the level of the lowest competitor. Elements must be performed in unison, simultaneously, or in a staggered consecutive "peel-off". A staggered element performed consecutively will receive difficulty value as a single element. Choreographed physical contact or linking will not receive difficulty value. Choreographed physical contact or linking during compulsories is prohibited.

g) Partner lifts and/or supports will be counted as free elements. Mixed Pairs and Trios are limited to a maximum of four partner lifts/supports, including the beginning and ending lifts. The support partner(s) must maintain a floor position with a part of their body in contact with the floor other than, or in addition to their hands and feet (kneeling, sitting, lying). Partners may not propel or pass one member to another, or propel themselves to another member or position. Partner lifts from a standing position are only allowed as a final pose.

Prohibited Movement List

Following is the list of prohibited movements:

- Standing turns greater than two revolutions
- Floor turns on knees or neck for one or more revolutions
- Front and Back Handsprings
- Backflip
- Handstand
- Standing, Sagittal or Frontal Balance Drop split
- Sag Ring
- Ring Balance
- Backbend
- Toe Hinge and Toe Hinge Spin
- Saltos
- Butterfly
- Cartwheel
- Aerial somersault and/or Dive Roll
- Ring Jump
- Bridge
- Kip
- Front and Back Walkover

Competition Divisions (Certain divisions may not be offered in every country).

USNAC Club Cup Challenge: The Club Cup Challenge is an entry-level competition for individual competitors and health clubs. Led by aerobics instructors, this event requires no prior preparation or training. For specific Club Cup Challenge Rules you have to contact ANAC.

Youth A competition for children and teens—ages 7 to 17. Junior=7-10, Junior Varsity=11-13, and Varsity=14-17.

Class I: The class I division offers competition in the categories of Men, Women, Mixed Pairs, and Trios. Competitors may select elements ranging in difficulty value from A=.1 to F=.6

Class II: The class II division offers competition for individual men and women requiring a lower degree of difficulty than Class I routines. Competitors may only choose from A=.1, B=.2, and a maximum of four (4) C=.3 elements from the element pool list.

Masters: The Masters Division is for individual men and women 35 years of age or older by the day of the competition. Competitors may only choose from A=.1, B=.2 and a maximum of C=.3 elements from the element pool list.

■

ATHLETICS

Chapter - 2

A combination of many sporting events like running, jumping, relay races, hurdles and throwing of javelin, discus, shot put and hammer.

History

The sport is governed by the IAAF today and operates in close cooperation with the International Olympic Committee. However, running is the earliest known Olympic sport and Athletics can be traced back to ancient Greek Olympics in the 13th century B.C. The first winner of a race in the earliest recorded Olympics in 776 BC was a sprinter named Coriobos. Originally races were run over a length of the stadium which was about 200 yds. Throwing and jumping may have been introduced later.

Like in many games England has been in the forefront for the development of athletics. In England, there are evidences of athletics in about 1154 AD. The first organised competitions were held at the Royal Military Academy, Woolwich, London, in 1849. The first modern track and field meet in the world took place in 1864, when Oxford and Cambridge Universities competed against each other. And it was in 1880, that Amateur Athletic Association was founded in England.

Hurdle Race

First evidence of athletics in America was in 1868, when the New York Athletic Club held a full-scale championship. And it was in 1896, during the first Modern Olympic Games in Athens, USA, UK, Sweden, Switzerland, Denmark, Germany, France, Greece and Hungary participated in athletics.

Following the growth and increase in interest, on 7 July, 1912, the International Amateur Athletic Federation (IAAF) was formed by the 17 nations, which participated in the athletic events in the Olympic Games at Stockholm.

In Asia, the Far-Eastern Athletic Championships were held in Manila in 1913. The first West Asiatic Games were held in New Delhi and finally the Asian Games Federation was founded in 1948, and the first Asiad was held in New Delhi in 1951. Growing popularity of the sports in Asia has also led to meets like South-East Asian Peninsular Games, South Asian Federation Games and Asian track and field championships.

EVENTS

Track Races

Sprints	*Middle distance*	*Long distance*
100 m	800 m	5000 m
200 m	1500 m	10000 m
400 m		
Relays	*Hurdles*	*Steeplechase*
4 × 100 m	100 m	3000 m
4 × 400 m	110 m	

Road Races

Marathon
Walks
20 km
50 km

Throwing Events

Javelin
Discus
Hammer
Shot Put

Jumping Events

Long Jump
Triple Jump
High Jump
Pole Vault

Combined Events

Heptathlon
Decathlon

Arena

The modern competition arena has distinct running tracks, specific areas for jumping and throwing events. These tracks are synthetic, all-weather surfaces. Cinder tracks are also in vogue.

Clothing and Shoes

Clothing: The competitors are allowed to wear clean clothing made of a material which is non-transparent even if wet. They must prominently display two numbers which must be worn on the breast and back except in pole vault and high jump events. In these events only one number is worn on the breast or back.

Shoes: The competitors are allowed to compete barefoot or use footwear in one or both feet. The shoes used, however, must not be so made as to give the competitor any additional assistance. No spring or device of any kind may be used in these shoes. Not more than eleven spikes are allowed to be used in the sole and heel of the shoes.

Competition Officials

One (or more) Referee for Track Events
One (or more) Referee for Field Events
One Referee for events outside the Stadium
One Chief Judge and three (or more) Judges for Track Events
One Chief Judge and three (or more) Judges for Field Events
Four (or more) Umpires for Track Events
Three (or more) Time-keepers
One (or more) Starter
One (or more) Recaller
One (or more) Starter's Assistant or Marksman
One (or more) Lap Scorer
One (or more) Recorder
One (or more) Marshal
One (or more) Wind Gauge Operator
One Chief Photo finish Judge
Two Assistant Photo finish Judges

One (or more) Measurement Judge (Electronics)
Additional Officials
One (or more) Announcer
One Official Surveyor
One (or more) Doctor
Stewards for Competitors, Officials and Press.

TRACK EVENTS

Track

The length of a running track should not be less than 400 m. The track should be not less than 7.3 m in width. Where it is not possible to have a raised border for the inner edge of the running track, it should be marked with lines 50 mm in width. A grass track shall be flagged at intervals of 5 m.

Sydney Olympic Stadium

In international meeting, the track should allow for at least six lanes; however, for major tournaments, eight lanes must be provided.

The starts should be staggered so that the distance from start to finish shall be the same for each competitor.

The 800 metres event shall be run in lanes as far as the end of the first bend, using the maximum number of available lanes. As the runners are permitted to leave their respective lanes on entering the back straight, the starting position must be taken into consideration for two factors. First, the normal echelon allowance which would be applicable were the race to be 200 m starting at the same point on

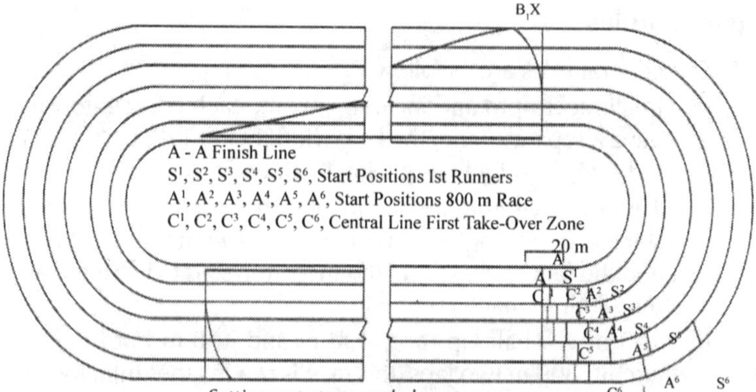

Setting out starts and change over areas

the track, secondly an adjustment to the starting point in each lane to compensate position on the track at the end of the back straight than those in the inside lane.

The following method of arriving at the starting position in each lane is recommended:

(a) Mark B_1 in the inside lane at the point of entry into the back straight 0.30 m from the inside kerb.

(b) Fix point *Y*, which is the point in the outer lane in prolonging of the line AB_1, 0.20 m from the inner line in the lane.

(c) Fix point *C*, which is the point on the path of the runner, namely 0.30 m from the inside kerb at which the back straight ends and the bend begins.

(d) With radius CB_1 describe an arc across the track B_1X. This line must be flagged at each end with a flag set on a post at least 1.50 m high on each side of the track and with a line 50 mm wide across the track. This indicates to the runners that they may leave their lanes at this stage.

For lanes 2 to 6 this point can be determined by the intersection of BIX and the path of the runner, which is 0.20 m from the line marking the inside of his lane.

(e) The correct adjustment to the starting positions can now be determined in the following way:

The normal starting position in each lane for 200 m race must be advanced by the distance the points of denouement from the lanes, viz B_2 B_3 B_4 B_5 B_6.

General Rules

1. The general rules are as follows:
   (a) In all races upto and incluing 400 m, each competitor shall have a separate lane, the lane width being 1.22 m to 1.25 m to be marked by lines having 5 cm width.
   (b) The track is 400 m per lap in all eight, resulting "staggered" starting points for the 200 m, 400 m, 400 m hurdles, 800 m and the four relays so that distance from start to finish remains the same for each competitor.
   (c) 200 m is a half lap race, 400 m and 400 m hurdles a full circuit, 800 m two laps (this race is run in lanes until the first bend is completed), 1500 m is 3¾ laps; 3000 m steeplechase is 7½ laps; 5000 m is 12½ laps and 10000 m is 25 laps.
   (d) **Starting**: The command for starting are "on your marks" (in the starter's mother tongue) and for races upto 400 m, "set", when all competitors are set, the pistol is fired. There is a pause between the call set and fire.
   (e) Each competitor is allowed one false start and one warning. He is disqualified for a second false start. However, if the start is generally a faulty one, then the starter may not fault any individual competitor.
   (f) **Finish:** Fully automatic timing equipment shall be used at all meets which is started automatically by the starter's gun or similar apparatus.

   The finish must be recorded through a camera with a vertical slit, on a continuous film for photo finish recording. The film must be synchronised with a uniformly marked time scale graduated in 1/100th of a second. The camera is positioned at the extension of the finish line.

   The winner is the one who reaches the near edge of the finish line with any part of his or her torso and not head or foot, arms and hands, etc.
   (g) **Timing:** The timing for races upto and 400 m is recorded to 1/100th of a second by electronic apparatus. The timings for races from 800 m to 1000 m are recorded to1/10th of a second. For the walks and the marathon the time is recorded to the whole second.
   (h) **Wind Factor:** No records will be allowed for races upto and inclusive of 200 m if the wind speed is over 2 m per second, i.e., 7.19 kmph.

100M Dash Florence Joyner

2. In all races upto and including 400 m each competitor shall have separate lanes.
3. In 4 × 400 m relay race, the first lap and upto exit from the first bend of the second lap will be run in separate lanes.
4. 800 m even shall be run in lanes as far as the end of the first bend. The starts are staggered so that each competitor completes the same distance.
5. In international meets the track should allow for eight lanes or at least six lanes.
6. Maximum allowance for lateral inclination of tracks shall not exceed 1:100 and the inclination in the running directions should not exced 1:1000.
7. For Olympics and other major games, the length of the track should not be less than 400 m and the width should allow for 8 lanes.

Hurdle Races

Hurdling in a rudimentary form took place in the first Steeplechase event in 1850. The first instance of 120 yards hurdles race was in the Oxford University sports in 1864. Sheep hurdles were used thus giving rise to the common usage of the word "Hurdling". In the four hurdle events there are ten flights of hurdles. The details of the hurdles are given as follows:

Distance of race	*Height of hurdles*	*Distance hurdles line*	*Distance between*	*Distance from last hurdle to finish*
		For men		
110	1.067	13.72	9.14	14.02
400	0.914	45	35	40
		For women		
100	0.840	13	8.50	10.50
400	0.762	45	35.40	40

Knocking down a hurdle unintentionally will not disqualify a competitor. The original rule, that a competitor overturning three or more hurdles should be disqualified, became obsolete after 1932. The IAAF stipulated that race hurdles should have a toppling moment of 3.6 kg at the centre of hurdle. Maximum width of a hurdle is 1.20 m, weight of the hurdle is not less than 10 kg.

Steeplechase

3000 m steeplechase is 7½ laps and it includes a total of 28 hurdle jumps and seven water jumps.

The water jump shall be the fourth jump in each lap. The water jumps are constructed on the arena inside or outside the track which causes shortening or lengthening the normal distance of the laps. Therefore, it is neither possible to lay down any rule specifying the exact length of the laps nor to state precisely the position of the water jump. However, it should be borne in mind that there must be sufficient distance from the starting line to the first hurdle and there should be at least 68 m distance from the last hurdle to the finish line.

In 2000 m steeplechase there are 18 hurdle jumps and five water jumps.

Hurdle specifications: The hurdle specifications are follows:

(a) Height	0.914 m ± 3 mm
(b) Weight	89 – 100 kg
(c) Width	3.96 m
(d) Base	1.20 – 1.40 m

Water jump pool has 70 cm depth and a spread of 3.66 m.

Relay Races

In the entire track and field events, relay races are the only group activity where four runners participate as a team. Each of them runs only one stage in the race. During the progress of the race the runners pass a baton to the next within a specified zone.

In the 4 × 400 m the first runner in each team has to cover the full lap in lane and the second runner has to keep in his lane until entry to the back straight.

The central line of the first takeover zones can be determined by advancing the normal starting stagger in each lane for 200 m race by the distance the points of denouement from the lanes, viz B_2 B_3 B_4B_5 B_6 are in advance of the line A_1 Y. The takeover zone will be within two lines set out 10 m either side of this central line in each lane. The takeover zones for the second and last takeovers will be the normal 10 m lines either side of the start/finish line AA. Lines shall be drawn across the track to mark the distances of the stages and to denote the scratch line.

The baton must be carried in hand throughout the race and must be passed within takeover zones. If dropped, it must be recovered by the athlete who dropped it. Teams may change their running order between preliminaries and finals. Teams may not, however, substitute reserves for those who originally started the competition, except in cases of injury or illness.

Relay Baton: Relay baton is a hollow circular tube made of wood or metal. Its length should be 28 cm to 30 cm and circumference 120 mm but weight should not be less than 50 gm.

Road Races

Standard distance for men and women are 15 km, 20 km, half marathon, 25 km, 30 km and marathon.

Walking

Walking is defined as a progress by steps so taken that unbroken contact with the ground is maintained. One of the feet must be on the ground, the legs must be straightened at least for one moment from the knee. Rules are as follows:

(a) 20 km – In 20 km road walk, maximum circuit permitted is three km.

(b) 50 km – In this event, refreshments are provided by the organisers at the refreshment stations at every five km mark. Refreshments may also be carried by the athlete himself but they shall be made available at the point nominated by competitors.

(c) For all walking events of 10 km or more, sponging points are made available at suitable intervals, if weather conditions warrant such provisions.

(d) Three judges preferably from three nationalities or two judges if one of them is elected as Chief Judge shall supervise the event.

(e) Disqualification is indicated by a red flag. A competitor may be cautioned once, indicated by a white flag.

Marathon

The marathon derives its name from the story of Phidippides, a Greek soldier. He was ordered to run from the battlefield of Marathon to Athens, a distance of 22 miles, to convey the message of Greek victory over the Persians in 490 B.C. The marathon was included in the first modern Olympics in Athens but the present distance of 26 miles 385 yd (42.195 km) was not standardised until 1908. In that year, marathon took place between Windsor and London measuring a distance of 26 miles and the runners were required to cover a further distance of 385 yd in order to finish the race opposite the Royal Box at the White City Stadium.

The start and finish are in the stadium. Competitors are allowed to have food and drink at the 7 miles (11 km) mark and thereafter 6 more times at every 3 miles (5 km) point. Sponging and water are available at intervals (2-3 kms) between feeding points, if weather conditions warrant such provisions. A competitor may carry his own food but that has to be approved by the committee.

COMBINED EVENTS

Decathlon (Men) and Heptathlon (Women)

Decathlon in Greek means "ten prize". Decathlon consists of 10 events which are held on two consecutive days in the following order from 1912 onwards:

(a) First day 100 m, Long Jump, Shot put, High Jump, 400 m.

(b) Second day 110 m hurdles, Discus throw, Pole Vault, Javelin throw, 1500 m

Heptathlon, instituted in 1984 in place of Pentathlon, consists of seven events, which are held on two consecutive days:

(a) First day 100 m hurdles, Shot put, High Jump, 200 m

(b) Second day Long Jump, Javelin throw, 800 m

Each competitor must compete in all events. General rules apply to each event except that only three attempts are allowed in the long jump and throws. Disqualification occurs on a third false start instead of two in the normal course. The wind assistance does not disqualify a record unless it is over 4 m/sec instead of 2 m/sec.

Scoring

Points are scored when a competitor completes his runs, jumps and throws. He is awarded points on the basis of timings, heights and distances.

The competitor who wins the maximum points is declared the winner. In case there is a tie, the competitor with the most points in any one event is the winner.

FIELD EVENTS

General Rules

In field events, there is a qualifying competition for which a standard is set. All those who qualify earn the right to appear in the final. If less than 12 qualify, the number is made upto 12. The finalists in the long jump, triple jump and four throws have 3 trials each. The leading 8 then earn 3 more trials.

High Jump

The minimum length of the runway is 15 m. The take off must be from one foot and the bar must be cleared. Crossing under the bar counts as a failure.

Three consecutive failures at any height disqualify a competitor. In case of a tie, the winner is the competitor with the fewest jumps at the tying height. If still equal, the winner will be the one with the fewest failures at any height. If still a tie persists it is only to be broken for the first place. The competitors shall have one jump at the height at which they failed. And if there is still no decision then bar shall be lowered and raised until the tie is broken.

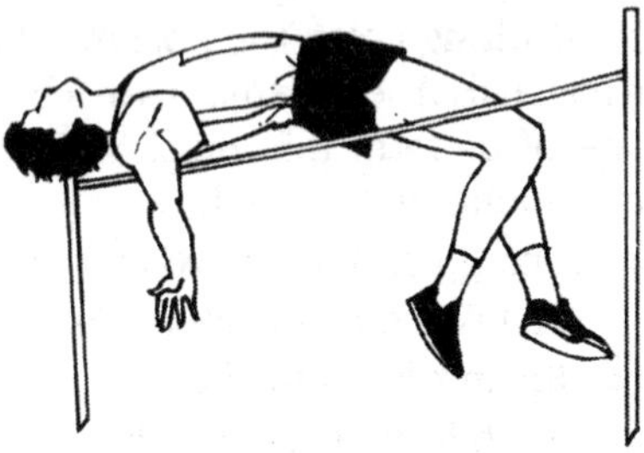

High Jump

The landing area should measure not less than 5 m long and 3 m wide.

Cross Bar: The length of a cross bar is 3.98 m to 4.02 m. The weight should not be more than 2 kg. The supports for it should be flat and rectangular having 60 mm length and 40 mm width. The distance between uprights must be 4 –4.04 m.

Pole Vault

Pole vault is probably a refinement of pole-jumping, a practice employed for many centuries in the Fen district of England for crossing marshy patches of ground. Competitive jumping can be traced back to the mid-nineteenth century in Ulverston, Lancashire.

Minimum length provided for the runway shall be 40 m. The landing area should not measure less than 5 m × 5 m. A large inflated cushion (air bed) has been introduced for the landing area. The length of the cross bar should be between 4.48 m and 4.52 m. The maximum weight permissible for the bar is 2.25 kg.

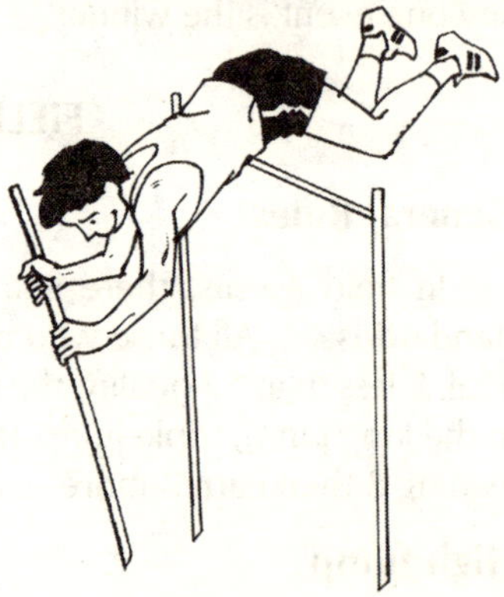

Pole Vault

Supports for Cross Bar: Pegs are used for supporting the cross bar and should be without notches or indentations of any kind. They should be of uniform thickness and not have more than 13 mm (½ in) diameter. They must not extend more than 75 mm (3 in) from the uprights. Cross bar rests on them in a fashion that if a competitor or his pole touches it, it will fall easily to the ground in the direction of the landing area.

Vaulting Pole: The pole may be of any material or combination of materials. The pole may have a binding only of two layers of adhesive tape of uniform thickness. Since 1962, the use of fibre glass has revolutionised the event.

A competitor is allowed three trials at each height. He fails if he:

(a) takes off and fails to clear the bar,

(b) knocks off the bar,

(c) shifts his hands on the pole after take off, or

(d) crosses the plane of the uprights with either his body or the pole.

A pole that passes under the bar after take off does not spoil a jump. The ties are broken in a similar manner as in high jump.

Long Jump

The take off board is 198 to 202 mm wide and 1.21 m to 1.22 m long. The edge of the board which is nearer to the landing area is called the take off line. All jumps are measured from the take off line to the nearest break in the landing area. The landing area should have a minimum width of 2.75 m. The distance from the take off and the end of the landing area should be at least 10 m. The take off board should not be less than one metre from the edge of the landing area.

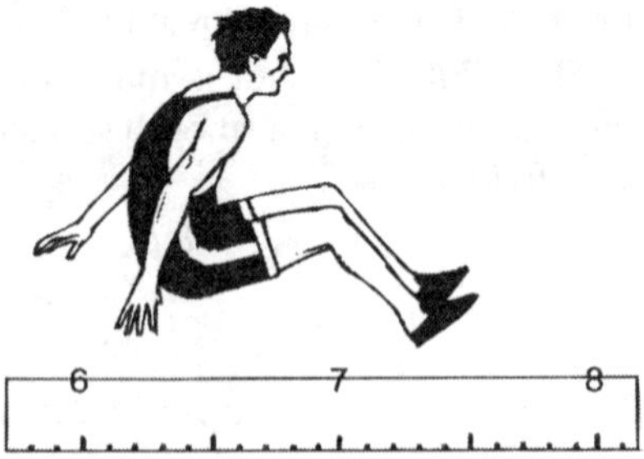

Long Jump

The jump shall be counted as failure if the competitor:

(a) touches the ground beyond the take off line,

(b) after a completed jump, walks back through the landing area.

Triple Jump

The general rules for triple jump are the same as for long jump except that in the "hop" the competitor must land on the same foot that he took off from and during "step" land on the other foot. The distance between the take-off board and the far end of the landing area shall be at least 21 m.

THROWING EVENTS

General Rules

In all throwing events from a circle, a competitor must commence the throw from a stationary position. The competitor must not leave the circle until the implement has touched the ground. Similarly, for a javelin throw, the competitor shall not leave the delivery area until the javelin has touched the ground.

In the case of discus, hammer and shot put, the implement must fall so that the point of impact is within the winner edges of the lines marking: sector of 40° set out on the ground in a fashion so that the radii lines cross at the centre of the circle. All sectors should be marked with sector flags. The implements must be carried back to the starting line, never thrown back .

The measurement of each throw should be made from the nearest mark made by the fall of the implement or head of the javelin or hammer to the inside of the circumference of the circle. In order to obtain a better grip competitors are permitted to use an adhesive substance. Gloves are allowed only for hammer throw.

Shot Put: The shot is made of solid iron or brass. It must be spherical shape with a smooth surface. The specifications of the shot are as follows:

Men *Women*

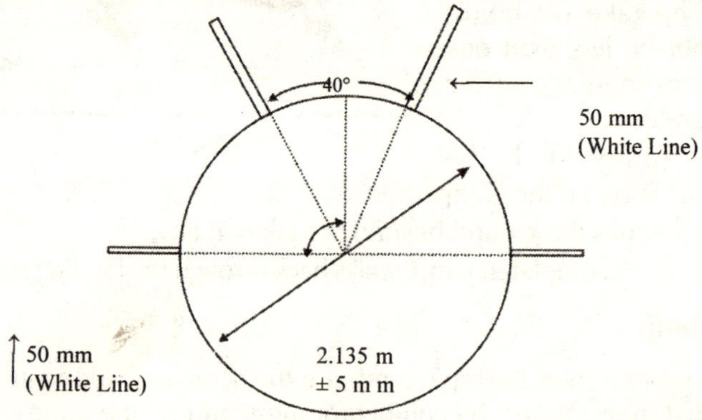

Shot put

(a) Weight	7.26 kg	4 kg
(b) Diameter of head	110-130 mm	95-110 mm

Circle for throw should have 2.135 m :f: 5 mm diameter. One should use only one hand and the put should be from the shoulder and not behind the shoulder.

Hammer: It must be completely spherical in shape made of solid iron or other metal not softer than brass. The handle shall be of single unbroken and straight length of spring steel wire not less than 3 mm in diameter. The specifications of the hammer are as follows:

(a) Weight	7.26 kg
(b) Diameter	117.5 – 121.5 cm
(c) Length	110 – 130 mm

All hammer and discus throws shall be made from an enclosure or cage.The cage should be U-shaped. The opening through which the throw is made should be 6 m wide. The minimum height of the netting panel for discus is 4 m and for hammer 5 m. The circle should be as for the shot put. The sector of landing area should be 40".

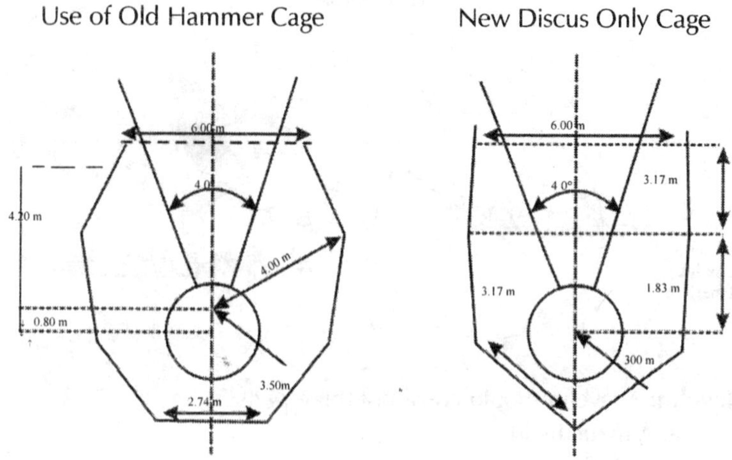

Plans of alternative discus cages

Discus: Discus is made of wood or other suitable material with metal plates set flush into the sides. The specifications of the discus are:

		Men	*Women*
(a)	Weight	2 kg	1 kg
(b)	Thickness of the centre	44-46 mm	37-39 mm
(c)	Outer diameter of metal rim	219-221 mm	180-182 mm
(d)	Diameter of metal plates	50-57 mm	50-57 mm

(e) Each side of the discus shall be identical and must be made without indentation or projection of any sharp edges.

(f) The circle for discus throw should be with diameter 2.50 m ± 5 mm. The layout of discus circle is shown in the following figure:.

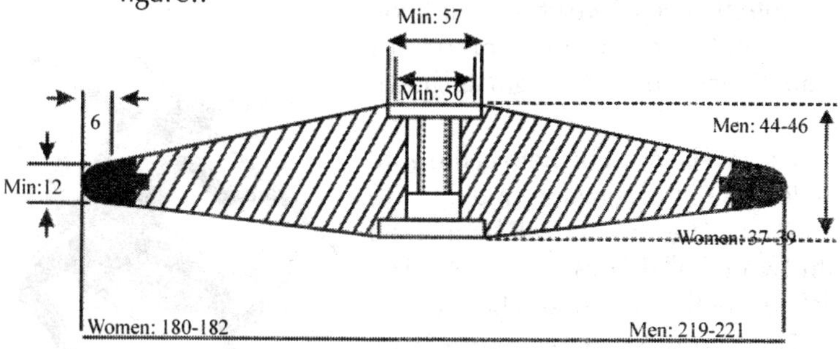

Discus

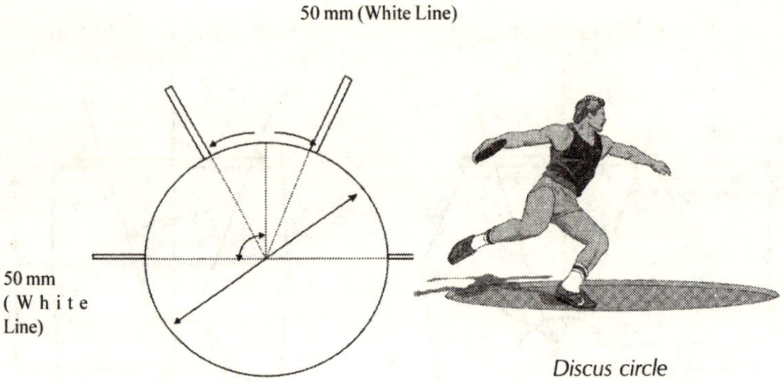

Discus circle

Javelin: A javelin should consist of three parts:

(a) A metal head

(b) A shaft

(c) A cord grip

The specifications of a javelin are given as follows:

		Men	*Women*
(a)	Weight	800 gm	600 gm
(b)	Length	2.60-2.70 m	2.20-2.30 m
(c)	Length of metal head	250-330 mm	250-330 mm
(d)	Weight of metal head	80 gm	80 gm
(e)	Distance from tip of metal head to centre of gravity	0.90-1.06 m	0.80-0.95 m
(f)	Diameter of shaft at thickest point	25-30 mm	20-25 mm
(g)	Width of cord grip	150-160mm	140-150mm

Note: Range of weights in addition to normal for all equipment for competitions is from 5-25 gm as shown above.

The javelin must be held at the grip. The length of the runway should be 30 to 36.5 m. The runway will be marked with two parallel lines 4 m apart. The thickness of the line should be 5 cm.

The throw shall be made from behind an arc of a circle drawn with a

Javeline Throw

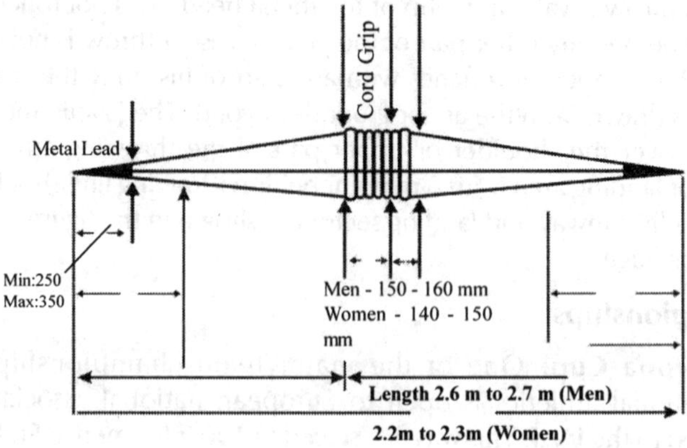

Javelin

radius of 8 m. This arc is painted white and is made of wood or metal. The width of the arc should be 7 cm. Two lines are drawn from end of the arcs at right angles to parallel lines. The length of these lines should be 0.75 m and width 7cm.

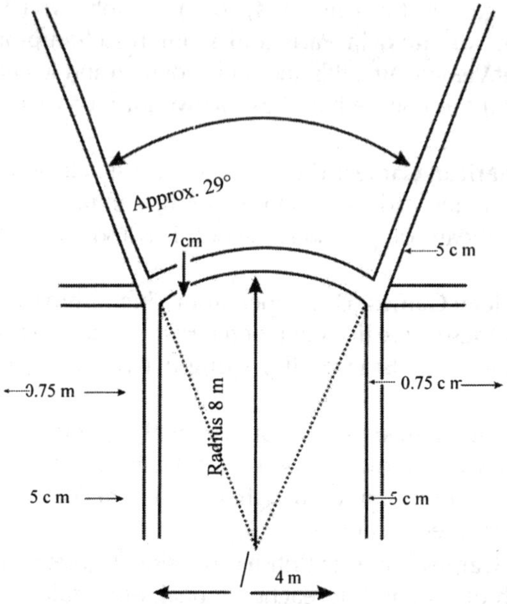

Javelin runway and landing sector

No throw is valid if the tip of the metal head does not touch the ground before any other part of the javelin. Also a throw is not valid when the competitor touches with any part of his body the strip or the lines drawn from the arc or grounds beyond. The javelin must be thrown over the shoulder or upper part of the throwing arm. The sector of landing area from 8 m point behind throwing line should be 29°. Javelin runway and landing sector are shown in the figure on the previous page.

Championships

Europa Cup: One of the major team championships of international athletics is open to European national associations affiliated to the IAAF. This was first staged in 1965, for men at Stuttgart and for women at Kassel. The competition consists of a qualifying round in three groups, followed by a semi-final round and a six-nation final. Each nation enters one competitor per event. The result is determined on a point scoring basis. It was held in Kiev in 1967, at Stockholm in 1970, at Edinburgh in 1973. Thereafter it is held every four years.

European Championships: A major athletics championship, it was first staged in Turin in 1934, for men only. In 1938, men's competition was held in Paris and women's championship was conducted at Vienna. After this, the venue for men and women became the same and the competition has followed a four-year cycle since 1974.

Pan-American Games: The Games were first held at Buenos Aires in 1951. Both men and women from North, Central, South America, and the Caribbean competed in athletics. This also follows a four-year cycle.

Pan-African Games: Developed from "Friendship Games" of the early 1960s, these were first held for the French-speaking countries of Africa in 1965, at Brazzaville, Congo; twenty-nine countries participated.

Lake Land Games: The UK professional athletics championship is held in the Lake District of North-West England. The games do not attract national interest now, though they were major sporting events in the late nineteenth century.

Border Games: Another British professional athletics meet is held in the South of Scotland. It reached a peak of popularity in the late nineteenth century.

Indoor Games: (a) The American Amateur Athletic Union Indoor championships, first held in 1906, are organised annually. However, the first indoor meeting was held at New York in 1868.

(b) European Indoor Games were first held in 1966. This is an annual fixture.

Asian Games: The Asian Games Federation was founded in 1948. The first Asian Games were held in 1951 at New Delhi. This follows a four-yearly cycle. Other venues were Manila (1954), Tokyo (1958), Jakarta (1962), Bangkok (1966, 1970, 1978), Teheran (1974), New Delhi (1982), Seoul (1986) and Beijing (1990).

Olympics: The first modern Olympic games were held in 1896 at Athens. It is held once every four years.

Commonwealth Games: The Commonwealth Games were originally known as the British Empire Games. Athletics is the main sport of these games. The Games were first held in Hamilton, Canada, in 1930. Women 's events were first introduced in 1934 at the London Games.

Names to be Remembered

Charley Paddock

Charley Paddock (USA,1900-1943): He was unofficially known as the world's fastest man. Between 1921 and 1926, he equalled the world's 100 yds record of 9.6 seconds six times. He won Olympic gold medals in 100 m and 4 × 100 m relay in 1920 games.

Sergey Bubka (USSR, b.4 December, 1964): A pole vaulter from the USSR with amazing skill. He is the only pole vaulter so far who has cleared the 6 m mark. He established a record jump of 6.06 m at Nice, France, on 10 July, 1988, and even better to 6.08 m later. He also won the Olympic gold at Seoul in 1988.

Valeri Borzov

Valeri Borzov (1949): He is arguably the greatest European sprinter of all times. He first won European championship of 100 m at Athens in 1969. During the next three years he remained unbeaten in any important athletic meet which included visits to the USA also. At Munich in 1972, he became the first man to win an Olympic sprint double by winning 100 m and 200m gold medals. His best 100 m timing of 10.00 seconds was also a European record then.

Emil Zatopek (Czechoslovakia, b.19 September, 1922): Emil was the son of a poor carpenter and had a difficult childhood. In 1941, at the age of 19, he entered a 3000 m cross country run and finished second in 9 minutes 12 seconds just three seconds behind the winner. His first success came in 1944, when he improved the 2000 m, 3000 m and 5000 m national records: In 1948, at the London Games, he broke the Finnish monopoly and won gold medal for 10000 m and silver for 5000 m. Zatopek won 38 consecutive 10000 m races between 1948 and 1954. After the Helsinki Olympics where he won gold medals for 5000 m, 10000 m and Marathon, his birthday was declared a national holiday in Czechoslovakia and his statue was erected near his home in Prague.

Sebastian Coe (UK, b. 29 September, 1956, London): Credit for Sebastian Coe's greatness may be attributed to his father Peter. Peter supervised his son's training right from the beginning. There was no compromise on the training schedule, not even on the day before the school examinations. In 1980, Coe won a gold in 1500 m and a silver in 800 m at the Moscow Olympics. His repeat performance in 1984, astonished the world when he again won the gold in 1500 m and silver in 800 m at Los Angeles. He held world records in 800 m, 1000 m and 1500 m.

Frederick Carlton Lewis (USA, b. 1 July, 1961, Texas): Carl Lewis' father, Bill, and mother, Evelyn, were professional coaches in different high schools in Willingboro, New Jersey. As a result his coaching began at home. In the 1984 and the 1988 Olympics he won a total of 8 gold medals in l00 m, 200 m, 4 × l00 m relay and long jump.

Francis Daley Thompson (UK, b.30 July, 1958, London): Daley Thompson is the son of a Nigerian father and Scottish mother. He joined the Farney School in 1965, where he learnt his first lesson in sports. In 1975, he started training under Bob Mortimer. He won the Decathlon gold in the 1980 Moscow Olympics and the 1984 Los Angeles Olympics. He has also won world championship in 1983. He came to Seoul in 1988, to create history but unfortunately he was injured during the pole vault event. However, his 8847 points in Decathlon still remains the world record.

Edwin Moses (USA, b. 31 August, 1955, Laguna Beach, California): On 26 August, 1977, Edwin Moses was beaten by Harald

Edwin Moses

Schmid of West Germany in 400 m hurdles. After that he remained unbeaten in this event till the 1984 Olympics. He won his first Olympic gold in 1976, and regained his title eight years later in 1984. With this gold in 1984, he won 105 races. He won World Cups in 1977, 1979 and 1981. He was injured in 1981, at Rome and thought about quitting. But he returned with renewed vigour and won the World Cup in 1983 at Helsinki. At the Koblenz international meet he improved his world record to 47.02 seconds in this event. His unmatched speed has destroyed the hopes of an entire generation of 400 m hurdlers. He returned to Seoul in 1988, to create history but at the age of 33 he had to be satisfied with a bronze only.

Francina "Fanny" Blankers-Koen (Holland, b. 26 April, 1918, Amsterdam): Fanny Blankers-Koen was only 18 when she competed in the Berlin Olympics, but could not achieve much. But 12 years later, she went to London in 1948, as a 30-year-old mother and won four gold medals in 100 m, 200 m, 80 m hurdles and 4 × l00 m relay. She is the only woman athlete to win four golds in one Olympic in the world.

Paavo Johannes Nurmi (Finland, 1897-1973): He is considered as the greatest distance runner of the Twentieth century. He broke 20 world records and accumulated 12 Olympic medals (9 gold and 3 silver). He was known to have ignored other competitors and ran with a stop watch in his hand to improve upon records. In 1924, he won both 1500 m and 5000 m within 90 minutes. His world records were established between 1921 and 1931. In 1932, he was disqualified for professionalism when he was a favourite for Olympic Marathon. In 1952, at Helsinki, he made his last Olympic appearance as the torchbearer.

Justin Gatlin (born February 10, 1982) is an American sprinter. He is an Olympic gold medalist in 2004 Olympics who shares the world record in the 100 m sprint (with Asafa Powell) with a time of 9.77 seconds.

Liu Xiang (born July 13, 1983) is a Chinese hurdling athlete and 2004 Olympic gold medalist who holds the current world record in the 110 metres hurdles with a time of 12.88 seconds. Born in Shanghai, China, his given name, means—appropriately for a hurdling champion—"to soar". In 2002 Asian Championships (Manila, Philippines) — 110m hurdles: GOLD medal. Asian Games (Busan, South Korea) — 110m hurdles: GOLD medal. 2003 IAAF World Championships (Paris, France) — 110m hurdles: BRONZE medal IAAF World Indoor Championships (Birmingham, UK) — 60m hurdles: BRONZE medal

Stefan Christian Holm (born May 25, 1976) is a Swedish athlete competing in the high jump. He has won 1 Olympic gold medal, 3 gold and 1 silver medals in the World Championships, 1 gold, 2 silver and 1 bronze medals in the European Championships. His personal record in high jump is 2.40 m (indoors 2005) and 2.36 m (outdoors 2004).

Timothy "Tim" Mack (born September 15, 1972 in Cleveland, Ohio) is an American pole vaulter who became Olympic champion in 2004. The same year he won the 2nd IAAF World Athletics Final with the result 6.01 m, thereby joining the exclusive "6 meters club" of pole vaulters who reached 6 meters. He is a graduate of St. Ignaitus High School, in downtown Cleveland.

Yulia Nestsiarenka, née Bartsevich (Belarusian: born June 15, 1979 in Brest) a sprinter from Belarus, is an Olympic champion. Nestsiarenka won the women's 100 metres race at the 2004 Summer Olympics in Athens, in 10.93 seconds, becoming the first white and first non-U.S. athlete to win this event since the American boycott of the games in 1980. She ran all four times (two qualification rounds, semifinal and final) under 11 seconds, and became one of the biggest sensations of the Olympic Games in Athens. At the 2006 European Athletics Championships in Gothenburg she was sixth in the 100m final and won a bronze medal in 4 x 100 metres relay.

■

BADMINTON

Chapter - 3

The game derives its name from the seat of the Duke of Beaufort at Badminton in England. The first rules of the game were drawn in Poona in the mid-eighteen seventies.

History

The game of Badminton came to India with British army officers, named after the Duke of Beaufort at Badminton in Gloucestershire where it is supposed to have been evolved in the 1870s. While the game originated in England, it was developed in India.The rules of the game were drawn up at Pune in the mid-eighteen seventies. The rules were not immediately adopted by other nations. But in 1893, fourteen clubs met at South Sea, Hampshire, and founded the Badminton Association. The tournament organised by the club, the All England Championship, was the beginning of the popularisation of this game.

Till the first decade of the last century, the game of badminton underwent many changes. Until 1901, the shape of the badminton court was like an hourglass, wide at the ends and narrow at the centre where the net comes. The present rectangular shape of the court came into existence during this time. The shuttlecocks or what is known as shuttles today were handcrafted and were not uniform in weight and balance.

The International Badminton Federation was formed in 1934, following which the rules of the game were standardised. It was a demonstration game at the 1988 Seoul Olympics and became a medal event in the Olympics in Barcelona in 1992.

Badminton Court

The court is laid out on a level and smooth surface, wood and composite flooring, being common. The floor must not be slippery. A sketch of the court is shown below with all the details.

(a) A minimum of 2 m clear space is essential on all four sides.

(b) The markings are in white paint or by white tape and must be 4 cm in width.

(c) For doubles play, the entire court is used but for the singles the court is 91 cm narrower, on the sides.

(d) **Net**: It is made of cord with a mesh of 1.5-2 cm . White tape should be doubled over the top and strained over the top of the post. The net is 1.550 m high at the post and 1.524 m high in the centre.

Shuttles

There are two types of shuttles — 14 to 16 feathers with light fan 64 mm to 70 mm and the other of nylon. The base of the feather shuttle is of cork, which is completely rounded except by what is generally known as the skirt weight 4.74 to 5.50 gm.

Shuttle

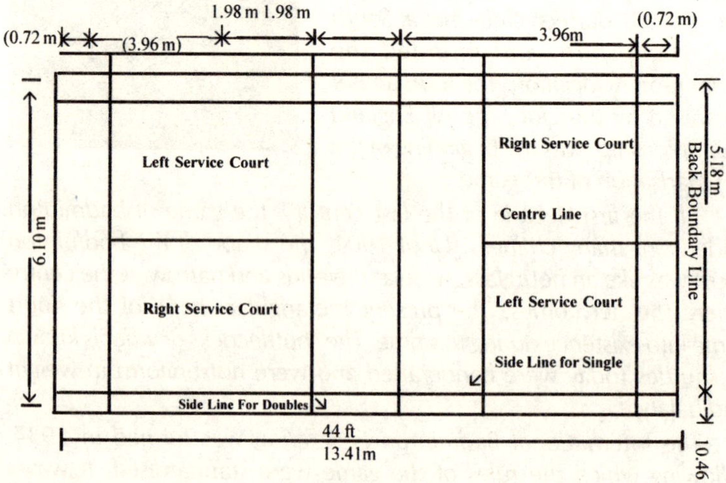

Badminton Court

Racket: The modern badminton racket is made of either hickory carbon alloys or steel. It has about 16 horizontal and vertical strands of thin gut strung tightly. It is 680 mm long and the head is 230 mm in

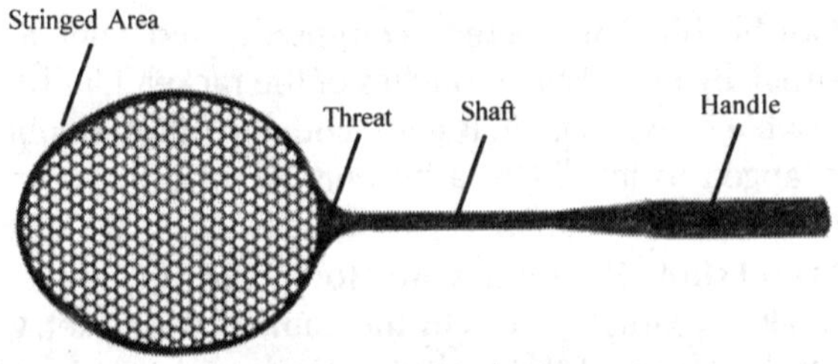

Racket

width. Though there is no stipulation in the rules as to its dimensions or composition, a racket weighs 92 gm to 156 gm .

Rules of Badminton

The following are the badminton rules in a nutshell:

1. Service in badminton must be delivered underhand. There are four types of service-short, high, drive and flick.
2. The server must stand with both feet within his service court and neither foot should touch the line.
3. The receiver may stand anywhere within his service court.
4. Some part of the feet must be in contact with the floor at the same spot, until the shuttle is hit.

5. Who will serve first is decided by tossing a coin.
6. Only the server can add to his/her score.
7. If the receiving side wins a rally, the score remains static but service change takes place.
8. In doubles, two partners serve consecutively except that at the starting of the game only one service is allowed. After both lose the service, the service changes to the other team.

9. A side loses the rally if:
   (a) the shuttle falls outside the boundary;
   (b) the service fault is committed;
   (c) the shuttle is held on the racket.
10. **Double hit**: This is a term commonly used when a shuttle is struck by two distinct touches of the racket. Until 1968, any double hit was a fault. But in 1968, the rule of double hit was changed to invalidate a hit only when a player made two strokes at the shuttle.
11. **Wood shot**: This term is used for mis-hits when the shuttle is totally or partially struck by the frame of the racket. Clean hits off the frame of the racket or the wood shot is valid since 1963.
12. A 'let' occurs only as a result of any unforeseen or accidental hindrance such as a shuttle from a neighbouring court interfering with play or a shuttle being caught in or held on the net. When a let occurs, the whole rally is replayed.
13. If the score reaches 14-all, the player or pair, which first reaches 14 points, has to give the defending player/pair the option of 'setting' the game for a further three points. If the game is extended by three points, then the score is called' love-all' and the first side to score three points wins the game. If 14-all, then the game may be completed straight or extension of three points may be allowed.
14. The women's singles game is of 11 points. If a game reaches 9-all, it may be set for three points and at 10-all, for two points.
15. In the third game the opponents change ends halfway through it, i.e., when one side's score reaches eight in a game of 15 and six in a game of 11.

Championships

All England Championship: First organised by the BAE in 1899, it may be regarded as an unofficial world championship. Since 1957, the championship is being held in Empire Pool, Wembley.

Uber Cup: The Uber Cup is the team trophy for women's international badminton championship instituted in 1956. The cup was donated by Mrs. H.S. Uber who represented England for twenty-five years. It was first won by the United States beating Denmark at Lytham St. Annes. Japan has the maximum of five victories in the Uber Cup.

Olympics: Badminton was a demonstration sport in 1988 Olympics at Seoul. It was included as a medal event in 1992 Olympics at Barcelona.

Thomas Cup: The Thomas Cup is the international badminton championship trophy for men. The cup was donated in 1939 by Sir George Thomas (1881-1972) who was largely responsible for the foundation of the International Badminton Federation. It was first held in 1948-49 in Preston and was lifted by Malaya beating Denmark.

Asian Games and Commonwealth Games: Badminton has been a part of Asian and Commonwealth Games since 1951, and 1930, respectively. The Asian championship was first instituted in 1962, at Kuala Lumpur.

Names to Remember

Yang Yang (China): The 24-year-old Chinese badminton player, Yang lived under the shadows of mighty Ran Jian, Luan Jin and Zao Zianhua. In 1985, he won the Hong Kong Open by beating Morten Frost and won the world championship in 1987 at Beijing by again beating Morten Frost.

H.S. Uber (England,1907-): She represented England for 25 years commencing from 1926. She was the donor of the Uber Cup. In 1923, she was British junior lawn tennis champion also.

Rudy Kurniawan Hartono (Indonesia): Hartono was regarded as the world's most celebrated singles badminton player. He first competed in All England championship in 1968, and continued the winning streak for six years consecutively. Later on he won the title two more times. He was also the main force behind Indonesia regaining the Thomas Cup in 1970.

Wong Peng Soon (Singapore and Malaysia,1918-): He is one of the finest badminton players the world has ever seen. He won All England singles championship four times. The last win was at the age of 37. He helped the Malaysian team to win the Thomas Cup between 1949 and 1955.

Erland Kops (Denmark,1937-): A well-known Danish badminton player, he won All England singles title seven times between 1958 and 1966 and the men's doubles title three times successively from 1967. He represented his country 40 times.

Kirsten Thorndahl (Denmark,1928-): Mrs. Thorndahl represented Denmark between 1946 and 1963. She won 11 All England championship titles.

Prakash Padukone (India): The Indian badminton champion, Padukone is labelled as the 'gentleman player' because of his mild behaviour. He was the national champion in a row for eight years from 1972. He won All England badminton championship in March 1980, when he was 25, and World Cup in 1981.

Taufik Hidayat (born August 10, 1981, Bandung, Jawa Barat, Indonesia): Hidayat is an Indonesian badminton player and his height is 176 cm. He is a former world champion and the current Olympic champion in the men's singles. He also won the Indonesian Open six times (1999, 2000, 2002, 2003, 2004 and 2006). Hidayat played badminton at the 2004 Summer Olympics in men's singles, defeating Hidetaka Yamada of Japan and Wong Choong Hann of Malaysia in the first two rounds.. In August 2005, he defeated world number one Lin Dan of China, 15-3, 15-7 in the men's singles final of the IBF World Championships.

Zhang Ning (born 19 May 1975 in Shenyang, Liaoning province) is a female badminton player from the People's Republic of China. Zhang played badminton at the 2004 Summer Olympics for China.She is also the winner of World Badminton Championships 2003 (Women's Single) at Birmingham. She beat the titleholder and Chinese compatriot Gong Ruina with 11-6, 11-3 in the final. At the 2006 IBF World Championships she reached the final again, this time losing against Xie Xingfang.

■

BASEBALL

Chapter - 4

Baseball is the most popular game in the USA. The game is played by a team of nine. Alexander Cartwright wrote the first set of rules in 1845.

History

Baseball is a nine-a-side bat-and-ball game generally regarded as the American national game. Modern rules for baseball were written in 1845, by Alexander Cartwright, a member of the Knicker-bocker Baseball Club of New York. The rules were revised in 1854. In 1858, the National Association of Baseball players was formed.

It is more or less sure that the game has evolved from the 'old English game of rounders and miscellaneous variants of games like town ball, one old cat, two old cats and four old cats, etc.

Baseball Field

The game is played on a field with four bases placed at an angle forming a 27.4 m. square. From the home plate, bases are counted anti-clockwise as the first, second and third. Two foul lines form the boundaries of fair territory. These lines start from home and extend past the first and third base till the entire length of the field and end at the fence. A sketch of baseball field is shown on next page.

Equipment

The Bat: The baseball bat is a wooden club elongated and rounded with a smooth finish. It is generally made of hardwood. Its length is 1.06 m, weight 5¼ ounce and diameter is not more than 7 cm at any point.

The Ball: The ball is covered with horsehide, hand sewn around a cork and rubber centre wound with woollen yarn, about 23 cm (9¼

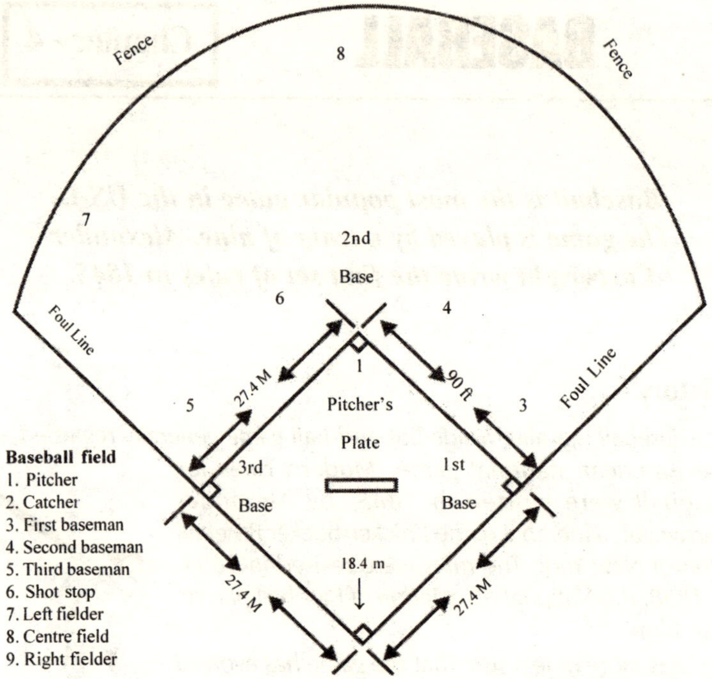

in) in circumference. Bases are made out of iron pegs covered with canvas. The first basemen use special large mitt and the catchers use well-padded mitt or pillow gloves. They also use chest protector, shinguards and a metal mask.

Rules of the Baseball

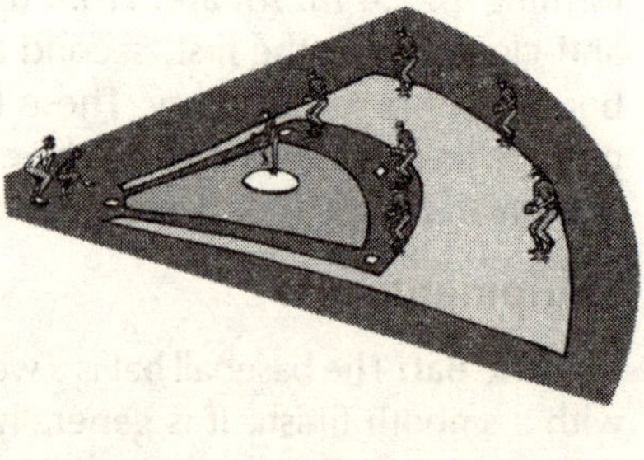

1. This is nine-a-side game and the object is to score maximum runs. A run is scored whenever a player circles all bases and reaches home.
2. A team consists of a pitcher and catcher called the battery. Infields are : first, second and third basemen and shortstop. Right, centre and left fielders are called the outfield.

3. The game is divided into innings and a game generally consists of nine innings.
4. A team is allowed three outs in each inning to bat and then must take up defensive position while the other team takes its turn to bat.
5. The pitcher throws the ball to his catcher from slab, called rubber, which is directly between the first and third base and 17 inches wide, flush to the ground. The rubber is 18.4 m away from the home plate. The pitcher must throw the ball through the strike zone, i.e., the ball should go over home plate and pass between batter's armpit and knees.
6. The batter tries to reach base safely after hitting the pitched ball into fair territory. Reaching the first base is called single, the second base a double, the third base a triple and a four-base hit is a home run. A fair ball hit over an outfield fence is automatically a home run.
7. **Progress of Base Runner:**
   (a) When his team hits the ball through fair territory.
   (b) By stealing from one base to another when a pitcher delivers the ball.
   (c) When a pitcher makes a wild pitch.
   (d) When a catcher allows the ball to pass.
   (e) When a pitcher makes an illegal move.
   (f) A batter is awarded his base if a pitcher delivers four pitches which do not pass through the strike zone, or if he is hit by a pitched ball, or if the opposing catcher interferes when he swings the bat.
8. Batters may be put out by the following means:
   (a) When a pitcher gets three strikes on him.
   (b) The ball is caught by the fielder before it drops on the ground.
   (c) Before the batter gets to a base, a fielder touches that base with the ball.
   (d) If he is forced to leave his base to make room for another runner and fails to reach the next base.
   (e) If he is hit by a team-mate's batted ball before it has touched or passed a fielder.

9. An umpire-in-chief calls balls and strikes from his position directly behind the catcher at home plate. In World Series games six umpires are used. When there is only one umpire, he stands behind the pitcher.
10. A strike is a pitch that crosses the plate in the strike zone, hit in the foul territory and any pitch that is struck and missed.
11. Substitute players may enter the game any time but once a player goes out, he cannot return.

Championships

Most prominent American baseball tournaments are:

1. American League (AL), formed on 25 January, 1901.
2. National League, formed on 2 February, 1876, at the Grand Central Hotel, New York.
3. Little League.
4. American Legion Junior Baseball.
5. American Amateur Baseball Congress.

Names to Remember

Tyrus Cobb (1886-1961): He played for Detroit, AL (1905-1926) and Philadelphia, AL (1927-1928). He held the highest batting average of 367. He led his League in batting 12 times and stole 892 bases.

Baseball at the 2004 Summer Olympics was held on two separate diamonds within the Helliniko Olympic Complex. Cuba won the Gold medal.

Danny Betancourt Chacón (born May 25, 1981 in Santiago de Cuba, Cuba): Betancourt Chacón was part of the winning team.. He is a young righthanded baseball pitcher who has played for Santiago de Cuba in the Cuban National Series, as well as the Cuban national baseball team.

■

BASKETBALL

Chapter - 5

The game was invented by Dr. James Naismith of the USA in 1891.

History

The earliest evidence of basketball game may be found in ancient Central and South American civilizations, dating back to the seventh century BC. But the Encyclopedia of Athletics *(1818) indicates a game played in Florida in which the players attempted to throw the ball into a basket attached to the top of a pole. However, the credit for the invention of the game as played today should go to the Canada-born Dr. James Naismith who formulated the first rules in December 1891. Basketball was included in the Olympics for the first time at the Berlin Games in 1936.*

Basketball Court

As per the FIBA (Federation International de Basketball Amateur) rules, the court should have a hard surface of wood, concrete or any suitable material, but grass covered courts are not permitted. It is 26 m long and 14 m wide. The court is divided into two halves marked by a centre line. On the centre line is a circle with a radius of 1.80 m. At each end are marked the free throw line, the restricted zone and the free throw lane. The goal is a "basket" consisting of a bottomless net of white cord which is suspended from an iron ring with an inside diameter of 45 cm painted orange in a horizontal plane 3.05 m above the surface of the court floor. This is rigidly fixed to the backboard 30 cm from its bottom edge. The dimension of the backboard is 1.80'm × 1.20 m. The lower edge of the board has to be 2.75 m above the floor.

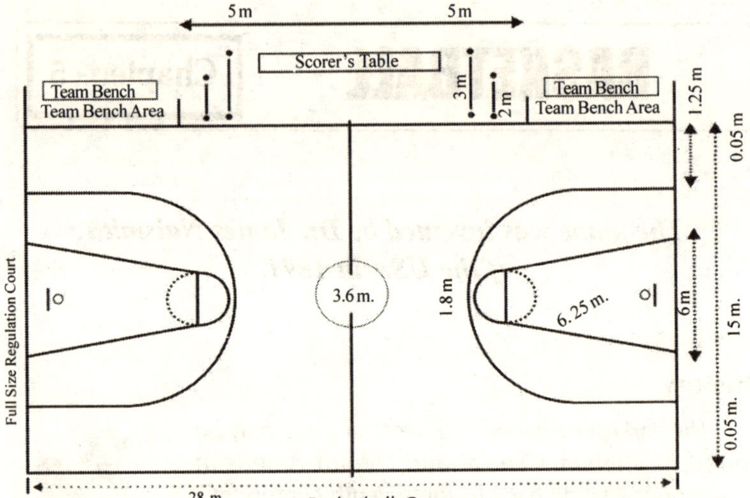

Basketball Court

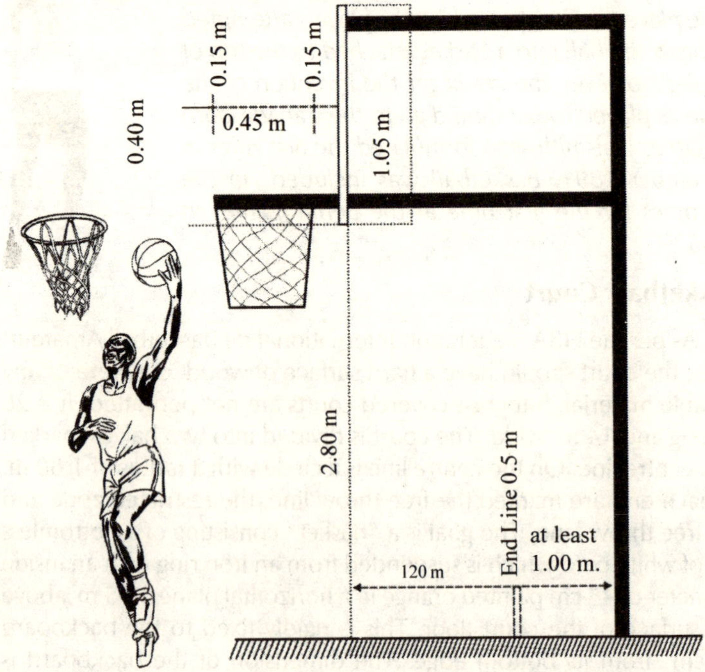

Basket and post

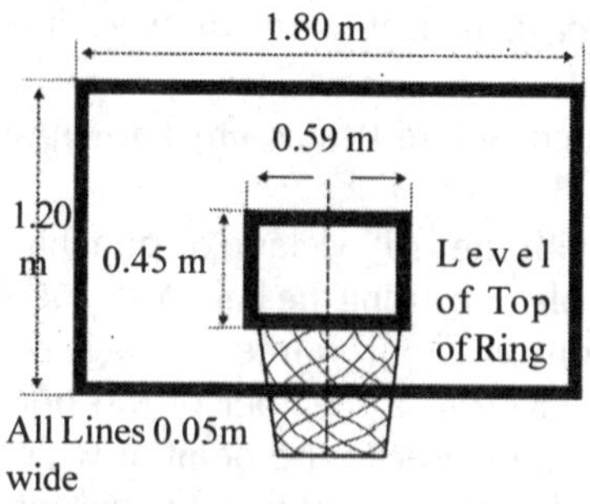

Regulations Backboard Marketing

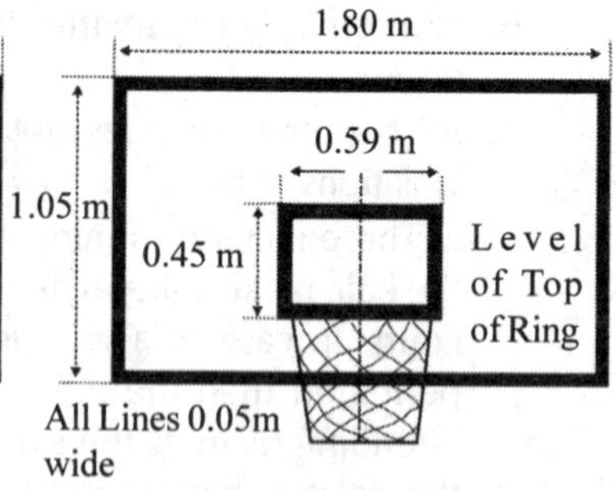

Specifications for all New Backboards

Basketball Rules

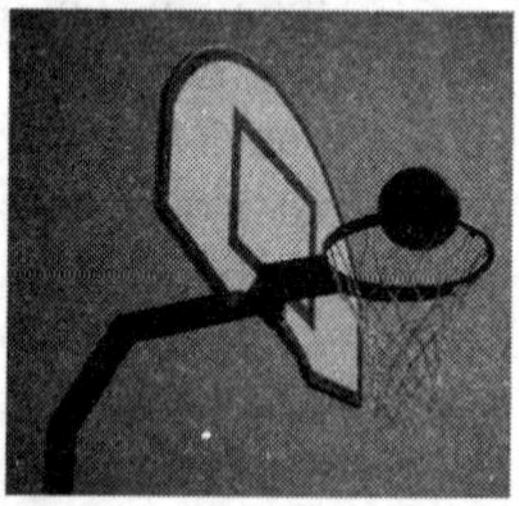

1. Each team consists of five players. Substitutes are allowed up to five. A team can have maximum12 players in such tournaments where more than three games are played.
2. The game begins with a jump ball at the centre circle with the two opponents' feet in the half circle.The referee tosses the ball upward (vertically) between them to a height greater than the players can reach. The jumpers are allowed two taps at the ball.

3. Penalty for technical foul by a player is two free throws. Penalty for technical foul by a coach or substitute, or a team follower is two free throws and the ball shall be thrown in by any player of free throw shooter's team from out of bounds at mid court of the side line opposite scorer's table.
4. A basket is worth two points. If a basket is scored from beyond the 3-point line, then it will be three points and if it is scored from a free throw it is one point.
5. Free throw taker must remain behind the free throw line until the ball hits the ring or the backboard. No other player is allowed to enter the free throw line until the throw has been taken, i.e., the ball has left the free thrower's hands.

6. Non-offending team may leave its right to free throws if it so desires.
7. All breaches of rules not considered fouls are known as violations.

   These include running with the ball, kicking or punching the ball, making illegal dribble or causing the ball to go out of court. In case of a violation or a foul, if free throw is not permitted then the ball is given to a member of the non-offending team at the sideline closer to the point at which the violation has occurred. That player must pass the ball into the court within five seconds.
8. Following a basket or a successful second throw, the opposing team puts the ball back into play from any point behind the end line.

9. Each player is numbered on the front and back of his vest. In international competitions only the numbers 4 to 15, both inclusive, are used.
10. The ball may be played only with hands and players are not allowed to carry it more than a single step.
11. Every player must try to avoid personal contact at all times and if such a contact occurs, a "personal foul" is charged against the player responsible.
12. If the player who had been fouled was in the act of shooting for goal, and if the shot proved unsuccessful, that player is awarded two free throws.
13. A "technical foul" is charged for an offence not involving personal contact. This would also result in two free throws.
14. If a player commits five fouls either personal or technical during a match, he is barred from taking part in the game. A substitute may be introduced in place of that player.
15. After a team has committed seven player fouls either technical or personal in a half all-subsequent fouls shall be penalised by one and one Rule.
16. The team in possession of the ball must advance the ball into its front court within ten seconds of having gained possession of the playing court. Infringement of this rule is a violation.

17. There is no limit to the number of substitutions that may be made during the game. Substitution can be made only when the ball is dead and the clock is stopped.
18. Time out: A team coach may request time out. He is allowed to have two time outs in each half and one in each extra period. Time out is granted when the ball is dead.
19. The basket is 3.05 m above the floor and the ball must enter it from the top.
20. A game consists of two periods of 20 minutes each with 10 minutes interval. Extra time is played for five minutes only.
21. In basketball there is no draw. At the end of 2.20 minutes period, if both the teams have equal points, five minutes extra period is given to break the tie. Even after five minutes extra time, the points are equal, a further five minutes extra time will be given. This process will continue, till the tie is broken.

Ball

The ball is between 74.9 and 78 cm in circumference and weighs between 567-650 gm. It is so inflated that when dropped on a hard surface from a height of 1.80 m it re-bounces to a height of between 1.20 -1.40 m. The ball is normally bright orange coloured with black panel markings. The width of the seams and for channels of the ball shall not exceed 0.635 cm.

Game Officials

The game is controlled by two officials (referee and umpire) aided by several assistants. The referee has the ultimate authority. The assistants are the time-keeper, the scorer and the 30-second operator. A technical commissioner may also be appointed.

The Scorer: The scorer keeps chronological summary of the score sheet. Along with points scored, he also notes all fouls, free throws, time outs, substitutions, etc.

The Time-keeper: The time-keeper controls the game clock. When an official sounds his whistle, the timekeeper stops the clock which is not restarted till the ball is once again in play and retouched by a player. The clock is also stopped during free throws.

The 30-Second Operator: The 30-second operator operates the 30-second device or clock. He ensures that the team in possession attempts a shot within 30 seconds of having gained control of the ball. If they fail to do so, the operator sounds signal to indicate a violation.

Rule Variation

Though the FIBA, founded in 1932, is the ruling body of international basketball competitions yet there are certain rules which do not conform to the National Basketball Association (NBA), the American Basketball Association (AHA) and the National Collegiate Athletic Association (NCAA) rules in the USA. The court markings in the USA also differ from the FIBA in various ways. In American professional league the 30-second rule is replaced by the 24-second rule.

Championships

NCAA Championship: Commenced in 1938.

Apart from the above, basketball forms an integral part of most organised regional sports meets like the Asian Games, etc.

European Cup for Champion Club: This competition began in 1958. In the USA, the professional NBA League started in 1949.

FIBA Championship: Organised by the FIBA, it was first held in 1950, in Argentina. Women's championship was instituted in 1953.

Olympics: In the 1928 Los Angeles Olympics, basketball was played as a demonstration sport and from the 1936 Olympics at Berlin, it was a regular medal-event game. The USA was the first Olympic champion in basketball.

Names to Remember

Nikos Gallis (1957): A Greek, at the age of 31 he steered Greece to the European basketball title in 1987, after beating the USSR in the finals. The press hailed him as the player of the 21st century because of his uncanny skill. He was fondly called as the "Gangster" by his teammates because of his mild behaviour.

George Mikan (USA,1929-): He played for Minneapolis Lakers and helped them win NBA championships. Mikan was elected to the Hall of Fame in 1959. In 1967, he was appointed as the League Commissioner of NBA.

Dr. James Naismith (1861-1939): Naismith was born in Canada. He was the inventor of basketball. He was a graduate in Medicine and Theology. He invented basketball while he was at the International

YMCA training school at Springfield. Naismith Basketball Hall of Fame was founded in his honour. Outstanding players and officials are elected to this elite organisation.

Dr. James Naismith

Wilton Norman Chamberlain (1936-): American professional basketball player. His height is over 7 ft. A graduate from Kansas University, he played for various American teams including Harlem Globe trotters, and was popularly known as "Wilt the Stilt". He became an all-time leading scorer reaching a total of 30,000 points in 1972. He also set the record of most points (4029) in one season during 1961-62. He was the first man to score 100 points in a single game in NBA league against NY Knickerbockers on 2 March, 1962.

Michael Jeffrey Jordan (born February 17, 1963) is a retired American professional basketball player. Considered by many to be the greatest basketball player of all times, he became the most effectively marketed athlete of his generation and was instrumental in spreading the appeal of the National Basketball Association around the world in the 1980s and 1990s. He is currently a part-owner of the Charlotte Bobcats.

A remarkable force at both ends of the floor, "M.J." ended his 15 NBA seasons with a regular-season scoring average of 30.12 points per game, the highest in NBA history (marginally ahead of Wilt Chamberlain's 30.06). He won six NBA championships with the Chicago Bulls (during which he won all six NBA Finals MVP awards), won 10 scoring titles, and league MVP five times. He was named to the All-NBA First Team 10 times, All-Defensive First Team nine times, and led the league in steals three times. Since 1983, he had been appearing on the front cover of Sports Illustrated a record 49 times.

Kareem Abdul-Jabbar: Kareem Abdul-Jabbar, formerly known as Lewis Alcindor, was one of players who graces a sport once in a lifetime. The basketball world might never again see an athlete dominate the sport for as long and as thoroughly as Abdul-Jabbar did. The 7-foot-2 Abdul-Jabbar established himself as basketball's most talented and recognizable figure. Upon his retirement in 1989, Abdul-Jabbar stood on top of the heap in nine NBA statistical categories, including points scored (38,387), seasons played (20), playoff scoring (5,762), MVP awards (6), minutes played (57,446), games played (1,560), field goals made and attempted (15,837 of 28,307) and blocked shots (3,189).

Rubén Oscar Wolkowyski (born September 30, 1973): Rubén is an Argentine professional basketball player. He is a 6'10", 275 pound center. Known for his above average shooting skills and leaping abilities, Wolkowyski has played professionally in Argentina, the United States, Russia, Spain, and Greece. He has also been a mainstay of the Argentina national basketball team, having participated in the 2001 and 2003 FIBA Americas Championships, the 2002 and 2006 FIBA World Championships, and the 1996 and 2004 Summer Olympics.

Carlos Francisco Delfino (born August 29, 1982, in Santa Fe, Argentina): Delfino is an Argentine professional basketball player for the Detroit Pistons who generally plays at the shooting guard and small forward positions. He stands 6 ft 6 in (1.98 m) tall and weighs 230 lb (104 kg). He began his professional career playing in the Argentine Basketball League for Olímpia de Venado Tuerto in the 1998-99 season. Delfino moved to Italy in 2000 and played four seasons in the Italian A-1 League. He was a member of Argentina's Under-21 National Team.

■

BEACH VOLLEYBALL

Chapter - 6

Till late 1990s and 2000s the game remained more or less unknown but then suddenly it gained popularity mostly due to media exposure.

History

It is presumed that Beach Volley Ball began in Santa Monica, California, in the 1920s. It began to make its appearances in Europe about a decade later. In the 1960s, an attempt to start a professional volleyball league was made in Santa Monica. It failed, but a professional tournament was held in France. During 1970s, a few professional tournaments in Santa Monica were sponsored by beer and cigarette companies. In the 1980s, Hermosa Beach, California, developed into beach volleyball capital of world with sand courts lining the beach.

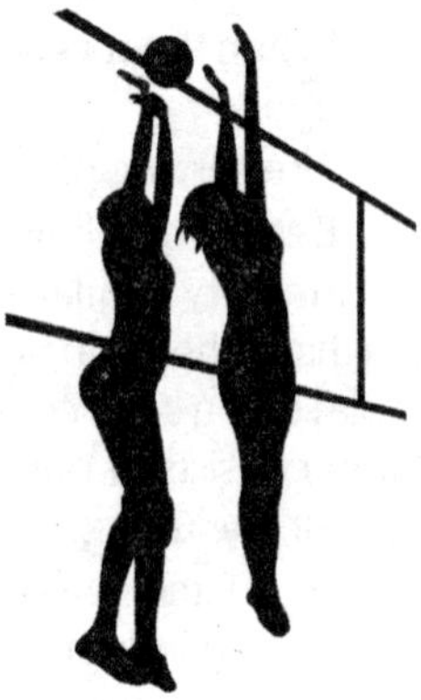

Till late 1990s and 2000s the game remained more or less unknown but then suddenly it gained popularity mostly due to media exposure. The. Beach volleyball was an exhibition sport at the 1992 Olympics, and became a separate Olympic event in 1996.

For decades, the two nations which have dominated international beach volleyball are Brazil and the United States. Recently, Australia has emerged as a distant third superpower, and each of these three nations owns a reasonably well developed national touring system which typically takes place during the summer months. Furthermore, these three are the only countries to win gold medal in an Olympic beach volleyball event since its debut at the 1996 Games. Specifically in the case of the more popular Women's event, each country has won once each, the Brazilians in 1996, the Australians in 2000, and the United States in 2004.

Other countries such as Greece, Germany and China have developed a large and competitive following.

Beach Volleyball is a sport played by two teams of two players each on a sand court divided by a net.

There are different versions available for specific circumstances in order to offer the versatility of the game to everyone.

The object of the game is to send the ball over the net in order to ground it on the opponent's court, and to prevent the same effort by the opponent.

The team has three hits for returning the ball (including the block touch).

The ball is put in play with a service: hit by the server over the net to the opponents.

The rally continues until the ball is grounded on the playing court, goes "out" or a team fails to return it properly. In Beach Volleyball, the team winning a rally scores a point (Rally Point System).

When the receiving team wins a rally, it gains a point and the right to serve.

The serving player must be alternated every time this occurs.

Beach volleyball evolved from indoor volleyball, and the two sports remain very similar. The most important differences between them are that rather than being played on indoor hard courts, beach volleyball is played on sand courts, and instead of teams of six, a beach volleyball team consists of only two players. There are many minor differences as well, including:

- Each half of the court measures 8 by 8 meters, not 9 by 9 as in indoor volleyball.
- Overhand finger passes are called very tightly when receiving or attacking. Unless executed very cleanly and square to the shoulders, they are ruled illegal. The exception is receiving a hard smash.
- The standard for double hits when using overhand finger passes and hand sets is much stricter than in indoor volleyball.
- The block always counts as the first contact.
- Open-hand dinks, where a player uses his or her finger tips to redirect the ball into the opponent's court, are illegal.
- It is legal to cross under the net as long as doing so does not interfere with the opponents' attempt to play the ball.
- Players are not required to rotate positions; they must alternate service, but there are no 'rotation errors'.

- Most players, either by choice or by requirement of the rules, play the game barefoot.

Playing Area

The playing area includes the playing court and the free zone.

Dimensions

- The playing court is a rectangle measuring 16 m x 8 m, surrounded by a free zone with a minimum of 3 m wide and with a space free from any obstruction up to a height of a minimum of 7 m from the playing surface.
- For FIVB World Competitions, the playing court is a rectangle measuring 16 m x 8 m, surrounded by a free zone with a minimum of 5 m and a maximum of 6 m from the end lines / side lines and with a space free from any obstruction up to a minimum height of 12.5 m from the playing surface.

Playing Surface

- The terrain must be composed of leveled sand, as flat and uniform as possible, free of rocks, shells and anything else, which can represent risks of cuts or injuries to the players.
- For FIVB World Competitions the sand must be at least 40 cm deep and composed of fine loosely compacted grains.
- The playing surface must not present any danger from injury to the players.
- For FIVB World Competitions the sand should also be sifted to an acceptable size not too coarse, free of stones and

Beach Volleyball Court

dangerous particles. It should not be too fine to cause dust and stick to the skin.

- For FIVB World Competitions a tarp to cover the central court is recommended in case of rain.

Line on the Court

- Two sidelines and two end lines mark the playing court. Both sides and end lines are placed inside the dimensions of the playing court.
- There is NO centerline.
- All lines are 5-8 cm wide.
- The lines must be of a colour, which contrasts sharply with the colour of the sand.
- For Court lines should be used ribbons made of resistant material, and any exposed anchors should be of soft, flexible material.

Service Zone

The service zone is the area behind the end line and between the extensions of the two sidelines. In depth, the service zone extends to the end of the free zone.

Net

The net is 8.5 m long and 1 m (+/- 3 cm) wide when it is hung taut, placed vertically over the axis of the center of the court. It is made of 10 cm square mesh. At its top and bottom there are two 7-10 cm wide horizontal bands made of two-fold canvas, preferably in dark blue or bright colours, sewn along its full length. Each extremity of the upper band has a hole through which passes a cord fastening the upper band to the posts to keep the top of the net stretched.

Within the bands, there are: a flexible cable in the upper one and a cord in the bottom one for fastening the net to the posts and keeping its top and bottom taut. It is permissible to have advertising on the horizontal bands of the net.

For FIVB World Competitions an 8.0 m net with smaller meshes and brandings displayed between the end sides of the net and the poles may be used provided that the visibility of the athletes and officials will be preserved. Publicity may be printed on the above items as per FIVB regulations.

Side Bands

Two colour bands, 5-8 cm wide (same wide as the court lines) and 1 m long, are fastened vertically to the net and placed above each sideline. They are considered part of the net. Advertising is permitted on the side bands.

Antennae

An antenna is a flexible rod, 1.8 m long and 10 mm in diameter. It is made of fiberglass or similar material. Two antennae are fastened to the outer edge of each side band and placed on opposite sides of the net. The top 80 cm of each antenna extends above the net and are marked with 10 cm stripes of contrasting colours, preferably red and white. The antennae are considered part of the net and laterally delimit the crossing space.

Height of the Net

The height of the net shall be 2.43 m for men and 2.24 m for women.

Posts

The posts supporting the net must be rounded and smooth, with a height of 2.55 m, preferably adjustable. They must be fixed to the ground at an equal distance of 0.7-1 m from each sideline to the post padding. Fixing the posts to the ground by means of wires is forbidden. All dangerous or obstructing devices must be eliminated. Posts must be padded.

Ball Characteristics

The ball shall be spherical, made of a flexible material (leather, synthetic leather, or similar) which does not absorb humidity, i.e. more suitable to outdoor conditions since matches can be played when it is raining. The ball has a bladder inside made of rubber or a similar material. Approval of synthetic leather material is determined by FIVB regulations.

Colour: Bright colours (such as orange, yellow, pink, white, etc.).

Circumference: 66 cm to 68 cm for FIVB international competitions.

Weight: 260 g to 280 g.

Inside pressure: 171 mbar to 221 mbar or hPa (0.175 $Kgcm^2$ to 0.225 Kg/cm^2).

Participant Teams Composition and Registration

A team is composed exclusively of two players.

Only the two players recorded on the scoresheet may participate in the match. For FIVB World Competitions, coaching is not allowed during a match.

Captain

The team captain shall be indicated on the scoresheet.

Player's Equipment

A player's equipment consists of shorts or a bathing suit. A jersey or "tank-top" is optional except when specified in Tournament Regulations. Players may wear a hat. For FIVB World Competitions players of a given team must wear uniforms of the same colour and style according to tournament regulations.

Player's uniforms must be clean.

Players must play barefooted except when authorised by the referees.

Players' jerseys (or shorts if players are allowed to play without shirt) must be numbered 1 and 2.

The number must be placed on the chest (or on the front of the shorts). The numbers must be of a contrasting colour to the jerseys and a minimum of 10 cm in height. The stripe forming the numbers shall be a minimum of 1.5 cm wide.

Scoring System to Win a Match

The match is won by the team that wins two sets.

In the case of a 1-1 tie, the deciding set (the 3rd) is played to 15 points with a minimum lead of 2 points.

To Win a set

A set (except the deciding 3rd set) is won by the team that first scores 21 points with a minimum lead of two points. In the case of a 20-20 tie, play is continued until a two-point lead is reached (22-20, 23-21 etc).

The deciding set is played according to the Rule above.

To Win a Rally

Whenever a team fails in its service or fails to return the ball, or commits any other fault, the opposing team wins the rally, with one of the following consequences:

If the opposing team served, it scores a point and continues to serve. If the opposing team received the service, it gains the right to serve and also scores a point.

Default and Incomplete Team

If a team refuses to play after being summoned to do so, it is declared in default and forfeits the match with the result 0-2 for the match and 0-21, 0-21 for the sets.

A team that does not appear on the playing court on time is declared in default with the same result as in the Rule above.

A team declared incomplete for the set or for the match loses the set or the match. The opposing team is given the points, or the points and the sets needed to win the set or the match. The incomplete team keeps its points and sets.

Preparation of the Match, Structure of Play, Coin Toss

Before the warm-up, the first referee carries out a coin toss in the presence of the two team captains.

The winner of the coin toss chooses:

a) Either the right to serve or receive the service or

b) The side of the court

The loser takes the remaining choice.

In the second set the loser of the coin tóss in the first set will have the choice of a) or b).

A new coin toss will be conducted for the deciding set.

Substitutions

There are NO substitutions or replacement of players.

Player's Positions

The moment the ball is hit by the server, each team must be within its own court (except the server).

The players are free to position themselves. There are NO determined positions on the court.

There are NO positional faults.

Service Order

Service order must be maintained throughout the set (as determined by the team captain immediately following the coin toss).

Ball in Play

The rally begins with the referee's whistle. However, the ball is in play from the service hit.

Ball out of Play

The rally ends with the referee's whistle. However, if the whistle is due to a fault made in play, the ball is out of play from the moment the fault was committed.

Playing Faults

Any playing action contrary to the Rules is a playing fault.

The referees judge the faults and determine the penalties according to these Rules.

Playing the Ball

Team Hits

Each team is entitled to a maximum of three hits for returning the ball over the net.

These team-hits include not only intentional hits by the player, but also unintentional contacts with the ball.

A player may not hit the ball two times consecutively; however, there are exceptions.

Ball in action

Characteristics of the Hit

The ball may touch any part of the body.

The ball must be hit, not caught or thrown. It can rebound in any direction.

Exceptions:

a) In defensive action of a hard driven ball: In this case, the ball can be held momentarily overhand with the fingers.

b) If simultaneous contacts by the two opponents leads to a "held ball": The ball may touch various parts of the body, only if the contacts take place simultaneously.

Faults at Playing the Ball

Four Hits: A team hits the ball four times before returning it.

Assisted Hit: A player takes support from a teammate or any structure/object in order to reach the ball within the playing area.

Held Ball: A player does not hit the ball unless when in defensive action of a hard driven ball or when simultaneous contacts by the two opponents over the net lead to a momentary "held ball".

Double Contact: A player hits the ball twice in succession or the ball touches various parts of his/her body successively.

Ball/Player Touching the Net

While crossing the net the ball may touch the net. A ball driven into the net may be recovered within the limits of the three team hits. If the ball rips the mesh of the net or tears it down, the rally is cancelled and replayed. Each team must play within its own court and playing space. The ball may, however, be retrieved from beyond the free zone.

Reaching beyond the Net

In blocking, a blocker may touch the ball beyond the net, provided that he/she does not interfere with the opponent's play, before or during the latter's attack-hit

A player is permitted to pass his/her hand beyond the net after his/her attack-hit, provided that his/her contact has been made within his/her own playing space.

Crossing into the Opponent's space, Court and/or Free Zone

A player may enter into the opponent's space, court and/or free zone, provided that this does not interfere with the opponent's play.

Contact with the Net

It is forbidden to touch any part of the net or the antennae.

Once the player has hit the ball, he/she may touch the posts, ropes or any other object outside the total length of the net this action does not interfere with play.

When the ball is driven into the net, which causes it to touch an opponent, no fault is committed.

Incidental contact of hair is not a fault.

Player's Faults at the Net

A player touches the ball or an opponent in the opponent's space before or during the opponent's attack-hit.

A player penetrates into the opponent's space, court and/or free zone interfering with the latter's play.

A player touches the net.

Service

The service is the act of putting the ball into play by the correct serving player who, positioned in the service zone, hits the ball with one hand or arm. The first service of a set is executed by the team determined by the coin toss. After the first service in a set, the player to serve is determined as follows:

a) when the serving team wins the rally, the player who served before, serves again.

b) when the receiving team wins the rally, it gains the right to serve and the player who did not serve last time will serve.

Time-outs

A Time-out is a regular game interruption and it lasts for 30 seconds.

For FIVB World competitions, in sets 1 and 2, one additional 30 second Technical Time-out is automatically allocated when the sum of the points scored by the teams equals 21 points. Each team is entitled to a maximum of one time-out per set.

Court Switches

The teams switch after every 7 points (Set 1 and 2) and 5 points (Set 3) played.

Intervals

The interval between each set lasts one minute. During the interval before a deciding set, the first referee carries out a coin toss. During court switches the teams must change immediately without delay.

Game Officials

The first referee carries out his/her functions seated or standing on a referee's stand located at one end of the net. His/her view must be approximately 50 cm above the net The second referee performs his/her functions standing at the post outside the playing court on the opposite side of and facing the first referee. The scorer performs his/her functions seated at the scorer's table on the opposite side of and facing the first referee. It is compulsory to have two linejudges in official international matches.

Names to Remember

Ricardo & Emanuel of Brazil defeated 2-0 Bosma & Herrera to win the Beach Volleyball Gold medal for men.. This was Brazil's first gold medal in men's beach volleyball.

Kerri Lee Walsh (born August 15, 1978). Walsh is an American beach volleyball player. Who won the gold medal in 2004 Olympics with her team mate Misty May. Walsh was born in the U.S. state of California to Tim and Margie Walsh, and grew up in Saratoga, California. As a high school student, she played on the varsity team at Archbishop Mitty High School in San Jose. Walsh continued on to Stanford University, where she won national titles in 1996 and 1997. She has played both indoor and beach volleyball. On July 23, 2006 Kerri Walsh topped $1 million in career earnings with a win (with her partner Misty May) at AVP McDonald's Chicago Open presented by Nautica.

Misty May-Treanor (born July 30, 1977) is an American professional beach volleyball player. In the 2000 Summer Olympics, May teamed with Holly McPeak, a highly ranked U.S. beach volleyball player, and they finished in fifth place. In the 2004 Summer Olympics with teammate Kerri Walsh, the number one ranked player, May won Gold after she and Walsh defeated the Brazilian team in the finals.

■

BILLIARDS

Chapter - 7

The game is played on green cushioned table with long cues hitting two white balls and a red one.

History

The earliest mention of billiards was in France in 1429. King Louis XI (1461-83), was reported to have a table which conformed to the present billiards table. The rubber cushion for the table was introduced in 1835, and the slate bed 1836. Jonathan Kentfield was the first professional from the early 19th century. British Empire championship used to draw players from India, Australia, New Zealand and South Africa. Interest in billiards declined with the introduction of snooker. During the last few years, both the governing bodies of amateur and professional billiards have made efforts to revive interest in the game. Presently the World Championship draws a lot of interest and the game has received a good financial boost.

Equipment Specifications: The purpose of specifications shall be to set standards for equipment used at all WPA World Championships, WPA World Tour events and other WPA sanctioned and/or recognised events. These specifications do not necessarily apply to tables manufactured for commercial home use. At its sole discretion, the World Pool-Billiard Association can sanction tournaments on tables not in compliance with these specifications.

Table Bed Height: Shall be between 29 ¼ inches [74.295 cm] and 31 inches [78.74 cm].

Design: Shall not have any sharp edges or materials that might cause injuries or damage. Construction should be adequate enough so that the table will remain stable and level under all conditions of play.

Slates: The thickness must be at least 1 inch [2.54 cm], and the playing surface must be capable, either by its own strength or a combination of its strength and that of the table base frame, of maintaining an overall flatness within + .020 inches [.508 mm] lengthwise and + .010 inches [.254 mm] across the width. Further this surface should have an additional deflection not to exceed .030 inches [.762 mm] when loaded with a concentrated static force of 200 pounds [90.7 kg] at its center. All slate joints must be in the same plane within .005 inch [.127 mm] after levelling and shimming. Tournament tables must have a set of slates consisting of three pieces of equal size with wooden frame of at least ¾ inch [1.905 cm] thick lumber attached underneath the slate. The slatc sections must be secured to the base frame with countersunk screws or bolts.

Playing Surface: The playing surface (area) must be rectangular, and symmetrical when the pocket configurations are included:

9 foot - 100 (+ 1/8) x 50 (+ 1/8) inches (except cushions)/ [2.54 m (+ 3.175 mm) x 1.27 m (+ 3.175 mm)]

8 foot - 92 (+ 1/8) x 46 (+ 1/8) inches (except cushions)/ [2.3368 m (+ 3.175 mm) x 1.1684 m (+ 3.175 mm)]

Rail and Cushion: The rail width must be between 4 [10.16 cm] and 7 ½ inches [19.05 cm] including the rubber cushions. 18 sights (or 17 and a name plate) shall be attached flush on the rail cap with:

12 ½ inches [31.75 cm] from sight to sight on a 9-foot regulation table.

11 ½ inches [29.20 cm] from sight to sight on a 8-foot regulation table.

The center of each sight should be located 3 11/16 (+) inches [93.6625 mm (+ 3.175 mm)] from the nose of the cushion. The sights may be round (between 7/16 [11.11 mm] and ½ inch [12.7 mm] in diameter) or diamond-shaped (between 1 x 7/16 [25.4 x 11.11 mm] and 1 ¼ x 5/8 inch [31.75 x 15.875 mm]). Any name-plates and score-counters should be flush level with rail top. All rail-bolts should be thus located that when properly torqued render a quiet and optimum rebound from any point of the cushion nose of the table.

Height of the Cushion: Rubber cushions should be triangular in shape with the width of the cloth-covered cushion being between 17/8 [4.76 cm] and 2 inches [5.40 cm] measured from the outer edge of the featherstrip to the nose of the cushion. Rail height (nose-line to table-bed) should be 63 ½% (+1 %) or between 62 ½% and 64 ½ % of the diameter of the ball.

Cushion Rubber: Table cushions should influence the speed of the table such that with placement of a ball on the head spot, shooting through the foot spot, using center ball with a level cue and firm stroke, the ball must travel a minimum of 4 to 4 ½ lengths of the table without jumping.

Pocket Openings and Measurements: Only rubber facings of minimum 1/16 [1.5875 mm] to maximum ¼ inch [6.35 mm] thick may be used at pocket jaws. The WPA-preferred maximum thickness for facings is 1/8 inch [3.175 mm]. The facings on both sides of the pockets must be of the same thickness. Facings must be of hard re-enforced rubber glued with strong bond to the cushion and the rail, and adequately fastened to the wood rail liner to prevent shifting. The rubber of the facings should be somewhat harder than that of the cushions.

The pocket openings for pool tables are measured between opposing cushion noses where the direction changes into the pocket (from pointed lip to pointed lip). This is called mouth.

Corner Pocket Mouth: between 4.5 [11.43 cm] and 4.625 inches [11.75 cm].

Side Pocket Mouth: between 5 [12.7 cm] and 5.125 inches [13.0175 cm].

The mouth of the side pocket is traditionally ½ inch [1.27 cm] wider than the mouth of the corner pocket.

Vertical Pocket Angle (Back Draft): 12 degrees minimum to15 degrees maximum.

Horizontal Pocket Cut Angle: The angle must be the same on both sides of a pocket entrance. The cut angles of the rubber cushion and its wood backing (rail liner) for both sides of the corner pocket entrance must be 142 degrees (+1). The cut angles of the rubber cushion and its wood backing (rail liner) for both sides of the side pocket entrance must be 104 degrees (+1).

Billiards Table

Shelf: The shelf is measured from the center

of the imaginary line that goes from one side of the mouth to the other—where the nose of the cushion changes direction—to the vertical cut of the slate pocket cut. Shelf includes bevel.

Corner Pocket Shelf: Between 1 [2.54 cm] and 2 ¼ inches [5.715 cm].

Side Pocket Shelf: between 0 and .375 inches [.9525 cm].

Pocket Liners: The pocket liners and boots should be of long wearing plastic, rubber or leather. The material the liners and boots are made of should not permanently mark (stain) the balls or cues. The upper part of the inner wall must be so fashioned that whenever a ball hits the pocket liner wall below the rim at the top of the rail, the ball is directed downwards.

Ball Return and Drop Pockets: Both drop pockets and automatic ball returns can be used, but must be as noiseless as possible. Drop pockets must have a basket capacity of at least 6 balls. Automatic ball returns must be properly installed so that pocketed balls are not trampolined back to the table or off the table.

Cloth: The cloth must be non-directional, nap-free billiard fabric which will not pill or fluff, composed of no less than 85% combed worsted wool and no more than 15% nylon. 100% combed worsted wool fabric is preferred. No backed cloth will be allowed. Only the colours of yellow-green, blue-green or electric blue are acceptable for WPA competition.

Fastening of the Cloth (Guidelines): Before cloth-covering the slate, a strip of canvas (or table-cloth) should be glued to the vertical pocket cuts of the slates and their underlying wooden slate liner. The table-bed cloth must be stretched for "proper tension" and mechanically attached to the underlying wooden slate liner with fully driven fasteners (staples or tacks) spaced a maximum of 1 inch on center approximately, with at least inch [.9525 cm] penetration into the wooden slate liner. Guidelines for proper tension are as follows:

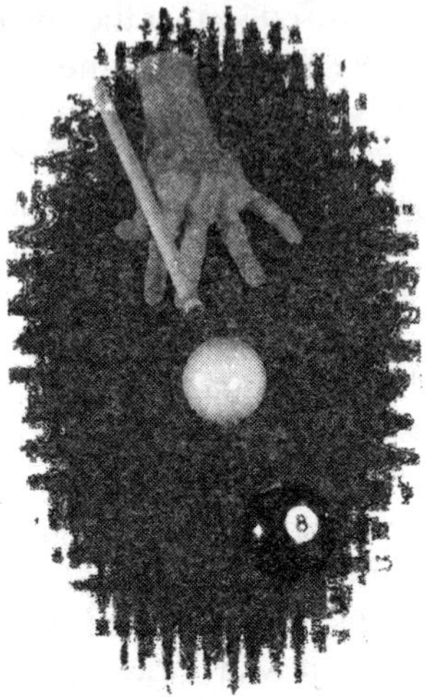

1. Length of the cloth should be manually stretched as tight as

possible, and then relieved ½ inch [1.27 cm] before attachment.

2. Width of the cloth should be manually stretched as tight as possible, and then relieved ¼ inch [.635 cm] before attachment.

When covering the cushions, the cloth must be lengthwise evenly and consistently well-stretched while inserting the featherstrip as well as thereafter. While the cloth is in a stretched condition lengthwise, the cloth must then be stretched in the width up to the moment when indentation of the nose of the rubber cushion is about to start and attached underneath the wooden rail with fully driven fasteners (staples or tacks) spaced a maximum of 3/4 inch [1.905 cm] on center approximately, with at least 3/8 inch [.9525 cm] penetration into the wood. At the side pocket openings, the rails are to be covered with a minimum overlapping of fabric over the facings. When doing overlappings, great care must be taken so that hidden folds, if any, do not cause balls to jump off the table during play. No folds are allowed in the cloth over the facings of the corner pockets.

Cleaning Table and Rail Cloth (Advised Preparation): The WPA recommends only green and blue colours for chalk. A soft (horse hair) brush, a cloth-cleaner made with billiard fabric, or a brushless (without rotating brush) vacuum cleaner are the recommended table and cushion cleaning devices. Brushes that shed bristles are not recommended.

Lights: The bed and rails of the table must receive at least 520 lux (48 footcandles) of light at every point. A screen or reflector configuration is advised so that the center of the table does not receive noticeably more lighting than the rails and the corners of the table. If the light fixture above the table may be moved aside (referee), the minimum height of the fixture should be no lower than 40 inches [1.016 m] above the bed of the table. If the light fixture above the table is non-movable, the fixture should be no lower than 65 inches [1.65 m] above the bed of the table. The intensity of any directed light on the players at the table should not be blinding. Blinding light starts at 5000 lux (465 footcandles) direct view. The rest of the venue (bleachers, etc.) should receive at least 50 lux (5 footcandles) of light.

Balls and Ball Rack: All balls must be composed of cast phenolic resin plastic and measure 2 ¼ (+.005) inches [5.715 cm (+ .127 mm)] in diameter and weigh 5 ½ to 6 oz [156 to 170 gms]. Balls should be unpolished, and should also not be waxed. Balls should be cleaned with a towel or cloth free of dirt and dust, and may also be washed with soap and water. Balls contaminated with any slippery substance—treated with a polishing or rubbing compound and/or waxed—must be cleansed and dewaxed with a clean cloth moistened with diluted alcohol before play.

Cue Sticks: Cue Sticks used at WPA competitions should comply with the following during play at table:

Length of Cue: 40 inches [1.016 m] minimum / No Maximum

Weight of Cue: No minimum / 25 oz. [708.75 gm] maximum

Width of Tip: No minimum / 14mm maximum

The cue tip may not be of a material that can scratch or damage the addressed ball. The cue tip on any stick must be composed of a piece of specially processed leather or other fibrous or pliable material that extends the natural line of the shaft end of the cue and contacts the cue ball when the shot is executed.

The ferrule of the cue stick, if of a metal material, may not be more than 1 inch [2.54 cm] in length.

Mechanical Bridge: The mechanical bridge, also called rake, crutch or rest, is an accessory of the billiard sports table and consists of a stick with a bridge head mounted at its end to support the shaft of the cue stick replacing the hand bridge during shots difficult to reach. The stick or handle of the mechanical bridge is very similar in shape to the cue stick. The bridge head has notches or grooves, usually at various heights, in which the cue shaft can rest. The contour of the bridge head should be smooth in order not to mar the cue shaft or rip the threads of the table-cloth when being used.

Spacing Between Tables: In WPA-sanctioned competitions a minimum measurement of 6 feet [1.83 m] is required between the outside edge of the table rail in every horizontal direction and obstacle (table, chair, rail, etc.).

Table Recognised by the WPA: Only tables that are recognised by the WPA can be used at a WPA-sanctioned or recognised event.

Rules of Billiards: The game is played by two players or pairs. The rules are given in a nutshell below:

1. Duration: Play lasts an agreed length of time or until one players or side reaches an agreed number of points. A match consists of agreed number of games.

2. Scoring:

(a) Cannon. Two points. When the striker's ball hits both the red and white ball, it falls or vice versa.

(b) In-off white. Two points. When the striker's ball after hitting the non-striker's white ball falls into a pocket.

(c) In-off white. Two points. Three points. When the striker's ball after hitting the red ball falls into a pocket.

(d) Pot white. Two points. The non-striker's white ball is forced into a pocket by the striker's ball.

(e) Pot red. Three points. The red ball forced into a pocket by the striker's ball.

(f) If more than one of the above occur and are made in the same strike all scores are counted.

(g) When an in-off is combined with a canon, the score will be four or five depending upon whether white or red was hit first.

3. Commencement of Game: The choice of the ball and order of play is generally decided by stringing.

4. Stringing: Each player plays the cue ball from the baulk line to the top cushion with the object of getting the ball as close to the bottom cushion as possible. The player whose ball stops nearer to the cushion starts the play.

5. Starting Position: The red ball is placed on the spot and the striker places his cue ball at any point in the 'D' and plays the first shot. While bringing a cue ball into play, no shot may be made to a ball directly in the baulk area. If both the balls are inside the cue area, the cue ball must strike the cushion outside, before it can touch another ball.

6. Pocketed Balls: If the non-striker ball is pocketed during a break, the ball remains off the table until the break ends. When the red ball is pocketed, it is brought back on the table and placed on the spot.

7. Balls Touching: If the striker's ball comes to rest against another ball, the red ball is placed on the spot, the non-striker's ball on the centre spot and the striker plays from the 'D'.

8. Spotting Red Ball: If the red ball is pocketed or forced off the table, it is placed on the spot. If the spot is occupied, it is placed on the pyramid spot. If this is also occupied then it is placed on the centre spot. If the red ball is pocketed twice from the spot or the pyramid spot consecutively, the ball should be placed on the centre spot.

9. Each time a player scores from a shot, he is entitled to another shot.

10. **Limitations:** (a) Consecutive cannons limited to 75.

(b) Consecutive hazards (in-off) limited to 15.

(c) Red may be pocketed three times in succession.

11. **Fouls and Penalties:** (a) A striker who makes a foul shot loses his turn and also the score in that break.

(b) A striker concedes points to his opponent for the following:

(i) Two points—Touching his ball more than once in a strike.

(ii) Three points—Forcing the ball off the table.

(iii) Two points—Not playing out of the baulk from 'D' correctly.

(iv) Two points making a push shot.

(v) For a miss, the striker concedes one point. A miss is foul except when the striker is in hand and there is no ball out of baulk. If the cue ball goes into a pocket after a miss, the striker concedes three points.

(c) The following fouls incur no penalty points:

(i) Playing with both feet off the ground.

(ii) Playing the balls before they are still.

(iii) Striking the ball with anything else than the cue.

(iv) Playing the wrong ball.

(v) Playing out of turn.

(vi) Playing from outside the 'D' when required to play from within it.

Game Officials

Referee: He is the sole judge of fair or unfair play.

Marker: The marker keeps the score on the scoreboard and assists the referee.

Championships

The major tournaments include World championships instituted in 1870, UK Title started in 1934, and English Amateur Championship started in 1888.

■

BOCCE

Chapter - 8

In 1896, a bocce Olympiad competition was held in Athens but it would be the middle of the 20th Century before any type of official organisation grew up around the game.

History

Bocce is based on one of the oldest diversions known to man—throwing something at a target. In the case of bocce, a small ball called a pallino is thrown onto the court. Players then bowl larger balls toward the pallino to see who can get the closest. A painting of two boys playing a similar type of game was found in an Egyptian tomb and dated to 5200 B.C.

From Egypt the game apparently made its way to Greece and then to Rome. Roman soldiers played a game like bocce during the Punic Wars in the Third Century B.C. In this version of the sport, stones were used instead of balls. Later, the Romans played the game with coconuts they brought back from Africa. Emperor Augustus (31 B.C.-14 A.D.) played the game and became the first in a long line of notable public figures who enjoyed bocce or a closely related type of sport.

Bocce shared a fate common to many games of the Middle Ages—it was banned both by kings and the church. In 1319, Roman Emperor Charles IV outlawed the game because it took people's attention away from military matters. King Carlos of Spain would issue a similar ban. Perhaps they were right. Legend says that English Admiral Sir Frances Drake was playing Bocce when he was told that an attack by the Spanish armada was imminent. His response: "First, we finish the game, then we have time for invincible armada."

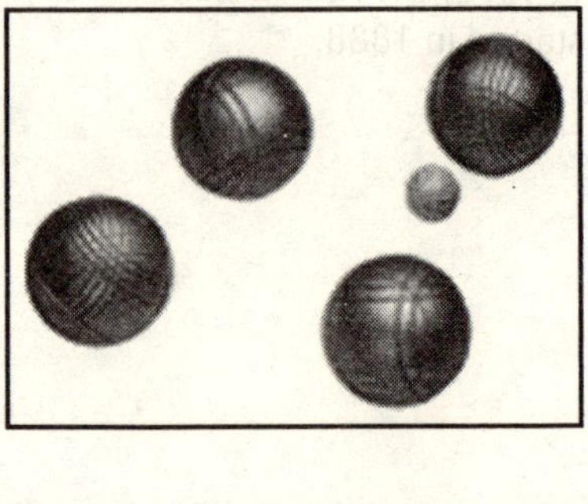

Just a few years before Sir Frances supposedly spoke those words, the Republic of Venice had also outlawed bocce in 1576. Those caught playing the game were fined and in some cases sent to prison. The Catholic Church also condemned bocce because it led to gambling.

Any game that people find competitive and enjoyable will overcome even official attempts to stop play. Bocce was no exception. It found a following in the streets, alleyways, parks and town squares of Europe, particularly in Italy and France.

Throughout history, some notable names have been associated with the game of bocce. Galileo and deVinci reportedly enjoyed the sport, as did Queen Elizabeth and George Washington. Washington is said to have built a bocce court on his Mount Vernon estate in the 1780s.

When famed Italian soldier Giuseppe Garibaldi was not busy fighting battles to unite Italy, he was an avid bocce ball competitor. In his military travels, he took the game with him and introduced it to new parts of the world..

In 1896, a bocce Olympiad competition was held in Athens but it would be the middle of the 20th Century before any type of official organisation grew up around the game. The first international bocce organisation was formed in 1946. The Federation International de Boules (FIB) started with four member countries: Italy, France, Switzerland and Monaco. Today, 39 nations belong to the FIB.

Formal local clubs were first organised around the town of Rivoli, Italy, and the first official Italian league was formed in 1947. The first world championships were held the same year in Geneva.

Two competing international organisations were stared in the 1980s. The Confédération Bouliste Internationale (CBI) was started in 1982 to promote bocce among European clubs that did not use metal balls. The FIB, CBI and a third organisation formed to promote the French version of the bocce called petanque were all trying to gain Olympic recognition.

The Olympic Committee balked at working with three separate groups, so an umbrella organisation was formed in 1985. The Confédération Mondiale Sports Boules works solely toward the goal of getting bocce and its related games into the Olympics.

Italian immigrants brought bocce to the United States and the game was most popular in urban centers that had large Italian-American populations. In the 1970s, the US game had a growth spurt, particularly in California. The Martinez Bocce Federation has 1200 players who *play on 14 permanent courts. The game is also popular in RV parks and campgrounds.*

In 1976, Chris Gerardo established the United States Bocce Federation. The United States has sent competitors to every world championship since 1977.

Phil Ferrari, a US national singles bocce champion, has formed the World Bocce League to promote the game. According to WBL, more than two million Americans play bocce regularly and 25 million have tried it at least once. The WBL is working to introduce the game to youth and to disabled veterans. Bocce is already part of the Special Olympics and the World Corporate Games.

What is Bocce?

Today's version of bocce has elements of bowling, horseshoes, shuffleboard and billiards. Bocce can be played on nearly any type of surface from grass to asphalt to sand, though officially it's played on packed dirt or gravel. The game requires strategy and accuracy and can be enjoyed by players of all ages and athletic abilities.

A bocce court is 10-13 feet wide and between 60 feet and 100 feet long. Boards that are four and one-half inches tall surround the court. Two to eight players can compete at a time. The pallino, sometimes called the jack or pig, is rolled onto the court. This ball becomes the target. Players roll larger balls to see who can come closest to the pallino. Players can move the pallino with their balls or knock opposing balls further away. This is where the strategy comes in. In a variation of the game called raffa, balls may be tossed rather than rolled.

BASIC RULES OF BOCCE

The Courts

For lawn bowling, you don't really use a court. Just choose any space of lawn that's large and reasonably level. Then step off about 20 adult paces and use that as a good playing distance. For bocce:

1. Backstops are placed 60 feet apart.
2. Backstops are 12 feet wide with sides 4 feet long.
3. Backstops and sides must be at least 4 ½ inches high.
4. A foul line is marked out 10 feet from each backstop.
5. Court surface between backstops can be stone-dust, dirt, clay, grass, or artificial surface.

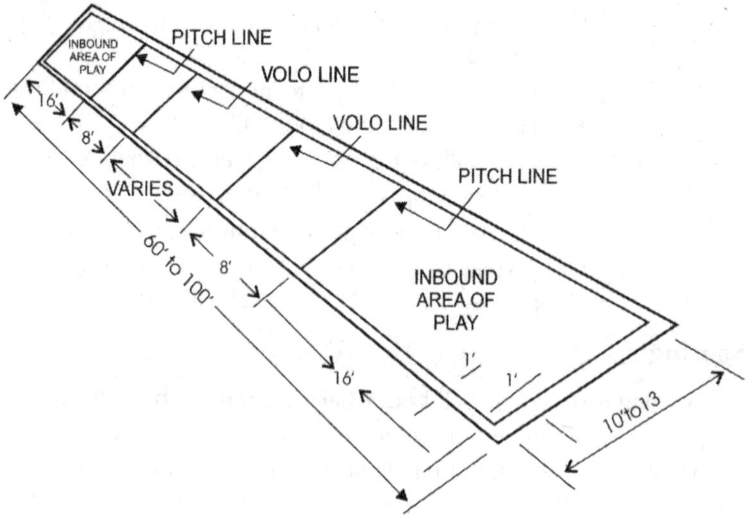

Equipment

Two sizes of balls are used to play bocce. The balls are usually made of a tough, composite material like small bowling balls (without the finger holes). The target ball is called the pallina or pallino and is about 2.25 inches in diameter. The team balls are called bocces and are about 4.25 inches in diameter. Four bocces are used for each team and are colour-coded by team. The pallina can be white, cream, or yellow but there may be contrasts in colour with the bocce balls.

The Rules to Play

1. Teams can consist of from 1 to 4 players on each side.
2. When multiple team members are present, a playing rotation is maintained throughout the game.
3. The first player (choose by coin toss or whatever), throws the pallina into the opposite court. That player also rolls the first bocce ball. The idea is to get as close to the pallina as possible. It doesn't matter if you hit the pallina, as long as you don't knock it out of the court. If that happens, it must be re-tossed by the opposing team.
4. Now the opposing team throws until they get a ball closer to the pallina. This is called getting "inside" your opponent's ball.

5. Play then returns to the first team who must try to get a ball "inside" that ball.
6. In each case, throwing by each team continues (in rotation) until a ball gets "inside" or all four balls are tossed.
7. The remaining balls of the opposing team are then rolled to try to get inside any opposing balls for points.
8. For "official" play, 1 and 2 player teams play to 12 points. 4 player teams play to 16 points. For casual play you can go to 21 and, optionally, a "win by 2 points" rule can be used.

Scoring

Scoring is done after all bocce balls are thrown by both teams. There is no minimum distance to the pallina. One point is awarded for each ball that is closest to the pallina and "inside" of any opponent's ball. Therefore, at least 1 and as many as 4 points may be awarded to a team in each frame.

Strategies

This is where experience and skill really pay off in bocce. There are a bunch of tactics, both offensive and defensive, that can be employed to out-manuever your opponent. A few of them are as follows:

1. Spot your ball directly in front of the pallina. Although this often invites a bomb (see next), it makes it difficult for your opponent to get around your ball and be closer.
2. "Spocking" or bombing. This involves intentionally knocking your opponent's ball away from the pallina. If this is done with skill, you can end up with your ball closest to the pallina while your opponent's ball rolls down the neighbor's driveway.
3. You can also spock the pallina if you wish to move it away from your opponent's ball and against the other three balls that you've carefully positioned in previous rolls.
4. Sometimes you have to sacrifice. If an opponent's ball is in a solid position against the pallina, you can spock it out of contention, taking your ball with it. The starting team must now re-establish the point ball which (hopefully) will be in a better position for you to get inside.

5. If you're playing on a bocce court with backstops and sides, all kinds of bank shots are possible, making ball placement more critical. Ideally, you knock the pallina into a corner and surround it with your balls.

If you would like more information, you can contact any of the following:-

- World Bocce League (WBL)
- United States Bocce Federation (USBF)
- Fédération International de Boules (FIB)
- Confédération Bouliste Internationale (CBI)
- Confédération Mondiale Sports Boules
- Bocce Federation of Australia.

■

BOWLING

Chapter - 9

Originally a European game bowling became popular in the USA in the 17th century. The 10th pin was added at a later date.

History

The European game Ninepin most likely originated in Germany. The game Heiden Werfen (knock down the pagans) was brought to the USA in the early 17th century. A tenth pin was added to evade the law. The American Bowling Congress (ABC) was established in New York on 9th September, 1895. This was the first body to standardise rules. In 1961, the ABC affiliated itself to the Federation International des Quilleurs (FIQ), an international organisation based at Helsinki which covers a number of bowling games.

Bowling Lane

The lane is 19.16 m long and 1.06 m wide. Maple is used at the ends.

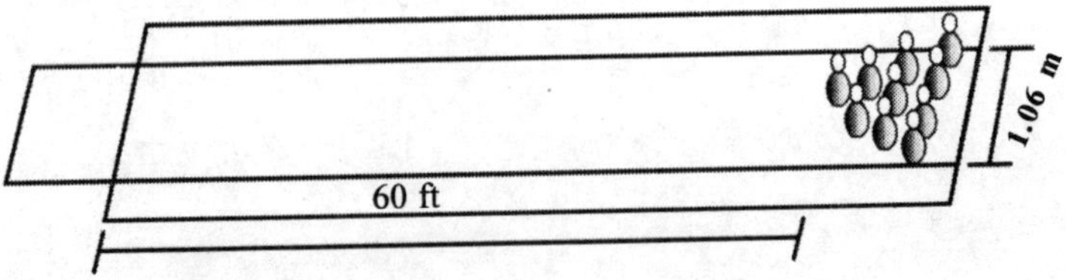

Pins

Pins are placed in a triangle with the apex being 18.29 m (60 ft) away at the end of the lane.

Bowling lane

Ball

Pins

Height	381 mm (15 in)
Circumference	14.97 in
Weight (wood)	1.42-1.64 kg
Weight (synthetic)	1.47-1.53 kg

Ball

Circumference	Not more than 685 mm (27 in)
Weight	Not more than 7.26 kg (16 1b)
Diameter	3½ in

It has one thumb hole and two finger holes.

Bowling

The name of the game is knocking down pins. Everyone can enjoy that, but many people are confused by the scoring system in bowling.

With ten pins and ten frames you might think the maximum score would thus be 100 — but, no, you can throw twelve strikes in one game of ten frames and you'll get a score of 300. The scoring system goes like this.

Frame

There are ten frames in one game. You have two chances to knock down the ten pins in each frame (see the explanations for strike and spare). Note that the tenth frame rewards you with a final bonus ball if you convert your spare (or make two strikes). You can thus throw nine strikes in the first nine frames and, if you get another two in the tenth, the bonus ball means the most strikes you can have in one game is twelve. This is called a perfect game.

Spare

Getting all ten pins down with one ball is not as easy as it seems! So, if you leave one or more pins standing after your first delivery, you get a second chance to knock all the pins down, this is your "spare" shot. If you knock all remaining pins down on the second shot you have made your spare. A spare is marked on the scoresheet with a "/". It takes skill to consistently make spares and the scoring system rewards you by adding in the pins from the next ball into the current frame. See also split.

Strike

When the bowler knocks down all ten pins with the first delivery of the ball it is called a strike. Clearly your score goes up by ten, but like a spare, you get a bonus — your next two deliveries are added to the score. Stringing strikes together will raise your score dramatically (turkey)—Marked on the scoresheet with an "X".

Pin Spotter

Pin Spotter is an automatic machine used to put up the pin again if the bowler knocks down all the ten pins.

Championships

Asian Games: Bowling was introduced in the Asian Games for the first time in the Xth Asiad at Seoul.

World Championship: This championship for men was instituted in 1954. For women the championship began in 1963.

Names to Remember

Sandra Jo Sherry (USA): In June 1987 at Helsinki she scored a record 4894 in 24 game series in women's championship.

Thomas Jordan (USA, b. 27 October 1966): For three sanctioned games and out of possible 900, he scored 899 on 7 March 1989 at Union, New Jersey, USA.

Albert Allie Brandt (New York,USA): He has the world record of scoring 886 out of possible 900 in the sanctioned 3 games on 25 October 1939.

Mark Roth (b.1950): In Professional Bowler Association competition he has won a record sum of £ 1,278,681.

Jeane Maiden (b.10 November 1957): At Saloon, Ohio, on 23 November 1976, she created world record for the women by scoring 864 in 3 games.

Ed. Luther (USA): At Milwaukee Wisconsin on 28 August 1971, he created a record of highest pin fall in the individual men's event scoring 5963 in 28 games.

■

BOXING

Chapter - 10

Jack Broughton of England formulated the first set of codes for prize ring competition of boxing. And it was the Queensberry rules which made boxing compulsory with gloves.

History

Pugilism was introduced in Greece in the Olympic games around 686 BC. However, the earliest evidence of boxing with gloves was found on a fresco on the Isle of Thera in Greece dating back to 1520 BC.

Jack Broughton, a British boxer from Bristol, formulated the first set of codes for prize ring competition and came to be known as the father of boxing. Thereafter, the Boxing came under Queensberry Rules of 1867 formulated for the 9th Marquess of Queensberry. Under this code, boxing with gloves was established for the first time. The Amateur Boxing Association was formed in 1880, in England. The Association Intemationale de Boxe Amateur (AIBA) was formed in 1946. This association controls the world amateur boxing. Boxing didn't, however, become a legal sport in Britain till the legal ruling by Justice Gronthan following the death of Billy Smith on 24 April,1901. Boxing of various classes was introduced in the Olympic Games at different periods.

Boxing Ring

Three of four rope rings of 6.10m square comprise the boxing ring.This ring is usually set on a stage. The floor should project not less than 457 mm outside the ropes and it should not be less than 91 cm or more than 1.22m above the ground or base. A sketch of boxing ring is shown here.

Boxing Ring

Gloves

Gloves should weigh 8 or 10 oz and the boxers' hands are further protected by wrapping and soft adhesive bandages. An amateur boxer wears shorts, a singlet and high-ankled soft leather boots and uses 8 oz gloves. The professional is stripped to the waist and in England his gloves should weight 6 oz.

Rounds

All rounds fought by both amateur and professional boxers are of 3 minutes duration followed by a minute's rest. Amateur bouts consist of three/five rounds. Professional bouts range from 6 to 15 rounds.

Weight Classification

The different weights in which the boxers are divided are as follows (according to Association Internationale De Boxe Amateur):-

1.	Light-Flyweight	Weight up to 48 kg
2.	Flyweight	Above 48-51 kg
3.	Bantamweight	Above 51-54 kg
4.	Featherweight	Above 54-57 kg
5.	Lightweight	Above 57-60 kg
6.	Light-Welterweight	Above 60-63.5 kg
7.	Welterweight	Above 63.5-67 kg
8.	Light-Middleweight	Above 67-71 kg
9.	Middleweight	Above 71-75 kg
10.	Light-Heavyweight	Above 75-81 kg

11. Heavyweight Above 81-91 kg
12. Super-Heavyweight Above 91 kg

Weighing of the competitors is carried out on the morning of the competition. One attempt is permitted to make the grade.In England, professional boxers are weighed at 1 p.m. for evening bouts and allowed one hour of grace period from that time to make the weight.

Rules of Boxing

Article VII, Section 107.6 — Judges

(1) Dress: The judges shall officiate in white clothing, similar to the referee. Female officials will be dressed in white blouse, white skirt or slacks, and preferably, white shoes. Officials working in USA Boxing Group Members' tournaments may wear the uniforms of that organisation at its competitions.

(2) Duties:

(a) Each judge shall independently judge the merits of the two boxers and shall decide the winner according to the rules.

(b) A judge shall not speak to a boxer nor to another judge nor to anyone else except the referee during the contest, but may, if necessary, at the end of a round, bring to the notice of the referee any incident which the referee may appear not to have noticed, such as the misconduct of a coach, loose ropes, etc.

(c) The number of legal scoring blows will be counted with the use of a tally counter or similar counting device. Two counting devices will be used. One device will count the scoring blows for the Red corner and the other device will count the scoring blows for the Blue corner. The number of legal scoring blows awarded to each boxer will be recorded on the score card at the end of each round. In addition, any warnings shall be entered by the judge on the scorecard immediately after the end of the round as indicated by Rule 107.7(1)(b) & (c). The scoring device must be reset to zero prior to the start of the next round.

(d) At the end of the bout, a judge shall total the scoring blows and nominate a winner.

(e) Judges shall not leave their seats until the result has been announced to the public.

(3) Each contest shall be marked by five USA Boxing judges who shall be seated separate from the public and immediately adjacent to the ring. Two of the judges shall be seated on the same side of the ring at a sufficient distance from one another, and each of the other three judges shall be seated at the center of one of the other three sides of the ring. When the number of officials available is insufficient, three judges instead of five may be used, but this shall not apply to the U.S. Championships or similar events.

(4) Before a contest begins, the referee and the judges should confirm the identity of each boxer, fill in the necessary preliminary entries on their score card, such as weight class, bout number, date and affix their signature to the bottom of the paper. Each official will print, in large block letters, the names of the boxers in the red and blue corners in the corresponding left and right columns on the scorecard.

Note: Competition organisers should strive to have all scorecards pre-printed or typed with names, club representation, weights, etc.

Article VII, Section 107.7 — Awarding of Points

(1) Directives: In awarding points, the following directives shall be observed.

(A) Concerning blows:

(1) Scoring blows: During each round, a judge shall assess the respective scores of each boxer according to the number of blows obtained by each. Each blow to have scoring value must, without being blocked or guarded, land directly with the knuckle part of the closed glove of either hand on any part of the front or sides of the head or body above the belt. 3lows landing as above described are scoring hits. The value of blows scored in a rally of infighting shall be assessed at the end of such rally and shall be credited to the boxer who has had the better of the exchanges according to the degree of said boxer's superiority.

(2) Non-scoring blows: Non-scoring blows are blows which are struck by a boxer:

(a) while infringing any of the rules;

(b) with the side, heel, or inside of the glove or with the open glove or any part other than the knuckle part of the closed glove;

(c) which lands on the arms;

(d) which merely connect, without the weight of the body or shoulder.

(B) Concerning fouls – "W," "X" and "J"

(1) There are three symbols the judge uses to annotate fouls on the score card – "W," "X" and "J".

(a) W – Referee's Warning: If the referee issues a "warning" against one (or both) of the boxers, the judge will indicate a "W" on the score card in the column of the offending boxer. The judge will also note the reason for the warning (i.e. W - holding).

(b) X – Judge disagrees with referee's warning: If the judge concludes "unequivocally" that the warning was inappropriate or in error, the judge will annotate an "X" in the appropriate column and indicate the reason for the warning (i.e. X – low blow). In this case, there will be no addition to the number of scoring blows awarded the "fouled" boxer. It must be noted if the judge did not see the foul or was unsure if it was a foul, the judge will accept the advice of the referee and issue a "W" for warning.

(c) J – Judge's warning: If the judge detects a foul, apparently unnoticed by the referee, the judge may impose a warning by writing a "J" on the score card in the column of the offending boxer. The judge will also note the reason for the judge's warning (i.e. J – ducking). A "J" warning carries the same penalty as a "W" warning.

(C) How to administer the penalty (foul)

(1) The purpose of using a tally counter or similar scoring device is to mimic the computer scoring system. Administering the penalty (foul) will also mimic the computer scoring system. These are the rules a judge must use to administer the penalty (foul).

(a) "W" - Two scoring blows will be added to the round score of the FOULED boxer. This will be done for each "W" occurring in that round.

(b) "X" - In this case no scoring blows will be added.

(c) "J" - Two scoring blows will be added to the round score of the FOULED boxer. This will be done for each "J" occurring in that round.

(d) When using tally counters or similar scoring devices, there will be no "offsetting" fouls. Two scoring blows will be added to the round score of any boxer fouled.

(e) The judge must immediately note the foul in the remarks column of the scorecard, when given by the referee. A judge's warning must be noted prior to the beginning of the next round.

(D) Concerning the award of scoring blows

(1) At the end of the bout the scores for each of the rounds will be totaled and the winner will be the one with the higher score.

(2) If, at the end of a bout, having marked each round, the judge finds that the boxers are equal in scoring blows after totaling the scorecard, the judge is required to select a winner. The judge must record the criteria for the selection of the winner. The judge must record the criteria for the selection of the winner in the remarks column next to the scorecard total of the winner. The criteria for selecting a winner is as follows:

(a) Who has done most of the leading off or was the effective aggressor? then —

(b) Who has shown the better defense (blocking, parrying, ducking, side-stepping, etc.) by which the opponent's attacks have been made to miss? If still equal:

(c) Who boxed cleaner and had the better style?

(d) A winner must be nominated in all USA Boxing competitions (in AIBA dual matches, a draw decision may be awarded).

(3) Knockdowns—No extra points shall be awarded for a knockdown.

Article VII, Section 107.8 — Method of Scoring

(1) A judge is advised to fixate in between the two boxers; do not develop a tendency to study or follow just one of the boxers.

(2) Never rely on past performance, reputations or titles earned by a particular boxer.

(3) Amateur boxing is scored on a point system, not on a round basis.

(4) The winner is decided on the majority of judges, i.e., 5-0, 4-1 or 3-2.

(5) Amateur boxing is scored on a legal scoring blow system not on a round basis.

(6) Decisions.

(A) Types of decisions:

(1) Win on points: At the end of a contest the boxer who has been awarded the decision by a majority of the judges shall be declared the winner.

(a) If both boxers are injured or down simultaneously and cannot continue the contest, the judges shall record the points gained by each boxer up to its termination, and the boxer who was leading on points up to the actual end of the contest shall be declared the winner.

(b) AIDS Stoppage Rule: If both boxers are bleeding or where one boxer is bleeding and the opponent has an open cut or abrasion, the referee may stop the bout and take the boxers to the doctor to be examined.

If the bout is stopped the boxer ahead on points shall be the winner.

(2) Win by retirement: If a boxer retires voluntarily owing to injury or other causes, or if a boxer fails to resume boxing immediately after the rest between rounds, the opponent shall be declared the winner. If a boxer retires during the rest between rounds, the referee will immediately notify the jury and the judges of the retirement and the other boxer is declared the winner.

(3) Win by referee stopping contest (RSC).

(a) Outclassed: RSC is a term used to stop a bout when a boxer is outclassed or unfit to continue.

(1) If a boxer, in the opinion of the referee, is being outclassed or is receiving unnecessary and excessive blows, the bout shall be stopped and the opponent declared the winner.

(B) Outscored—RSC-OS is only used with the Computer Scoring System and stops a bout when a boxer is outscored as follows:

(1) If one boxer has a 20-point advantage (for Open and Under 19/Junior men), or a 15-point advantage (for Women and Junior Olympics/Cadets) over their opponent, the bout must be stopped except in the last round, and the boxer with the advantage is declared the winner.

(C) Injury

(1) If a boxer, in the opinion of the referee, is unfit to continue because of injury or other physical reasons, the bout shall be stopped and the opponent declared the winner. The right to make this decision rests with the referee, who may consult the doctor. Having consulted the doctor, the referee must follow the doctor's advice.

(2) When a referee calls a doctor into the ring to examine a boxer only these two officials should be present. Coaches should not be allowed into the ring or on the apron.

(3) The ringside physician has the right to request the bout be suspended if the physician thinks, for medical reasons, the bout should not be allowed to continue.

(D) Compulsory Count Limits:

When a male boxer has three compulsory counts in the same round or four counts during the same bout, the match must be stopped. When a female boxer has two compulsory counts in the same round or three counts during the same bout, the match must be stopped. A count issued for a harm foul is not included in this number.

RSC(H): If a boxer is down due to head blows, and fails to box within eight to 10 seconds, whichever is applicable, the opponent shall be declared the winner by RSC(H). For more information on awarding RSC(H), see section 107.1.

Win by disqualification: If a boxer is disqualified, the opponent shall be declared the winner. A boxer is automatically disqualified for not making weight or for committing three warnings in a bout. If both boxers are disqualified, the decision shall be announced accordingly. A disqualified boxer is eliminated from the tournament and shall not be entitled to any prize, medal, trophy, honourable award or grading, relating to any stage of the competition in which the boxer has been disqualified.

No contest: A bout may be terminated by the referee inside the scheduled distance owing to a material happening outside the responsibility of the boxers, or the control of the referee, such as the ring becoming damaged, the failure of the lighting supply, exceptional weather conditions, etc. In such circumstances the bout shall be declared "no contest" and in the case of championships, the jury shall decide the necessary further action.

Win by walkover: Where the boxer presents themselves in the ring fully attired for boxing and the opponent fails to appear after the opponent's name has been called out by the public address system, the bell sounded and a maximum period of two minutes has elapsed, the referee shall declare the first boxer to be the winner by a walkover.

Professional Boxing

Professional boxing is handicapped due to the absence of world body boxing like AIBA. Closest to world authority are two associations, World Boxing Council (WBC) and World Boxing Association (WBA). WBC was started in Mexico city in 1963, and reconstituted in 1969,whereas its chief at WBA, previously the National Boxing Association, was formed in 1920. Dissensions between these two bodies continue and they issue their individual monthly ratings of boxers in all divisions even today.

Boxing as Practised in Other Countries

Chinese Boxing: China had a well-developed system of boxing encouraged by the emperors of the Tang Ching and Ming dynasties. Chinese boxing is divided into two schools—soft and hard. Out of the hard form, Ing Kuen (Red Fist) was adopted by the Japanese and became popular. The soft school was formulated by Chan Tuan. Chinese boxing tournaments are held once in two years. The 1967 championship was held at Taiwan. At present Chinese boxing is practised widely in Asia and in all Chinese communities of Western countries.

Thai Boxing: Thailand also has its own style of boxing in which blows with the feet, knees and elbows are permitted along with normal gloved first used in boxing ring.

Championships (Amateur)

	Professional Championship (Introduced in)	*Olympics*
Light-Flyweight	—	1968
Flyweight	1909	1904
Bantamweight	1888	1904
Featherweight	1889	1904
Lightweight	1868	1904
Light-Welterweight	1951	1952
Welterweight	1892	1904
Light-Middleweight	1951	1952
Middleweight	1884	1904
Light-Heavyweight	1903	1920
Heavyweight	1881	1904

European Amateur Championship

It was inaugurated in 1924, in Paris. From 1953, this championship has been dominated by Polish and Russian boxers. In 1961, the Russians won five European amateur titles, seven in 1963, and in 1965, eight out of the ten weights. The name of Lagutin (Light-middleweight) is famous among boxers from the USSR. The Poles won 5 Olympic and 18 European titles from 1953 to 1969. The majority of boxers taking part in Olympics and European amateur championships never turn professional. This may be due to the fact that no country in the communist bloc practises any professional sports.

Names to Remember

Muhammad Ali (Cassius Clay, 1942) Heavyweight boxer from the USA, who won the world heavyweight title in 1964 four years after winning the Olympic light-heavyweight championship. His licence to box was withdrawn because of his adherence to Black Muslim faith and refusal to serve in the US Armed Forces. Cassius

Muhammad Ali

Clay is a vital figure in the field of sports because of his controversial character. He regained heavyweight title twice when he defeated George Foreman on 30 October 1974, and Leon Spinks on 15 September 1978.

Floyed Patterson (1935-): American boxer who became the youngest world heavyweight champion in 1956, at the age of 21. He won the Olympic middle weight championship in 1952. He was defeated in June1959, by Ingemar Johansson of Sweden but a year later he scored a fifth-round knockout over Johansson.

Rocky Marciano

Rocky Marciano (USA,1923-1969): He won the world heavyweight title in 1952, and remained undefeated in 1956, with a record of 49 professional fights. His irresistible attack and powerful right-hand punch were considered most dangerous for his opponents. Only five of his opponents lasted to the final bell. Marciano was killed in an air crash in 1969.

Joe Louis

Joe Louis (1914 -1981): He was known as the 'Brown Bomber' in American boxing circle. A large body of supporters claim Joe Louis as the greatest of all champions in the history of boxing. He was heavyweight champion from 1937 to 1949, with a record number of successful defences of his title. Louis remained undefeated till 1949, but shortage of money brought him back to the ring that year. He suffered a point's defeat at the hands of Ezzard Charles in a championship fight. His last defeat came in 1951, when he was knocked out by Marciano. Thereafter he retired for good.

Alexander Povetkin (born in Kursk, Russia on September 2, 1979): He is a Russian boxer. His height is 188 centimeters (6 feet and 2 inches). As an amateur, Povetkin won all of the possible tournaments in the super heavyweight division including: national titles, international title, both European and Asian titles, Intercontinental title, world title in 2003, he also won the gold medal in super-heavyweight (>91 kg) boxing at the 2004 Summer

Olympics in Athens, Greece. His amateur record is 125 wins and 7 defeats. Povetkin avenged all of his defeats before turning professional. Before his amateur boxing career he has also won 1999 World kickboxing championship and a 2000 European title in professional kickboxing.

Odlanier Solis Fonté (born April 5, 1980 in Havana, Cuba): He is a Cuban Amateur boxer. His first international success was in 1998 the title at the Panamerican Juniors championship in Toluca and the Juniors' World championship in Buenos Aires. In 1999 he won the Cuban championship beating Félix Savón. Until 2004 he defended his title five times consecutively. In 2005 he switched from heavyweight to super heavyweight and lost in the finale to Michel López Núñez. In 2006 he won the title again for a seventh time.

■

BRIDGE

Chapter - 11

Popular card game played by four players.

History

The name Bridge may have been derived from the Russian card game Biritch which is not in vogue now. Auction bridge was invented in 1902. which is based on the highest bidder, who names the trump. The contract principle as seen in planfond (a French game) was introduced by Harold S. Vanderbilt, an American millionaire, on 1st November 1925, during a Caribbean voyage aboard SS Finland. References also indicate that the British soldiers, based in India, had substantially contributed towards the growth of bridge. The game became extremely popular after the famous challenge match between the UK and USA at Almach's Club, London. Romania-born Ely Culbertson and Lt. Col Walter Thomas More Buller shot into fame throughout the world.

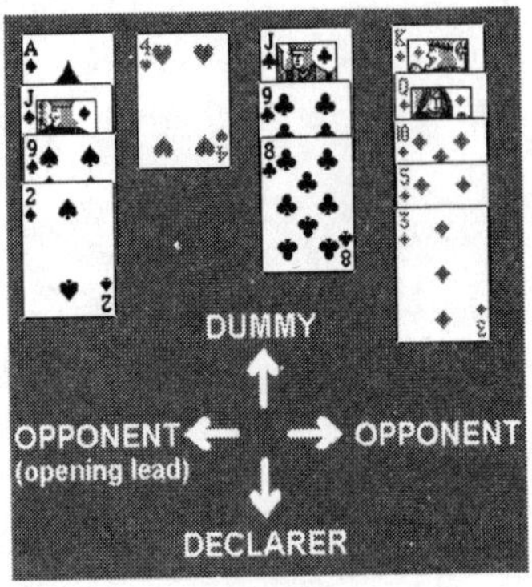

The contract bridge which was played throughout the world replaced the auction bridge in the 1920s. In 1927, a new code, essentially based on the 1926 laws of auction bridge, was adopted. Subsequently, in 1928, the first laws of duplicate bridge were published.

The first recognised championships were held in 1935 and the other landmarks were the organisation of the first post-war world championship series in 1950, followed by the foundation of the World Bridge Federation in 1958 and the first team of four Olympiad in 1960.

The World Bridge Federation controls competitive bridge all over the world through the respective national associations of the country.

Besides competitive bridge, rubber bridge is played for enjoyment and skill at homes throughout the world. The laws of duplicate bridge differ marginally from the rubber bridge which is played for relaxation. The basic rules of the game are common to both rubber bridge and duplicate bridge.

Rules of the Game

1. The game is played by four players out of which one becomes the Dummy when the play starts.

2. A pack of cards is thoroughly shuffled before the play starts and there is a cut if either opponent so desires.

3. Opponent *to* the left of the dealer shuffles the cards and passes to his partner to cut for the next deal.

4. There are two packs of cards which are used alternately. The cards of each suit rank in descending order starting from Ace followed by King, Queen and so on. The suits are also ranked. Spade is the highest followed by Hearts, Diamonds and Clubs. There is also the 'No Trump' which is ranked the highest.

5. The dealer distributes one card face down at a time, starting from his immediate left opponent. After all the 52 cards have been equally dealt among all the players, the cards are picked up by each player.

How to Bid?

1. After the cards have been dealt the dealer makes the first call and thereafter each player in turn from the dealer's left calls. When there are 3 passes in continuation following a call, the auction is deemed to have closed and the contract decided.

2. Each bid has to denote a number of tricks from 1 to 7 as well as a denomination of the suit including "No Trump". The next bid to be followed must supersede the previous bid if it names the same number of odd tricks in a higher ranking denomination suit including "No Trump" or a greater number of odd tricks in any denomination.

3. A player may also double a preceding bid and a player following may re-double but that bid must have been made by an opponent.

4. Partnership that names the highest ranking denomination with the greatest number of tricks wins the auction. The player who named the first denomination of the suit that won the auction becomes the declarer.

Scoring System in Bridge

In rubber bridge each game constitutes a minimum of 100 points. The partnership that wins two of the three games wins a "rubber". A standard scoring table has been devised. Scores are kept on a sheet of paper for each hand played. The scoring table currently in operation is as follows:

BRIDGE SCORING TABLE

Trick Score

Scored by declarer's side if the contract is fulfilled:
If Trumps are
For each odd trick bid and made

Undoubled	20	20	20	30
Doubled	40	40	60	60
Redoubled	80	80	120	120

At a No Trump Contract
For the first odd trick bid and made
For each additional odd trick

Undoubled			
Doubled	40	80	160
Redoubled	30	60	120

A trick score of 100 points or more made on one board is *Game*.
A trick score of less than 100 points is a *Part-score*.

Premium Score

Scored by declarer's side:
Slams

For making a slam	Not Vulnerable	Vulnerable
Small Slam (12 tricks)		
bid and made	500	750
Grand Slam (all 13 tricks)		
bid and made	1000	1500

Overtricks

For each *Overtrick* (tricks made in excess of contract)

	Not Vulnerable	Vulnerable
Undoubled	Trick Value	Trick Value
Doubled	100	400
Redoubled	200	400

Premiums for Game, Part-Score, fulfilling Contract

For making *Game,* vulnerable	500
For making *Game,* not vulnerable	300
For making any *Part-score*	50
For making any doubled, but not redoubled contract	50
For making any redoubled contract	100
For winning rubber in two games	750 bonus
For winning rubber in three games	500 bonus

Undertricks/Penalties

Scored by declarer's opponents if the contract is not fulfilled:
Undertricks
(Tricks by which declarer falls short of the contract)

	Not Vulnerable			Vulnerable		
	Un-doubled	Doubled	Re-doubled	Un-doubled	Doubled	Re-doubled
For first undertrick	50	100	200	100	200	400
For each additional undertrick	50	400	100	300	600	
Bonus for the fourth and each subsequent undertrick	0	100	200	0	0	0

A *Game* can be made by 3 no trumps, 4 spades, 4 hearts, 5 diamonds and 5 clubs.

Tournament Scoring

The tournament scoring varies from the rubber bridge as a number of boards are played in a tournament and each board has to be evaluated separately. Bonues—of 50 points for each part game, of 300 for non-vulnerable game, and of 500 points for each vulnerable game are given. There is no change in the slam bonuses or for other overtricks gained or undertricks conceded, doubled or redoubled.

International Matchpoint Scoring

In international matchpoint scoring, on each board the total point, difference between the two scores compared is converted into IMPs according to the following scale:

Difference in points	IMP	Difference in points	IMP	Difference in points	IMP
0-40	1	370-420	9	1500-1740	17
50-80	2	430-490	10	1750-1990	18
90-120	3	500-590	11	2000-2240	19
130-160	4	600-740	12	2250-2490	20
170-210	5	750-890	13	2500-2990	21
220-260	6	900-1090	14	3000-3490	22
270-310	7	1100-1290	15	3500-3990	23
320-360	8	1300-1490	16	4000 and upwards	24

The difference in the total of two teams may be further converted into a victory point scale.The aim of conversion into IMPs and victory points is to eliminate the element of luck as far as possible.

In pairs tournament either a travelling score sheet or a pick up slip is used. Each pair that defeats another pair on the same board in the same direction scores one point. Thus in a field comprising 16 pairs, maximum points which a pair can obtain on a particular board would be 15. These points at the end of the game are totalled and the pair which scores the highest number of these match points is declared the winner.

Conventions

In a tournament the players cannot hide the convention from the opponents. They have to declare the same. The following are some of the popular conventions:

1. Strong club system with variations
2. Relay system
3. Roman club
4. Blue club
5. Standard American (Forerunner of Culbertson system) also known as Goring system.
6. Precision club
7. Strong no trump convention
8. Acol system
9. *Bonus for Honours* (Applicable only for Rubber Bridge). Five top cards are the honours cards, i.e., Ace, King, Queen, Jack and Joker.
10. To be eligible for bonus for honours, a minimum of 4 honours cards must be held in any one hand.

This is awarded to anyone, regardless of the fact that contract is made or not.

(a) Four Aces in no trumps	150
(b) Five of trump suit	150
(c) Four of trump suit	150

Duplicate Bridge

Idea of playing Duplicate Bridge was derived from whist. The application of duplicate to contract bridge was developed rapidly. In the US, the first national championship was held in 1928 under the auspices of the American Bridge League.

In this form of Bridge the same hand is played more than once by the competing units who have to try to perform better than the one before. It can be played either as a team of four, pairs or individuals. In a team of 4 the same boards are played by the two teams sitting in compass directions on two tables, opposite to one another.

Types of Bridge

Contract Bridge was invented in the 1920's and in the following decades it was popularised especially in the USA by Ely Culbertson. Bridge currently occupies a position of great prestige, and is more comprehensively organised than any other card game. There are clubs, tournaments and championships throughout the world.

Rubber Bridge is the basic form of Contract Bridge, played by four players. Informal social bridge games are often played this way, and rubber bridge is also played in clubs for money.

Duplicate Bridge is the game normally played in clubs, tournaments and matches. The game is basically the same but the luck element is reduced by having the same deals replayed by different sets of players. At least eight players are required for this. There are some significant differences in the scoring. Two types of duplicate bridge will be covered:

- teams of four
- pairs

Chicago Bridge is played by four people (like rubber bridge), but a game is complete in four deals.

Contract Bridge developed from Auction Bridge, which is different mainly in the scoring. In Auction Bridge, overtricks count towards making game, so it is only necessary to bid high enough to win the contract - there is no incentive to bid all the tricks you can make.

Before Auction Bridge there was Bridge-Whist or Straight Bridge (at the time this game was just called Bridge). Earliest published rules of Bridge, which appeared in 1886 under the name Biritch or Russian Whist. In Bridge-Whist there is no bidding at all — the dealer either names a trump suit or passes, in which case the dealer's partner must choose trumps. In either case the dealer's partner is dummy. Either opponent may double before the lead to the first trick, and if doubled, the dealer's side may redouble. In the earliest form of the game, after any redouble, the other side can redouble again, and this can continue indefinitely.

Championships

Venice Trophy: World bridge championship for women was played for the first time in 1974 at Venice and began as a challenge match. This is also played on zonal basis like Bermuda Bowl.

World Team Olympiad: This was started in 1960 and is played once in 4 years.

Bermuda Bowl: Annual world team championship, the symbol of supremacy in bridge. It was played for the first time in 1950 in Bermuda (USA).

Names to Remember

Ely Culbertson (1891-1955): Romania-born US bridge player Culbertson became famous after the US *vs* Britain bridge match at Almack's Club, London. His method and instruction for playing bridge is consulted even today by the world bridge players.Other well-known bridge players are:

(a) Terrence Reese (UK)
(b) Edgar Kaplan (USA)
(c) Charles Goren (USA)
(d) Dorothy Haydon (USA)
(e) Bento Garozzo (Italy)
(j) Robert Hamman (USA)

Giorgio Belladonna (b. 7 June 1923): Italy-born bridge player who was in Italy's winning team in all the three Olympiads.

■

CARROM

Chapter - 12

A popular Indian indoor game played by two or four players.

History

Carrom has been a popular Indian indoor game for a long time. But its origin is not known exactly. Surprisingly the game had been played mostly following similar rules, yet there were no set rules. In 1956 the Indian Carrom Federation was established which for the first time wrote down the rules of Carrom for universal application. The first unofficial international Carrom championship was held in Colombo in 1961 and India won both the men's and women's titles. Substantial changes in the rules were made in 1969 and the first edition of the Laws of Carrom was published in 1970. The International Carrom Federation was established in 1989. The first official International Carrom Federation Cup was held in 1989, and the first three places were won by India.

Carrom Board

Playing surface of the Carrom Board (CB) should be of plywood or made out of birch wood or any other good wood with thickness not less than 8 mm. The size of the board is 73.66 cm (29 in) square. A CB shall be able to have at least three and a half runs of a normally smooth striker made of ivory when struck with the maximum possible force from one of the base lines to the opposite frame of the CB.

Dimensions of the CB are given below:

(a) **Frames** (adjoining playing surface)

Height	2.54 cm
Width	6.35–7.62 cm
Thickness of outer frame	3.81 cm, –5.72 cm

(b) **Pockets**:Round inwardly. Diameter 4.45 cm—variation not more than 0.16 cm.

(c) **Base Lines:** Length 47 cm. Lower base line 10.16 cm away from the frame.The upper base line 3.18 cm away from the lower base line. Base lines are closed by circles with 3.18 cm diameter at both ends.

Within this circle 2.54 cm in diameter shall be coloured in red. They are called base circles.

(d) **Arrows**: At each corner of the CB at an angle of 45°. Length 26.67 cm.

(e) Centre circle	3.18 cm diameter
(f) Inner circle	16.19 cm diameter
(g) Outer circle	21.27 cm diameter

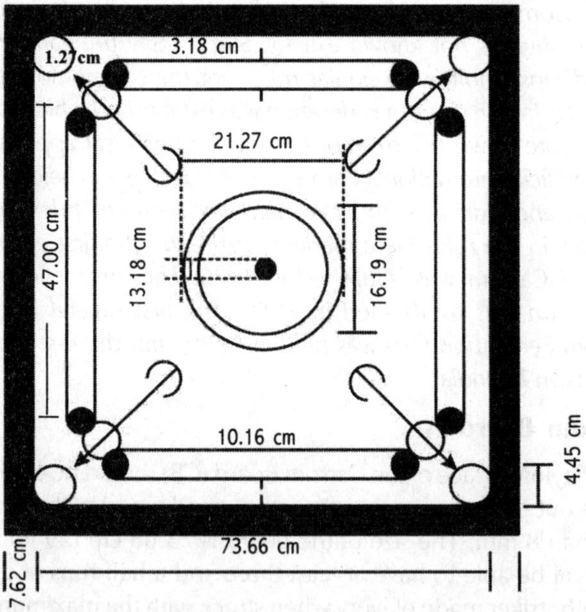

Standard carrom board

Carrom Men (C/M)

Shape	Circular
Material	Wood

Diameter	2.86-3.18 cm
Thickness	0.64-0.95 cm
Weight	5.25-6.00 gm
Number	Nine white, nine black, one red

Striker

Material	Ivory, plastic, ebony wood
Shape	Round
Diameter	Not more than 4.13 cm
Weight	Not more than 15 gm

Carrom Board Stand

Height 63.50-67.22 cm

Stool or Chair for Players

Height 40.64-48.26 cm

Nets

Pockets are covered with nets.

Light

Bulb preferably transparent white between 60 and 100 watts should be at a convenient height above the centre position.

Two, three or four people can play. In singles, your opponent sits across from you; in doubles, you play opposite your partner. With three, you can play for points.

How to arrange the pieces on the board

Line up the double whites to aim 'dead-on' into a corner pocket.

Whoever plays first, or breaks, is always white. The object of the game is to sink all of your pieces, using the heavier 'striker', in any of the pockets before your opponent. Your turn continues as long as you keep sinking your pieces — luck shots count and all combinations are permitted.

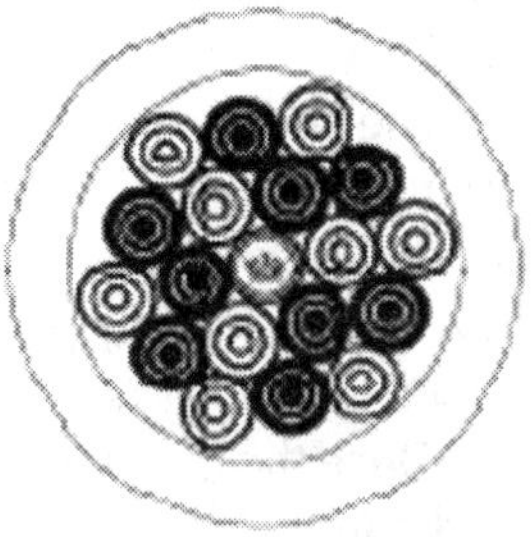

When placing the striker on the board to shoot, the striker must touch both 'base lines' (see left diagram), either covering the red circle completely, or not touching it at all. The striker may not touch the diagonal arrow line.

Shooting styles are very personal — whichever 'grip' works for you is fine as long as you 'flick' the striker and don't push it. Generally, it's best to orient your body in order to see the line of your aim while shooting comfortably; you may not move or leave your chair.

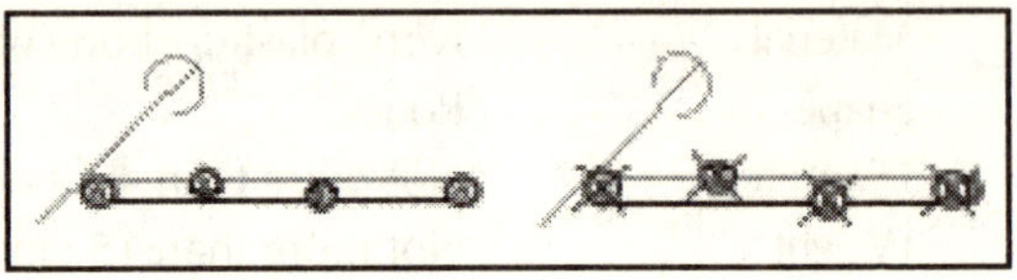

For forward shots, you can use your index finger, middle finger, or even the 'scissors' shot (right).

Tip on technique: Before shooting, try touching the striker with your fingernail, to be sure that it's really on line. This will improve your accuracy and prevent you from hurting your finger.

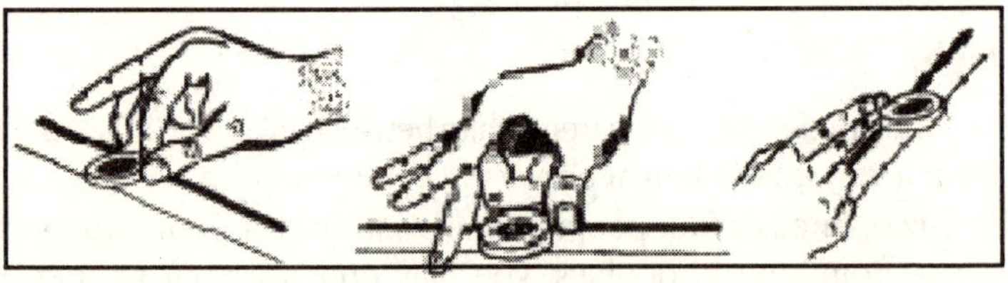

For 'back-shots' you may only use your thumb or the scissors technique.

No part of your body, except your hand, may cross the imaginary diagonal line (wrong in illustration) nor may your elbow protrude over the frame in front of you. Even your feet or knees may not leave your quadrant.

The red piece, or 'queen,' can be pocketed at any time after sinking your first piece but must be sunk before your last one. After pocketing the queen, you must sink one of your pieces, thereby 'covering' it, into any pocket in the next shot, or she is returned to the center spot.

Once the queen is covered, whoever clears their pieces first wins the 'board'.

The winner of a board collects one point for each of the opponent's pieces left at the finish and three points for the queen if covered by the winner (if covered by the loser, no-one gets those points). No more points are collected for the queen after your score reaches 22.

A game consists of 25 points or eight boards, whichever comes first.

Miscellaneous Rules

- Sinking the striker costs you one piece and your turn. But, if you sink a piece in the same shot, then two come up and you shoot again.
- After sinking the striker, your opponent places the due piece(s) within the center circle. If you haven't sunk one yet, you owe one.
- If while shooting for the queen you also sink one of your pieces, the queen is automatically covered, no matter which went first.
- If a piece jumps off the board, it is placed on the center spot. If pieces land on end or are overlapping, they are left that way.
- If the center spot is partially covered when replacing the queen or a jumped piece, the piece should cover as much red as possible. If totally covered, the piece is placed opposite the next player behind the red spot.
- If you sink your opponent's piece, you lose your turn. If you sink their last piece, you lose the board and three points.
- If you sink your last piece before the queen, you lose the board, three points and one point for each of your opponent's pieces left.
- If the striker does not leave both lines, go again. You get three tries to break before losing your turn.

Rules to Play

(1) In singles, the players shall sit opposite to each other. In doubles, four persons comprising two teams, the partners shall sit opposite to each other, occupying all four sides.

(2) Before the break, carrom men are arranged in the inner circle with the queen (red) always occupying the centre circle and the rest placed around; keeping the white and black alternately. In the second row three white carrom men will form the shape 'Y' with the white carrom men of the first row. The remaining space is filled up by placing white and black alternately.

(3) Break is taken by a player who has chosen to strike first. The player who is to break will have whites during that board. The queen shall be common.

(4) Winner of the toss has the option to choose side or to break.

(5) Even if the striker touches slightly any carrom man, it is considered that the break has been made.

(6) Two trial boards are played before a match.

(7) A player's turn will continue, as long as he pockets his own carrom men and/or queen according to the law.

(8) Black and white carrom men change in alternate boards both for singles and doubles. However, in the second game the player who did not have his first turn in the first game shall have his first turn.

Scoring

Each carrom man has one point if pocketed by the striker.

Queen value is three and value of the queen for a player is lost if he reaches 22.

A game shall be of 25 points. A player who scores 25 wins the game. All matches are decided by the best of three games.

Each game consists of eight boards or 25 points whichever is earlier. A player leading at the end of the eighth board will be the winner. In the case of a tie at the end of the 8th board, 9th board will be played as a tie breaker.

In the third game the players shall change sides after reaching 13 points or after completion of the 4th board whichever is earlier. This is applicable till pre-quarter final stage. From quarter-final onwards, change of side takes place after a player scores 13 points irrespective of the number of boards.

Scoring the Queen

(1) The player can pocket the queen and cover it, provided one C/M of his own has already been pocketed and is not brought out as due or penalty in the stroke.

(2) If the queen is pocketed before any C/M of the player is pocketed, the queen will be taken out for placing on the CB. If the queen is not covered it will be taken out.

(3) If the queen and one C/M of the player are pocketed together in one stroke, the queen is covered.

(4) When all nine C/Ms are on the CB, if queen and one C/M are pocketed the queen is not covered.

(5) If the queen, a C/M and the striker are pocketed together, they and an additional C/M will be taken out, the player will continue his turn.

(6) When all nine C/Ms are on the CB, if the queen and striker are pocketed together, the queen will be replaced, a due will be declared. The player will lose his turn.

(7) The player can pocket the C/M together with his striker while covering the queen. The C/M plus one will be taken out. The player shall continue his turn. If subsequently he cannot pocket any C/M, the queen will be taken out for placing.

(8) If the queen along with the last C/M of the player and the opponent are pocketed together, the queen is scored.

(9) If the queen is on the CB and the player pockets the remaining C/M of the opponent, he will lose the Board by the number of his C/Ms plus the points of the queen.

(10) If the queen is on the CB and the player pockets the last of his and the opponent's C/M, he loses the Board by three points.

(11) If while covering the queen, the C/M of his own and his opponent's are pocketed together, he wins by three points or I point if score is 22 or more.

(12) If the player pockets all his C/Ms leaving the queen on the Board, the opponent will win the Board by three points.

(13) If the player pockets the queen and while covering pockets the last C/M of his opponent, he shall lose the Board by the number of his C/Ms on the Board plus the points of the queen.

(14) If the player pockets the last C/M of his own together with the striker leaving the queen on Board, he loses the Board by three points.

(15) If the player pockets the queen, his last C/M, opponent's last C/M and the striker together, he loses the Board by three points.

(16) If the player pockets his and his opponent's last C/M along with the striker, he will lose the Board by one point, if the queen has already been covered by him or by three points if the queen has been covered by his opponent.

Dues or Penalties

The following are the dues and the penalties:

Dues	*Penalty*
1. If the striker is pocketed	Loss of turn and one C/M will be taken out.
2. If the striker is pocketed	Play will continue. The C/M along with his C/M and an additional C/M will be taken out.
3. If the striker along with Opponent's C/M is pocketed	Loss of turn. One C/M will be taken out for placing.
4. If the striker and the last C/M on the board is pocketed	The Board is completed. The C/M on the board plus one will be the point.
5. If a C/M of the opponent pocketed	Same is considered is and one of his C/Ms will be taken out as due or penalty.
6. If a C/M is pocketed due to an additional C/M	This and an additional C/M will be taken out.
7. If the striker and a C/M are pocketed	Lose the turn. The C/M and an additional C/M will be taken out.

SCORE CARD

Organised by__________________________

Tournament/championship____________________

Event______ Round______ Date________ Time______

Allotted C/Bood No______ Game No.______	Player/s Name______ Club ______	Players Name______ Name______

Board No.	1 Break By	2 Queen	3 No. of C/M	4 Grand Total	5 Queen	6 No. of C/M	7 Grand Total
1							
2							
3							
4							
5							
6							
7							
8							

Remarks of Reference____________________

Match Won by Loser's Signature Reference Sig.

Dues or penalty C/M shall be taken out for placing as and when available and it will be placed as and when the space is available. While placing a C/ M, no other C/M or queen should be touched.

C/M over Board

If a C/M or the queen jumps out of the board or jumps but falls back on the Board, the C/M or queen shall be placed by referee in the centre circle, covering it fully or partially as the case may be.

C/M Rolling and Overlapping

1. If a C/M or the queen stands on its rim, it shall be allowed to remain as it is. If two C/Ms and/or the queen overlap each other, they shall be left undisturbed.
2. If the striker rests on a C/M, it will be removed by the referee.
3. If a C/M rests on the striker, the striker will be removed by the referee and the C/M positioned at the correct place.
4. If a C/M resting at the mouth of the pocket falls into the pocket due to any reason, it is considered pocketed.

■

CHESS

Chapter - 13

The game of Chess or Chaturanga originated in India.

History

It is more or less established that the game of Chess originated in India and its name was Chaturanga. It is believed that a Brahmin philosopher of India named Sesac, from the court of King Balhit, in AD later 4th century or early 5th century, was the inventor of the game.

May be the game was named Chaturanga because in those days armies in India were divided into four parts, viz. cavalry, elephants, chariots and the infantry.

The game from India went to Persia. From Persia the game was handed over to the Arabs in about AD 650 and it started gaining popularity as it spread. When the Arabs conquered Spain, they introduced the game to the European mainland. From Spain the Byzantines carried it to Italy and France and from there it quickly spread to the Scandinavian countries and England. From England the immigrants carried the game to America. Federation Internationale 'des Echees (FIDE) was established in 1924.

The Rules of Chess

Chess is a game, played by two players. One player plays with the white pieces, and the other player plays with the black pieces. Each player has sixteen pieces in the beginning of the game: one king, one queen, two rooks, two bishops, two knights, and eight pawns.

The game is played on a chessboard, consisting of 64 squares: eight rows and eight columns. The squares are alternately light (white) and dark coloured. The board must be laid down such that there is a black square in the lower-left corner. To facilitate notation of moves, all squares are given a name. From the view of the white player, the rows are numbered 1, 2, 3, 4, 5, 6, 7, 8; the lowest row has number

1, and the upper row has number 8. The columns are named, from left to right, a, b, c, d, e, f, g, h. A square gets a name, consisting of the combination of its column-letter and row-number, e.g., the square in the lower left corner (for white) is a1.

Black

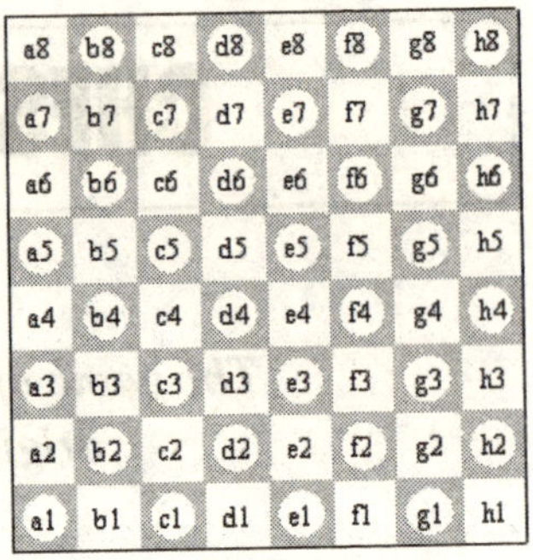

White

Alternately, the players make a move, starting with the white player (the player that plays with the white pieces.) A move consists of moving one of the pieces of the player to a different square, following the rules of movement for that piece — there is one special exception, named castling, where players move two pieces simultaneously.

A player can take a piece of the opponent by moving one of his own pieces to the square that contains a piece of the opponent. The opponents piece then is removed from the board, and out of play for the rest of the game. (Taking is not compulsory.)

At the start of the game, the position of the pieces is as follows:

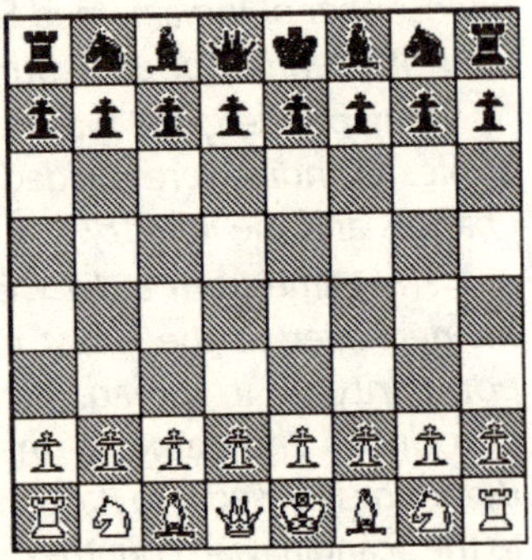

Thus, at the second row, there are eight white pawns, at the seventh row, there are eight black pawns. At the first row, from left to right, we have a: rook, knight, bishop, queen, king, bishop, knight, and rook. Note that the queens start of squares of their own colour, with a dark square in each players left hand corner.

Movement of the pieces

Rook

The rook moves in a straight line, horizontally or vertically. The rook may not jump over other pieces, that is: all squares between the square where the rook starts its move and where the rook ends its move must be empty. (As for all pieces, when the square where the rook ends his move contains a piece of the opponent, then this piece is taken. The square where the rook ends his move may not contain a piece of the player owning this rook.)

Bishop

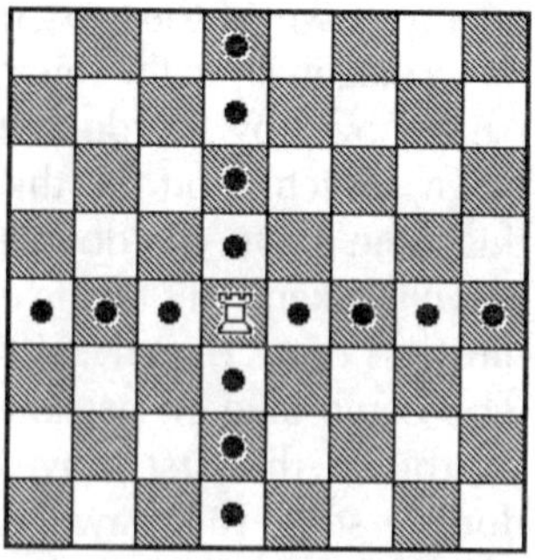

The bishop moves in a straight diagonal line. The bishop may also not jump over other pieces.

Queen

The queen has the combined moves of the rook and the bishop, i.e., the queen may move in any straight line, horizontal, vertical, or diagonal.

Knight

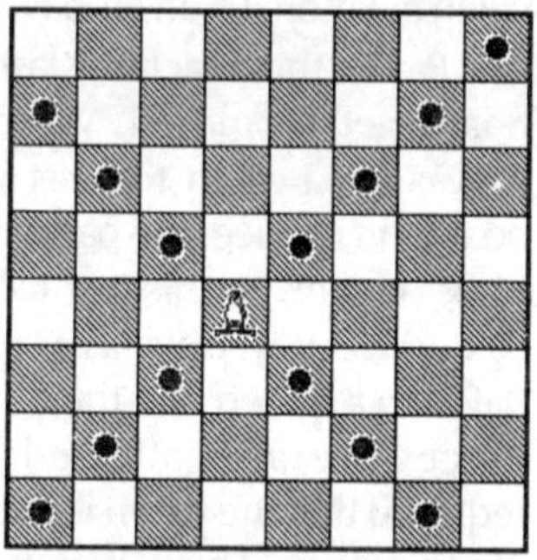

The knight makes a move that consists of first one step in a horizontal or vertical direction, and then one step diagonally in an outward direction. The knight jumps: it is allowed that the first square that the knight passes over is occupied by an arbitrary piece. For instance, white can start the game by moving his knight from b1 to c3. The piece that is jumped over is further not affected by the knight: as usual, a knight takes a piece of the opponent by moving to the square that contains that piece.

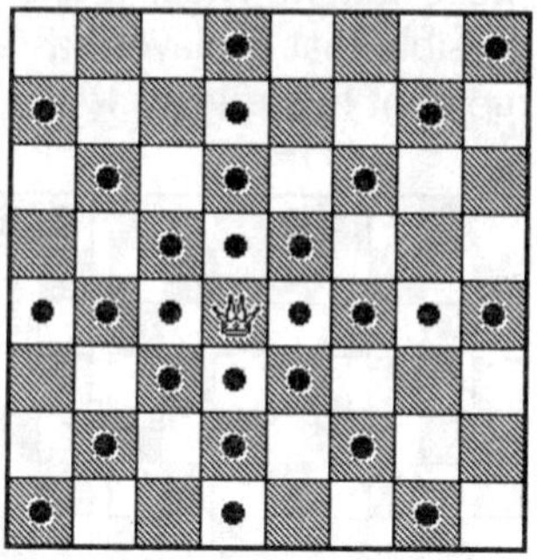

Pawn

The pawn moves differently regarding whether it moves to an empty square or whether it takes a piece of the opponent. When a pawn does not take, it moves one square straight forward. When this pawn has not moved at all, i.e., the pawn is still at the second row (from the owning players view), the pawn may make a double step straight forward. For instance, a white pawn on d2 can be moved to d4.

When taking, the pawn goes one square diagonally forward.

There is one special rule, called taking en-passant. When a pawn makes a double step from the second row to the fourth row, and there is an enemy pawn on an adjacent square on the fourth row, then this

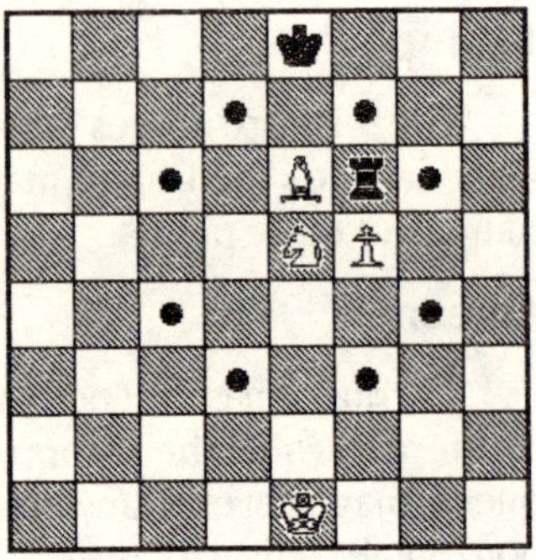

enemy pawn in the next move may move diagonally to the square that was passed over by the double-stepping pawn, which is on the third row. In this same move, the double-stepping pawn is taken. This taking en-passant must be done directly: if the player who could take en-passant does not do this in the first move after the double step, this pawn cannot be taken anymore by an en-passant move.

Pawns that reach the last row of the board get promoted. When a player moves a pawn to the last row of the board, he replaces the pawn by a queen, rook, knight, or bishop (of the same colour). Usually, players will promote the pawn to a queen, but the other types of pieces are also allowed. (It is not required that the pawn is promoted to a piece taken. Thus, it is for instance possible that a player has at a certain moment two queens.)

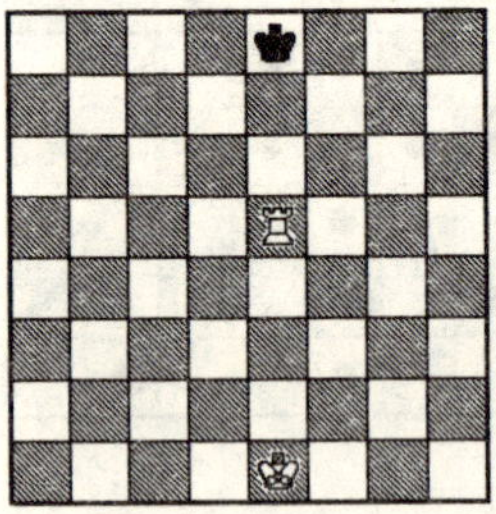

King

The king moves one square in any direction, horizontally, vertically, or diagonally. There is one special type of move, made by a king and rook simultaneously, called castling.

The king is the most important piece of the game, and moves must be made in such a way that the king is never in check.

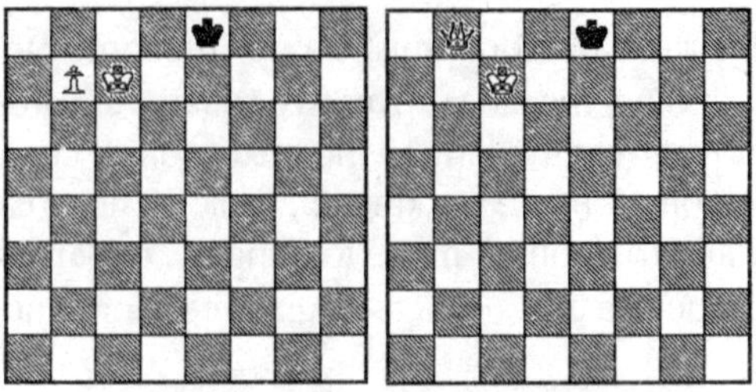

Before and after a promotion

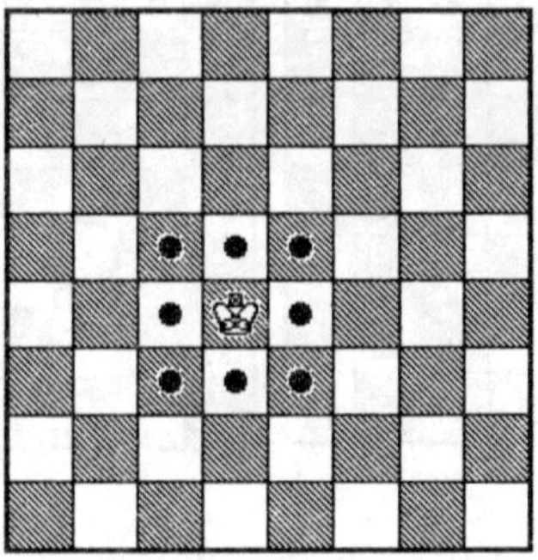

Castling

Under certain special rules, a king and rook can move simultaneously in a castling move.

The following conditions must be met:

- The king that makes the castling move has not yet moved in the game.
- The rook that makes the castling move has not yet moved in the game.
- The king is not in check.
- The king does not move over a square that is attacked by an enemy piece during the castling move, i.e., when castling, there may not be an enemy piece that can move (in case of pawns: by diagonal movement) to a square that is moved over by the king.
- The king does not move to a square that is attacked by an enemy piece during the castling move, i.e., you may not castle and end the move with the king in check.
- All squares between the rook and king before the castling move are empty.

- The king and rook must occupy the same rank (or row).

When castling, the king moves two squares towards the rook, and the rook moves over the king to the next square, i.e., black's king on e8 and rook on a8 move to: king c8, rook d8 (long castling), white's king on e1 and rook on h1 move to: king g1, rook f1 (short castling).

Position before and after castling: white short, and black long.

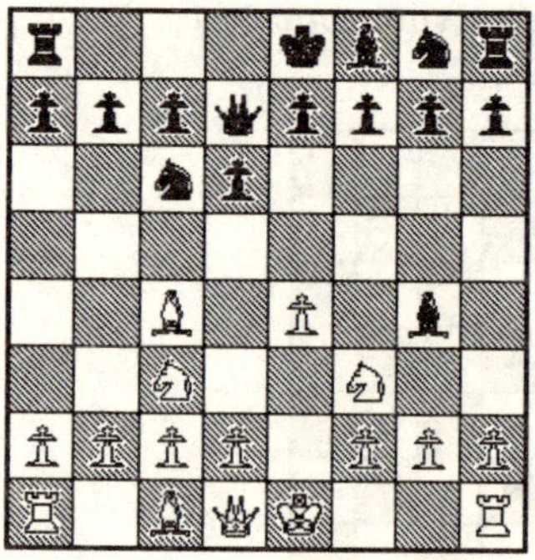

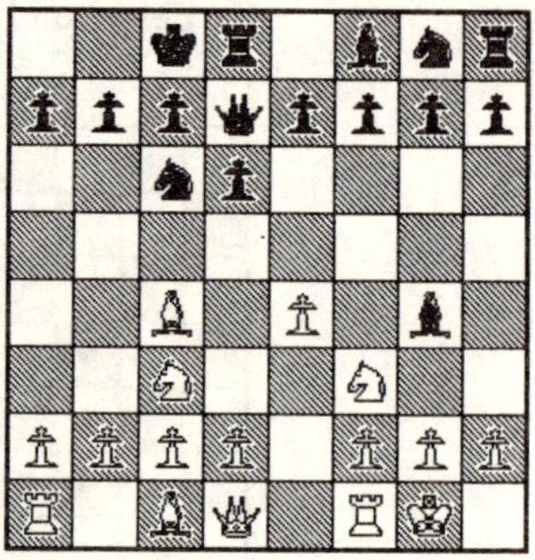

Neither white nor black may castle: white is in check, and the black king may not move over d8.

Check, mate, and stalemate

Check

When the king of a player can be taken by a piece of the opponent, one says that the king is in check. For instance, the white player moves his rook to a position such that it attacks the black king, i.e., if black doesn't do anything about it, the rook could take the black king in the next move: we say that the white rook gives check. It is considered good manners to say check when one check's ones opponent.

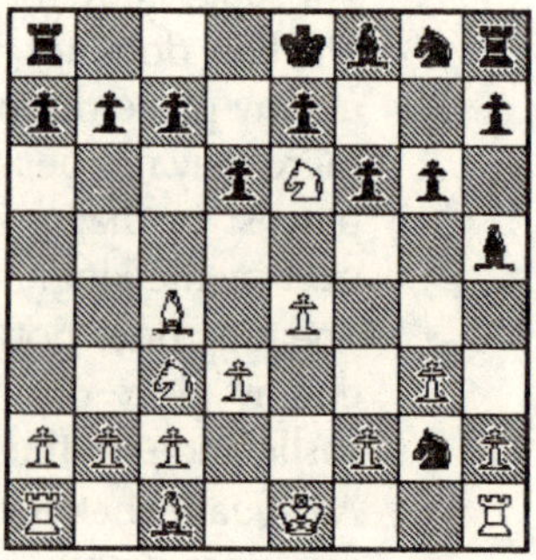

It is not allowed to make a move, such that one's king is in check after the move. If a player accidently tries to make such a move, he must take the move back and make another move (following the rules that one must move with the piece one has touched.)

Mate

When a player is in check, and he cannot make a move such that after the move, the king is not in check, then he is mated. The player that is mated loses the game, and the player that mates him wins the game.

Note that there are three different possible ways to remove a check:

1. Move the king away to a square where he is not in check.
2. Take the piece that gives the check.
3. (In case of a check, given by a rook, bishop or queen:) move a piece between the checking piece and the king.

Stalemate

When a player cannot make any legal move, but he is not in check, then the player is said to be stalemated. In a case of a stalemate, the game is a draw.

When black must move, the game is a stalemate.

Other rules

Resign and draw proposals

A player can resign the game, which means that he has lost and his opponent has won.

After making a move, a player can propose a draw: his opponent can accept the proposal (in which case the game ends and is a draw) or refuse the proposal (in which case the game continues).

Repetition of moves

If the same position with the same player to move is repeated three times in the game, the player to move can claim a draw. (When the right to make a certain castling move is lost by one of the players between positions, then the positions are considered to be different. For the fine points of this rule, please see the official rules of chess.)

One case where the repetition of move occurs is when a player continues to give check forever.

50 moves rules

If there have been 50 consecutive moves of white and black without

- any piece taken
- any pawn move

then a player can claim a draw. For the fine points of this rule, see the official rules of chess.

Touching pieces

When a player touches one of his own pieces, he must, if possible, make a legal move with this piece. When a player touches a piece of the opponent, he must, if possible, take this piece.

Chess clocks and time

Often players play the game with chess clocks. These clocks count the time that each player separately takes for making his own moves. Additional rules are then used, saying how many (possibly all) moves must be made before a player has used a certain time for his moves. For details, see the official rules of chess.

Other Rules

There are other rules, telling what should happen on special occasions, like that players started the game with a wrong setup, etc. These are not so important for friendly games; for details, see the official rules of chess.

Names to Remember

Anatoly Karpov (USSR, b. 23 May 1951): He remaind world champion from 1975 to 1985. During this period he averaged 45.2 competition games per year played in 32 tournaments and came first in 26 of these.

Nona Gaprindashvili (USSR, b.3.May 1941): She held the world title 1962 to 1978. She defended her title four times successfully.

Bobby Fischer: He was born in Chicago on 9 March 1943 and may be reckoned as the greater grandmaster on the officially adopted ELO system with a 2785 rating.

Garry Kasparov (USSR, b.13. April 1963): He is the youngest world champion, won the title on 9 November 1985. He is currently the highest ranked grandmaster.

Dr. Emanues Laskar (Germany, 1868-1941): He had the longest undisputed world championship tenure for 27 years — from 1894 to 1921.

Vera Menchik Stevenson (USSR,1906-1944): She held the women's world championship from 1927 until her death. She defended her world title 7 times successfully.

■

CRICKET

Chapter - 14

A game of national passion in many of the English speaking countries incluing India.

History

The cricket playing nations are not many in the world yet the game evokes tremendous interest among the common people. Cricket is now played in two forms—the Test series and one day matches. With the availability of flood lit grounds the game is not restricted to-day time matches only..

The name Cricket probably means "throwing at a stick", though it is not certain. The practice of trying to knock down a stick which was defended by a second player having another stick may plausibly be thought of as the earliest form of the game. The word "Cricket" appears in the 15th century literature but it became a well-known game only by the 17th century in the south eastern part of England. In those days the wicket comprised only two stumps, each being one foot high, but with a wide gap. Some accounts say two feet between them; a third stump or bail lay across the top. To bowl a man out the wicket had to be broken. The bat also could be of any size or width. For a long time it was curved. Hence accurate batting in the modem sense was impossible, especially on the rough wickets of those days.

Oval

Cricket is a team sport for two teams of eleven players each. A formal game of cricket can last anything from an afternoon to several days.

Although the game play and rules are very different, the basic concept of cricket is similar to that of baseball. Teams bat in successive innings and attempt to score runs, while the opposing team fields and attempts to bring an end to the batting team's innings. After each team has batted an equal number of innings (either one or two, depending on conditions chosen before the game), the team with the most runs wins.

(Note: In cricket-speak, the word "innings" is used for both the plural and the singular. "inning" is a term used only in baseball.)

Equipment

Cricket Ball

Hard, cork and string ball, covered with leather. A bit like a baseball (in size and hardness), but the leather covering is thicker and joined in two hemispheres, not in a tennis ball pattern. The seam is thus like an equator, and the stitching is raised slightly. The circumference is between 224 and 229 millimetres (8.81 to 9.00 inches), and the ball weighs between 156 and 163 grams (5.5 to 5.75 ounces). Traditionally the ball is dyed red, with the stitching left white. Nowadays white balls are also used, for visibility in games played at night under artificial lighting.

Cricket Bat

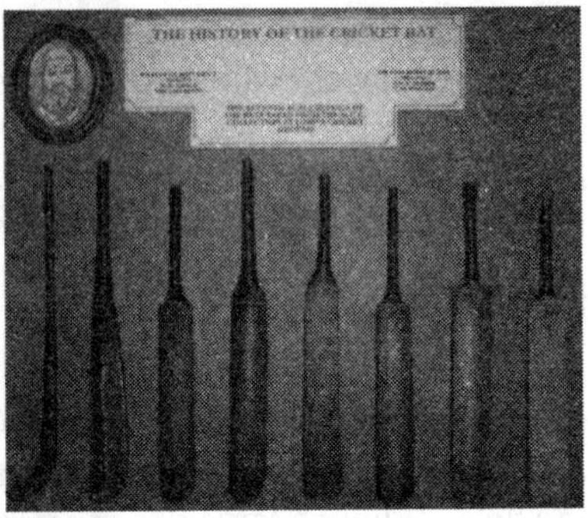

Blade made of willow, flat on one side, humped on the other for strength, attached to a sturdy cane handle. The blade has a maximum width of 108 millimetres (4.25 inches) and the whole bat has a maximum length of 965 millimetres (38 inches).

Wickets

There are two wickets - wooden structures made up of a set of three stumps topped by a pair of bails. These are described below.

Stumps

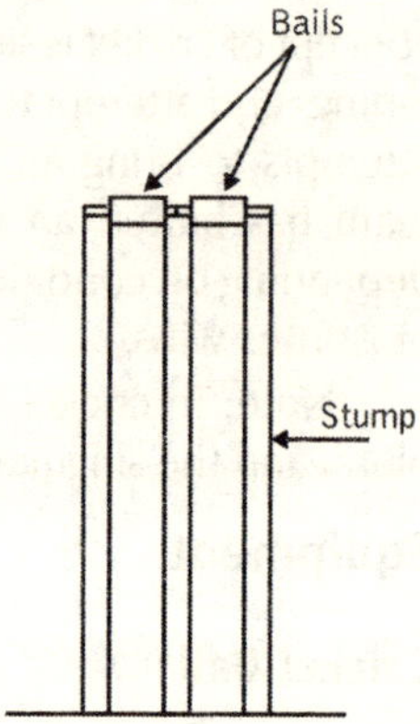

Three wooden posts, 25 millimetres (1 inch) in diameter and 813 millimetres (32 inches) high. They have spikes extending from their bottom end and are hammered into the ground in an evenly spaced row, with the outside edges of the outermost stumps 228 millimetres (9 inches) apart. This means they are just close enough together that a cricket ball cannot pass between them.

Bails

Two wooden crosspieces which sit in grooves atop the adjacent pairs of stumps.

Protective Gear

Pads, gloves, helmet, etc., for batsmen to wear to prevent injury when struck by the ball.

Shoes

Leather, usually with spiked soles for grip on the grass.

Clothing

Long pants, shirt (long or short sleeved depending on the weather), possibly a sleeveless or long-sleeved woollen pullover in cold weather. For games played with a red ball, the clothing must be white or cream. With a white ball, players usually wear uniforms in solid team colours. Add a hat or cap to keep the sun off. There are no regulations regarding identifying marks or numbers on clothing.

The Field

A cricket field is roughly an elliptical one of flat grass, ranging in size from about 90 to 150 metres (100-160 yards) across, bounded by an obvious fence or other marker. There is no fixed size or shape for the field, although large deviations from a low-eccentricity ellipse are discouraged. In the centre of the field, and usually aligned along the long axis of the ellipse, is the pitch , a carefully prepared rectangle of closely mown and rolled grass over hard packed earth. It is marked with white lines, called creases.

The dimensions are in centimetres (divided by 2.54 for inches).

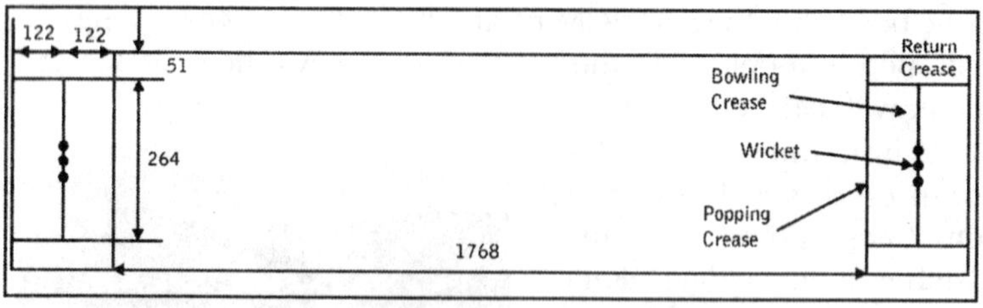

The Play

The order in which the teams bat is determined by a coin toss. The captain of the side winning the toss may elect to bat or field first.

All eleven players of the fielding team go out to field, two players of the batting team go out to bat. The remainder of the batting team wait off the field for their turn to bat. Each batsman wears protective gear and carries a cricket bat.

The game progresses by the bowling of balls. The sequence of events which constitutes a ball is as follows:

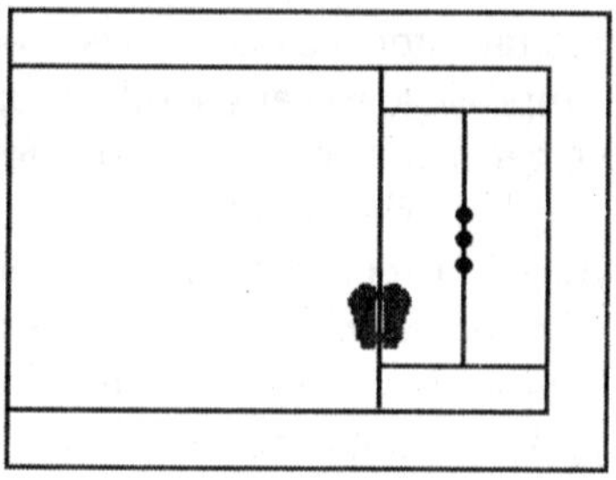

The fielding team disperses around the field, to positions designed to stop runs being scored or to get batsmen out. One fielder is the bowler. He takes the ball and stands some distance behind one of the wickets (i.e. away from the pitch). Another fielder is the wicket-keeper, who wears a pair of webbed gloves designed for catching the ball and protective pads covering the shins. He squats behind the opposite wicket. The rest of the fielders have no special equipment — gloves to assist catching the ball are not allowed to anyone but the wicket-keeper.

One batsman stands behind each popping crease, near a wicket. The batsman farthest from the bowler is the striker, the other is the non-striker. The striker stands before his wicket, on or near the popping crease, in the batting stance.

The ball is considered to be in play from the moment the bowler begins his run-up. It remains in play until any of several conditions occur after which it is called dead. The ball is also dead if it lodges in the striker's clothing or equipment. Once the ball is dead, it is returned to the bowler for the next delivery (another name for the bowling of a ball). Between deliveries, the batsmen may leave their creases and confer with each other.

When one bowler has completed six balls, that constitutes an over. A different member of the fielding team is given the ball and bowls the next over — from the opposite end of the pitch. The batsmen do not change ends, so the roles of striker and non-striker swap after each over. Any member of the fielding team may bowl, so long as no bowler delivers two consecutive overs. Once a bowler begins an over, he must complete it, unless injured or suspended during the over.

Another possibility during a ball is that a batsman may get out. There are ten different methods of being out — these will be described in detail later. If a batsman gets out, the ball is dead immediately, so it is impossible to get the other batsman out during the same ball. The out batsman leaves the field, and the next batsman in the team comes in to bat. The not-out batsman remains on the field. The order in which batsmen come in to bat in an innings is not fixed. The batting order may be changed by the team captain at any time, and the order does not have to be the same in each innings.

When ten batsmen are out, no new batsmen remain to come in, and the innings is completed with one batsman remaining not out. The roles of the teams then swap, and the team which fielded first gets to bat through an innings. When both teams have completed the agreed number of innings, the team which has scored the most runs wins.

Scoring Runs

Whenever a batsman hits the ball during a delivery, he may score runs. A run is scored by the batsmen running between the popping creases, crossing over midway between them. When they both reach the opposite crease, one run is scored, and they may return for another run immediately.

If the batsmen are attempting to take runs, and a fielder gathers the ball and hits a wicket with it, dislodging one or both bails, while no batsman is behind that wicket's popping crease, then the nearest batsman is run out. Specifically, the batsman must have some part of his body or his bat (provided he is holding it) grounded behind (not on) the crease.

The batsmen carry their bats as they run, and turning for another run is accomplished by touching the ground beyond the crease with an outstretched bat. The batsmen do not have to run at any time they think it is unsafe — it is common to hit the ball and elect not to run.

The batsmen usually stop taking runs when a fielder is throwing the ball back towards the pitch area. If no fielder near the pitch gathers the ball and it continues into the outfield again, the batsmen may take more runs. Such runs are called overthrows. If the ball reaches the boundary on an overthrow, four runs are scored in addition to the runs taken before the overthrow occurred.

Runs scored by a batsman, including all overthrows, are credited to him by the scorer. The number of runs scored by each batsman is an important statistic.

If, while running multiple runs, a batsman does not touch the ground beyond the popping crease before he returns for the next run, then the umpire at that end will signal one short, and the number of runs scored is reduced by one.

Ways of Getting Out

Here is a full list of the ten different ways of getting out that calls for a few necessary definitions:

The wicket is said to be broken if one or both of the bails have been dislodged and fallen to the ground. The field is notionally split into two halves, along a line down the centre of the pitch. The half of the field in front of the striker is called the off-side, the half behind is called the leg-side, or sometimes the on-side. Thus, standing at the bowler's wicket and looking towards a right-handed striker's wicket, the off-side is to the left and the leg-side to the right (and vice-versa for a left-handed striker). The stumps of the striker's wicket are called off-stump, middle-stump, and leg-stump, depending on which side they are on.

When a batsman gets out, no matter by what method, his wicket is said to have fallen, and the fielding team are said to have taken a wicket.

Now, the ways of getting out

Caught

If a fielder catches the ball on the full after the batsman has hit it with his bat. However, if the fielder catches the ball, but either during the catch or immediately afterwards touches or steps over the boundary, then the batsman scores six runs and is not out.

Bowled

If the batsman misses the ball and it hits and breaks the wicket directly from the bowler's delivery. The batsman is out whether or not he is behind his popping crease. He is also out bowled if the ball breaks the wicket after deflecting from his bat or body. The batsman is not out if the wicket does not break.

Leg Before Wicket

If the batsman misses the ball with his bat, but intercepts it with part of his body when it would otherwise have hit the wicket, and provided several other conditions are satisfied. An umpire must adjudicate such a decision, and will only do so if the fielding team appeal the decision. If the ball has hit the bat before hitting the batsman, then he cannot be given out LBW.

Stumped

If a batsman misses the ball and in attempting to play it steps outside his crease, he is out stumped if the wicket-keeper gathers the ball and breaks the wicket with it before the batsman can ground part of his body or his bat behind his crease.

Run Out

If a batsman is attempting to take a run, or to return to his crease after an aborted run, and a fielder breaks that batsman's wicket with the ball while he is out of the crease.

Hit Wicket

If, in attempting to hit a ball or taking off for a first run, the batsman touches and breaks the wicket. This includes with the bat or dislodged pieces of the batsman's equipment — even a helmet or spectacles!

Handle The Ball

If a batsman touches the ball with a hand not currently holding the bat, without the permission of the fielding side. This does not include being hit on the hand by a delivery, or any other non-deliberate action.

Obstructing The Field

If a batsman deliberately interferes with the efforts of fielders to gather the ball or effect a run out. This does not include running a path between the fielder and the wicket so that the fielder cannot throw the stumps down with the ball, which is quite legal, but does include any deliberate attempt to swat the ball away.

Hit The Ball Twice

If a batsman hits a delivery with his bat and then deliberately hits the ball again for any reason other than to defend his wicket from being broken by the ball. If the ball is bouncing or rolling around near the stumps, the batsman is entitled to knock it away so as to avoid being bowled, but not to score runs.

Timed Out

If a new batsman takes longer than two minutes, from the time the previous wicket falls, to appear on the field.

These methods of getting out are listed in approximate order of how commonly they occur. The first five are reasonably common, the last five quite rare. The last three methods are almost never invoked.

If a batsman is out caught, bowled, LBW, stumped, or hit wicket, then the bowler is credited with taking the wicket. No single person is credited with taking a wicket if it falls by any other method.

Officials

The game is adjudicated by two umpires, who make all decisions on the field and whose word is absolutely final. One umpire stands behind the non-striker's wicket, ready to make judgements on LBWs and other events requiring a decision. The other umpire stands in line with the striker's popping crease, about 20 metres (20 yards) to one side (usually the leg side, but not always), ready to judge stumpings and run-outs at his end. The umpires remain at their respective ends of the pitch, thus swapping roles every over.

If the technology is available for a given match, a third umpire is sometimes used. He sits off the field, with a television replay monitor. If an on-field umpire is unsure of a decision concerning either a run out or a stumping attempt, he may signal for the third umpire to view a television replay. The replay umpire cannot be used for any decisions other than run outs and stumpings.

The game is also presided over by a match referee, who watches from outside the field. The referee makes no decisions of relevance to the outcome of the game, but determines penalties for breaches of various rules and misconduct. In professional games, these penalties are monetary fines.

The most serious misconduct in a cricket match is of the order of a rude gesture to an opponent or throwing the ball into the ground in disgust. Such gross misbehaviour would attract large fines and possibly match suspensions. Penalties for physical violence can only be guessed at, but would possibly be a career suspension.

Extras

Extras are runs scored by means other than when the ball is hit by a batsman. Extras are not credited to any batsman, and are recorded by the scorer separately. The total number of runs for the innings is equal to the sums of the individual batsmen's scores and the extras. There are four types of extras: no balls, wides, byes, and leg byes.

The Bowling Action

The bowling action itself has to conform to several restrictions. The bowler's arm must be straight when the ball is bowled (so no throwing is allowed). The ball must be bowled overarm, not underarm.

A warning is also given if the umpire believes the bowler is bowling at the body of a batsman in a deliberate attempt to injure the batsman. After two warnings a bowler is barred from bowling for the rest of the innings.

If any rule governing the bowling action is violated, a no ball results.

The bowler may bowl from either side of the wicket, but must inform the umpire and the batsmen if he wishes to change sides. Bowling with the bowling arm closest to the wicket is called over the wicket, and is most common. Bowling with the non-bowling arm closest to the wicket is called around the wicket.

A delivery may also be aborted by the striker stepping away from his stumps, if distracted by an insect or dust in the eye, for example.

Fielding

There are several named field positions, and the fielding captain uses different combinations of them for tactical reasons.

The following diagram shows the rough positions of all of the simply named field positions. In this diagram, the pitch is indicated by three '#' marks; the striker's end is at the top. The approximate field positions are marked with numbers or letters, according to the key on the right of the diagram. The three marks: '+', '*', and '~' indicate that the adjective shown at the bottom of the list can be used to describe a modification of that position, as shown in the example.

Other modifiers used to qualify positions:

square: close to a line perpendicular to the pitch, through the batsman;

fine: close to a line straight along the pitch;

short: close to the batsman.

The only restriction on field placements is that, at the time the ball is delivered, there must be no more than two fielders in the quadrant of the field backward of square leg. (This rule exists mainly for historical reasons — see the Bodyline section below.)

Injuries and Substitutions

In case of injury, substitutes may replace any number of fielders. A substitute may only field — he may not bowl, nor bat. A substitute may not keep wicket. A substituted player must return to the field as soon as he is able to resume playing without danger.

If a batsman is injured, he may retire and resume his innings when fit again, so long as his team's innings is not over. If a batsman is too injured to bat when no other batsmen remain to come in after a wicket falls, his innings must be forfeited and his team's innings ends. If a batsman is able to bat, but not run, then another player may run for him.

If a bowler is injured during an over and cannot complete it, another bowler must bowl the remaining deliveries in that over. The bowler chosen to finish the over must not be the bowler who bowled the previous over, and must not bowl the over immediately following either.

Umpire's Signals

The umpires signal various events with gestures, as follows:

Out

When a batsman is out, the umpire making the decision raises one hand above his head, with the index finger extended.

Not Out

There is no formal signal to indicate that a batsman is not out. The umpire can either shake his head `no' or not signal at all.

Four

A four scored by the ball reaching the boundary is signalled by an arm extended horizontally and waved briefly back and forth in a horizontal arc.

Six

A six is signalled by raising both arms straight over the head.

No Ball

A no ball is signalled by holding an arm out horizontally.

Wide

A wide is signalled by holding both arms out horizontally.

Byes

Runs scored as byes are signalled by raising one arm over the head, palm open.

Leg Byes

Leg byes are signalled by raising one leg and tapping the knee with one hand.

Dead Ball

If the umpire has to signal dead ball to prevent the players from assuming that the ball is still alive, he waves both arms across each other in front of his abdomen.

One Short

One short is signalled by touching the tip of one hand to the same shoulder.

TV Replay

If an umpire wishes the third umpire to make a decision based on a TV replay, he signals by drawing a large square shape in the air with both hands, spreading them out high in the air in front of him, bringing them down, and then together again.

The Two Forms of Cricket

Cricket is played in two very distinct forms. The first is limited duration, in which a specific number of hours of playing time are allocated and each team plays two innings.

The second is limited overs, in which each team plays one innings of a pre-determined number of overs.

First Class Cricket

First class cricket matches are the most prestigious games, played at a professional level. The top level games are international Test matches, played betwen countries.

Test matches are played over five days, with six hours play each day. Each day's play is divided into three sessions of two hours each,

with a 40 minute break between the first two sessions for lunch, and a 20 minute tea break between the last two sessions.

Each team has two innings, usually played in alternating order. Each innings is over when either ten batsmen are out, or the captain of the batting side declares the innings closed (for strategic reasons, more later).

On each day of play in a Test match, a minimum of 90 overs must be bowled if a day's play ends early because of poor weather conditions, all calculations are reset for the next day.

One-Day Cricket

One-day cricket differs significantly from first class cricket. A one-day match is played on a single day. Either a red or a white cricket ball may be used, and play under artificial lighting is allowed.

Each team gets only one innings, and that innings is restricted to a maximum number of overs. Usual choices for the number of overs are 50, 55, or 60. Each innings is complete at the end of the stipulated number of overs, no matter how many batsmen are out. If ten batsmen are out before the full number of overs are bowled, the innings is also over. If the first team's innings ends in this manner, the second team still has its full number of overs to score the required runs. The timing of the innings and the break between them are not regulated.

Whichever team scores the most runs wins. A tied score stands. There is no draw result. If the match is washed out, so that the innings are not played, the game is declared a no-result.

One-day competitions are played either as Series between pairs of international teams, round-robin competitions between groups of international teams, or round-robins between domestic teams. A World Cup one-day competition is played between all the Test nations every four years.

Cricket Twenty 20

Twenty20 is the newest form of cricket where each team bats for a maximum of only 20 overs a side, with each innings lasting for 75 minutes. Twenty20 cricket was first introduced at county level by the England and Wales Cricket Board in 2003 and such was the success of the format of the sport, the game quickly spread around the world with the first men's full Twenty20 international taking place in February 2005 between New Zealand and Australia.

The ICC Board agreed to the inclusion of an ICC World Twenty20 competition at a meeting in April 2006. It was agreed that the inaugural event would take place in South Africa in September 2007, with the second event scheduled for England and Wales during the ICC's Centenary Year in 2009.

The remaining period up to 2015 will be taken up either by one or two further ICC World Twenty20, depending on the success of those first two events. The ICC Board also agreed in April 2006 to cap the number of matches each Full Member can play within a 12 month period to a maximum of three home matches, including no more than 2 series.

That decision was based on the desire to preserve the primacy of the existing formats of Test and One-Day International cricket, the views of some Members that Twenty20 should be viewed more as a development tool and the need to ensure player workloads were kept under control.

India Won the First Twenty 20 World Cup. India created history by winning the first twenty 20 World Cup in September 2007 at South Africa under the captainship of M S Dhoni beating Pakistan by five runs in the finals.

T20 cricket has caught the imagination of the public and this win will herald a new era. Just as there were one-day specialists trying to make a mark in the early90's, there will be a set of players who will train their thoughts and mind entirely to suit the demands of this format.

Typical bowling speeds are:

Fast bowler

130-140 km/h (80-90 mph)
Medium pace bowler:
100-130 km/h (60-80 mph)

Spin bowler

70-90 km/h (45-55 mph)

Bouncer

A ball bounced short so that it bounces high, usually chest height or higher as it passes the batsman.

Yorker

A ball bounced very close to the batsman's crease. This is difficult to score from and often gets batsmen out, but is difficult to bowl without accidentally bowling a full toss.

Batsman's Shots

The different types of shots a batsman can play are described by names:

Block

A defensive shot played with the bat vertical and angled down at the front, intended to stop the ball and drop it down quickly on to the pitch in front of the batsman.

Drive

An offensive shot played with the bat sweeping down through the vertical. The ball travels swiftly along the ground in front of the striker. A drive can be an on drive, straight drive, off drive, or cover drive, depending in which direction it goes.

Cut

A shot played with the bat close to horizontal, which hits the ball somewhere in the arc between cover and gully.

Edge, or Glance

A shot played off the bat at a glancing angle, through the slips area.

Leg Glance

A shot played at a glancing angle behind the legs, so that it goes in the direction of fine leg.

Pull

A horizontal bat shot which pulls the ball around the batsman into the square leg area.

Sweep

Like a pull shot, except played with the backmost knee on the ground, so as to hit balls which bounce low.

Hook

Like a pull shot, but played to a bouncer and intended to hit the ball high in the air over square leg — hopefully for six runs.

French Cut

An attempt at a cut shot which hits the bottom edge of the bat and goes into the area behind square leg.

Reverse Sweep

A sweep with the bat reversed into the point area.

Most of these shots can also be lofted, in an attempt to hit the ball over the close fielders (or the boundary). The batting strokes can be divided into two categories: Straight bat and cross bat. The straight bat shots are played with the bat held close to the vertical, and are the blocks, drives and glances. Cross bat shots are played with the bat held more horizontally, like a baseball bat. These include cuts, pulls, sweeps and hooks.

The following terms are used more informally and are not standard:

Hoik

A wild swing intended only to hit the ball as hard and as far as possible, usually with little or no control.

Agricultural Shot

Any shot played with very little skill.

Statistics and Good Performances

The following statistics are recorded:

Batsmen

Number of runs scored, time spent batting, number of balls faced, how out (and by which bowler and catcher if appropriate).

Bowlers

Number of overs bowled, number of maidens bowled, number of wickets taken, number of runs conceded (i.e. scored off his bowling).

Team

Extras, total runs, wickets fallen, overs bowled, total at each fall of wicket.

Batting Average

The aggregate number of runs scored divided by the number of times the batsman has been out. The higher, the better.

Bowling Average

The aggregate runs scored against a bowler divided by the number of wickets taken. The lower, the better.

Each of these averages is kept separately for Test cricket, first class cricket in general, and one-day cricket. A batting average above 30 is very good, 40 excellent, and 50 is legendary. Mention must be made of the Australian batsman Sir Donald Bradman, whose career average was a record 99.94, far and away the greatest batsman ever to play the game. A bowling average below 25 is considered excellent.

Teams Which Play Cricket

The official Test Cricket nations are currently: England, Australia, West Indies, South Africa, India, Pakistan, New Zealand, Sri Lanka, and Zimbabwe and Bangladesh.

Minor cricketing nations (which do not play Test cricket, but do compete for a place in the World Cup One-Day competition) include: Kenya, Canada, The Netherlands, Ireland.

The most famous Test cricket Series is The Ashes, played every two years between Australia and England. The Ashes trophy is a small urn containing "the ashes of English cricket" (in reality the ashes of a set of bails), which "died"' in a match in 1882 when Australia beat England for the first time. The Ashes are currently held by Australia.The physical trophy is kept permanently in a room at Lord's Cricket Ground in London.

Important Tournaments

Apart from Test matches, the following are the prominent one-day cricket championships of the world:

World Cup. The Prudential World Cup was inaugurated in 1975. This is held after a four-year interval. It was won by the West Indies in 1975 and 1979, by India in 1983 and by Australia in 1987. This Cup was known as the Reliance World Cup in 1987.

Benson & Hedges Cup. Benson & Hedges World Series Cup, inaugurated in-l979-80, is held annually in Australia.

Sharjah Cup. The Cup was instituted in 1984 by Sheikh Abdur Rahman Bukhatir in Sharjah (United Arab Emirates).

Championships

Duleep Trophy: This Trophy named after Duleepsinhji, a nephew of Ranjitsinhji, was instituted in 1961-62. He was also the chairman of All India Council of Sports. The trophy is awarded to the winners of an Inter-Zone knock-out competition.

Ranji Trophy: The Trophy was instituted in memory of Ranjitsinhji in 1934. This is awarded to the national champions of Indian cricket. This is contested annually.

Names to Remember

Sunil Manohar Gavaskar: Sunil Gavaskar (born in Bombay on 10 July 1949) has the unique distinction of scoring 34 centuries in 125 Test matches which is a world record. He made his debut during India's tour of the West Indies in 1971. During this tour, he became the first Indian to score a century and a double century in the same match besides scoring 774 runs in four Tests. A recipient of the Arjuna Award and Padma Bhushan, he has authored. books like *Sunny Days, Runs'n Ruins, One-day Wonders*.

Sir Garfield St. Aubrun Sobers (1936 0): A well-known cricketer from West Indies. Possibly, the finest all-rounder. He scored 8,132 runs and took 221 wickets. He holds the world record of highest Test score (365 not out against Pakistan) in Test matches.

Sir Leonard Hutton (1916-1900): An English cricketer, he scored 364 not out against Australia in an innings in 13 hours and 17 minutes. He became the first professional cricketer to captain England in 1953. He made a record 1,294 runs in a month in June 1949. He was knighted on retirement in 1956.

Ranjitsinhji (1872-1933): Jam Sahib of Nawanagar. Played for England, Sussex and Cambridge University. In 1899, he became the first cricketer to score 3,000 runs in a season. He captained Sussex from 1899 to 1903.

Sir Donald George Bradman (1908–) A legendary figure in cricket. His batting records are still unbeatable. As captain of Australia, he never lost a rubber. His 452 not out stood as the highest first class innings for 29 years. Also his 29 Test centuries and overall average of 99.94 (6,996 runs) remained a record for a long time. He was the first Australian cricketer to be knighted.

Sachin Tendulkar: Sachin Ramesh Tendulkar (born 24 April 1973) is a current Indian cricketer who was rated by Wisden (2002) as the second greatest Test batsman ever after Sir Don Bradman. He made his international debut in 1989 and holds several batting records in both Test Cricket and ODI Cricket. Rajiv Gandhi Khel Ratna award in 1997-1998. Many commentators and fellow players regard him as one of the greatest batsmen the game has seen. While not a regular bowler, Sachin Tendulkar has taken 38 wickets in 135 Tests and 146 wickets in 377 ODIs.

Sourav Chandidas Ganguly is an Indian cricketer. Born 8 July 1972, lives at Barisha in Kolkata, formerly Calcutta, West Bengal. He made his One Day International debut against Australia in 1992, and a Test debut versus England in 1996. He went on to become the captain of Indian cricket team from 2000 to 2005. He has led India to the World Cup 2003 finals, and holds the Indian captaincy record for the most Test victories. Following an exit from the national team in early 2006, he was recalled to the Indian Test side in December, staging a successful comeback in the 2006 — 2007 Indian tour of South Africa. Ganguly has scored over 10,000 runs in One Day Cricket and over 5,000 runs in Test cricket, including 12 centuries in Tests and 22 in ODIs.

Kapil Dev Ramlal Nikhanj (born 6 January 1959, Chandigarh), better known as Kapil Dev, is a former Indian cricketer regarded as one of the greatest all-rounders to have played Cricket. Kapil Dev was named by Wisden as the Indian Cricketer of the Century in 2002 [2] for captaining India to their maiden and only Cricket World Cup in 1983 and holding the record for the most Test match wickets between 1994 and 1999. Kapil Dev had a rather prosaic stint as India's national cricket coach for 10 months between October 1999 and August 2000.

■

CROQUET

Chapter - 15

Very interesting game but not played by many.

History

The game of Croquet was not very well known and its popularity is fairly uncertain.It may be assumed that the game originated in France, because a number of its earlier terminologies were in French. It was John Jacques in 1857, who made the first croquet set and wrote a book on this game. In 1867, Walter Johnes Whitmore organised the first croquet championship at Evesham, Worcestershire, and in 1870 ,this championship was transferred to All England Croquet and Lawn Tennis Club at Wimbledon. The game was not popular because it was never a spectator's sport. After the Second World War, the younger generation players started paying attention to this age-old game. In 1967, the Croquet Association was formed with Rackitt as its president. The game is also played in Ireland, Australia, New Zealand, South Africa.

Croquet Court: The diagram of croquet court is given on the next page.

Hoops

There are a total of six hoops.These are made of rounded iron 5/8 1.59 cm thick and have a square crown painted white. The crown of the first hoop is blue and the last hoop or rover is red. The hoops stand 30.5 cm high above the ground with inside measurement being 9.53 cm.

Flags

Four flags are positioned at four corners of the court with the following colours:

First Corner	Blue
Second Corner	Red

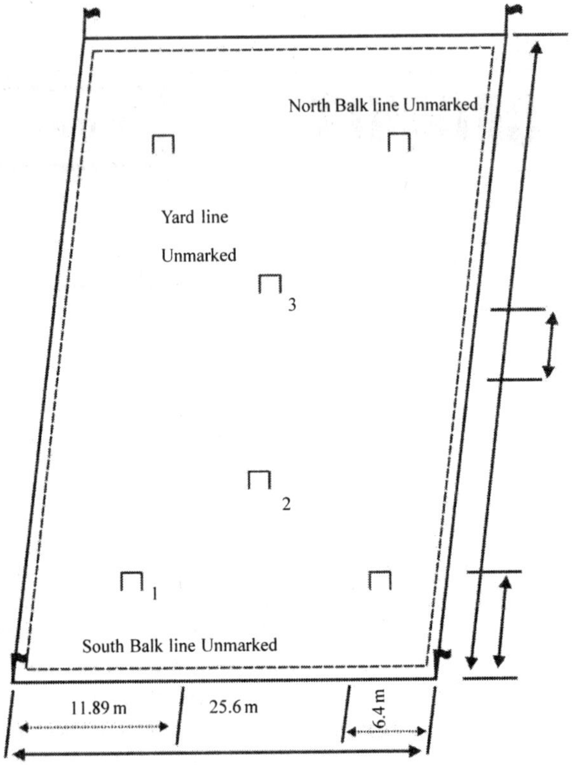

A sketch of a croquet court–1. first hoop– blue,2. last hoop or rover –red, 3 peg.

Third Corner	Black
Fourth Corner	Yellow

Corner Pegs

Two corner pegs are placed at each side of the flag in all four corners at a distance of 91cm.

Centre Peg

A wooden peg is positioned at the centre which is 3.8 cm in diameter and 45.72 cm high above the ground. This has a detachable portion on the top capable of holding clips.

Clips

Four coloured clips are used to indicate the next hoop for each ball. For the first six hoops or first round, they are attached to the crown or horizontal bar of the hoop. And to the vertical bar of the hoop for return hoops.

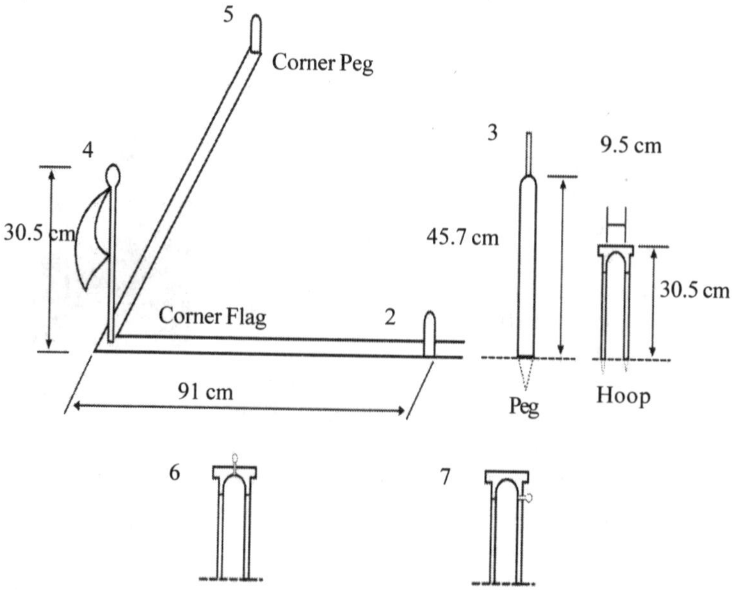

Peg, flags, hoop and clips

Croquet Equipment

Mallet: Mallets are made of wood and weigh between 1.24–1.70 kg. The size of the mallet head is 22.86 cm long and between 2¼-2½ in (5.71-6.35 cm) square. Round headed mallets are also in use. Both types of mallets are bound with brass about ¼ inch from each face to avoid splitting of the mallet head. The shaft of a mallet is generally made of hickory with ash or malacca. Metal and nylon shafts may also be used but they are not popular because of its springiness.

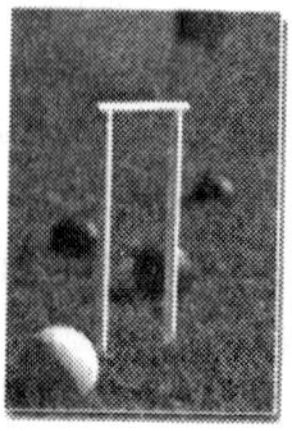

Ball: There are four coloured balls which are in use in croquet, i.e., black, blue, yellow and red. They weigh approximately I lb and are 9.2 cm in diameter. The balls are made of compressed cork covered with a layer composition or plastic.

Dress

Players should wear rubber-sole flat heeled shoes and white clothes for competitions.

Rules of Croquet

The following are the croquet rules:

1. The game consists of 26 points. One point for each hoop and one point for the peg. Therefore, each ball has to carry out 12 hoops and touch the peg finally, thus scoring 13 points. Each player plays with two balls, thus the total score is $2 \times 13 = 26$.
2. Four balls are always used whether playing singles or doubles. The blue and the black balls are partners against the red and the yellow.
3. When all four balls are in play, the sides play alternately but the balls need not be played in sequence. In doubles, each player plays the same ball throughout.
4. One player of a partnership can play several consecutive turns for his side.
5. A toss decides who plays first and who has the choice of balls. The striker plays either of his balls from a point on the balk line. The second player does the same. The third and the fourth balls are played into the court in similar fashion.
6. The game can start from either of the balk line.
7. **Croquet Route**:Routes for the balls are shown in Croquet routes diagram above.
8. A turn consists of one strike. But this is extendable by a croquet or a hoop.
9. **Roquet**: When the striker's ball hits one of the other three balls, a player is entitled to two further strikes — a croquet strike and an ordinary strike which is called continuation strike. Each ball may be required to be hit once in one turn unless a hoop is scored.
10. Scoring a hoop also entitles a player or an ordinary strike and he gains a right to roquet the other three balls again.
11. Thus each time a hoop is scored, the sequence of roquet and croquet can continue.

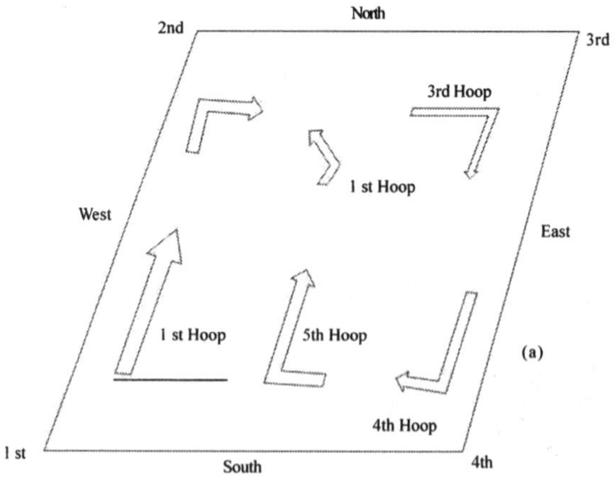

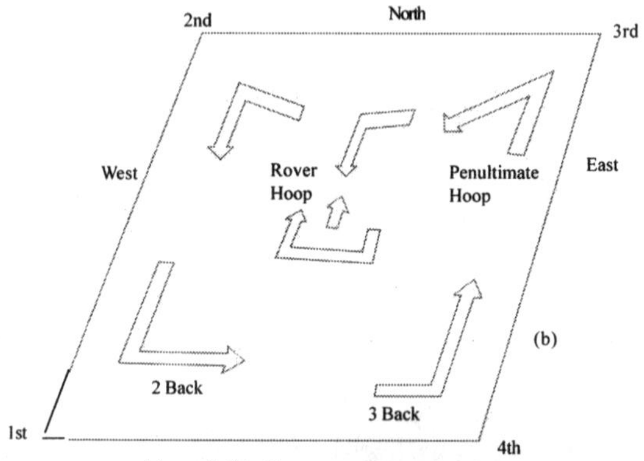

(a) and (b) Croquet routes

12. **Croquet Shot**: The striker plays his ball alongside the roqueted ball. A foul will occur if the croqueted ball does not shake. In that case, the balls are replaced and the turn ends.
13. Any ball crossing the boundary or coming to rest within 91cm is to be replaced on the yardline before the commencement of play. If a striker's ball goes out after a croquet shot or after a hoop he loses the turn.
14. A ball is deemed to be out of play when it touches the inside edge of the boundary line.

15. A turn ends after one strike or if a croqueted ball goes outside or the striker's ball goes out of play after a croquet shot.
16. A ball cannot be pegged out until it has made the last or the 12th hoop. After completing the 12th hoop, the ball becomes a rover ball.
17. Another ball cannot peg out a ball unless it is also a rover.
18. The end of the game may be in a fashion that both balls become rover. One ball may be croqueted to the peg followed by its partner.

Duration: The game ends when one side completes both its balls and scores 26 points. If there is no winner after an agreed time, the person on play finishes his turn and his opponent has a turn and thus the winner is the side with the maximum points.

Championships

Stoker Bowl: This was introduced in 1967 for the championship of champions in which the winner of the President's Cup challenged the winner of the Open Championship. However, this was withdrawn subsequently.

MacRobertson Trophy: Croquet competition between Australia and England was first played in 1925.

Inter-State and Dominion Championship: Exclusively played in Australia and governed by the Australian Croquet Association since 1950.

Names to Remember

Humphrey Osmond Hicks (1904–): Between 1932 and 1966, he won seven open championships, nine men's, seven open doubles, four mixed doubles and the President's Cup. He represented England in the MacRobertson Trophy in 1950, 1956 amd 1963.

Edmond Patrick Cotter (1904–): A versatile sportsman of the UK who played bridge and croquet for England. He won the President's Cup in 1948, and captained England in the MacRoberston Trophy during 1956 and 1963. He was known for his attacking approach to croquet.

John William Solomons (1931–): In 1959, Reckitt wrote of him as perhaps the greatest player of all times. In 1973, Solomons had a total of 46 titles including 10 each open singles and doubles and was the Champion of Champions for four years consecutively since its inception in 1967.

Dorothy Dyne Steel (1884–1965): A legendary woman in the game of croquet. She won four open championships, four Beddow Cup (succeeded by the President's Cup). She played in the MacRobertson Trophy for England in 1925, 1928 and 1937 and between 1919 and 1939 won 15 women championships, five open doubles and seven mixed doubles.

■

CYCLING

Chapter - 16

Cycle races are held in a Velodrome. The first Velodrome with cement track was built in Putney, London.

History

Velocipedes or the bone shakers were much different from the modern generation cycles. But these velocipedes began the cycling era. Modern cycles were evolved from these velocipedes. A velocipede race was first counducted on 31 May, 1868, over 1.2 km at the Parc de St Cloud, Paris, for the first time and was won by James Moore. The longest distance covered in 1 hour was 76 miles 604 yards by Leon Vanderstuy ft (Belgium) on 30 September, 1928.

Cycle racing became popular from 1890, in countries like the USA, Australia, France and Germany. Subsequently the first velodrome with cement track was built in Putney, London, in 1891. The International Cyclist Association was formed in 1892. World Cycling championships started in 1893 at Chicago.

Since 1868 cycle sport in one form or the other has been in vogue. Cycle manufacturers like Dunlop, Humber and Swift started promoting cycle racing to advertise their products. In the 1890s cycle racing became popular in the US, Australia, France and Germany. The International Cyclist Association was formed in 1892 with England, Germany, France, Denmark, Holland, the US and Canada as members. World cycling championships started in 1892 at Chicago at the behest of ICA. The championships consisted of three amateur events —1 mile, 10 miles and 62.137 miles race.

The Cycle

Diagram of road race bicycle is given below:

Cycle Races

Cycle races may be divided into road and track races. However, various types of other cycling events are also in vogue like bicycle

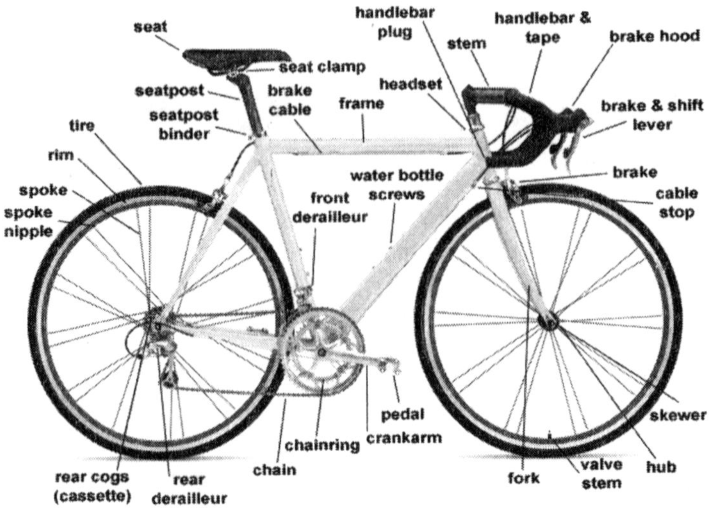

Road race bicycle

polo, cycle ball, the cross country sport of cycle cross and the simulated racing of cycle roller contest. Various types of cycle races are described below.

Road Racing

Road racing may cover any distance from 32 lap to more than 4828 km. This type of race is by an individual from start to finish. But generally for a long distance race, six to twelve riders compete as a group with one as the leader and two or three other members as protected riders. The rest of the members from the supporting group are widely known as domestiques.'Domestiques help to close the gap, if a rival brakes away to pace the leader to the break, to exchange bicycle if the leader has mechanical trouble or his bicycle is punctured. And in a mass finish, they lead the leader in the final sprint. Therefore, the moves in a road race are difficult to interpret because of their constantly changing pattern. During the race the leader may change because he may not be well placed to win. Sometimes a domestique after attaching himself to a strong break away group may not have any alternative other than contesting the finish.

The food is organised by the organisers and is contained in a Musetta, a light cotton satchel. The rider snatches the food as he rides and transfers it in his racing jersey pockets. Clothing worn in road races, generally, consists of racing jersey with large pouches across the chest and hip, cotton racing cap and mitts, tight fitting woollen shorts, lighweight perforated shoes with metal insets laminated between the layers of the sole and white ankle socks.

Criterium and Kermesse

Criterium is a form of race which passes through closed streets of a town or road, linking a group of villages. This has the laps of 3.2-6.4 miles generally. Kermesse race uses even smaller laps in urban area.

Time Trialling

Time Trialling is a system of bicycle racing in which riders start singly at one-minute intervals and are individually timed on completing the course.The French term for time trial is "Course Centre la montre" or race against the watch.

Track Events

For the track events a track is specially constructed in a velodrome which is symmetrical and approximately oval in shape but with two straight sections, a back straight and a finishing straight parallel with its longer axis. The track is generally banked all through more steeply on the curves than on the straight.

1. **Outdoor Tracks:** The circumference of the outdoor track is less than 1 km, but distances of 250, 333 1/3,400 and 500 m are popular.

The outdoor track is generally made of concrete, shale, asphalt or occasionally wood.

2. **Indoor Tracks:** Indoor tracks are generally made of wooden slates or plywood panels. The circuit is often under 200 m and rarely over 300 m having shorter length and steeper banks which may be angled upto 50° to 55°.

3. **Track Marking:** The circumference of a track is measured along the gaugeline which is a 20 mm blue band painted 20 cm from the inner edge of the track. A black or white sprinters line 40 mm wide is marked concentrically 90 cm from the inner edge. A blue stayer's line of the same width is marked concentrically 90 cm (35 in) from the inner edge. A blue stayer's line of the same width is marked at one-third of the breadth of the track from the inner edge.

Types of Track Events

There are various types of track events of which six form the basis of competition at world championships. These are:

1. **Sprint Races:** This is organised on knockout basis, with three riders on the track in the earlier rounds and two or three in the finals. Each race is held over 1 km but only the last 200 m is timed.

2. **Tandem Sprint:** Covers the same distance and takes the same general form as single sprints. The front man controls the racing. The man behind who provides the extra power is often called the stoker.

3. **Individual Pursuit:** This event is contested by professionals over 5 km, by amateurs over 4 km and by women over 3 km. Two riders take part in each race starting from stations on opposite sides of the track. Victory goes to the first rider to reach his home station on completing the distance or to the rider who overtakes his opponent.

4. **Madison Racing:** This is a contest between teams of two or three riders.Only one of whom is in the race at any given moment whereas his partner circles slowly above the stayer's line. After two or three laps the resting partner will relay him to the race by some form of physical contact. This can be prolonged for many hours. The object of the race is to gain laps.

5. **Devil Take the Hindmost**: This is an elimination race in which after a predetermined lap the last man across the finishing line drops out. The process continues until only two men are left to contest the final sprint.

6. **Australian Pursuit:** This is a form of individual pursuit in which a number of riders start from equidistant stations around the track. Any rider who is overtaken is eliminated and the winner is the first man home.

7. **Italian Pursuit:** This is a variation of the team pursuit in which each team sheds one rider at the competition of every lap until one man remains for the final circuit.

8. **Omnium:** This is a contest to find the best all-rounder of a track meetings. Points are given for placings in four or five events.

9. **Six-Day Race:** This is a highly specialised event staged on indoor tracks during the winter months and is confined to an exclusive circle of professional riders. Madison racing remains at the heart of the six-day race.

10. **Cycle Speedway:**This is a form of racing modelled on motorcycle speedway and is generally conducted on shell tracks 85 to 125 yards in circumference. Riders compete in fours.

11. **Motor Paced Races:** Motor paced races are the longest track event. The championship distance for professionals is 100 km. Each competitor is paced by a specially built motorcycle. A competitor can maintain an average speed of 80 km/hour or more while riding in the shelter of the motorcycle driver. Each competitor is totally dependent upon his pace maker's appreciation of the situation. In France motor paced is known as 'demi-fond' or middle distance.

12. **Grass Track Racing:** This type of racing is generally associated with country fetes and fairs. National championships are held at 800 m and 5 km for men and 800 m for women.Tyres of these cycles are heavily studded with treads.

Championships

Vuelta A Espagna (Tour of Spain): A professional cycling stage race which was founded in 1935. This race is held before the tours of Italy and France and covers approximately 3060 km in 16-18 stages.

Asian Games: Cycling was a part of the first Asian Games. Only 1000 m time trial, 4000 m team pursuit and individual road race competitions were held. Other cycling events were introduced subsequently.

Giro D'Italia (Tour of Italy): This is an annual stage race first held in 1909, for professionals. It was modelled on Tour de France. The Giro competition takes place between the French and Spanish tours and lasts for about three weeks. This race takes a different route each year.

Tour de France: This was founded by Desgranges, a newspaper editor, in 1903 as a six-stage race of 2410 km. In 1970, the Tour was 4,345 km and spread over 24 days.Now it is restricted to 20 stages whose average length should not be more than 200 km to 260 km.

Tour of Britain: In 1951, *The Daily Express* newspaper instituted this race exclusively for amateur cycling stage race. In 1958, it was revived by the Milk Marketing Board. The race covers 2410 km approximately in 13-15 days.

Tour of Flanders (Belgium): Annual one-day race for professional cyclists, it was instituted in 1913. It starts in Ghent and returns to a village near the city. The route changes every year but roughly covers 241 km.

World Championship: This is held annually. This was first staged in 1893 for the amateurs and in 1895, for the professionals.

Olympics: Cycling has been a part of the modern Olympics since 1896. However various cycling events were introduced in different Olympics at a later period.

Names to Remember

Baron Yon Drais-de-Sauerbrun: A German engineer who made the most significant progress towards invention of the modern bicycle by introducing a pivoting front wheel which allowed him to steer the machine by a handle bar. An arm rest was also introduced by him against which he could press forward as he thrust back his feet. He could manage a speed of 8 mph.

Paolo Bettini (born April 1, 1974): He is an Italian road cyclist with the Belgian Quick Step-Innergetic professional cycling team. He is the gold medal winner of the 2004 Athens Olympics road race and of the 2006 World Road Race Championship. Bettini is a 3-time champion of the UCI Road World Cup series consecutively in 2002, 2003 and 2004. He has also won stages of the Tour de France, Giro d'Italia, and Vuelta a España. He finished in 9th place at the 2000 Summer Olympics, and won a silver medal at the 2001 World Championships in Lisbon, Portugal. He is nicknamed "Il Grillo" ("The Cricket") for his propensity to attack repeatedly, and for his sprinting style.

Sara Carrigan (born September 7, 1980 in Gunnedah, New South Wales): He is a professional cyclist from Australia, who commenced her cycling career in 1996 at the age of fifteen. Her greatest success as a road cyclist has been in the 2004 Summer Olympics Women's Road race where she won the gold medal. She was awarded the Order of Australia Medal (OAM) in the 2005 Australia Day Honours List. Other awards include Australian Female Road Cyclist of the Year in 2002, 2003, 2004

Leontien van Moorsel (born March 22, 1970, Boekel): He is a Dutch cyclist. She is also known under her married name, Leontien Zijlaard-van Moorsel.Van Moorsel started her professional career in the late 1980s, and soon was one of the best cyclists in the world. She won major races both on the track, and on the road. In the first half of the 1990s, she won the Tour Feminin twice, after fierce competition with her main rival in that time, Jeannie Longo. At the 2000 Summer Olympics in Sydney, Van Moorsel was one of the most successful athletes. She won gold medals both on the road (road race and time trial), and on the track (3km pursuit). At the 2004 Summer Olympics, she was again one of the favorites in the road race, but she fell in the penultimate lap. Although she was injured, she started in the time trial three days later, and successfully defended her title. With 4 gold, 1 silver, and 1 bronze Olympic medals.

Bradley Wiggins, OBE (born April 28, 1980): He is a professional track and road bicycle racer. He won three medals on the track at the 2004 Summer Olympics. The son of a professional cyclist, Gary Wiggins, Bradley Wiggins was born in Ghent, Belgium but grew up in Maida Vale, London. He won gold in the 4km individual pursuit in Athens before winning a silver in the team pursuit, and a bronze with Rob Hayles in the Madison. At the Sydney 2000 Summer Olympics, Wiggins won bronze in the team pursuit. Wiggins rode for the French professional road cycling team Cofidis in 2006, and participated in the 2006 Tour de France. He was created an OBE for services to sport.

Sarah Ulmer (born March 14, 1976 in Auckland): He is a New Zealand cyclist who won a Gold medal and set new world records at the 2004 Summer Olympics at Athens, the first New Zealander to win an Olympic cycling gold medal. When she left Athens at the end of the games, Ulmer held the Olympic title, the Olympic and world records, the Commonwealth Games title and the Commonwealth Games record for the 3000m individual pursuit.

■

DIVING

Chapter - 17

It was in 1893 in England that diving became a competitive sport.

History

In 1893 , the first diving stage in England was erected at the Highgate Ponds, London, when the Amateur Swimming Association started the diving championship. It was a firm board fixed at a height of about 4.6 m above the surface. The competition was open to men only and comprised standing and running dives from heights of 4.6 m and 10 m. Fancy diving which was subsequently followed by spring board diving was included in the 1904 Olympics Games at St. Louis. Women's diving competition was included for the first time in Olympic Games in Stockholm in 1912, and the spring board Women events were included in the 1920 Olympics at Antwerp.

Diving Pool

The diving area in the modern pool complex is usually separated from the swimming pool. This enables the required water temperature to be maintained at 28° to 30°C as against 24°C required for swimming area. Depth of water over a specified area for each height of board is laid down by the *Federation Internationale de Nation Amateur* (FINA). These are given as follows:

(a) Depth of water at plummet:

		Depth requirement minimum
Spring boards	1 m	3.00 m
	3 m	3.00 m

Platforms	5.00 m	3.80 m
	7.50 m	3.80 m
	10.00 m	3.80 m

(b) Minimum distance depth ahead of plummet:

		Distance	*Depth*
Spring boards	1m	5 m	3.40 m
	3 m	6 m	3.70 m
Platforms	5 m	6 m	3.70 m
	6 m	8 m	4.40 m
	8 m	11 m	4.75 m

(c) Depth at 12 m ahead of plummet for a 10 m platform is 4.25 m.

(d) Distance from plummet to pool wall ahead:

		Distance
Spring boards	1 m	3.70 m
	3 m	10.25 m
Platforms	5 m	10.25 m
	7.5 m	11.00 m
	10 m	13. 50 m

(e) Distance from plummet back to pool wall:

		Distance
Spring boards	1.00 m	1.80 m
	3.00 m	1.80 m
Platforms	5.00 m	1.25 m
	7.5 m	1.50 m
	11.00 m	1.50 m

(f) Minimum distance from plummet to adjoint plummet:

		Distance
Spring boards	1 m/l m	2.40 m
	3 m/3 m/l m	2.60 m
Platforms	5 m/3 m/l m	2.50 m
	7.5 m/5 m/3 m/lm	2.50 m
	10 m/7.5 m/5 m/ /3 m/l m	2.75 m

(g) Distance from plummet to side pool wall:

		Distance
Spring boards	1 m	2.50m
	3 m	3.50m

Platforms	5 m	4.25m
	7.5 m	4.50m
	10 m	5.25m

Dress

Men must wear swimming trunks and women one-piece swimming costumes. Caps are optional.

Types of Dives

Various types of dives are shown here.

Diving Groups

1. **Forward Group:** The diver takes off with body facing the water and dives forward.
2. **Back Group:** The diver takes off with body facing the diving board platform and dives backward.
3. **Reverse Group:** The diver takes off with body facing the water and dives backward.
4. **Inward Group:** The diver takes off with body facing the diving board platform and dives.
5. **Twist Group:** Any dive from any of above four groups with the body simultaneously twisting horizontally (alongwith the lateral somersaulting action).
6. **Armstand Group:** Only for Platform Diving. The diver stands on edge of platform in an armstand prior to any forward/backward fall or rotation.

High Board

A rigid platform covered with coir-matting or other non-slip material. The 10 m platform should be 2 m wide and 6 m long. The front of the platform must project at least 1.50 m beyond the edge of the bath. The back and sides must be surrounded by hand rails with crossbars. Mechanical surface agitation must be installed to aid divers in their visual perception of the surface

of the water. It is installed at heights of 5 m, 7.5 m, and 10 m above water level.

Spring Board

The modern spring board is a flexible tapered, precision instrument made of timber strips glued together and totally encased in fibre glass. Now it has been superseded by more springy aluminium alloy board. The most advanced is Aerodynamic, in as much as it has upto 210 perforations to overcome air resistance and drag during depression and its recoil. The spring boards are at least 4.8 m long and 0.5 m wide covered with rough coconut matting (in case of wooden boards only). The fibre glass and aluminium alloy diving boards are provided with a non-slip surface coating.

Diving Competitions

Spring Board: The men's spring board competition comprises five dives selected from five different groups to the total degree of difficulty of which shall not exceed 9.5, and six voluntary dives selected from five groups without limit. Women's spring board competition comprises five dives selected from five different groups to the total degree of difficulty of which shall not exceed 9.5, and five voluntary dives selected from five groups.

High Board: Men's high board competition comprises four voluntary dives selected from four different groups, the total degree of difficulty of which shall not exceed 7.6, and six voluntary dives without limit. In each section each dive is selected from a different group. The dives may be performed from 5 m or 10 m platform. In World Championship and Olympics only dives from 10 m shall be executed. Women's high board competition comprises four dives with limit of 7.6 total degree of difficulty selected from different groups, and four voluntary dives without limit selected from different groups.

Scoring

In Olympic and World Championships there are seven judges, for other competitions five may be adequate. Points are awarded as under:

(a) Completely failed	0 /
(b) Unsatisfactory	1/2-2 points
(c) Deficient	2½-4½ points
(d) Satisfactory	5-6 points

(e) Good 6½-8 points
(f) Very good 8½ -10 points

Results

To find the score for each dive, the highest and lowest scores are cancelled. The remainder is totalled and multiplied by the official degree of difficulty for the dive. The winner is the one with the highest total number of points in the final round.

Irina Kalinina (USSR, b.8 February 1959): She won five medals (three gold, one silver, and one bronze in 1973, 1975 and 1978).

Names to Remember

Greg Louganis (USA): He was considered to be the best diver, he won five world titles in 1978, and in 1982 won both high board and spring board titles. He scored over 700 points for the 11 dive spring board event. In the 1984 Olympics he won two gold medals and set a total record of 754 points for spring board and 710.91 points for high board diving.

Patricia Joan McCormick (USA): She won four diving events in the 1952 and 1956 Olympics. She thus holds the world record of winning maximum gold medals by a woman.

Peng Bo.(b. February 18, 1981, China -): He is a Chinese diver who competed at the 2004 Olympic games and won the men's 3m springboard diving event with a score of 787.38. He also competed in the men's synchronised 3m springboard diving event along with his partner, Kenan Wang and was placed 8th with a score of 283.89. He started competing in 2000. He and Wang have won a few medals in diving events. Peng is also known as Peng Bo.

Hu Jia is a Chinese diver who won the gold medal at the 2004 Summer Olympics in the men's 10 metre platform. He was in sixth place at the end of the preliminary round, and fourth place after the semi-finals, but put in an excellent performance in the finals to take first place. Jia also won two silver medals at the 2000 Summer Olympics in Sydney, Australia in the 10m Platform and 10m Platform Synchronized.

Guo Jingjing (Chinese, born 1981): She is an athlete from the People's Republic of China. She competes in diving 2002 Asian Games – 1st 3m Springboard/Synchronized Springboard 2003 Fina Diving Grand Prix (Australia/China) – 1st 3m Springboard/Synchronized Springboard

2003 World Championships – 1st 3m Springboard/Synchronized Springboard 2004 World Cup – 1st 3m Synchronized Springboard; 2nd 3m Springboard 2004 Olympic Games – 1st 3m Springboard & Synchronized Springboard 2006 Asian Games – 1st 3m Synchronized Springboard 2007 World Championships – 1st 3m Springboard.

Chantelle Newbery (born May 6, 1977 in Melbourne, Australia): She is an Australian diver, who won two medals at the 2006 Melbourne Commonwealth Games. She finished fourth in synchronised 3m springboard at the 2000 Summer Olympics, and she has medalled in multiple World Championships and Grand Prix events. She was gold medalist in 2004 Summer Olympics. Her husband, Robert Newbery, is also an Olympic medallist.

■

DRAUGHTS

Chapter - 18

The game is played by two players with 24 coins, 12 black and 12 white on a Chess Board.

History

The origin of draughts or checkers as it is called in the USA is not exactly known. It is believed that it was played in Egypt in the 2nd century BC. Antonio Torqemada of Valencia, Spain, in 1547, wrote the first book on draughts. The game can be traced back to Britain during the16th century though the rules then were different. The game as it is played today was established in the 19th century in Europe but is played with a number of variations in different countries.

English Draughts

The rules of draughts according to the 1991 EDA Handbook:

The Numbered Board

At the start of the game the black pieces occupy squares 1-12 and the white pieces occupy squares 21-32.

Draughts Board and Men

1. The draughts board is square in shape and is divided into 64 squares of equal size,alternately light and dark in colour(technically called black and white).

2. The board is placed between the two players such that the bottom left-hand corner square is black.

3. The game is played only on the black squares, which for the purpose of reference are assigned numbers from 1 to 32.

4. Each player starts with 12 discs, or "men", all of equal size. One player has dark coloured men (called black) and the other has light coloured men (called white).**Note...** The colours of the men must make a distinct contrast with the colours of the squares of the board.

5. At the start of play the black men occupy squares 1 to 12 and the white men occupy squares 21 to 32.

Order of Play

6. To start the first game the players decide by the toss of a coin which colour they will play. In subsequent games the players alternate colours.

7. The first move in each game is made by the player with the black men; thereafter the moves are made by each player in turn.

The Moves

8. There are fundamentally 4 types of move: the ordinary move of a man, the ordinary move of a king, the capturing move of a man and the capturing move of a king.

Ordinary Move of A Man

9. An ordinary move of a man is its transfer diagonally forward left or right from one square to an immediately neighbouring vacant square.

10. When a man reaches the farthest row forward (the king-row or crownhead) it becomes a king, and this completes the turn of play. The man is crowned by the opponent, who must place a man of the same colour on top of it before making his own move. (It may be necessary to borrow from another set if no captured man is available for the purpose).

Ordinary Move of A King

11. An ordinary move of a king (crowned man) is from one square diagonally forward or backward, left or right, to an immediately neighbouring vacant square.

Capturing Move of A Man

12. A capturing move of a man is its transfer from one square over a diagonally adjacent and forward square occupied by an opponent`s piece (man or king) and on to a vacant square immediately beyond it.

(A capturing move is called a "jump"). On completion of the jump the captured piece is removed from the board.

Capturing Move of A King

13. A capturing move of a king is similar to that of a man, but may be in a forward or backward direction.

Capturing in General

14. If a jump creates an immediate further capturing opportunity, then the capturing move of the piece (man or king) is continued until all the jumps are completed. The only exception is that if a man reaches the king-row by means of a capturing move it then becomes a king but may not make any further jumps in the same turn. At the end of the capturing sequence, all captured pieces are removed from the board, in the order in which they were jumped.

15. All capturing moves are compulsory, whether offered actively or passively. If there are two or more ways to jump, a player may select any one he wishes, not necessarily that which gains most pieces. Once started, a multiple jump must be carried through to completion.

Touching the Pieces

16. Either player, on intimating his intention to his opponent, is entitled to adjust his own or his opponent`s pieces properly on their squares at any time during the course of the game.

17. If a player on his turn to move touches a piece he must play that piece, unless he has given an adjustment warning. If the piece is not legally playable, rule 19.2 applies.

18. If any part of a playable piece is played over a corner of the square on which it is stationed, the move must be completed in that direction.

False, Improper or Illegal Moves

19. A player making a false, improper or illegal move shall be cautioned for the first offence, and the move recalled. He shall forfeit the game for any subsequent false, improper or illegal move made in that game.This applies, for example, if a player:

19.1. Omits to capture or to complete a multiple capture. (This supersedes the old "huff" rule).

19.2. On his turn to play touches an unplayable piece.

19.3. Moves a piece, either in an ordinary move or in a capturing move, on to a wrong square.

19.4. Moves an uncrowned man backwards.

19.5. When capturing, removes an opponent`s piece or pieces not in a position to be captured by that move.

19.6. When capturing, inadvertently remove one or more of his own pieces.

19.7. Continues a capturing move through the king-row with a man not already crowned.

19.8. Moves a piece when it is not his turn to play.

20. If any of the pieces are accidently displaced by the players or through any cause outside their control, the pieces are replaced without penalty and the game is continued.

21. A player who refuses to adhere to the rules shall immediately forfeit the game.

Result of the Game

22. There are only two possible states to define: the win and the draw.

Definition of A Win

23. The game is won by the player who can make the last move; that is, no move is available to the opponent on his turn to play, either because all his pieces have been captured or his remaining pieces are all blocked.

24. A player also wins if his opponent:

(1) Resigns at any point;

(2) Forfeits the game by contravening the rules.

Definition of A Draw

25. The game is drawn if at any stage both players agree on such a result. (This usually occurs when neither side can force a win).

26. 50-move rule. The game shall be declared drawn if, at any stage of the game, a player can demonstrate to the satisfaction of the referee that both the following conditions hold:

26.1. Neither player has advanced an uncrowned man towards the king-row during the previous 50 moves;

26.2. No pieces have been removed from the board during the previous 50 moves.

Note... . For the purposes of this rule, a move shall be said to consist of one black move and one white move.

Types of Draughts

1. **Spanish:** The board is placed in such a fashion that there is a black square in each player's right-hand corner. The pieces are then set up as for the standard game using the black squares. A king is made in the usual way and it is then allowed "long move".

2. **German:** The game is played by keeping the board in the conventional position. But, as in the spanish game, kings are entitled to the "long move". Ordinary men move forward normally but they can, when capturing, move backwards or forwards.

3. **Russian:** The board is set up as in standard games. A king on being crowned after reaching the back row of the opponent, can in the same move make any possible capture. It is entitled to the "long move" in this game also.

4. **Italian:** As in the Spanish game, the board is kept in such a way that a black square remains to the back rank right-hand corner of each player. A king has the long move. Kings in this game cannot be captured by a single piece.

5. **Turkish**: It uses 16 men instead of 12. And these are placed on the second and third ranks.

6. **Polish:** It uses a board having 100 squares (10 × 10) instead of 64 as in the case of conventional draughts. Each player has twenty men. They are arranged at the four back rows of the board.

7. **Losing:** The player tries to lose as many pieces as possible instead of capturing. Capturing is compulsory. The winner is the one who loses all his men or cannot move.

Championships

British Championship (Biennial): This competition was inaugurated in 1886. Samuel Cohen (London, 1905-1972) won the Championship six times, in 1924, 1927, 1929, 1933, 1937 and 1939.

World Championship: A record eight World Championships were won by Walter Hellman (USA) between the period 1948-1975.

Charles Walker: At New Orleans Centre, Louisiana, USA, on 5 November, 1988, he played a record 201games simultaneously, winning 189 and drawing 12.

Con McCarrick (Ireland): On 14 March, 1982, he made a unique record. He is reported to have played 154 games simultaneously. Out of which he won 136, drew 17 and lost only 1 game.

■

EQUESTRIAN

Chapter - 19

Played by the horse but controlled by the rider is what is known as Equestrian.

History

The Equestrian sports as we know them today, particularly the Olympic disciplines of jumping, dressage and eventing, were born in the 19th century. The Societe Hippique Francaise was founded in 1865.

The first serious attempt to include riding as an Olympic discipline was made by a group of Swedish officers led by Count Clarence von Rosen. He appealed to Baron de Coubertin at the IOC meeting in 1906, and, as a result, he was asked by the Baron to draft an Olympic equestrian programme. This was presented to the Olympic Congress at The Hague in 1907, and was accepted for the 1908 Games to be held in London.

However, when the Organising Committee received the entries from 88 riders from eight nations, it took fright and backed down. Fortunately, the next Games of 1912 were awarded to Stockholm and there was no difficulty about accepting the programme proposed by Count von Rosen in 1907.

In the autumn of 1911, the invitations were sent out to the military departments and to the national Olympic committees. The Three-Day Event was limited to military officers but the jumping and dressage competitions were open to civilians. Some 62 competitors from 10 nations with 70 horses eventually took part in the competitions, but they were all officers. They knew each other; they probably knew all the judges and they were quite prepared to accept any local variations to the fairly simple rules which existed at the time. With the advent of the Olympic Games, it became obvious that some internationally recognised rules for the three Olympic disciplines were becoming essential. Eventually, in May 1921, delegates from ten national equestrian organisations met in Lausanne to discuss the formation of an international federation.

Equestion

The FEI is the sole authority for all international events in the three Olympic equestrian disciplines—Jumping, Dressage and Three-Day Event, as well as Driving, Endurance Riding, Vaulting and Tent Pegging.

Jumping, Dressage, Driving and Endurance Riding as sports disciplines have their origin in the daily occupation with the horse. The Three-Day Event was created to test the officers' horses, combining all variations of riding, such as dressage, endurance riding, steeplechase, cross-country riding and jumping. Also vaulting and tent-pegging have their origins in the military, the former as training for the inexperienced rider, the latter as a game.

The rules and regulations cover competitions for Seniors (over 18 years), Young Riders (18-21), Juniors (14-18) as well as Pony Riders (under 16 years of age). The Young Riders category, created in 1981, bridges the Junior category with the Seniors. In FEI terms "Event" refers to the complete "Show, Concours, Championship or Games" under the control of an Organising Committee. The term "competition" refers to each individual class in which competitors are placed. The term "discipline" refers to each individual type of event or competition for which rules are established. The term "category" refers to the group of competitors for whom events or competitions are organised. The term "series" refers to a number of competitions held successfully at different events leading to a final classification. The term "phase" refers to separate competitions at the same event which are taken together to arrive at the final classification. The term "round" refers to two or more consecutive circuits over the same, or similar, course as part of a single competitions. Each movement is marked individually by the judges and the total marks of each are then added to give each horse's final score. All tests are judged in an area that is measuring 60 m × 20 m. Dressage was first included in the Olympic Games of 1912.

Marking

There are ten points for each movement with the scale as under:

Excellent	10 points
Very good	9 points
Good	8 points
Fairly good	7 points
Satisfactory	6 points
Sufficient	5 points
Insufficient	4 points
Fairly bad	3 points
Bad	2 points
Very bad	1 point
Not performed	0 point

Forty collective marks are for paces, impulsion, submission and position of the rider, 10 for each.

Errors

First error	2 marks
Second error	4 marks
Third error	8 marks
Fourth error	Elimination

Show Jumping

In show jumping, the horse and the rider jump a set of course of fences specially designed and built for each contest and has *three* main categories of competition:

(a) Primarily test jumping ability but use time as the deciding factor in order to reach a final result.

(b) Test jumping ability alone.

(c) Jumps which put a premium on speed and ability. In certain jumping events, water jumps are also included.

Most competitions come into the first category. Time counting is in the first round or more frequently, in the first or second jump off. Jumping ability is of prime importance. However, time counts only when there is equality of faults. A horse with a slow clear round may beat a fast one with four faults. As a rule the winner is one who incurs the least number of penalties and/or completes the course in the fastest time and/or gains the highest number of points, depending on the type of competition. These competitions are judged and faults are incurred as follows:

(a) Fence knocked down		4 faults
(b) One or more feet in the water or the landing tape		4 faults
(c) Refusals:	First	3 faults
	Second	6 faults
	Third	

Elimination

(d) Fall of horse/rider: first second	6 faults
(e) For each second over the time allowed	1/4 faults
(f) Exceeding the time limit	Elimination

There are over 20 types of show jumping competitions that can be conducted to provide variety as also to test the various kinds of jumping abilities of horses. The "Puissance" which is very popular all over the world is meant to test the power of horses to jump high obstacles. It is equivalent to the high jump where each time an obstacle is cleared at a certain height, it is raised further for the next round which is open only to horses who cleared the previous one without incurring a fault. The world record in this presently stands at 8 feet 2 inches. Similarly, to test speed over obstacles, there is the "Top Score" competition in which a certain time is allowed for the horse and the rider during which they have to clear as many obstacles as they can in a course. These obstacles have points according to their degree of difficulty which if cleared go into the score accumulated at the end of the time. The highest scorer is the winner.

Show jumping has been described as a test in which the course designer is the examiner and the competitors examinees. Since courses are specially designed for each individual competition, the rider's ability to "read" the problems correctly is vital. These problems relate to the positioning of the fences just as much as to their height and width. Combination fences, which comprise two or more jumps within 12 m of each other, become considerably more difficult when a distance problem is involved.

Show jumping is the most competitive discipline in the world today. It attracts the largest audiences and media coverage due to its spectator appeal. At the highest level it is now almost totally professional with large amounts of prize money and the horses attract huge prices.

Three-Day Event

This is a competition designed to test the all-round ability of the horse and the rider. The event consists of three distinct phases, which test the horse in dressage, speed, endurance, cross country, and finally show jumping. The phases take place on three separate days, hence the name. The dressage phase consists of a series of movements at the walk, trot, and canter which the rider must memorise. Points are deducted if the rider forgets the test or does in the wrong order. The second phase, the endurance 'phase, is the most important as well as the toughest part of the competition. The length of the course varies but the maximum is 32.3 km (20 miles). The course is divided as follows:

1. Roads and tracks 16-20 km speed 220 m/minute
2. Steeplechase 3.105 to 3.450 km speed 690 m/minute
3. Cross-country 7.4 to 7.9 km speed 570 m/minute

The two roads and track sections should each be completed within the allotted time of 220 m per minute. Exceeding the time allowed incurs a penalty of one per second. The first acid test comes on the steeplechase course, for it is here that time plays a vital role. Exceeding the time allowed is penalised by penalties. The ideal result is obtained when a horse

completes the course in the specified time, and it is, therefore, a waste of effort to go faster on the second Roads and Track sections.Competitors then set out on the cross-country course, containing between 30 and 35 fixed obstacles, by far the most difficult part of the test. The height for cross-country obstacles is limited to 1.2 m (3 ft 11 in). A typical course would include one or more jumps into water, obstacles built in a steep down hill gradient, and several "drop-fences" where the landing is considerably lower than the take-off. This is an acid test of the horse's stamina, jumping ability and strength.

Penalties in the cross-country and steeplechase courses are incurred as follows:

1.	Refusals:	
	(a) First	20 penalties
	(b) Second (at the same obstacle)	40 penalties
	(c) Third (at the same obstacle)	Elimination
2.	Fall of horse and/or rider within the "penalty zone"	60 penalties
3.	Second fall of horse and/or rider within the "penalty zone" in the steeplechase course	Elimination
4.	Third fall of horse and/or rider within the	Elimination
	"penalty zone" in the cross-country course	Elimination
5.	Taking the wrong course	Elimination
6.	Exceeding the time allowed in steeplechase	0.8 penalty/sec.
7.	Exceeding the time allowed in cross-country	0.4 penalty/sec.

Show jumping penalties in the three-day event are incurred as follows:

1.	Fence knocked down.	5 penalties
2.	One or more feet in water or on the landing tape	5 penalties
3.	Refusals:	
	(a) First	10 penalties
	(b) Second	20 penalties
	(c) Third	Elimination
4.	Fall of horse and/or rider	60 penalties
5.	For each second over the time allowed	0.25 penalty
6.	Exceeding the time limit	Elimination

Tent Pegging

Purpose: A test to demonstrate the horse's freedom, energy, skill and obedience in galloping straight on the track while the rider skilfully picks up a peg with a lance.

Arena: The competitor has to gallop, with speed not less than 800 m per minute along a track marked in the centre of the ground which is 100 m long from start to finish and 60 m wide.

Conduct: A competitor riding the same horse will make four runs at a 60 cm peg and four runs at a 4 cm peg.

Important Rules

1. The riders will only use their right hand for carrying the lance.

2. The lance must be minimum 2.4 m long and shall not exceed 2.75 m with a clear point not jagged nor serrated or with edges.

Marking

Marking will be done as follows:

Rider carrying the peg for more than 15 m	5 points
Peg is drawn out but falls within 15 m	3 points
Peg is struck but not lifted out of the ground	1 point
Correct peg neither struck nor taken	1 point
0.25 penalties incurred for each commenced second over the time allowed	Deduction

Tie Breaker: If there is a tie after the eight runs over two sessions of four runs each, one or more extra runs will be made as required on the 3 cm peg until the decision is arrived at.

General Points

1. If a competitor drops his lance at any place between the start and finish lines, he will not be awarded any points for that run.

2. In the event of a lance breaking during the run, the run will hold good and points will be awarded as per the rules.

3. In case either a horse or a rider or both have a fall between the starting and the finishing lines, no points will be awarded for that particular run.

The One-Day Event

To progressively prepare the horses for the Three-Day Event, One-Day Event has been introduced for the novice horses. This event comprises a dressage test, followed by a cross-country test and one round of show jumping, all normally carried out in one day. There are no road and track tests (Phases A and B) or steeplechase (Phase C) of the endurance test, as in the Three-Day Event, but only cross-country (Phase D). For administrative or other

conveniences, the One-Day Event may be conducted over two days. Generally penalties as for Three-Day Event apply to the One-Day Event as well.

Endurance Ride

Endurance riding was introduced in India for the first time in 1988, as a part of the Horse Trials. It has only recently become an international competitive sport. To date, only a couple of World Cups have been organised in this event. The International Equestrian Federation introduced this as a demonstration event in the 1992 Olympics in Spain.

Endurance rides normally are of 80 or 160 km. The point to note is that to win, not only has the rider to cross the finish line first but at the end of the ride his horse should be in a fit condition, as laid down in the rules.

Driving

The FEI established the first rules for driving events in 1970. They provide for three types of competitions:

1. Dressage (and possibly presentation)
2. Marathon
3. Obstacle driving

A combination of any of these is known as combined driving competition. The championships comprise all three competitions and are held, at present, for teams of four horses and four pairs. There are also competitions for singles and tandems.

The object of the presentation, which is normally not part of a combined driving competition any more, is to judge the turn out, cleanliness, general condition and impression of the horses, harness and vehicle. The teams are judged at the halt.

The object of the dressage is to judge the freedom, regularity of paces, harmony, lightness, and ease of movement, impulsion and the correct positioning of the horses on the move. The driver will be judged on his style of driving accuracy and general command of his team.

The object of the marathon is to test standard of fitness and stamina of the horses and the judgement of pace and horse mastership of the driver.

The object of the obstacle driving is to test the fitness, obedience and suppleness of the horses after the marathon and the skill and competence of the driver.

In all competitions, with the exception of the marathon, the dress of the driver and the passengers (grooms) must conform to the style of carriage and harness used. A different vehicle may be used in the marathon.

The individual classification will be obtained by adding together the penalties obtained in each competition.The team classification will be obtained by adding together the scores of the best two (of three) drivers in each of the three competitions, provided a team member is not eliminated in one of the three competitions.

The length of the marathon in international events should not be less than 23 km and not more than 27 km. Section E of the marathon (approx. 10 km) will have upto eight artificial obstacles.

Vaulting

The origin of vaulting goes back to the intention to train people to ride by getting used to the movements of the horse, to give them the feeling of balance. At several Cavalry Schools, vaulting was obligatory for beginners.

At championships (world or continental) separate vaulting competitions for males and females must be organised. In the team vaulting competition, male and female vaulters may compete together. *Pas-de-deux* competitions (which are not part of championships) may be held for male pairs, female pairs or for mixed pairs.

A vaulter may take part in team vaulting competitions until the end of the calendar year in which he or she reaches the age of 18.

In individual competitions they may take part from the beginning of the calendar year in which they reach the age of 16. There is no upper age limit for individual vaulters.

A vaulting team is composed of eight vaulters and one reserve vaulter, one longeur and one horse. The horse canters left hand on a circle with a minimum diameter of 13 m. Both the individual and the team vaulting competitions consist of two parts, the compulsory test and the free test.

Championships

The President's Cup: Instituted in 1965, and awarded annually, it is based on the results of Nations Cup and may be called the World team championship.

World Championship: The principal individual contest next to the Olympic Games instituted in 1953. This is open to riders from each nation. The title is decided during three preliminary competitions and a final in which four qualifiers ride their own and each other's horse. However, changing of horse is not allowed for women championship.

Nations Cup: This is open to international team of four riders and is decided over two rounds. The worst score of the two are discarded. This is held as per the rules laid down by the FEI.

Olympics: Show jumping was included in the 1900 Olympics. Show jumping (team) dressage, three-day event was introduced in the Olympics of 1912. But dressage (team) was included only in 1928.

Names to Remember

Anky van Grunsven (born 2 January 1968 in Erp): He is a Dutch Dressage champion who won the gold medal in the 2000 Olympics with her horse Bonfire and gold in the 2004 Olympics with Salinero. Anky is married to her trainer/coach Sjef Janssen who entered the world of horses at the age of 28 and introduced new views on training. . Germany was the world leader in dressage for decades until the Dutch team, including Van Grunsven, won the Nations Cup in Aachen in 2005.

Leslie Law (born May 5, 1965, Hereford): He is a British eventer, who won the individual gold medal in the 2004 Summer Olympic Games. He started riding at age 10, competing with his brother, and participated in his first accredited event in 1982. By 1989, he was a widely respected competitor, and that year was placed 8th at the

Badminton Horse Trials. After a period of consolidation, by the late 1990s he was counted amongst the sport's elite, placing him in the top ten at Badminton, Burghley and the British Championship on a number of occasions.

He was a member of the British team that won silver at the 2000 Olympic Games and bronze at the 2002 World Equestrian Games

Rodrigo Pessoa (born November 29, 1972 in Paris, France): He is an equestrian from Brazil, who's an important name in the world of show jumping as well as an accomplished rider backed by his six Grand Prix winnings and a total of $700,000 (•590,000) in prize money. In 1998 he rode Gandini Lianos to be World Champion of show jumping at the World Equestrian Games, in Rome. He later claimed the title and prize for the world's best rider and in addition to the Show Jumping Year trophy. In 2000 at the Olympic Games in Sydney, he again won the bronze team medal.

■

FENCING

Chapter - 20

Art of ancient fighting with swords has been transformed into a specialised sport.

History

Swordsmanship as a mode of defence was practised throughout the world. The excitement in duelling kept this art alive. However competitive fencing as a sport commenced in the continent of Europe in the last quarter of the 19th century. Fencing has been an Olympic sport since the first modern Olympic games held in Athens in 1896. There are records of women fencing since the 18th century. The women's individual foil event was first included in the Olympic games in 1924. The women's fencing team event was added in the Olympics of 1960.

Sometime before 1540, King Henry VIII granted permission to form a Corporation of Masters of Defence, which became the first governing body for fencing. Subsequently in 1902 the Amateur Fencing Association was formed with Captain Hulton as its first President. World governing body for the Fencing Federation Internationale d'Escrime was founded in Paris on 29 November 1913.

Sword

The weapons used are of three types—"the foil", the "epee" and the "sabre".

In each case the weapon consists of a blade and mounting. The different types of fencing weapons are shown here.

The "foil" used in duels has a maximum length of 110 cm and a maximum weight of 500 gm. It has quadrangular tampering blade and a small, bell shaped guar.

The "epee" is a duelling sword, invented for practising actual duelling in schools.

Maximum weight 770 gm

Maximum length 110 cm

It has larger bell-guard and stiffer triangular, fluted blade.

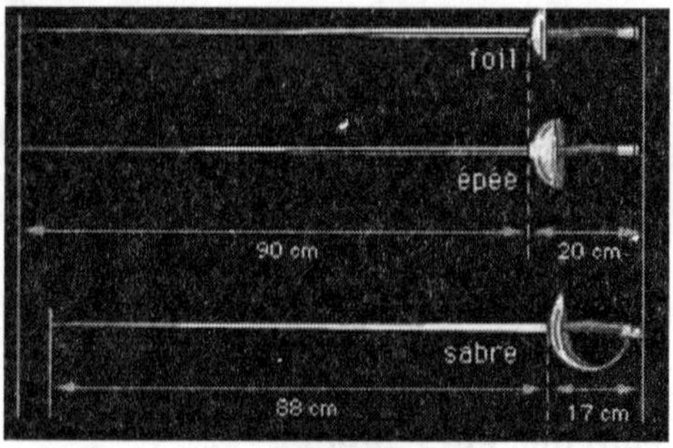

Fencing Weapons

The "sabre" is the out and thrust weapon evolved from the backsword and the heavy cavalry sabre. It has a maximum length of 105 cm and weighs not more than 500 gm. It has a flattened V-shaped blade with a blunted cutting edge and a point folded over to form a button.

Dress

Fencing equipment consists of the weapon, a mask, a jacket, gloves, breeches and stockings. Fencing does not pose any danger to a competitor provided he is well protected and a mask and gloves are worn at all times.

Piste

Piste is the competition area for fencing. The area is flat and the surface can be made of wood, cork, plastic, linoleum or metal based compound. This must be 14 m long and 1.8-2 m wide. At each end of the piste there should be an extension 1.5-2 m long.

Piste is marked as:

1. Centre line
2. On-guard line—2 m each side of the centre line.
3. Warning line for epee and sabre—5 m each side from centre line.

4. Foil warning line—6 m from centre.
5. Rear limit—7 m for all weapons.

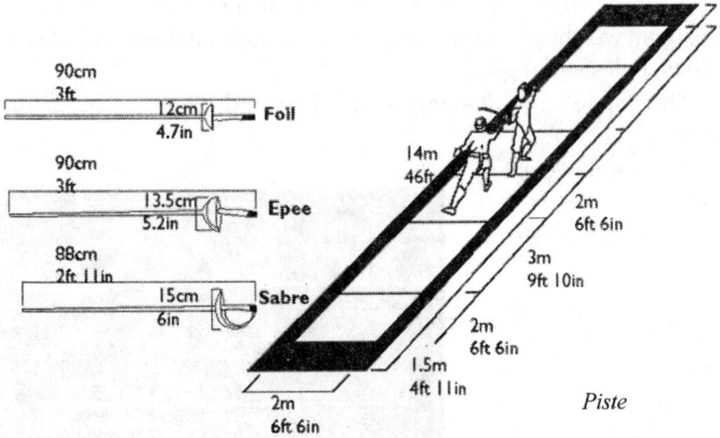

Piste

Fencing Phraseology

1. Fencing demands quick thinking, poise, balance and muscular control combined with mental discipline, rather than strength.
2. In bouts, the fencer takes up a stance called the "guard" with his arms, weapons, body and feet so placed as to give him the best possible balance for attack or defence movement forward or back, or "the lunge".
3. When the fencers cross swords they are said to be "engaged" otherwise they are fencing with "absence of blade".
4. When they are in the "on guard" position, the distance between the two constitutes the "fencing measure". The distance normally maintained is that where the fencer feels safe from a direct attack yet in a position to launch attack of his own.
5. A "lunge"is the extension of the sword arm, body, and legs to carry the point or edge of the weapon forward from the "on guard" position to score a hit on the opponent target.
6. The sequence of fencing movements exchanged during a bout is called a "phrase".
7. A "hit" is an offensive action which lands the point or edge of the weapon on the opponent. If it lands on the opponent's

target, it is a "valid hit"; otherwise it is "non-valid"or "off-target" hit.

8. The lunge and recovery from the lunge to the "on guard" position are known as the "development" and the "return to guard".
9. A hit made with any part of the front edge or third of the back edge of the sabre is known as a "cut".
10. A "stop-hit", as the name suggests, is a hit made to stop the oncoming hit.
11. A "parry" is a defensive action which deflects an attacker's blade clear of the target. There are three types of parry:
    (a) Simple or direct parry
    (b) Indirect parry
    (c) Circular or counter parry
12. "Riposte" is an offensive action following a successful parry. If riposte is parried by an opponent then the next offensive by the defender is known as counter riposte.
13. **Feint:** This is an offensive movement to draw a reaction from the opponent.
14. **In Quartata**: This is an attacking movement carried out while moving the body out of line, with a side step.
15. **Pamanta Sotto:** This is an action of avoiding an attacker's blade by ducking below it.
16. **Sentiment de Fer:** It is the term used for feeling an opponent's reactions through contact of the blades.
17. **Doighte:** It means finger play. Controlling and directing the weapon by using the fingers only.
18. **Targets:** Targets differ for different weapons and hits are also restricted accordingly. Target hits are explained below:
    (a) **Foil:** Valid hits are restricted to those made with the point on the trunk. Hits on legs, arms and head are not good.
    (b) **Epee:** Hits may be made with the points on any part of the opponent or his equipment.
    (c) **Sabre**: Hits may be scored with the whole of the *front* edge or third of the back edge as well as with point. Valid hits are restricted to those hits which are delivered on the arms, head or trunk up to hip line.

Competition Judging and Scoring

The time limits for a bout are six minutes for men and five minutes for women. The competitors are warned when one minute remains. The competitions take place on a 'piste' which is 2 m wide and 14 m long.

The bout goes to a player who scores five hits first. But for the women the number is four. If the time limit expires at foil or sabre, the fencer leading at that time wins the bout.

Senior foil and epee competitions are judged by an electrical judging apparatus, in which the blade is connected to a thin wire through the handle. The body wire runs through sleeve of the jacket and emerges at the back where it is plugged to a wire from the piste. The central apparatus registers hits by light and sound signals. Hits on ground are not registered. For foil fencing the competitor wears a metallic jacket exactly covering the valid target. A hit on the target is shown by a coloured light whereas hit on head, arm, etc., is indicated by a white light. All epee fencing is judged by an electrical apparatus. However no electrical apparatus at present is used for judging sabre. It is therefore necessary to have two pairs of judges.

Championships

European Championship: European championship for different weapons started in 1921. However the first European championship to include all weapons with both teams and individual events started in 1930.

World Youth Championship: First held in 1950, this is organised annually.

World Championship: The championship is held annually but not during the Olympic years. This includes all weapons—both teams and individual events.

Olympics: Fencing has been part of the Olympic Games since 1896. Women's individual foil event was included in 1924 whereas the women's team event was included in 1960.

Names to Remember

Rene Lacroix: The name of this French fencer will never be forgotten because it was only due to his initiative that the Federation Internationale d'Escrime was formed at the Automobile Club in Paris on 29 November, 1931.

Brice Guyart (born March 15, 1981 in Suresnes): He is a foil fencer from France. He won the following:- 2000 – Team Olympic Champion 2001 – Team World Champion with France 2001 – World Bronze Medal 2003 – World Bronze Medal 2004 – Olympic Champion 2005 – Team World Champion

Timea Nagy (born August 22, 1970 in Budapest): He is a Hungarian fencer who has won two Olympic gold medals in Individual Épée. She is left-handed, and became world champion in the Épée discipline at the 2006 World Fencing Championships. In 2000 she also ranked 4th in Team Épée, and she became world champion in this particular discipline in 1992, 1993, 1995, 1997 and 1999 and bronze medallist in 2001 and 2003.

Mariel Zagunis (born March 3, 1985): She is an American Olympic sabre fencer, won the Gold in 2004 Olympics. She competed in the 2004 Athens Women's sabre competition, and was the first American to win an Olympic fencing gold medal in 100 years. Daughter of an Olympian, Zagunis has numerous unique accomplishments. She was the first American fencer to hold the Jr. World Cup Champion title (2002), and she did so 3 years in a row (2002, 2003, 2004).

■

FIELD ARCHERY

Chapter - 21

Archery is an ancient sport. Target archery is shooting of a specified number of arrows at a target.

History

Archery as a sporting event came much later than its use for survival for early man. Bow and arrow were invented primarily for hunting to find food. Gradually it became an instrument to wage war as well. The mesolithic cave paintings in Spain provide the earliest pictorial evidence of the existence of bow. Archery known as the mesolithic skill can claim to be the oldest of any sports. It is not certain when the bow was invented, but there is proof of its use in different parts of the world 50,000 years ago. In Indian mythology there are many references to the bow and arrow. It was both used for competition and to wage war. There is a reference to the bow as a weapon in the 48th chapter of Genesis, the first book in the Holy Bible. As we stated earlier, it is believed that the invention of the bow and arrow may have been inspired by primitive spring traps used to capture animals in the forest.

A refinement of the primitive bow was the English long bow of the Middle Ages which was made of the evergreen coniferous vew tree (Taxia baccata) or similar types of wood.

The oriental composite bow, in use in Asia and Near East from about 2500 BC,was cleverly constructed from material in layers glued together to provide additional strength. The modern bow was designed by an American Research Engineer, Hickman, and Klipsleg, a University Professor.

The ancient Scorton Arrow may have been the oldest sporting trophy instituted in 1673. In August 1844, the first Grand National Archery Meeting was held in York followed by the formation of a society in 1861.

International archery started during 1931, when Poland took the initiative and held the first international tournament. In the same year, Federation International De Tir al (FITA) was formed. The original members of the FITA were Belgium, France, Poland and Sweden. Other nations joined the FITA later. Archery was first included in the Olympic games in 1900, but was discontinued after 1920. It was, however, re-introduced in 1972, at the Munich Olympics.

In India the first national archery championship was held in Lucknow in 1973, under the auspices of the National Rifle Association.

Shamlal of Rajasthan, who won the bronze medal for the 50 metres competition at the 5th Asia Cup Archery Championship held in Calcutta in January 1988, became the first Indian to get a medal in an international event.

Range

The archery range is laid out preferably on a plain ground with closely cropped grass. Adequate safety zone behind the target must be provided for.

Athens Olympic Archery Range

The ranges for men and women are separated by a clear lane with width of five metres. The range is divided into lanes with five metres width. For men, target lines are marked at 90 m, 70 m, 50 m, and 30 m. For women, target lines are at 70 m, 60 m, 50 m, and 30 m. These distances are measured from the shooting line to a point vertically below the centre of the target.

In each lane of the range, generally, two targets are

placed. However, if required, one or up to three targets can be placed. There is a permanent shooting line and a waiting line is marked for all national or international tournaments. For club level tournaments the shooting and waiting line may be moved up for each distance, keeping the targets at a fixed point.

Targets

There are two types of targets used in target archery. They are:

(a) Target with 122 cm diameter is used for distances 90 m, 70 m, and 60m.

This circular target is divided into 10 scoring zones of equal width of 6.1 cm.

(b) Target with 80 cm diameter are used for distances 50 m and 30 m.

This circular target is divided into 10 scoring zones of equal width of 4 cm.

(c) Both the targets are divided into five colour zones. The scores for each Zone are given below:

		Points
(i)	Gold (inner)	10
(ii)	Gold (outer)	9
(iii)	Red (inner)	8
(iv)	Red (outer)	7
(v)	Blue (inner)	6
(vi)	Blue (outer)	5
(vii)	Black (inner)	4
(viii)	Black (outer)	3
(ix)	White (inner)	2
(x)	White (outer)	1

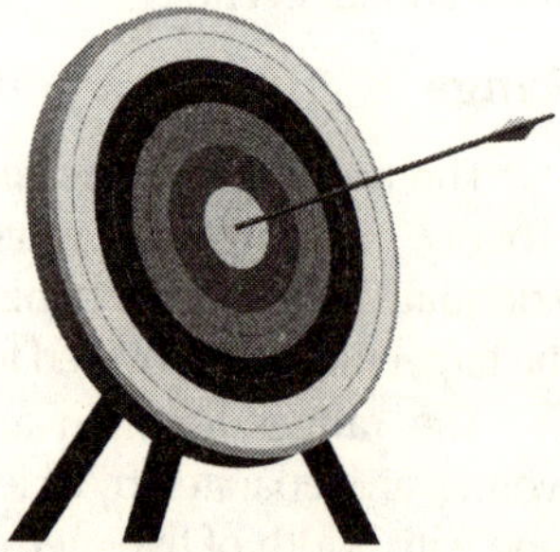

Buttresses: When a target is placed on the buttress, the centre of the gold should be at a height of 130 cm from the ground.

The dimensions of the buttresses are as follows:

(a) Overall dimension not to exceed 12.

(b) Setting up angle 15° to the vertical.

Equipment

Bow: A bow is something that is curved or something that bends. Grading of a bow weight is determined by the number of pounds, effort required to draw back an arrow to its optimum limit.

Men generally use bows weighing 32 to 42 lb (14.51 to 19.05 kg) and women use bows which weigh 26 to 34 lb (11.79 to15.42 kg).

Arrow: Old arrows used to be made of wood but modern arrows are made of aluminium alloys, aluminium carbon or fibre glass tubing furnished with a steel point (Pile). Their weight is generally less than 28 g. The notch or nock are moulded out of nylon. The vanes (fletchings) numbering three or four are made from wing feathers of turkeys and are usually dyed in various colours. These may be cut out of plastic also.

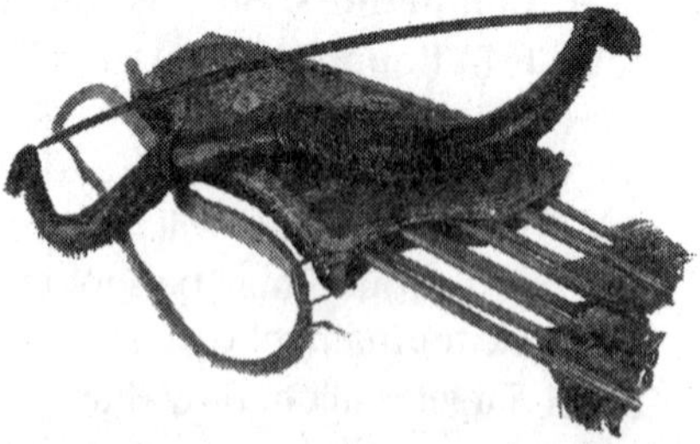

Other Equipment: Following equipments may be used for archery other than bow and arrow:

(a) Glove for the drawing hand.
(b) Finger stalls or tape used for protection.
(c) Ordinary glove for the bow hand.
(d) Visual aids like field glasses may be used to spot an arrow.
(e) Sun glasses and correcting eye glasses may be used but they must not be used to assist aiming.
(f) Among the other accessories are:
  (i) Belt quiver (case to carry arrow)
  (ii) Bracer
  (iii) Dress shield

Dress

The competitors may wear any comfortable dress for the competition. But they must wear target numbers on their backs.

Officials

(a) Scorer
(b) Chief Scorer
(c) Director of Shooting
(d) Deputy Director of Shooting
(e) Judges
(f) Jury of Appeal
(g) Chairman
(h) Tournament Director

Rules of Target Archery

Rules, in a nutshell, are given below :

(a) **Competitors:** Archers compete as individuals and as teams.

(b) **FITA Round**: A FITA round consists of 3 dozen of arrows shot from four distances, i.e. 90 m, 70 m, 50 m and 30 m for men and 70 m, 60 m, and 30 m for women.

A tournament will have either one or two FITA rounds. A single round may be shot in one or two days as decided by the tournament officials:

(c) Target is allotted by draw.

(d) Three or four archers are allotted one target.

(e) Six sighting arrows may be shot, which are not scored.

(f) Archers shoot in turn. During one end, an archer shoots three arrows within 2½minutes. A warning signal is given after two minutes. After shooting he returns to the waiting line when the other members of the group participate in shooting.

(g) **Penalty**: Any arrow shot outside the time limit shall cause forfeiture of the highest scoring arrow of that end.

Scoring

An arrow head touching a colour zone of the target scores that many marks. Scoring in various other situations are given below:

(a) In World and Olympic championships, the scores are counted after every second end, at distances 90 m, 70 m, and 60 m. It can be counted after each end also. Whereas at 50 m and 30m, scores are counted after each end.

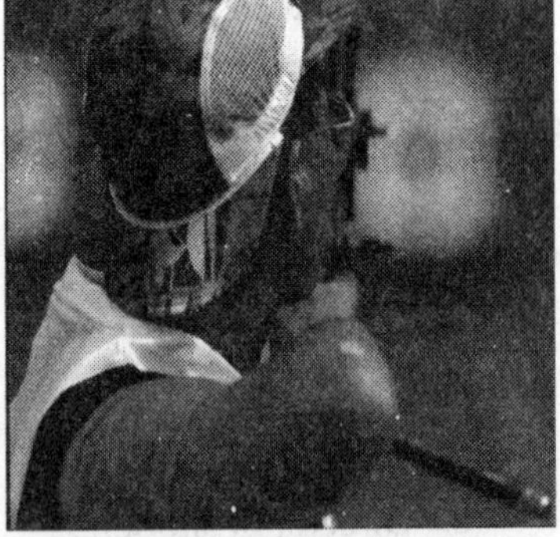

(b) An arrow which gets embedded in another arrow on the target will score the same as the previous arrow.

(c) An arrow, deflected from the target or another arrow, will score, if the deflection mark can be clearly identified.

(d) An arrow hitting the wrong target will not score.

(e) An archer shooting more than three arrows within the allotted time will score only the lowest three. Repeated offence of similar nature may cause disqualification.

(f) All holes are marked on the target after the arrows are withdrawn from it.

(g) An arrow touching two colour zones will score more marks.

(h) **Winner:** The archer who scores the highest wins the competition.

In case of a tie: If there is a tie, the winner will be the one with the greatest number of scoring shots. If the tie is not broken, then the winner will be the one with maximum hits in gold, then the maximum shots scoring 9 points

Other Types of Archery

Field Archery: The rules of shooting for field archery as adopted by the FITA are now generally recognised as the standard form. There are two types of field archery—Freestyle and Barebow. In Freestyle, the equipment for target archery may be used but in Barebow competition no artificial aiming devices are allowed.

Range: The range is laid out on a natural terrain in sequence in two courses. Direction and shooting distances vary.

Duration: A tournament consists of two rounds – a field round and a hunter's round.

Targets: Four circular targets are used with 60 cm, 45 cm, 30 cm and 15 cm diameter. All these targets are divided into three parts — centre spot, inner ring and outer ring. Except the competitions held under FITA rules, the target may be drawn on animal figures, where the centre spot is clearly visible.

Rovers: Rovers type of competition is held in the rough country where the stances are unspecified. This has similarities to field archery.

Clout Shooting: In clout shooting arrows are shot high in the air to fall on a target at a distance of 146.30-182.8 m for men and 109.72-146.30 m for women. The target is marked with a flag. The diameter of the target is 24 ft and has five scoring areas defined by rings of 1 Y2 ft (0.457 m), 3 ft (0.914 m), 6 ft (1.829 m), 9 ft (2.743 m) and 12 ft (3.658 m) respectively.

Flight Shooting: This type of shooting envisages reaching maximum distance. There are three classes of competition- Target Bow class, Flight Bow class and Freestyle class.

Popinjay Shooting: Rarely found outside Europe. The target in this type of archery consists of a series of wooden cylinders onto which feathers are attached. Variously they are called cocks, hens and chicks. The cylinders are set on a frame called a roost, on top of a mast 85 ft (25.908 m) high. The object is to dislodge these birds, by shooting blunt headed arrows from the base of the mast, each of which has a score value.

Championships

Asia Cup: This competition was inaugurated at Eden Gardens, Calcutta, in 1980. In 1989, the competition was held in Beijing. Team gold was won by India's Limba Ram, Shamlal, Skalzang and Rajinder Gurya.

Olympics: Archery was included in the Olympics in 1900, for men and in 1904, for women. The events held at that time were also different from the modern Olympic archery events. However, women's archery was discontinued after the 1908 Olympics and men's after 1920. Men's and women's archery once again became a regular fixture in the Olympics since the Munich Games in 1972.

Asian Games: Archery first made its appearance in the Asian Games as a demonstration game in 1962, at Jakarta. It became a regular event since the 1978 Bangkok Asiad.

European Championship: This competition is held regularly among European countries.

Great Britain International Trial: This tournament is held every year in the UK in which top archers from various parts of the world are invited.

World Championship: World championship in archery started in 1931, and is held every two years. In 1969, the first world championship in field archery was held.

Names to be Remembered

Kim Suo Nyung (South Korea, b. 5 April, 1971): This teenager captured five gold medals in the 1988 Asia Cup along with the individual championship. Currently she holds four individual world records and another record in the team event.

Hubert Van Innis (Belgium,1866-1961): Innis won the most Olympic medals in archery. In all he won six gold and three silver medals in the 1900 and 1920 Olympic Games. At the 1900 Paris Olympics he won two individual gold medals and a silver and at the

1920 Antwerp Olympics, while his individual tally was two gold and a silver, he also had a similar tally of two gold and a silver in the team events for Belgium.

Darrell Pace (USA, b. 23 October, 1956): Pace is one of the finest archers of the late twentieth century. He shot into fame in the 1976 Montreal Olympics at the age of twenty, when he won the gold medal by scoring 2571 points, creating a new world record. Pace again won the gold at the Los Angeles Olympics in 1984 scoring 2616 points, creating a new Olympic record. His individual single FITA round world record achieved in 1979, by scoring 1341 points out of 1440 still holds good. He also holds the world record for highest championship score of 2617 points out of a possible 2880. Pairing with compatriot Richard McKinney at Long Beach, California, on 21-22 October, 1983, Pace also created a world record in indoor double FITA rounds at 25 metres in 1985, by scoring 589 points out of a possible 600 points.

Alfred Horace Ford (UK,1822-1880): He won the British Archery Championship 12 times, from 1849 to 1859 and in 1867. No one has equalled this achievement so far. In 1859, he wrote *Archery: Its Theory and Practice* in which he presented a logical and intelligent application of simple principles to this art of shooting.

Alice Balanche Legh (UK, 1855-1948): Most famous archer from the UK, she won the British Archery Championship 23 times. Her mother was also a champion archer and won the British Championship from 1882 to 1885. Because of her mother Ms Legh did not compete during these years. She first won the championship in 1881, thereafter from 1886 to 1892, 1895, 1898 to 1900, 1902 to 1909,1913, 1921 and 1922.

Hans Deutgen (Sweden, b. 28 February, 1917): In the late nineteen forties Deutgen dominated the world of archery by winning four consecutive world titles. He won the world men's title in 1947, 1948, 1949 and 1950. This achievement of winning four world titles is still unsurpassed.

Justin Huish (born January 9, 1975 in Fountain Valley, California) is an internationally known archer. When he was fifteen he won his first local tournament and made the US archery team at eighteen. Huish won gold medals for the Men's Individual and Team Competition in the 1996 Summer Olympics. He had a somewhat dramatic appearance, with wraparound shades, a background baseball cap, a ponytail, and an earring. He tried out for the 2004 Olympics, but failed to make the U.S. team.

Simon Fairweather (born October 9, 1969): is an athlete born in Adelaide, South Australia. He is 175 centimetres tall and weighs 71 kilograms. He competes in archery. Fairweather won the individual gold medal at the World Championships in Poland in 1991. Fairweather was declared the Young Australian of the Year in 1991 and 1992. After an early Olympic career in which he was generally considered not to have lived up to his promise, Fairweather shot back into Australia's national consciousness with a gold medal in men's individual archery at the 2000 Summer Olympics. Fairweather competed at the 2004 Summer Olympics in men's individual archery. He was defeated in the first round of elimination, placed 52nd overall.

Marco Galiazzo (born May 7, 1983): He is an athlete from Italy. Galiazzo competed at the 2004 Summer Olympics in men's individual archery. He won his first three elimination matches, advancing to the quarterfinals. In the quarterfinals, Galiazzo faced Vic Wunderle of the United States, defeating Wunderle 109-108 in the 12-arrow match and advancing to the semifinals. There, he faced Laurence Godfrey of Great Britain, defeating Godfrey 110-108. Galiazzo then competed against Hiroshi Yamamoto of Japan in the gold medal match, winning 111-109 to earn the gold medal. Galiazzo was also a member of the 7th-place Italian men's archery team at the 2004 Summer Olympics.

■

FOOTBALL

Chapter - 22

May be the most popular sport in the world. Eleven a side the game was standardised in 1870. FIFA was founded in Paris on 21 May, 1904.

History

China's game of "Tsu Chu" played 2,500 years ago could be the forerunner of modern football or soccer as it is called in many parts of the world. Tsu may be translated as "to kick the ball with feet" and Chu as "a ball made of leather and stuffed". There are also early depiction of this game in many other countries. But the organised football with acceptable common rules was started at Cambridge in 1846. The game was standardised with the formation of the Football Association in England on 24 October 1857. Eleven per side the game was standardised in 1870. The Federation Internationale de Football Association (FIFA) was founded in Paris on 21 May 1904.

The Field of Play

Dimensions

The field of play must be rectangular. The length of the touch line must be greater than the length of the goal line.

Length: Minimum 90 m (100 yds), maximum 120 m (130 yds).

Width: Minimum 45 m (50 yds), maximum 90 m (100 yds).

International Matches

Length: minimum 100 m (110 yds), maximum 110 m (120 yds)
Width: minimum 64 m (70 yds), maximum 75 m (80 yds)

Field Markings

The field of play is marked with lines. These lines belong to the areas of which they are boundaries.

The two longer boundary lines are called touch lines. The two shorter lines are called goal lines.

All lines are not more than 12 cm (5 ins) wide.

The field of play is divided into two halves by a halfway line.

The centre mark is indicated at the midpoint of the halfway line. A circle with a radius of 9.15 m (10 yds) is marked around it.

The Goal Area

A goal area is defined at each end of the field as follows: Two lines are drawn at right angles to the goal line, 5.5 m (6 yds) from the inside of each goalpost. These lines extend into the field of play for a distance of 5.5 m (6 yds) and are joined by a line drawn parallel with the goal line. The area bounded by these lines and the goal line is the goal area.

The Penalty Area

A penalty area is defined at each end of the field as follows: Two lines are drawn at right angles to the goal line, 16.5 m (18 yds) from the inside of each goalpost. These lines extend into the field of play for a distance of 16.5 m (18 yds) and are joined by a line drawn parallel with the goal line. The area bounded by these lines and the goal line is the penalty area.

Within each penalty area a penalty mark is made 11 m (12 yds) from the midpoint between the goalposts and equidistant to them. An arc of a circle with a radius of 9.15 m (10 yds) from each penalty mark is drawn outside the penalty area.

Flagposts

A flagpost, not less than 1.5 m (5 ft) high, with a non-pointed top and a flag is placed at each corner.

Flagposts may also be placed at each end of the halfway line, not less than 1m (1 yd) outside the touch line.

The Corner Arc

A quarter circle with a radius of 1 m (1 yd) from each corner flagpost is drawn inside the field of play.

Goals

Goals must be placed on the centre of each goal line.

They consist of two upright posts equidistant from the corner flagposts and joined at the top by a horizontal crossbar.

The distance between the posts is 7.32 m (8 yds) and the distance from the lower edge of the crossbar to the ground is 2.44 m (8ft).

Both goalposts and the crossbar have the same width and depth which do not exceed 12 cm (5 ins). The goal lines are the same width as that of the goalposts and the crossbar. Nets may be attached to the goals and the ground behind the goal, provided that they are properly supported and do not interfere with the goalkeeper.

The goalposts and crossbars must be white.

II - The Ball

Qualities and Measurements
The ball is:

- spherical
- made of leather or other suitable material
- of a circumference of not more than 70 cm (28 ins) and not less than 6 8 cm (27 ins)
- not more than 450 g (16 oz) in weight and not less than 410 g (14 oz) at the start of the match.
- of a pressure equal to 0.6 - 1.1 atmosphere (600 - 1100 g/cm2) at sea level (8.5 lbs/sq in 15.6 lbs/sq in).

The Number of Players

A match is played by two teams, each consisting of not more than eleven players, one of whom is the goalkeeper. A match may not start if either team consists of fewer than seven players.

Official Competitions

Up to a maximum of three substitutes may be used in any match played in an official competition organised under the auspices of FIFA, the confederations or the national associations.

The rules of the competition must state how many substitutes may be nominated, from three up to a maximum of seven.

Other Matches

In other matches, up to five substitutes may be used, provided that: the teams concerned reach agreement on a maximum number, and the referee is informed before the match. If the referee is not informed, or if no agreement is reached before the start of the match, no more than three substitutes are allowed.

Substitution Procedure

To replace a player by a substitute, the following conditions must be observed:

- the referee is informed before any proposed substitution is made;
- a substitute only enters the field of play after the player being replaced has left and after receiving a signal from the referee;
- a substitute only enters the field of play at the halfway line and during a stoppage in the match;
- a substitution is completed when a substitute enters the field of play;
- from that moment, the substitute becomes a player and the player he has replaced ceases to be a player;
- a player who has been replaced takes no further part in the match; and
- all substitutes are subject to the authority and jurisdiction of the referee, whether called upon to play or not.

Changing the Goalkeeper

Any of the other players may change places with the goalkeeper, provided that:

- the referee is informed before the change is made;
- the change is made during a stoppage in the match.

IV - The Players Equipment

Basic Equipment

The basic compulsory equipment of a player is:

- a jersey or shirt
- shorts—if thermal undershorts are worn, they are of the same main colour as the shorts
- stockings
- shinguards
- footwear

Shinguards

- are covered entirely by the stockings;
- are made of a suitable material (rubber, plastic, or similar substances);
- provide a reasonable degree of protection.

Goalkeepers

- Each goalkeeper wears colours which distinguish him from the other players, the referee and the assistant referees.

V - The Referee

The Authority of the Referee

Each match is controlled by a referee who has full authority to enforce the Laws of the Game in connection with the match to which he has been appointed.

Powers and Duties

The Referee:

- enforces the Laws of the Game;
- controls the match in co-operation with the assistant referees and, where applicable, with the fourth official;

- ensures that the ball meets the requirements of Law 2;
- ensures that the players' equipment meets the requirements of Law 4;
- acts as timekeeper and keeps a record of the match;
- stops, suspends or terminates the match, at his discretion, for any infringements of the Laws;
- stops, suspends or terminates the match because of outside interference of any kind;
- stops the match if, in his opinion, a player is seriously injured and ensures that he is removed from the field of play;
- allows play to continue until the ball is out of play if a player is, in his opinion, only slightly injured;
- ensures that any player bleeding from a wound leaves the field of play; the player may only return on receiving a signal from the referee, who must be satisfied that the bleeding has stopped;
- allows play to continue when the team against which an offence has been committed will benefit from such an advantage and penalises the original offence if the anticipated advantage does not ensue at that time;
- punishes the more serious offence when a player commits more than one offence at the same time;
- takes disciplinary action against players guilty of cautionable and sending-off offences; he is not obliged to take this action immediately but must do so when the ball next goes out of play;
- takes action against team officials who fail to conduct themselves in a responsible manner and may at his discretion, expel them from the field of play and its immediate surrounds;
- acts on the advice of assistant referees regarding incidents which he has not seen;
- ensures that no unauthorised persons enter the field of play
- restarts the match after it has been stopped; and
- provides the appropriate authorities with a match report which includes information on any disciplinary action taken against players, and/or team officials and any other incidents which occurred before, during or after the match.

Decisions of the Referee

The decisions of the referee regarding facts connected with play are final.

VI - The Assistant Referees

Duties

Two assistant referees are appointed whose duties, subject to the decision of the referee, are to indicate:

- when the whole of the ball has passed out of the field of play;
- which side is entitled to a corner kick, goal kick or throw-in;
- when a player may be penalised for being in an offside position;
- when a substitution is requested;
- when misconduct or any other incident has occurred out of the view of the referee;
- when offences have been committed whenever the assistants are closer to the action than the referee (this includes, in particular circumstances, offences committed in the penalty area);
- whether, at penalty kicks, the goalkeeper has moved forward before the ball has been kicked and if the ball has crossed the line; in the event of undue interference or improper conduct, the referee will relieve an assistant referee of his duties and make a report to the appropriate authorities.

Assistance

The assistant referees also assist the referee to control the match in accordance with the Laws of the Game. In particular, they may enter the field of play to help control the 9.15 m distance.

VII - The Duration of the Match

The match lasts two equal periods of 45 minutes, unless otherwise mutually agreed between the referee and the two participating teams. Any agreement to alter the periods of play (for example to reduce each half to 40 minutes because of insufficient light) must be made before the start of play and must comply with competition rules.

Half-Time Interval

Players are entitled to an interval at half-time.

The half-time interval must not exceed 15 minutes.

Competition rules must state the duration of the half-time interval.

The duration of the half-time interval may be altered only with the consent of the referee.

Allowance for Time Lost

Allowance is made in either period for all time lost through:

- substitution(s)
- assessment of injury to players
- removal of injured players from the field of play for treatment
- wasting time
- any other cause

The allowance for time lost is at the discretion of the referee.

Penalty Kick Timing

If a penalty kick has to be taken or retaken, the duration of either half is extended until the penalty kick is completed.

Extra Time

Competition rules may provide for two further equal periods to be played. The conditions of Law 8 will apply.

VIII - Kick-off

A kick-off is a way of starting or restarting play:

- at the start of the match;
- after a goal has been scored;
- at the start of the second half of the match; and
- at the start of each period of extra time, where applicable.

A goal may be scored directly from the kick-off.

Dropped Ball

A dropped ball is a way of restarting the match after a temporary stoppage which becomes necessary, while the ball is in play, for any reason not mentioned elsewhere in the Laws of the Game. Play restarts when the ball touches the ground.

IX - Ball Out of Play

The ball is out of play when:

- it has wholly crossed the goal line or touch line whether on the ground or in the air;
- play has been stopped by the referee.

Ball In Play

The ball is in play at all other times, including when:

- it rebounds from a goalpost, crossbar or corner flagpost and remains in the field of play; and
- it rebounds from either the referee or an assistant referee when they are on the field of play.

X - The Method of Scoring

A goal is scored when the whole of the ball passes over the goal line, between the goalposts and under the crossbar, provided that no infringement of the Laws of the Game has been committed previously by the team scoring the goal.

XI - Offside

Offside Position

It is not an offence in itself to be in an offside position. A player is in an offside position if:

- he is nearer to his opponents' goal line than both the ball and the second last opponent.

A player is not in an offside position if:

- he is in his own half of the field of play or
- he is level with the second last opponent or
- he is level with the last two opponents.

XII - Fouls and Misconduct

Fouls and misconduct are penalised as follows:

Direct Free Kick

A direct free kick is also awarded to the opposing team if a player commits any of the following four offences:

- tackles an opponent to gain possession of the ball, making contact with the opponent before touching the ball;
- holds an opponent;
- spits at an opponent; and
- handles the ball deliberately (except for the goalkeeper within his own penalty area).

A direct free kick is taken from where the offence occurred.

A penalty kick is awarded if any of the above offences is committed by a player inside his own penalty area, irrespective of the position of the ball, provided it is in play.

Indirect Free Kick

An indirect free kick is awarded to the opposing team if a goalkeeper, inside his own penalty area, commits any of the following offences:

- takes more than six seconds while controlling the ball with his hands, before releasing it from his possession;
- touches the ball again with his hands after it has been released from his possession and has not touched any other player;
- touches the ball with his hands after it has been deliberately kicked to him by a team-mate; and
- touches the ball with his hands after he has received it directly from a throw-in taken by a team-mate.

An indirect free kick is also awarded to the opposing team if a player, in the opinion of the referee, commits any of the following three offences:

- plays in a dangerous manner;
- impedes the progress of an opponent;
- prevents the goalkeeper from releasing the ball from his hands; and
- commits any other offence, not previously mentioned in Law 12, for which play is stopped to caution or dismiss a player.

The indirect free kick is taken from where the offence occurred.

Sending-Off Offences

A player is sent off and shown the red card if he commits any of the following seven offences:

1. is guilty of serious foul play;
2. is guilty of violent conduct;
3. spits at an opponent or any other person;
4. denies an opponent a goal or an obvious goal-scoring opportunity by deliberately handling the ball (this does not apply to a goalkeeper within his own penalty area);
5. denies an obvious goal-scoring opportunity to an opponent moving towards the player's goal by an offence punishable by a free kick or a penalty kick;
6. uses offensive, insulting or abusive language; and
7. receives a second caution in the same match.

A player who has been sent off must leave the vicinity of the field of play and the technical area.

XIII - Ball Enters the Goal

A goal can be scored only if the ball subsequently touches another player before it enters the goal.

Direct or indirect free kick to the defending team:

- all opponents are at least 9.15 m (10 yds) from the ball;
- all opponents remain outside the penalty area until the ball is in play;
- the ball is in play when it is kicked directly beyond the penalty area; and
- a free kick awarded in the goal area is taken from any point inside that area.

Indirect free kick to the attacking team:

- all opponents are at least 9.15 m (10 yds) from the ball until it is in play, unless they are on their own goal line between the goalposts;
- the ball is in play when it is kicked and moves; and
- an indirect free kick awarded inside the goal area is taken from that part of the goal area line which runs parallel to the goal line, at the point nearest to where the infringement occurred.

Free Kick Outside the Penalty Area

- all opponents are at least 9.15 m (10 yds) from the ball until it is in play;
- the ball is in play when it is kicked and moves; and
- the free kick is taken from the place where the infringement occurred.

XIV - The Penalty Kick

A penalty kick is awarded against a team which commits one of the ten offences for which a direct free kick is awarded, inside its own penalty area and while the ball is in play.

A goal may be scored directly from a penalty kick.

Additional time is allowed for a penalty kick to be taken at the end of each half or at the end of periods of extra time.

XV - The Throw-In

A throw-in is a method of restarting play.

A goal cannot be scored directly from a throw-in.

A throw-in is awarded:

- when the whole of the ball passes over the touch line, either on the ground or in the air;
- from the point where it crossed the touch line; and
- to the opponents of the player who last touched the ball.

XVI - The Goal Kick

A goal kick is a method of restarting play.

A goal may be scored directly from a goal kick, but only against the opposing team.

XVII - The Corner Kick

A corner kick is a method of restarting play.

A goal may be scored directly from a corner kick, but only against the opposing team. A corner kick is awarded when the whole of the ball, having last touched a player of the defending team, passes over the goal line, either on the ground or in the air, and a goal is not scored in accordance with the rule of the game.

Procedures to Determine the Winner of a Match

The Golden Goal and taking kicks from the penalty mark are methods of determining the winning team where competition rules require there to be a winning team after a match has been drawn.

The Golden Goal

Procedure

- During the period of extra time played at the end of normal playing time, the team which scores the first goal is declared the winner.
- If no goals are scored the match is decided by kicks from the penalty mark.

Kicks from the Penalty Mark

Procedure

- The referee chooses the goal at which the kicks will be taken.
- The referee tosses a coin and the team whose captain wins the toss takes the first kick.
- The referee keeps a record of the kicks being taken.
- Subject to the conditions explained below, both teams take five kicks.
- The kicks are taken alternately by the teams.
- If, before both teams have taken five kicks, one has scored more goals than the other could score, even if it were to complete its five kicks, no more kicks are taken.

- If, after both teams have taken five kicks, both have scored the same number of goals, or have not scored any goals, kicks continue to be taken in the same order until one team has scored a goal more than the other from the same number of kicks.

- A goalkeeper who is injured while kicks are being taken from the penalty mark and is unable to continue as goalkeeper may be replaced by a named substitute provided his team has not used the maximum number of substitutes permitted under the competition rules.
- With the exception of the foregoing case, only players who are on the field of play at the end of the match, which includes extra time where appropriate, are allowed to take kicks from the penalty mark.
- Each kick is taken by a different player and all eligible players must take a kick before any player can take a second kick.
- An eligible player may change places with the goalkeeper at any time when kicks from the penalty mark are being taken.
- Only the eligible players and match officials are permitted to remain on the field of play when kicks from the penalty mark are being taken.
- All players, except the player taking the kick and the two goalkeepers, must remain within the centre circle.
- The goalkeeper who is the team-mate of the kicker must remain on the field of play, outside the penalty area in which the kicks are being taken, on the goal line where it meets the penalty area boundary line.
- Unless otherwise stated, the relevant Laws of the Game and International F.A. Board Decisions apply when kicks from the penalty mark are being taken.
- When a team finishes the match with a greater number of players than their opponents, they shall reduce their numbers to equate with that of their opponents and inform the referee of the name and number of each player excluded. The team captain has this responsibility.
- Before the start of kicks from the penalty mark the referee shall ensure that only an equal number of players from each team remain within the centre circle and they shall take the kicks.

The Technical Area

The technical area described in Law 3, International F.A. Board Decision no. 2, relates particularly to matches played in stadia with a designated seated area for technical staff and substitutes as shown below.

The Fourth Official

- The fourth official may be appointed under the competition rules and officiates if any of the three match officials is unable to continue.

Important Tournaments

European Championship (Nations Cup): It was started between 1958 and 1960, and is staged every fourth year. Each tournament takes two years to run with the semi-final and the final played in the same country.

European Champions Club Cup: A cup for the league champions of the respective nations was approved by the FIFA on 8 May, 1955, and is run by the UEFA (Union of European Football Association). Real Madrid won the first final.

European Cup Winners Cup: A tournament for the national cup winners, started in 1960-61.

UEFA Cup: This tournament began in 1955. It was originally known as the International Inter City Industrial Fairs Cup. It became an annual tournament in 1960-61 and has been replaced by the UEFA cup.

South American Championship: South American Championship began unofficially in 1916, in Buenos Aires, and officially in 1917, in Montevideo. Since 1947, this championship has been a two-yearly event.

South American Cup (Copa de Los Libertadores): The tournament was introduced unofficially in 1960, to enable a team of South America to meet the winners of the European Cup.

World Cup: The World Cup (Jules Rimet Cup, FIFA Cup) was instituted by the FIFA on 13 July, 1930, in Montevideo (Uruguay), and is held every four years.

World Club Championship: This club tournament began in 1960, between the winners of the European cup and the Copa Libertadores, the South American equivalent.

FA Cup (England): It was first played on16 March, 1872.

Olympics: Football was included in the 1908 Olympics in London.

India

IFA Shield: In 1893, four years after the Traders Cup competition began, the IFA Shield was constituted. Mohun Bagan was first allowed to play in the IFA Shield in 1909, after they had won the Traders Cup for the three previous years consecutively. Mohun Bagan won the IFA Shield in 1911.

Rovers Cup: The Rovers cup tournament, started in 1891, used to be dominated by British regiments until 1937, when the Bangalore Muslims became the first Indian team to win the cup.

Durand Cup: Durand Football Tournament, now staged annually, was inaugurated in 1888, by Sir Mortimer Durand and was first designed for competition between military teams. Most of the tradition of the trophy was built up at Anandale in Simla. Mohammedan Sporting was the first Indian team to win the Durand Cup.

Names to Remember

Diego Maradona (b.30 October, 1960): He is known as the world's most valuable footballer from Argentina. Argentina won the 1986 World Cup due to his superior skill and superb scheming capability. The largest amount of transfer fee quoted for him by Barcelona was 840 million pesos equal to £ 5 million.

Pele (1940-): Pele was the finest inside forward in the history of football. He was only 17 when he scored two goals for Brazil in the World Cup Final of 1958. He played for Brazil in the 1962, 1966 and 1970 World Cup. On 19 November, 1969, he scored his 1000th goal in senior football. This was a penalty goal for Santos against Vasco da Gama at the Maracana Stadium in Rio de Janeiro.

Sir Stanley Mathews (1915-): One of the finest footballers in the history of this game. He became a professional at the age of 17 only when he played for Stoke City. At the age of 50 he played his last first division match when he helped Stoke City to beat Fulham. In 33 years of eventful career he played 886 first class matches which included 54 internationals for England, 701 League and 86 League matches.

Lev Yashin (1929-): Association football player for Moscow Dynamo and probably the greatest goalkeeper in the history of the game. He played for the USSR in the 1958, 1962 and 1966 World Cup and was in the national team that won the Olympic gold in 1956. He played in FIFA XI team in England at Wembley in 1983, to mark FA's centenary celebration.

Michael Platini (1957-): Platini was a member of the Nancy Lorrane club where his father Aldo was a coach. He scored for it 98 goals in 175 games. He became a key figure in the 1978 World Cup and in 1982 France came very close to winning the World Cup. He steered France to win in the European cup in 1984, and led Juventus of Italy to win the European Champions Cup with a 1-0 victory over Liverpool of England.

Rund Gullit (Holland, 1964-). One of the most gifted footballers of recent years. He was named the "Footballer of the Year" in 1987 and "Netherlands Sportsman of the Year" in 1987.

Fereno Puskas (1927-): Played for Hungary, Real Madrid, Honved and Kispet. He played at inside left and was known for his left-footed goal-scoring capabilities. In 1956, he left Hungary and joined the Real Madrid. His goalscoring capacity was phenomenal.

Gordon Banks (1937-): English goalkeeper, played for Chesterfield, Leicester City and Stoke City. In the 1966 World Cup his performance earned him the rank of the finest goalkeeper of the world. In the 1970-71 season he was made captain of Stoke City. In March 1972, he met with a car accident and injured his eyes and subsequently retired.

Waldemar Peraira Didi (1928-): Brazilian footballer who played for Botafogo (Rio). Represented Brazil in the 1958 and 1962 World Cups.

Ferreira da Silva Eusebio (1943-): Portuguese footballer for Benfica (Lisbon) and Portugal. He was the leading scorer in the 1966 World Cup held in England.

Franz Beckenbauer (1945-): Superstar from West Germany. He played for Bayern Munich. He was captain of the West German team in 1974, which won the World Cup. He also played in the 1966 and 1970 World Cup. He played for the Rest of the World *vs* Brazil in 1968 in Rio de Janeiro. He was the Manager of the West German team which won the 1990 World Cup (Italy).

Ronaldo: Ronaldo was born in the poor suburbs of Rio de Janeiro under the name Luis Nazario de Lima. Driven by his childhood hero Zico, the youngster entered football early in his life. By his 12th birthday he was playing in an organized youth club called Tennis Club Valqueire. With Valqueire, he played "futebol de salão" or small-sided football with a miniature ball. This was considered an important step in Ronaldo's development as playing with a smaller ball is said to rapidly increase skill.

Hristo Stoichkov: Hristo Stoichkov is the most successful Bulgarian soccer player of all times. He debuted in professional football with CSKA Sofia and was later spotted by European giant FC Barcelona.

Stoichkov earned global acclaim after winning the Spanish Primera Division four consecutive times and taking his club to Champions League glory in 1992. He retired from soccer in December of 2003.

Zinedine Zidane: Zinedine Zidane was born in France on the 23rd of June in 1972. His parents of Algerian descent had a total of five children. By the age of 16, a scout by the name of Jean Varraud recruited the youngster to Cannes. One year later, Zizou made his debut with the club's senior squad in the French First Division. He was declared best footballer in World Cup 2006.

David Beckham: Beckham signed with the youth squad of Manchester United in July of 1991, at the tender age of sixteen. It took him about five years of playing with the youth squad, reserves and on loan (with Preston North End) until he got permanently established in the first Man U team. By the 1997/8 season, he attracted enough attention to get selected for England's World Cup team.

Pavel Nedved: Pavel Nedved was born in the town of Cheb, near Prague, the capital of former Czechoslovakia. Parents Vaclav and Ana raised Pavel along with his older sister and encouraged him to become an accountant. By the age of 19, Nedved debuted with Dukla Praga and less than a season later he was recruited by rivals Sparta. At Sparta, success also came promptly and the club took three consecutive league titles between 1992 to 1995.

Raul Gonzalez: Raul Gonzalez Blanco was born on June 27th 1977 in Madrid, Spain. He was brought up in a modest quarter of the city, the colony of San Cristobal de los Angeles. Raul is a product of Atletico Madrid's youth system but was picked up by rivals Real during a financial slump at his former club. Real's coach Jorge Valdano introduced him to the starting lineup at 17, and the youngster did not disappoint scoring six goals in his first 11 games.

Luis Figo: Luis Filipe Madeira Caeiro Figo was born on the 4th of November, 1972 as the only son of parents Antonio and Maria Joana. He grew up in a modest family in Almada, the working-class district of Lisbon. Luis began his career as a street footballer at Os Pastilhas, before joining Sporting Lisbon at the age of 11. As a youngster, Figo won the U-16 European Championship and the 1991 World Youth Cup.

Famous Football Clubs

Juventus: From Turin, Italy, founded in 1897. It has emerged as the most dominant club in Italy and has appeared regularly in European club competitions. Some of its leading players are—Sivori, Bonipetti, Combi, Rosetta, Caligar's, Monti, Orsi, Parola. Platini was also a regular player of the Juventus. Club colours—black and white strips shirts and white shorts.

Liverpool: It was founded in 1892. Ground: Anfield Road, Liverpool. Club colours—red shirts, white trimmings and red shorts. England's foremost club during the present days.

Fluminense: Brazilian club founded in 1902, in Rio de Janeiro. It won the Rio League in 1906, 1907, 1908, 1909. Club colours—white shirts with green and red diagonal strips and white shorts.

Hamburger: Sv. German club, founded in 1887. It was the champion in West Germany in 1923, 1928, and 1960 and frequently played in European Champions Club Cup and European Cup Winners Cup. Club colours—white shirts and red shorts.

■

GOLF

Chapter - 23

In India the Royal Calcutta and Royal Bombay Golf Clubs were formed in 1829 and 1892 respectively.

History

Though no convincing evidence has been obtained to prove the origin of golf, it is believed to have started between 1424 and 1457. The Romans had a cognate game called Paganica which may have been carried to Britain around 400 AD. The Chinese Golf Association also claims that the game is of Chinese origin. Chui Wan or ball hitting game was prevalent in the 3rd century BC. Initially the game used to be played with gutta-percha balls which were replaced with feather balls in 1848. In 1899, Col. W.N. Hskell of the USA invented rubber cored ball which was introduced in 1902. Steel clubs were authorised in the USA in 1925, and in Britain in 1929. The first club, the Honourable Company of Edinburgh Golfers, was formed in 1744, and ten years later the Royal and Ancient Golf Club was formed. In 1764, St.Andrews Royan and Ancient Golf Club came to be recognised as supreme authority in golfing matters. In India, the Royal Calcutta and Royal Bombay Golf Clubs were formed in 1829, and 1892, respectively. The ladies too were not very far behind. Mary Queen of Scots was said to have played golf. In 1972, the first ladies club was formed in Musselburgh and in 1893, the first Ladies Golf Union (British) was formed.

Golf Course

A golf course, usually between 4500-6500 m in length, is divided into 18 separate holes. Each one of it may be anything between 90-

550 m. A hole comprises the following features:

1. A flat teeing ground to make the initial stroke.
2. A fairway of 27-90 m wide of grass extending upto the green or brown in places of dry areas.
3. Green or brown — a prepared putting surface into which a hole of 108 mm diameter is sunk and marked by a flag.

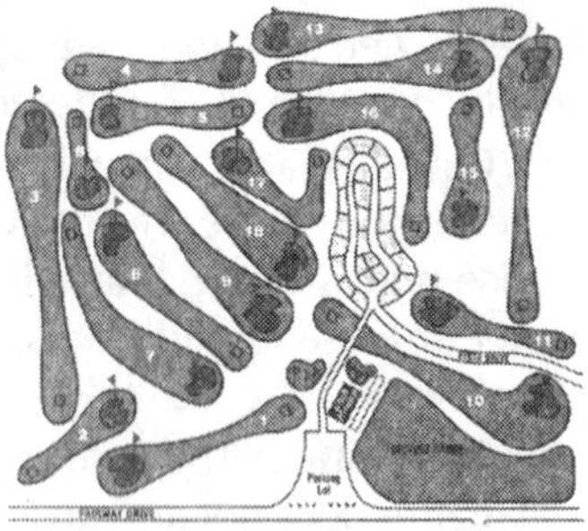

Golf Course Layout

In addition, the architect introduces features like streams, ditches, sand filled bunkers, ponds, trees, shrubs and other natural or created hazards offering a fair challenge to golfers of every level of skill.

From the golfing point of view he should provide three or four par 3 and par 5 holes and the remainder of par 4s of varying lengths, running in various directions subjecting the player to different wind conditions. The distances for determining par are as follows:

1. Par 3 — upto 250 yds (228.6 m)
2. Par 4 — 251 to 475 yds (223 — 434.3 m)
3. Par 5 — 475 and above (435 m) and above.

Definition of Terms

Addressing the Ball:A player has addressed the ball when he has taken his stance and has also grounded his club, except that in a hazard a player has addressed the ball when he has taken his stance.

Ball in the Play: A ball is in play as soon as the player has made a stroke on the teeing ground.

Caddie: A caddie is one who carries or handles a player's clubs during play and otherwise assists him in accordance with the rules.

When one caddie is employed by more than one player, he is always deemed to be the caddie of the player whose ball is involved, and equipment carried by him is deemed to be that player's equipment, except when the caddie acts upon specific directions of another player, in which case he is considered to be that other player's caddie.

Casual Water: Casual water is any temporary accumulation of water on the course which is visible before or after the player takes his stance and is not in water hazard. Snow and ice are either casual water or loose impediments, at the option of the player. Dew is not casual water.

Committee: The committee is incharge of the competition or, if the matter does not arise in a competition, the committee is incharge of the course.

Competitor: A competitor is a player in a stroke competition. A "fellow competitor" is any person against whom the competitor plays. Neither is partner of the other.

Course: The course is the whole area within which play is permitted.

Flagstick:The flagstick is a moveable straight indicator with or without bunting or other material attached, centred in the whole to show its position. It is circular in cross-section.

Forecaddie: A forecaddie is one who is employed by the committee to indicate to players the position of balls on the course, and is an outside agency.

Hazards: A hazard is any bunker or water hazard.

Hole: The hole shall be 108 mm (4¼ in) in diameter and at least 100 mm (4 in) deep. If a lining is used, it shall be sunk at least 25 mm (1 in) below the putting green surface unless the nature of the soil makes it impracticable to do so; its outer diameter shall not exceed 108 mm (4½ in).

Holed: A ball is holed when it is at rest within the circumference of the hole and all of it is below the level of the lip of the hole.

Honour: The side entitled to play first from the teeing ground is said to have the honour.

Marker: A marker is one who is appointed by the committee to record a competitor's score in stroke play. He may be a fellow-competitor. He is not the referee.

Move or Moved: A ball is deemed to have moved if it leaves its position and comes to rest in any other place.

Penalty Stroke: A penalty stroke is one added to the score of a player or side under certain rules. In a threesome or foursome, penalty strokes do not affect the order of play.

Referee: A referee is one who is refering for the hole being played which is specially prepared for putting or otherwise reported to him.

Rub of the Green: A rub of the green occurs when a ball in motion is accidentally stopped by any outsider.

Stipulated Round: The stipulated round consists of playing the hole of the course in the correct sequence unless authorised by the committee. The number of holes in a stipulated round is 18 unless a smaller number is authorised by the committee.

Handicapping System: This is based on a rating known as the standard scratch score (SSS) and is defined as the score in which a scratch player is expected to go round the course. Like par is the rating of a hole, SSS is the rating of a course depending upon the total length of the course according to the following table:

Distance	SSS	*Distance*	SSS
6942 m (7100 yd)	74	6309 m (6900 yd)	73
6126 m (6700 yd)	72	5944 m (6500 yd)	71
5716 m (6300 yd)	70	5578 m (6100 yd)	69
5395 m (5900 yd)	68	5212 m (5700 yd)	67
5029 m (5500 yd)	66	4846 m (5300 yd)	65
4663 m (5100 yd)	64	4481 m (4900 yd)	63
4298 m (4700 yd)	62	4115 m (4500 yd)	61
3932 m (4300 yd)	60	3749 m (4100 yd)	59

Thus a player with a handicap of 12 on a course with SSS 65 should go round in 77 strokes. The highest for men being 24 and for women 36. The handicap is valid for his own course.

Golf Ball

This is made of elastic thread wound under tension around a central core covered by a plastic coating having dimples approximately 3.302 mm deep.

The weight and diameter of the ball has been fixed to a maximum weight of 46 gm (1.62 oz) and minimum diameter of 43 mm (1.681 in).

Golf Clubs

The implement used to strike the ball is called the "club". A player is allowed to use a maximum of 14 golf clubs, consisting of "woods" and "irons". The following table shows the number, length, angle of loft and the average distance, in normal condition:

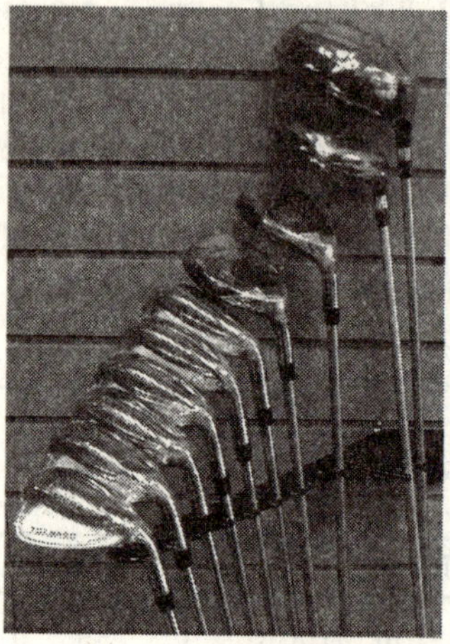

No.	Length	Angle of loft	Average distance
1. (Wood)	1092 mm	11	210 m
2. (Wood)	1080 mm	13'	200 m
3. (Wood)	1063 mm	16'	185 m
4. (Wood)	1050 mm	19'	175 m
1. (Iron)	1016 mm	IT	180 m
2. (Iron)	10 10 mm	20'	170 m
3. (Iron)	1003 mm	23'	160 m
4. (Iron)	991 mm	21'	150 m
5. (Iron)	978 mm	31'	140 m
6. (Iron)	965 mm	35'	130 m
7. (Iron)	952 mm	39"	120 m
8. (Iron)	940 mm	43'	110 m
9. (Iron)	927 mm	41'	100 m
1. (Wedge)	912 mm	51'	90 m
2. (Sadwedge)	912 mm	56'	–
3. (Putter)	Various	4'-10'	–

Golf Rules

1. **Winner**
   (a) **Match Play:** In match play the game is played by holes. A hole is won by the side which holes its balls in the fewest strokes. And a match which consists of a stipulated round is won by the side which is leading by number of holes greater than the number of holes remaining to be played.
   (b) **Stroke Play:** The competitor who plays the stipulated round or rounds in the fewest stroke is the winner.
2. **Practice**
   (a) **Match Play:** On any day of a match play competition a player may practise on the competition course before a round.
   (b) **Stroke Play:** A competitor is not allowed to practise on the competition course or test the surface of the putting green before a round or playoff.
3. **Strokes Taken:** The number of strokes a player has taken includes any penalty strokes incurred. In both match play and stroke play a player who has incurred a penalty should inform his opponent/marker as the case may be.
4. **Order of Play:** The side which shall have the honour at the first teeing ground is determined by the order of the draw or decided by lot in both match play and stroke play.
5. **Teeing:** Teeing ground is the starting place for the hole to be played. In teeing, the ball may be placed on the ground, on a tee, rand or other substance in order to raise it off the ground.
6. **Ball Falling off Tee**: If a ball, when not in play, falls off a tee or is knocked off a tee, it may be re-teed without penalty.
7. **Identifying Ball:** The responsibility for playing the proper ball rests with the player.
8. **Stroke**: A stroke is the forward movement of the club made with the intention of fairly striking at a moving ball. A player is not allowed to play while his ball is moving.
9. **Playing a Wrong Ball:** In match play if a player plays a stroke with a wrong ball except in a hazard he shall lose the hole. In stroke play, he shall add two penalty strokes to his score and shall then play the correct ball.

10. **Ball in Motion Deflected or Stopped:** If a ball is accidentally deflected *or* stopped by any outside agency no penalty is incurred. But if the ball is deflected *or* stopped by the player, his partner or either *of* their caddies *or* equipment in a match play will lose the hole. In stroke play the competitor shall incur a penalty of two strokes.
11. **Ball Unplayable:** At any place *on* the course except in a water hazard a player may declare his ball unplayable. He shall be under penalty of one stroke and play his next stroke as nearly as possible at the spot from which tne original ball was played. Drop a ball within two club lengths of the spot where the ball lay but not nearer the hole.
12. **Lifting Dropping:** A ball to be lifted under rules may be lifted by the player, his partner or another person authorised by the player. When a ball is required to be dropped, the player shall stand erect, hold the ball at shoulder height and at arm's length and drop it. It shall be dropped as near as possible to the spot where the ball lay, but not nearer the hole.
13. **Ball Lost:** A ball is lost if:
    (a) It is not found or identified as his by the player within five minutes after the player's side has started to search for it.
    (b) The player has put another ball into play under the rules, even though he may not have searched for the original ball.

Other Forms of Play

1. **Three-some:** A match in which one plays against two, and each side plays one ball.
2. **Four-some:** A match in which two play against two and each side plays one ball.
3. **Three-Ball Match Play:** In a three-ball match, each player plays two distinct matches.
4. **Four-Ball Stroke Play:** In four-ball stroke play two competitors play as partners, each playing his own ball. The lower score of the partners is the score for the hole.
5. **Bogey, Par and Stableford Competition**: These are forms of stroke competition in which play is against a fixed score at each hole.

Championships

Eisenhower Trophy: International amateur golf tournament for men. Played in alternate years.

The Open Championship: This was inaugurated in 1860 at Prestwick, Starthclyde, Scotland.

US Open Championship: This was inaugurated in 1895.

US Masters: It was instituted at Augusta National Golf Course, Georgia, in 1934.

World Cup: This was formerly known as the Canada Cup and was started in 1935.

Walker Cup: A competition between the US and the UK instituted in 1922. It is held biennially.

Ryder Cup: Initially professional match between the USA and Great Britain; inaugurated in 1927. Now this competition is held between the US and European professionals.

Curtis Cup: Women's golf tournaments played in alternate years between women amateur golfers of the UK and the USA.

Names to Remember

Tony Jacklin: A British golfer. He won the open championship in 1969 and won the US open championship in 1970. He is also a World Cup and Ryder Cup player.

Bill Casper (USA, 1931): A famous American golfer who won the US master in 1970, and US open championship in 1959. Probably the highest earning professional golfer in his time, he won about 40 sponsored events during his first 16 years in the game.

Samuel Ryder.(1859-1936): British golfer 'businessman' a donor of the Ryder Cup, instituted in 1927, played in alternate years between USA and British professionals.

Christy O'Connor (1926-): Professional golfer from Ireland. Played in the Ryder Cup from 1955 to 1969. He won the World Cup in 1958 with Brodshow as his partner.

Tom Morris Sr.(1821-1908) and Tom Morris Jr.(1850-1875): Father and son, both renowned Scottish golfers. The father was known as old Tom who won four open championships. But it was the son who created history by winning the first open championship at the age of 16. He won the championships consecutively for four years. Between them, they won a total of eight open championships. Unfortunately, the son died at the age of 24.

Catherine Lacoste (1945-): French amateur golfer. Daughter of Wimbledon lawn tennis championship Rene Lacoste. She won US women's open in 1967, French open in 1967 and 1969 and British championship in 1969.

Beth Daniels (b.14 October 1956): Professional woman golfer whose record earning in 1980 touched the figure of $ 231,000.

Byron Nelson (1912-): US professional golfer. He won US open championship in 1939, Master's championship in 1937, 1942 and 1945. He won 18 professional championships. He was also a Ryder Cup player.

Harry Vardon (1870-1937): British golfer and winner of a record six open championships and one US open championship. It may be said with certain amount of certainty that he was the father of plodern golf. "Vardon grip" is well known in this game.

Sandy Lyle (1958-): An outstanding golfer from Scotland who at the age of 9 participated in his first golf tournament. He turned professional at the age of 19 and was a member of the Walker Club team. He was also a member of the Ryder Cup winning side in 1985 and 1987. In 1978 he won the Golf Rookie award of the year. He won the Master's in 1988 at Augusta National.

Jack Nicklaus (1940—): American professional golfer whose name features in the *Guiness Book of World Records*. He has won the maximum number of major championships. Apart from holding several records his maximum earnings have been rated as exceeding 4 million dollars in 1983.

Tiger Woods: (Dec. 30, 1975, in Cypress, California). The world had never before seen a golfing phenomena—the likes of Tiger Woods. A golfer whose amazing youth and amateur exploits were followed up by equally amazing professional exploits.

In 1997, he won the Masters for his first major. Woods won just once in 1998, but in 1999 he began a string of consecutive Player of the Year awards that didn't end until Vijay Singh won the title in 2004.

He won 8 times in 1999, then 9 more times in 2000. Woods' 2000 season is arguably the best ever on the PGA Tour. He became the second golfer to win three professional majors in one year and broke Byron Nelson's more-than-50-year-old scoring average record. In 2001, when he won the Masters, Woods became the first golfer to hold all four professional majors at the same time.

■

GYMNASTICS

Chapter - 24

Gymnastics were known in Greece and Rome. But modern Gymnastics were developed in Germany.

History

Gymnastics were well known to the Greeks and some activities like rope climbing were part of the ancient Olympics. With the rise of the Roman Empire the Greek method of physical culture spread. The sport declined for nearly 1,500 years and it was revived by men like Guts, Muthsan and Ling. However, most of the correct competitive exercises may be attributed to the German, Friedrich Ludwig Jahn. Though modern gymnastics was developed in Germany, the most successful countries in this discipline have been Russia, Czechoslovakia and Japan. In 1881 the International Gymnastic Federation was formed and the first championship was held in 1903 at Antwerp.

Dress

Men: Men must wear a jersey (shirt) in all events. They must wear white pants in the events performed on rings, parallel bars, pommel horse and horizontal bars. They should wear gymnasium shoes and socks. For vault and floor exercise short-pants may be worn.

Women: Women wear leotards. As long as the general appearance remains the same, precise tailoring to suit an individual is permitted.

Types of Competitions

Competition 1: This is a team competition involving six members performing two sets of exercises on each apparatus.

Competition 2: This is in the individual all round championship. The competitors perform an optional exercise on each apparatus.

Competition 3: Individual championships on each apparatus. In Olympics, eight best competitors from the team competitions participate in the competition.

Events

At national and international levels there are six men's events:

(a) Floor exercise

(b) Pommel horse

(c) Rings

(d) Vault

(e) Parallel bars

(f) Horizontal bar

Women's events are four:

(a) Vault (b) Uneven bars

(c) Beam (d) Floor exercise

Scoring

Each competitor's performance on an apparatus is marked from 0 to 10 marks. The gymnast's score in the men's section is obtained by averaging the two intermediate scores awarded by four judges. The highest and lowest scores are disregarded. In the women's section average of the middle four judges is considered as the final score after eliminating the highest and the lowest scores.

Officials

Women's meet:

(a) Six judges and a head judge

(b) Scientific technical collaborator

(c) Assistants

Men's meet:

(a) Four judges (b) One superior judge

(c) One superior judge assistant (d) Assistants

FLOOR EXERCISES

The floor exercises consist of handsprings, cart-wheels, somersaults, back flip, back somersaults and other blended leaps, springs and balances. Women exercise with music and their movements must be synchronized with the music. There are lots of dancing movements, dancing poses, leaps and jumps.

The "mat" for floor exercises is 14 square metres but the working area is 12 square metres. The mat is made of four layers. The uppermost layer is of carpet cover, under this is the cushion layer and under that floor plate and elastic supports. The total height of the floor mat is 120 mm.

Men perform for 70 seconds and women with musical accompaniment from 70 to 90 seconds.

Vaulting Horse

The vaulting horse is also shared by both men and women.

(a) **Construction:** Leather-covered body similar to a pommel horse but without the pommels.

(b) **Height:** For men 1.35 m above the floor and placed length-wise. For women 1.20 m above the floor and placed breadth-wise.

(c) **Run-up**: 25 metres.

Vaulting Horse

The vault execution differs from person to person but marks are awarded for the degree of difficulty, smoothness and good position making. Vaults are categorised into four categories: A, B, C and D. The D is the most difficult.

Pommel Horse

Pommel Horse

The pommel horse is an almost trapezoidal, leather-covered body on which only men compete, since it requires great strength.

Its upper surface is 1.10 m above the floor. The pommels are 0.12 m high and 0.28 m wide, and 0.40 to 0.45 m apart.

Ring

Ring

The ring, like the pommel horse, is practised only by men.

The two rings are 0.50 m apart and suspended by two thin but strong cables. They are hung 2.75 m above the floor level.

The competitor has to show at least two handstands-one, using his momentum and the other using his strength.

The gymnast starts with a leap upward to grasp the rings, one in each hand, and then on conclusion of his exercise must land on both his feet together.

Parallel Bars

Parallel Bars

The parallel bars, in their original form, are used only by men. The bars are of the following specifications:

(a) Shape of material	Oval, wood
(b) Vertical thickness	0.051 m
(c) Width	0.40 m
(d) Length	3.50 m
(e) Distance	0.42-0.52 m (apart)
(f) Height	1.70 m (above the floor)

Assymetric Bars

Assymetric Bars

The women use the assymetric bars which are also known as "uneven bars". Length 240 cm. The upper bar in this case is 2.35 m high and the lower one is 1.55 m high.

Horizontal Bar

Horizontal Bar

The horizontal or high bar probably produces the most exciting moments in gymnastics. Only men compete on it and this exercise is one which does not allow use of strength, because it hinders the smooth flow otherwise. The high bar is 2.75 m high from ground level.

Balance Beam

Balance Beam

The balance beam is used only by women in competitions. The beam is 5 m long, 0.10 m wide, and 0.16 m thick. It is at a height of 1.20 m above the ground.

Modern Rhythmic Gymnastics

This form of gymnastics is performed by women which incorporates exercises with different hand-held apparatus such as ribbons, balls, ropes, hoops and clubs. This was included for the first time in the 1984 Olympic Games.

Important Competitions

Olympics: Gymnastics has been a part of the modem Olympics since 1896. But after the Second World War at the 1948 Olympics it really became a popular world sport.

World Championship: The first world championship of gymnastics was held in 1934, in Budapest.

World Cup: It was instituted in 1975.

European Championship: This is generally held during a non-Olympic world championship year.

Modern Rhythmic Gymnastics

Maximum overall titles in world championship — 3 by Maria Gigova (Bulgaria). Maximum individual apparatus titles — 9 by Maria Gigova and Galina Shugurova. Maximum medals — 14 by Galina Shugurova.

Famous Names

Boris Shakhlin: Russian gymnast who has won the maximum gold medals in Olympics and world championship. He won 10 individual and 3 team championships.

Olga Korbut: 17-year-old Olga Korbut, a Russian, hypnotised the Munich Olympic crowd by her superb skill. She won three gold medals (beam, floor exercise and team event).

Nadia Comaneci: At the 1976 Montreal Games, 14-year-old Comaneci, a Romanian, became the first gymnast to be awarded a perfect score of 10 in Olympic competition. She now resides in the US.

Oana Mihaela Ban (born January 11, 1986 in Cluj-Napoca): She is a retired Romanian gymnast. Oana's career highlight came at the 2004 Summer Olympics in Athens, where she, along with teammates Monica Rosu, Alexandra Eremia, Catalina Ponor, Daniela Sofronie and Silvia Stroescu, won the gold medal in the team competition.

Monica Rosu (born May 11, 1987 in Bacau): She is an artistic gymnast from Romania, who started gymnastics in 1991 at age four and trained during her early years at CSS Bacau. Rosu's finest hour came during the 2004 Olympics in Athens. With Catalina Ponor, Daniela Sofronie, Oana Ban, Alexandra Eremia and Silvia Stroescu, she was a part of the Romanian team who successfully defended their Olympic Team Title.

Paul Elbert Hamm (born September 24, 1982 in Waukesha, Wisconsin): He is a US gymnast and Olympic gold medalist. In 2003, he became the first American man to win the all-round title at the world championships. He competed at the 2004 Summer Olympics in Athens, alongside his twin brother Morgan. He won the silver medal in the team event and the high bar, and was awarded gold in the individual all-around competition.

■

HANDBALL

Chapter - 25

A seven-a-side ball game played by hand. In 1931 the game was included in Olympics.

History

Handball or handball like games were played all over the world in ancient days. A depiction of the game was found on the town walls of Athens in 1926. The game is believed to have been of 600 BC. Handball as played today was first introduced in 1890 by a German gymnastics master, Konrad Koch. The first countries to play modern handball were those of West Europe. During the 1928 Olymic games a demonstration handball match was played and in 1931 the International Olympic Committee decided to include handball in the Olympics. Today handball is played by more than 50 nations all over the globe. In 1946, the International Handball Federation was formed at Copenhagen. In 1926 at Berlin it was an 11-a-side outdoor game, but when reintroduced in 1972 at Munich it was an indoor game with seven-a-side, the standard size of team since then.

Handball Court

Goals: Goals are positioned on the centre of the goal line. This is also like a football goal.The height of the vertical posts is 2 m. They are placed 3 m apart, joined by a horizontal cross-bar. Cross-section of the posts and crossbars should be 8 × 8 cm in cross-section. The bars must be painted in contrasting bands of colours. Goals are attached with nets.

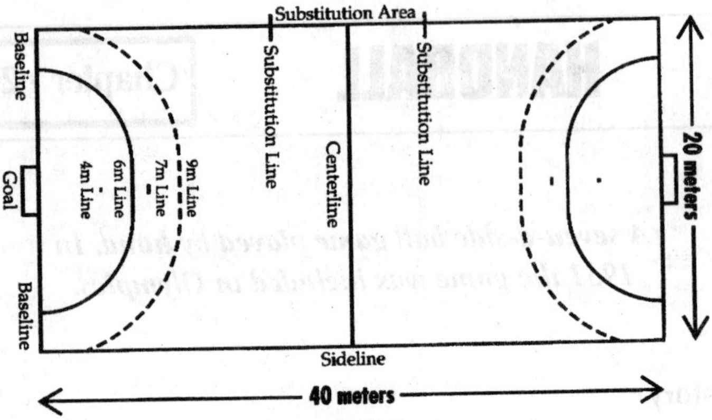

Handball Court

Ball: This is a round inflated synthetic leather ball, weighing 425 – 475 gm and with circumference of 58-60 cm. For women weight of the ball is 325-400 gm and circumference 54-56 cm.

Dress: A team must wear identical uniforms, except the goalkeeper who must wear a dress by which he can be recognised easily. Each player must wear a number, 10 cm high on the front of his shirt and 20 cm high on the back. Numbers from 1 to 20 are used-1, 12 and 16 are reserved for goalkeepers. The captain must wear an arm band approximately 4 cm wide.

Rules of Handball

1. A team consists of 10 court players and two goalkeepers out of which only seven can be in the play at any time, i.e., six court players and one goalkeeper.

2. **Substitute:** Any number of substitutions is permitted during the game. They need not notify the time-keeper provided the player being substituted has left the field of play.

3. **Duration:** The game consists of two periods of 30 minutes each with a ten-minute interval for both men and women above the age of 18. For juniors the two periods are of 25 minutes each and the interval is of 10 minutes.

4. **Start:** Each period commences with a throw-off by the team entitled to do it.

5. **Scoring:** Shots for goal must be executed from outside the goal area. A goal is scored if the ball has travelled (in the air or on the ground) completely over the goal line between the posts.

6. **Rules of the Game**

(a) A free throw is awarded for various infringements like a faulty handling of the ball, a faulty approach to an opponent, a faulty attitude to the referee and so on. If the place where the free throw awarded is in between the free throw line and the goal area line (9 m and 6 m lines) then the free throw must be taken from the nearest spot outside the free throw line.

(b) A player is allowed to hold the ball for three seconds only. They are allowed to hit the oncoming ball with the fist, but not to throw it up and fist it away.

(c) A player holding the ball may take not more than three steps and must pass it or bounce it with one hand.

(d) Once the ball has been caught or bounced with one hand, no more bouncing is allowed, and it has to be passed within three seconds.

(e) Lobbing, hooking, hugging, tripping, in any way is forbidden.

(f) Indiscipline in the field or court of play or bad behaviour towards the referee is also punishable. If such offences are repeated, a player may be suspended for two minutes, disqualified or excluded.

(g) In three fundamental respects handball differs from football. There are no offside rules, the ball may not be played back into the goal area or to the goalkeeper and lastly no goal melee is possible as no player is allowed inside the goal area.

(h) Only the goalkeeper is allowed to move around freely within the goal area and to come out of the goal area without the ball.

Game Officials

The game is conducted by two referees, one scorer and a time-keeper.

Important Tournaments

(a) **European Cup**

(b) **Baltic Cup**

(c) **World Cup**—Inaugurated in 1938 (now named World Championship).

(d) **Olympics** — Handball was first included in the 1932 Olympics.

(e) **Super Cup** — This is contested between the Olympic champions and the World champions.

■

HOCKEY (FIELD) Chapter - 26

The word Hockey became popular in 19th century. Hockey association was formed in 1886 and Federation Internationale De Hockey Sur Gazon came into being on 7 January 1924.

History

In Egypt, on a wall in an ancient tomb at Bern Hasan in Nile Valley, there were drawings indicating men engaged in a game similar to hockey. That is how it may be stated that the origin of hockey dates back to about 2000 BC. The sticks they were holding resembled the early twentieth century hockey sticks.

Hockey thus may be the forerunner of all modem sports played with an implement. An early form of hockey also used to be played in Argentina. They played a game called "Chouca" (the twisted end), which took its name from the stick with a twisted end. Their ball had a leather case. As the civilisation progressed, gradual evolution of the game also took place. The word "hockey" came into use in the 19th century. The game gradually became organised and modernised in England and the Hockey Association was formed in 1886 and Federation Internationale De Hockey Sur Gazon was inaugurated on 7 January 1924. Men's hockey was included in the modem Olympic Games in 1908.

Hockey Field

The game was originally played on grass in most parts of the world. However, the synthetic turf has become popular and is now the official surface in international hockey. A sketch of the hockey field is shown with all its details in Fig. 23.1.

(a) Boundary lines — white
(b) Width of all lines — 3 in (8 cm) wide.
(c) Straight line drawn at 25 yd from each goal line.
(d) Goal placed in centre of goal line.
(e) The goal is made of two perpendicular posts, 4 yd (3.66 m) apart, joined together by horizontal crossbar 7 ft (2.13 m) from the ground.
(f) Width of goal post and crossbar — 2 in (5 cm) and not more than 3 in (8 cm) deep and the sides facing the field of play are rectangular.
(g) **Goal Net.** The net is attached at intervals of not more than 6 in (15 cm) to the goal posts, the crossbar and the ground behind the goal.
(h) The goals are completed by fixing three boards which are of 18 in (46 cm) height each inside the netting.

Hockey Ball

Hockey ball is white in colour which weighs between 5¾ oz (163 gm) and 5½ oz (155 gm) and has a circumference between 9¼ in (23 cm) and in (22 cm). Regulation ball is to be made of natural or artificial material, either white or painted white or as agreed and the inside core made of cork and twine.

Hockey Stick

There are no rules as to the length of the hockey stick but the weight must be between 12 and 28 oz (340-794 gm). The stick must be able to pass through a ring with a diameter of 2 in (5 cm) and have a flat face on its left side, rounded edges and wooded head.

Dress

Players wear shirts, shorts and socks with the colour of the team. In addition goalkeepers wear pads, kickers, masks and gauntlet gloves.

Hockey Rules

Each player carries a "stick", normally a little over 3 feet (90 centimetres) long and traditionally made of wood but now often made with fibreglass, kevlar and carbon fibre composites, with a rounded handle flattening out on one side and with a hook at the bottom. New rules (2006) limit the curve of the stick so as to limit the power with which the ball can be flicked. The stick is only allowed to have a bow smaller than or equal to 25 mm, otherwise this is deemed to be illegal. The flat side of the hook is used to push, dribble, or hit a hard plastic ball. This ball is often covered with indentations to reduce hydroplaning that can cause an inconsistent ball speed on wet surfaces. Each field player normally wears a mouth guard and shin guards. Although the only equipment required for goalkeepers (under FIH rules, local variants may require more) is a helmet and a stick, invariably they wear extensive protective equipment including chest guards, padded shorts, heavily padded hand protectors, leg guards, and foot guards (called "kickers").

Artificial turf or synthetic turf, is a grass-like man-made surface manufactured from synthetic materials. It is most often used in arenas for sports that were originally or are normally played on grass, however, it is now being used on residential lawns and commercial applications, as well.

Field Hockey Formations

Formations provide structure to a hockey team on the pitch. They help players understand and share the defensive and attacking responsibilities. Although higher level teams may select from a wide range of formations, teams containing inexperienced players or teams which see frequent changes to their players are likely to select from a more limited range of formations such as 4-3-3, 5-3-2 and 4-4-2. (The numbers refer to the number of players arrayed across the pitch, starting in front of the goalkeeper with the defenders, then midfield and then attack.) The 2-3-5 formation, used predominantly in Australia from relatively lowly interschool to

professional interstate competitions, provides common language for many players and helps explain why "centre half" is often a name used for a player in the centre of a defence with 4 or 5 players.

Because hockey teams have 1 goalkeeper plus 10 outfield players as does association football (soccer), there are many common formations between the two sports.

One important difference in modern hockey is the absence of an offside rule. This allows attackers (often a lone attacker) to play well up the pitch, stretching the opponents' defence and using the large spaces to be found there. To counter this, defences usually keep a matching number of defenders.

Rules of Play

Throughout most of the world the rules set by the FIH are used. However in the United States, NCAA have their own rules for inter-collegiate competitions, and high school associations similarly play to different rules. This article assumes FIH rules unless otherwise stated.

Players are permitted to play the ball with any part of the stick other than the rounded side (back). The flat side is always on the "natural" side for a right-handed person — there are no "left-handed" hockey sticks (for actual use in play, some have been made as novelties).

Positions

Teams consist of eleven players on the field, and up to five substitutes. Substitutions are not limited but may not be made during a penalty corner. There are no set positions other than goalkeeper, but most teams arrange themselves into fullbacks, midfielders and forwards. Many teams include a single sweeper, who plays behind the fullbacks.

One player from each team is designated the goalkeeper. Goalkeepers must wear a suitable helmet with full face mask and are also permitted to wear protective padding, including large leg guards, kickers and gloves. Although goalkeepers may block or deflect the ball with any part of their bodies, and propel the ball with their feet, they must always carry a stick, and normal stick rules apply. Goalkeepers are permitted to play the ball outside their defensive circle (scoring area or "D"), but must only use the stick in this circumstance.

General Play

For the purposes of the rules, all players on the team in possession of the ball are attackers, and those on the team without the ball are defenders.

The match is officiated by two field umpires. Traditionally each umpire generally controls half of the field, divided roughly diagonally, although now experiments are being made where either umpire can make any decision anywhere on the field. These umpires are often assisted by a technical bench including a timekeeper and record keeper.

Prior to the start of the game, a coin is tossed and the winning captain can choose a starting end or start with the ball. The game time is divided into two equal halves of 35 minutes each, with five minutes for half-time. At the start of each half, as well as after goals are scored, play is started with a pass from the centre of the field. All players must start in their defensive half, but the ball may be played in any direction. Each team starts with the ball in one half, and the team that conceded the goal has possession for the restart.

Field players may only play the ball with the face of the stick. Tackling is permitted as long as the tackler does not make contact with the attacker or his stick before playing the ball (contact after the tackle may also be penalised if the tackle was made from a position where contact was inevitable). Further, the player with the ball may not deliberately use his body to push a defender out of the way.

Obstruction typically occurs in three circumstances - when a defender comes between the player with possession and the ball without first performing a legitimate tackle; when a defender's stick comes between the attacker's stick and the ball or makes contact with the attacker's stick; and also when (usually deliberately) blocking the opposition's passage to the ball (called third party obstruction).

When the ball passes over the sidelines, it is returned to play with a sideline hit, taken by a member of the team whose players were not the last to touch the ball before crossing the sideline. If it crosses the backline after last touched by an attacker, a 15 m hit. A 15 m hit is also awarded for offenses committed by the attacking side within 15 m of the end of the pitch they are attacking.

Field Hockey Tactics

The main methods by which the ball is moved around the field by players are: the "dribble", where the player controls the ball with the stick and runs with the ball, pushing the ball along as they run; the "push", where the player uses their wrists to push at the ball; the "flick" or "scoop", similar to the push but with an additional wrist action to force the stick through at an angle and lift the ball off the ground; and the "hit", where a backlift is taken and contact with the ball is made quite forcefully. In order to produce a much stronger hit, usually for travel over long distances, the stick is raised higher and swung at the ball, known as a "drive". Tackles are made by placing the stick into the path of the ball. To increase the effectiveness of the tackle, players will often place the entire stick close to the ground horizontally, thus representing a wider barrier. To avoid the tackle, the ball carrier will either pass the ball to a teammate using any of the push, flick, or hit, or attempt to maneuver or "pull" the ball around the tackle, trying to deceive the tackler.

When passing and maneuvering between players, certain commands are used to ensure understanding of movements and plays among teammates. Although these vary depending on which country the game is in, there are a few standard calls. By calling "through" or "straight" the ball is passed straight ahead to another player. "Flat" or "square" signifies a pass made to the right or left of the player with the ball at a 90 degree angle. Passes made backward are occasionally signified by a call of "drop". A hit made forward at an angle is recognized as "up".

In recent years, the penalty corner has gained importance as a vital part of the game as a goal scoring opportunity. Particularly with the advent and popularisation of the drag flick, penalty corners are highly sought after. Some tactics or set plays used involve the aforementioned drag flick, the straight hit, deflections towards goal, and various more complex plays, using passes before shots at goal.

At the highest level, hockey is a fast-moving, highly skilled sport, with players using fast moves with the stick, quick accurate passing, and hard hits, in attempts to keep possession and move the ball towards the goal. While physically tackling and otherwise obstructing players is not permitted, collisions are common, and the speed at which the ball travels along the ground (and sometimes through the air, which is legal if it is not judged dangerous by the umpire) requires the use of padded shin guards to prevent injury. Some of the tactics used resemble football (soccer), but with greater speed — the best players maneuver and score almost quicker than the eye can see.

Free Hits

Free hits are awarded when offences are committed outside the scoring circles. The ball may be hit or pushed once in any direction by the team offended against. Opponents must move 5 m from the ball when a free hit is awarded, and for attacking free hits within 5 m of the circle all attackers other than the one taking the hit must also be 5 m away.

As mentioned above, a 15 m hit is awarded if an attacking player commits a foul forward of that line, or if the ball passes over the backline off an attacker. These hits are taken in line with where the foul was committed (taking a line parallel with the sideline between where the offence was committed, or the ball went out of play). If the attack commits a foul in the circle they are attacking, the defence additionally has the option to take the free hit anywhere in that circle.

Long Corner

A long corner is awarded if the ball goes over the backline after last being touched by a defender. Long corners are played by the attacking team and involve a free hit on the sideline five yards from the corner of the field closest to where the ball went out of play.

Short Corner

The short or penalty corner is a rather complicated set play that is awarded against a defending team when any offence is committed in the defensive circle, and may be awarded when a deliberate offence is committed in the defending 23 m area, or when the defending team deliberately plays the ball over the back line.

Short corners begin with five defenders (including the keeper) arranged along the backline. All other defenders must return to the centre line until the ball is in play. Attacking players begin the play standing outside the scoring circle, except for one attacker who starts the corner by playing the ball from a mark 10 m either side of the goal (the circle has a 14.63 m radius). This player puts the ball into play by pushing or hitting the ball to the other attackers outside the circle; the ball must pass outside the circle before the attackers attempt to get a shot or deflection into the goal. For safety reasons, the first shot of a penalty corner must remain under 460 mm high unless it is flicked.

Penalty Stroke

A penalty stroke is awarded when defenders commit a deliberate foul in the circle which deprives an attacker of possession or the opportunity to play the ball, when an accidental breach prevents a certain goal, or if defenders repeatedly "break" or start to run from the backline before a penalty corner has started. This penalty pits a single attacker against the goalkeeper, and is taken from a spot 6.4 m out and directly in front of the goal. The goalkeeper must stand with heels on the goal line, and cannot move his feet until the ball is played. On the umpire's whistle, the striker may take one step and push or flick the ball at the goal, which the goalkeeper attempts to save. The attacker is not permitted to take more than one step, more than one shot, to fake or dummy the shot, or to move towards or interfere with the goalkeeper once the shot is taken. Hitting or dragging the ball is also forbidden. If the shot is saved, play is restarted with a 15 m hit to the defenders; if a goal is scored, play is restarted in the normal way.

Scoring In Field Hockey

The teams' object is to play the ball into their attacking circle and, from there, hit, push or flick the ball into the goal, scoring a point. The team with more goals after two 35-minute halves wins the game.

Tie Breaker

Conditions for breaking ties are not laid down in the rules of hockey, but many associations will follow the procedure laid down in FIH tournament regulations which mandate 7.5 minutes each way of "golden goal" extra time (i.e. the game ends as soon as one team scores). If scores are still level, then the game will be decided with penalty strokes, in much the same way that association football penalty shoot outs are conducted.

Other competitions may use alternative means of breaking a tie, for example, an extended period of golden goal extra time with a progressive reduction in the number of players each team can have on the field (usually termed "drop-offs"); if no goal is scored at the end of such extra time periods, again a result would be achieved using penalty strokes.

Dangerous Play and Raised Balls within Field Hockey

If the ball is raised off the ground in a manner that is, in the umpire's opinion, dangerous, the ball is turned over to the other team and they receive a free hit from the point of contact. The definition of a "dangerous ball" is a matter of interpretation by the umpires. Guidance in the rules states "a ball is considered dangerous when it causes legitimate evasive action by players" — but it also depends on the speed of the ball, the height at which it is raised, and the number of players near its path.

It is, however, legal to raise the ball when making a shot on goal (by hitting or flicking), or to make an 'overhead' pass (providing opposition players are greater than 5 m from the player, and the ball is not dangerous). The ball may only deliberately be raised using a hit if the player is shooting at goal.

Dangerous play rules also apply with relation to the usage of the stick. Players may not attempt to play at the ball above their shoulders (unless saving a goal on the goal line). It will generally be considered dangerous play to hit the ball while it is in the air; the ball must be controlled first in this circumstance.

Warnings and Suspensions within Field Hockey

Hockey uses a three-tier card system of warnings and suspensions. A Green card is a warning, while a Yellow card is a temporary suspension for a minimum of 5 minutes duration without substitution. As in association football, a Red card is a permanent exclusion from the rest of the game, without substitution, and in many circumstances will also result in the player being banned for a certain period of time or number of matches (this is governed by local playing conditions, rather than the rules of hockey). Unlike football, a player may receive more than one card of the same colour, although a second and subsequent card cannot be of a "lower" colour than one previously issued, and in the case of a second yellow card the temporary suspension would be expected to be of considerably longer duration than the first. However, local playing conditions may mandate that cards are awarded only progressively, and not allow second awards.

Signals by the Umpires

1. **Bully:** Make a "bully" movement with both hands.
2. **Obstruction:** Make a circular movement with one arm in front of the body.
3. **Kicks**: Slightly raise a leg and touch it with the hand.
4. **Off-side**: Stand on the line of the decision and raise arm horizontally pointing towards the direction.
5. **Goal:** Turn, point both arms horizontally towards the centre of the ground.
6. **Free-hit push-in:** Indicate the direction with one arm raised horizontally, downwards with the other arm.
7. **Corner:** Point an arm at the corner flag closest to the point where the ball has crossed the back line.
8. **16 yd hit:** Extend both arms sideways.
9. **Penalty-corner:** Point both arms towards the goal.
10. **Penalty-stroke:** The left arm points to the penalty spot. The right arm points straight up in the air.
11. **Dangerous play or bad tempers:** Stop play. Make palming indications by raising both hands horizontally, palm downwards in front of the body moving slowly up and down.
12. **Time stopped:** Turn towards the other umpire and time-keeper and cross fully extended arms at the wrist above the head.
13. **Start/Restart:** Raise one arm in the air and await other umpire's acknowledgement before starting play.

Major International Tournaments in Field Hockey

The biggest two field hockey tournaments are undoubtedly the Olympic Games tournament, and the Hockey World Cup, which is also held every 4 years. Apart from this, there is the Champions Trophy Cup held each year for the six top-ranked teams. Field hockey is also played in the Commonwealth Games. Amongst the men, India has won 8 Olympic golds and Pakistan have lifted the World Cup 4 times. Amongst the women, Australia has 3 Olympic golds while Netherlands has clinched the World Cup 6 times. Sultan Azlan Shah Hockey Tournament held annually in Malaysia is becoming a prominent Hockey Tournament where teams from around the world participate to win the cup.

Championships

Champions Trophy: Instituted in 1979. Top six teams of the previous Olympics/World Cup qualify.

Olympics: Hockey was included in the 1908 Olympics in London. But, the game was not included in the 1912 Stockholm Games and 1924, Paris Olympics due to the absence of an international body. The FIH was formed in 1924 and the game was reinstituted in 1928. India has won the maximum number of gold medals in Olympics (8).

World Cup: First instituted in 1971. Pakistan has won the cup three times in 1971, 1978 and 1982. Women's World Cup was instituted in 1974.

Names to Remember

Leslie Walter Claudius (b.25 March, 1927): Indian hockey player. He won three Olympic gold medals in 1948, 1952 and 1956, he also won a silver medal in 1960.

Udham Singh (b. 4 August, 1928): Indian hockey player. He is also a winner of 4 Olympic medals. Three golds in 1952, 1956 and 1964 and a silver in 1960.

Eric Broome Penniger (1902-): Indian hockey player, who played for Punjab, North-western Railway and Delhi Rangers. He was the Indian captain in the 1928 Olympic semi-final and final. He won his second gold medal in the 1932 Olympics.

Brig. Manzoor Hussain Atif (1929): Pakistan Olympic hockey player. He represented Pakistan in four Olympic Games 1952, 1956, 1960 and 1964. He won one gold medal and two silver medals. He captained Pakistan in: the 1962 Asian Games and the 1964 Olympics. He was selector, coach and manager of Pakistan hockey team.

Richard J. Allen (1902-): Indian hockey goalkeeper who along with Dhyan Chand holds a record of winning three Olympic gold medals in 1928, 1932 and 1936. He didn't concede a single goal during the 1928 Olympics.

Randhir Singh Gentle (1923-81): Indian hockey player. An outstanding full-back who played for Tatas (Bombay) and Independents also. He also won three Olympic gold medals in 1948, 1952 and 1956. He played in the Indian National championship 29 times. After retirement, he became a renowned hockey coach.

John Valentine Conroy (1928-): Born in India, he was the first Anglo-Indian to be selected for the British Hockey team. He played in

55 internationals — 23 for Great Britain and 32 for England and participated in the 1952 and 1956 Olympics. He won a bronze medal in 1952. He is regarded as the best forward of Britain.

Floris-Jan Bovelander (1966-): Dutch player who has earned over 120 caps. The most effective penalty-corner striker in modern hockey. Almost single-handedly he helped Holland to win the seventh World Cup in Lahore in 1990.

Brig. Abdul Hamid (1927-): A brilliant inside left of Pakistan hockey team. He captained the Olympic gold meda!-winning team of Pakistan in 1960 and Asian Games in 1958. He played in the 1948, 1952, 1956 and 1960 Olympics. "Hamidi" became a coach and manager of Pakistan National team.

Maj. Dhyan Chand (1905-79): One of the greatest hockey players the world has ever seen. He represented India and played in every continent. He won the Olympic gold in three successive Olympics (1928, 1932 and 1936). He had an amazing capability to score goals. He scored 133 goals during India's 1932 world tour and scored 201 goals during Australia-New Zealand tour in 43 games. In the 1936 Olympics, he scored six goals in the final to defeat Germany 8-1.

Michael Brennan (born October 15, 1975 in Toowoomba, Queensland): A field hockey midfielder from Australia, Brennan was a member of the team that won gold at the 2004 Summer Olympics in Athens. Four years earlier, when Sydney hosted the Summer Games, he finished in third spot with The Kookaburras , as the Men's National Team is called. Brennan made his international debut when selected to compete at the 1996 Champions Trophy in Madras. He is nicknamed Mouse, and played club hockey for the Queensland Blades in his native country and for Oranje Zwart in Eindhoven, The Netherlands.

Travis Brooks (born July 16, 1980 in Melbourne, Victoria): A field hockey forward from Australia, Travis Brooks won the golden medal with the Men's National Team at the 2004 Summer Olympics in Athens. He made his international debut in Canberra, on February 15, 2003, during the second Test of the series against the Netherlands, and played a starring role in The Kookaburras Sultan Azlan Shah Cup win in January 2004 with two goals in the final.

■

HORSESHOE PITCHING Chapter - 27

English peasants were playing both horseshoes and quoits and would later export both games to North America.

History

The history of horseshoe pitching can be traced back to Roman soldiers. During their idle hours, the soldiers occupied themselves with games that consisted of tossing metal rings over stakes pounded into the ground. Whether these first metal rings were actually horseshoes is a matter of some debate.

There's no doubt that the games of horseshoes and quoits are closely related. A quoit is a metal disk with a hole in the middle that may at one time have been a weapon.

Either way, we know that quoits was being played in England in the 14th Century, much to the chagrin of the English rulers who felt the games distracted men from military training, particularly archery. The game was outlawed in 1388. By the 16th century, English peasants were playing both horseshoes and quoits and would later export both games to North America.

Early tournaments had no rule regarding the weight, size or even shape of the horseshoe. A competitor in a 1911 tournament used a shoe that was four inches longer on one side. When the Grand League of American Horseshoe Pitchers Association (now that's a name) formed in 1919, it determined that a competition horseshoe should weigh between two pounds and two pounds, two ounces. Today's competition shoes can weigh up to two pounds, 10 ounces.

In 1919, a second governing body for horseshoe pitching was formed. The National League of Horseshoe and Quoit Pitchers (NLHPQ) merged with the GLAHPA in 1921. The new organization wisely shortened its acronym to the NHPA—the National Horseshoe Pitchers Association.

Over the years, the distance between the pegs and the scoring of horseshoes have changed slightly. The stakes in men's competition are now 40 feet apart. Women's courts have 30 feet between the stakes. In terms of scoring, ringers are now worth three points, a learner (a shoe touching the stake) or a shoe that comes to rest with any part six inches or closer to the stake counts one point. The last major rule change in horseshoes was instituted in 1982. It determined that games would be played to 40 points.

Men's world champion titles have been awarded since 1909. A women's world championship tournament was started in 1920. Today, championships are also awarded in boys', girls' and senior divisions.

Horsehoe Courts

Indoor pitching: When indoor courts are constructed, the height of pitching boxes shall not be over six (6) inches above floor level. Ceiling height shall be at least twelve (12) feet.

Layout of courts: A court shall consist of two pitchers' boxes with a stake in the center of each and shall cover a level area overall of ten (10) feet width and fifty (50) feet in length.

Pitchers' box: The pitchers' box shall be six (6) feet square, with stake in the exact center.

The stake area of the pitchers' box shall be filled to a depth of six (6) to ten (10) inches with potter's clay or substitute of like nature and kept in a moist and puttylike condition in the stake area.

Stake Distance: The distance shall be forty (40) feet between stakes, measured from the pitcher's platform level, from the center of each stake.

Foul lines surrounding the pitcher's box shall be clearly defined.

When a number of courts are constructed as required in tournament play, the stakes shall be a minimum of ten (10) feet apart between courts and front pitching box foul lines shall preserve a straight line across the entire layout. Construction should be made to permit north-south pitching.

A.H.P.A. Horseshoe Court Layout

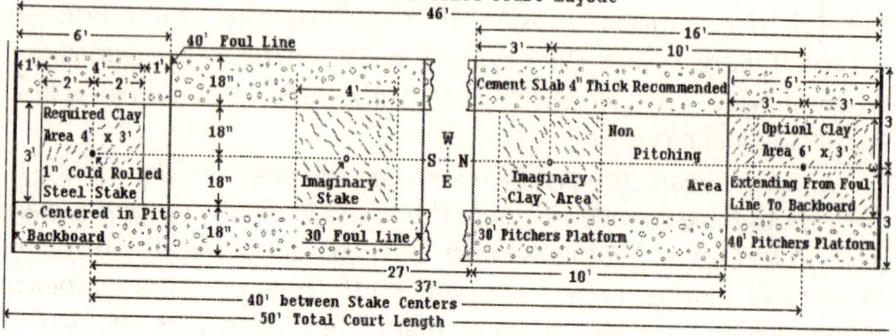

Pitching distance for women, juniors, senior men and handicapped persons shall be a minimum 30 feet with a foul line 27 feet from the stake. When women, juniors, short distance men and handicapped persons play on a court constructed for 40-foot pitchers, foul lines shall be marked 10 feet in front of the 40-foot foul lines with an imaginary stake marked three (3) feet behind the 30-foot foul line.

The pitcher's platform shall consist of an area: The maximum distance to the right or left of the stake or imaginary stake is three (3) feet. The minimum distance right or left of the stake or imaginary stake is eighteen (18) inches. The maximum distance in front of the stake or imaginary stake is three (3) feet.

Horseshoe Equipment

Stakes: The stakes shall be of cold rolled steel, one (1) inch in diameter, and shall extend no shorter than fourteen (14) inches and no higher than fifteen (15) inches above the clay surface with a three (3) inch incline toward the opposite stake.

Official Shoe: A shoe shall not exceed 7 1/4 inches in width, 7 5/8 inches in length, and shall not weigh less than 2 lb. 4 oz. and not more than 2 lb. 10 oz.. On a parallel line 3/4 of an inch from a straight edge touching the points of the open end of a shoe, the opening shall not exceed 3 1/2 inches. A 1/8 inch tolerance to 3 5/8 inches is allowed on used shoes.

Score Board Diagram

110 points to be used as a base of 50 shoes, 90% of the difference between actual score and 110. Three games or 150 shoes to be used to establish handicap. EXAMPLE: A player has 240 actual points for his three games, an average of 80 actual points per game, 110 minus 80 actual, equals 30, 90% of 30 being 27 handicap 80 actual plus 27

handicap a total of 107 with handicap. Round totals when calculating averages and handicaps. EXAMPLE: If pitcher's average is between 79.50 and 79.99 round their average up (80). If the average is between 79.01 and 79.49 round their average down (79). Handicap points to be used in full, starting with first round.

Handicap Points

AVG-HC	AVG-HC	AVG-HC	AVG-HC	AVG-HC	AVG-HC	AVG-HC
110-0	94-14	78-29	62-43	46-58	30-72	
109-1	93-15	77-30	61-44	45-59	29-73	14-86
108-2	92-16	76-31	60-45	44-59	28-74	13-87
107-3	91-17	75-32	59-46	43-60	27-75	12-88
106-4	90-18	74-32	58-47	42-61	26-76	11-89
105-5	89-19	73-33	57-48	41-62	25-77	10-90
104-5	88-20	72-34	56-49	40-63	24-77	9-91
103-6	87-21	71-35	55-50	39-64	23-78	8-92
102-7	86-22	70-36	54-50	38-65	22-79	7-93
101-8	85-23	69-37	53-51	37-66	21-80	6-94
100-9	84-23	68-38	52-52	36-67	20-81	5-95
99-10	83-24	67-39	51-53	35-68	19-82	4-95
98-11	82-25	66-40	50-54	34-68	18-83	3-96
97-12	81-26	65-41	49-55	33-69	17-84	2-97
96-13	80-27	64-41	48-56	32-70	16-85	1-98
95-14	79-28	63-42	47-57	31-71	15-86	

A master sheet is made by each State Secretary or Statistician, each player's record of games pitched, actual points, average and handicaps must be recorded, and kept up-to-date.

Playing Rules

Games can be played on Singles, Doubles and Team basis.

A regulation game consists of the pitching of fifty (50) shoes in all contests.

Choice of Pitch: Choice of first pitch shall be determined by the toss of a coin or shoe.

In successive games between the same players, the loser shall have choice.

First pitch alternates, as it evens up advantage of pitching against iron.

In delivering the shoe the pitcher must stand within the pitcher's platform.

A player, when not pitching, must remain on the opposite side of the stake to the player in action and to the rear of the pitcher's platform.

No contestant shall walk to the opposite stake or be informed of the position of shoes prior to the completion of an inning.

Broken Shoes: When a shoe lands in fair territory, and is broken in separate parts, it shall be removed and the contestant allowed to pitch another shoe in its place.

All fair shoes will be counted where they lay, even though they may have been hit by a foul or a fair shoe.

Foul Lines: Any shoe delivered while the pitcher's foot extends on or over the raised foul line shall be declared foul and removed from counting distance.

In delivering a shoe, the pitcher must remain behind the foul line until the shoe has left their hand.

A foul shoe shall not be scored or credited except in the score sheet column headed "shoes pitched".

Foul Shoes: A shoe pitched while the contestant stands beyond the box foul line limits. A shoe striking outside the opposite pitching box or on the hard surface area when courts are so constructed.

Foul shoes will be removed from the pitcher's box.

A shoe must be pitched over if it hits the tent or any foreign object. (Providing it is less than 12 feet high.)

Measurements: Measurements to determine points scored shall be made with official device and straight edge.

Conduct of player and members—No contestant, while opponent is in pitching position, shall make any remark or utter any sounds within the hearing of opponent, nor make any movement that does or might interfere with the opponent's playing.

Penalty: Both shoes of the offender shall be declared foul in the inning complained of.

Any member of the American Horseshoe Pitchers Association of America who indulges in heckling or unfair rooting against a pitcher in a tournament or league play, whether with malicious intent or otherwise, shall be expelled from the grounds and from the American Association.

Any player repeatedly violating rules or guilty of unsportsmanlike conduct may be barred from further participation in the contest. 1st offense—warning, 2nd offense—disqualified.

Winner of games, and final tournament standing is governed by most total points.

Names to Remember

Alan Francis : He won 10 world horseshoe pitching titles including the 2004 World Championship.

Ted Allen: He also won 10 world horseshoe pitching championships. His last win was in 1958.

Vicki Winston: She is the only woman who has won 10 women's world championship . Her last competition participation was in 1981.

Sue Snyder : With a win of 2004 championship her tally of world championship went upto 5.

Luralanhan: This remarkable sports woman won 6 world championship by the year 1928.

■

ICE HOCKEY

Chapter - 28

In 1879 Ice Hockey rules were formulated by Robertson and Smith of McGill University, Montreal.

History

Ice Hockey is played on a rectangular sheet of mechanically frozen or natural ice. A team consists of six players and the game is played with sticks and a rubber puck. Due to the fast speed of the game substitution becomes necessary and generally a team consists of 11 to 18 players.

The game was invented in Canada in the 2nd century. It could have originated from a game played by the Englishmen in Kingston Harbour at Ontario in 1860. They used a puck which is a total deviation from a ball to play the game. Most of these Ice Hockey pioneers were Crimean war veterans from a regiment of the Royal Canadian Rifles.

In 1879 W.F. Robertson and R.F. Smith of Mc Gill University, Montreal, formulated the first set of rules and regulations for the game to be played with nine players on each side. The first recognised team, formed in 1880, was called the McGill University Hockey Club. By 1893, about 100 clubs were established in Montreal alone. In 1893, the game was first played in the USA at Yale University. The famous Stanley Cup was also introduced during this year. The US Amateur Hockey League was founded in New York City in 1960.

It was during the Great Freeze of 1895 that the two future Kings, King Edward VII and King George V, were members of the Palace team in a match against Lord Stanley's side which included five Stanley brothers. The first five team competitions were held in England in 1903. And the UK won the first European championship in 1910 at Las Avanta in the Swiss Alps. The International Ice Hockey Federation was formed in 1908.

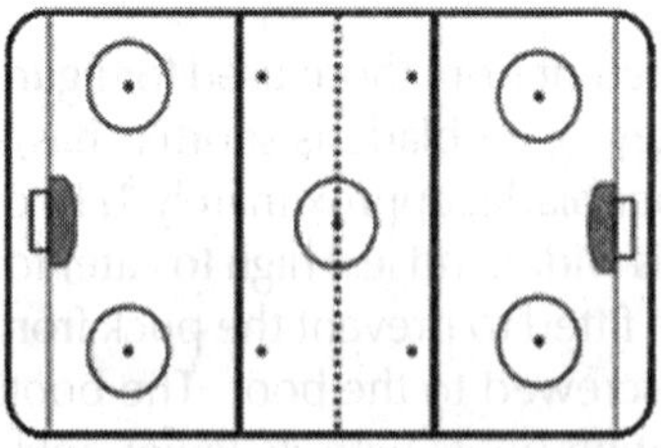

Ice Hockey Rink

Goals

The goals consist of posts, cross bar and net. Posts and cross bar and the external surface of the supports are painted red. The interior support must be painted white. The measurements (interior) of the goal must be: height 1.22 m, width 1.83 m and depth 0.6-1 m at the deepest point.

Equipments

Sticks: Ice Hockey sticks are made of wood without notches or projections. Sticks are of 1.35 m handle and 37 cm) blade. The goalkeeper may have a wider and heavier stick. Sticks are generally not made of one standard. They are made to a player's individual specifications and made in different lines (the angle between the blade and the handle varies). The length is considered correct, if the top of the shaft just touches the player's chin when the stick is held upright with the blade touching the ice. Black friction tape wound round the length of the blade increases the stick's durability. A knob of tape round the top of shaft allows a firmer grip in the gloved hand.

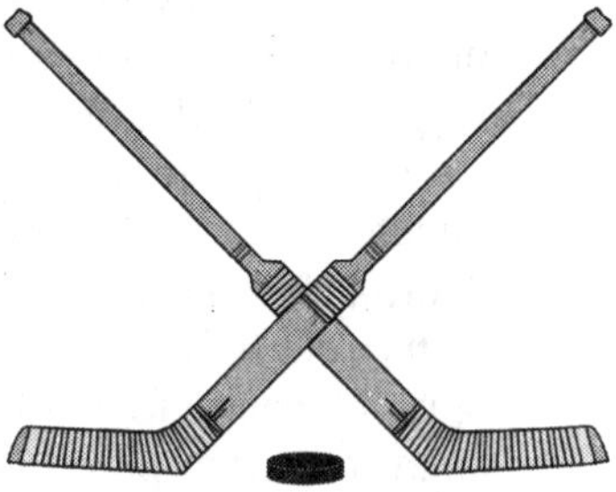

Puck: The puck or disc-shaped

object is used in the game due to its suitability on the ice. This is made of vulcanised rubber 7.6 cm in diameter and 2.5 cm thick. Before the match, it should be frozen to minimise its resilience.

Skates: Ice Hockey skates are different from those used for figure skating and speed skating. Ice Hockey skate blade is shorter, has a plain pointed end in front and a thinner blade, approximately 1/16 of an inch wide. The goalkeeper's skate is wider and less high to cater for easy balance.Extra stanchions are also fitted to prevent the puck from passing under the boot. The skate is screwed to the boot. The boots are also different from the figure skating boots with its lower ankle support.The materials used are calf or nubuck. The boot should fit correctly over one pair of woollen socks.

Clothing: Specialised clothing is used for this sport. All players wear knee pads, shin guards, elbow pads, shoulder guards, thick gauntlet-type gloves, long stockings that fit over the knee pad, a special type of shorts and sweaters in team colours. Helmets are optional but generally used to minimise head injuries. Apart from these, the goalkeepers use large leather leg guards, a chest protector and padded gloves.

Rules of Ice Hockey

1. Only six players are allowed on the ice rink at one time, i.e., a goalkeeper, two defenders and three forwards.
2. It is not obligatory to keep the goal minder throughout the game. During the final second half all six players may move up for all-out effort to score.
3. A game is divided into three periods of 20 minutes each. Between three playing periods there are two intervals of 15 minutes duration. During intervals ice is surfaced.
4. **Starting:** Play is commenced by a face off. The puck is dropped by the referee in the centre of the rink between the sticks of opposite centre forwards. They must stand one stick length apart. No other player is allowed within 4.5 m of the two face off players.

5. The puck stays in play whenever or wherever it hits the barrier boards including behind the goal.
6. The puck becomes dead only when it is hit over the barrier or when the whistle is blown for an infringement.
7. A goal is scored when the whole of the puck passes over the goal line between the goal posts.
8. A goal is not allowed if an attacker throws the puck in the goal or if an attacking player is in the goal crease when the puck passes over the goal line.
9. Goal judges stand behind each goal and indicate a goal by switching on an overhead red light.
10. A shut-out occurs when a goalkeeper concedes no goal during the match or during the 20 minutes period.
11. A player may stop the puck with hands, body or skates at any time and in any position. But he cannot hold the puck with his hand for more than three seconds.
12. Two blue lines divide the area into three zones—defence, neutral and attacking zone. Only three players may be in their own defence zone when the puck is outside that zone.
13. A player may enter the attacking zone only in line with or behind the puck or puck carrier.
14. To decide off side, the position of the player's skates is the determining factor.
15. The time taken for penalty shot is not included in the regular playing time.
16. After the failure of a penalty shot a goal cannot be scored from a rebound.
17. Players are penalised for infringements of the rules by being sent off for 2, 2, 10 minutes. A player can even be suspended for the rest of the game.

18. If a goalkeeper is penalised for misconduct, he is not required to leave the rink but a team member is withdrawn instead. However, a match penalty against a goalkeeper has to be served by himself and his place in the goal will be taken by another player.

Championships

National Hockey League: The National Hockey League of North America is Ice Hockey's major professional competition between clubs in the USA and Canada. Inaugurated at Montreal in November 1917, the first seasonal championship was won by Toronto Arenas in 1918. From 1943, the League settled to a regular contest among big six teams. The Champion wins the Prince of Wales Trophy.

World Championship: This was first held in 1920, for conjunction with the Olympic Games which were also considered as World Championship till 1968. From 1977, World Championships have been open to professionals.

Stanley Cup: The Stanley Cup was instituted in 1893, by Lord Stanley of Preston, then Governor-General of Canada. This is a permanent senior trophy which has become the most famous prize of Ice Hockey.

Allan Cup: Allan Cup in Canada is regarded as the chief trophy for non professional teams. First won in 1908 by Ottawa Cliffsides.

European Championship: Started in 1910, the UK won the first championship.

Olympics: Ice Hockey was included in the Antwerp Winter Olympics in 1920.

Names to Remember

Mattias Öhlund : (born September 9, 1976, in Piteå, Sweden): He is a professional Swedish defenceman with the Vancouver Canucks in NHL. Öhlund has represented his home country of Sweden at virtually every level of international play. He has played for Swedeen three times for the World Championship, once for the World Cup, and three times at the Olympics. He was a part of the Swedish Olympic Men's Ice Hockey team that won gold in the 2006 Turin Winter Olympics.

Nicklas Erik Lidström : (born April 28, 1970, in Västerås, Sweden): He is a Swedish professional ice hockey defenceman. Lidstrom is by many considered the top NHL defenseman of the 21st century, having won the Norris Trophy as the NHL's best defenseman in three consecutive seasons from 2000-01 to 2002-03 and again in 2005-06. He has been nominated for the award a total of seven times throughout his career. As of 2006, Lidstrom has played all of his thirteen NHL seasons for the Detroit Red Wings. He was a member of three Stanley Cup winning teams in 1996-97, 1997-98, and 2001-02

Christian Bäckman (born April 28, 1980 in Alingsås, Sweden): He is a Swedish professional ice hockey defenceman with St. Louis Blues in the National Hockey League. Since 2003-04 he has been a regular for St. Louis recording 37 points goals, 25 assists), and 64 penalty minutes in 121 games. During season 2005-06 Bäckman led St. Louis with an average of 24 minutes, 48 seconds of ice time per game.

Kenny Jönsson (in North America often called Kenny Jonsson, born October 6, 1974 in Ängelholm): He is a Swedish ice hockey player playing for Rögle BK in the Swedish tier two league HockeyAllsvenskan. He was voted Best Defender of the Tournament at the 2006 Winter Olympics where Sweden won the gold medal.

■

ICE SKATING

Chapter - 29

A graceful sporting event on Ice.

History

The story of Skating can be found in Scandinavian Literature. And it has been clearly established that in Holland also Skating used to be practised. But the most intcresting part of the history belongs to St. Lydwina of Schiedom who in 1396, broke a rib while skating at the age of 16. She died in 1433, and subsequently became the patron saint of the Skaters. The first skating club was formed in England in 1742, and 1772, the first instructional book on skating was writen and published by Captain Roberts Jones. The London Skating club was founded in 1842. The first all iron skate which was clipped to the boot was invented in 1850, by Bushnell of Philadelphia. By the end of 19th century a number of skating rinks came up in many cities including Melbourne and Johannesburg. International Skating Union (ISU) was formed in 1892, at Schweringer, Holland. ISU stardardized regulations in figure skating, speed skating and dancing on ice.

Types of Skates and Boots

Skates and Boots for Speed Skating: Speed skating skates are comparably longer than figure skating skates. The blades are as thin as 1/32 in (0.794 mm) reinforced with steel tubing for lightness and Strength. These are usually 12 to 18 in long and designed to travel in a straight line. The boots for speed skating are lighter in weight than those for figure skating. These are made of thin leather and have longer heel supports.

Skates and Boots for Figure Skating: The skate blade for figure skating is very slightly curved from heel to toe and is usually set on a 7 ft (2.13 m) radius. The underpart of the blade is not flat but has a hollow ridge right along the centre. The sides of the hollow ridge are called the edges of the skate. The blade is about 1/8 in wide and slightly longer than the length of the boot. Men use black leather boots whereas women use boots of white suede or nubuck. The boots have strong support reinforced with a stiffening material around the heel and under the arch which prevents the foot from slipping to the side. Boots should not be larger but must fit tightly.

Speed Skating

Speed skating is always performed in open air. International championship meets are normally of two days duration. On the first day 500 m and 5000 m events are held and on the second day 1500 m and 10000 m.The best allround performer over these four distances, calculated on point basis, is declared the overall champion. Ice speed skating record holders are the fastest self-propelled human beings over land. They can exceed 30 kmph.

Speed Skating

Figure Skating

In senior championships, solo competitors are required to skate three specific ice skating figures, followed by a short programme of prescribed free skating elements and finally a freestyle performance accompanied by music lasting five minutes for men and four minutes for women. Pair skaters perform a series of prescribed free skating movements followed by a selfdevised freestyle performance. Out of the 41 figures officially recognised by the ISO, there are some best known.

Figure Skating

Each figure skates three times. When a skater completes a figure the judges examine the pattern left by the skates. A bulge in a circle or a flattening of the skate or an improper change from one blade edge can be counted against the competitor. The position of hand, fingers and non-skating foot are also taken into consideration. Points upto six are awarded for each figure. These marks are subsequently multiplied by a factor of one and six according to the recognised standard of the figure.

Free Skating

Free skating is the climax of the competition. In this type of skating, intricate footwork is combined with jumps and spins, which are spaced between spirals and linking steps. Some of the jumps are explained as:

1. **Three-Jump:** This comprises a half turn in mid-air, taking off from the forward outside edge of one skate and landing back on the outside edge of the other.

2. **Loop Jump:** This requires a full revolution in the air.

3. **Spread Eagle Jump**: A spread eagle jump is a two-footed glide in which the feet are positioned in line with each other, heels together and toes pointing outwards. Two turns frequently used are the "bracket", a half turn from one edge to the opposite edge of the same skate, with the body turning inside the circle, and the "counter", a half turn maintaining the same edge.

4. **Flip Jump:** This is a toe jump, and involves a take off from the back outside edge of the skating blade and rotating in mid air before landing.

5. **Axel:** This is a jump involving one and a half turns in the air named after its originator Axel Paulsen, a figure and speed skater from Norway.

6. **The Lutz:** This is a jump in which the skater takes off from the back outside edge, helped by the toe point of the free foot rotating in mid air clockwise before landing on the back outside edge of the original foot.

7. **The Salchow:** This is a jump named after its originator.

8. **The Split Jump:** This is a toe jump in which the skater takes off from a back inside edge, half turns in mid air while swinging the legs up into a horizontal position and closes them before landing.

Some of the spins are explained below:

1. Single flat-foot spin is performed on the flat of the skate.

2. Sit spin starts as a standing spin. The skater immediately sinks on his knees with free leg extending in front.

3. Camel spin is a one foot spin holding the body and the non-skating leg in a horizontal position parallel to the ice.

4. Lay back spin is another one foot spin where the body is bent backwards, spinning parallel to the ice.

5. Cross foot spin is performed on the flat of both skate blades, with the legs in crossed position, toes together and heels apart.

6. Flying sit spin and flying camel, a jump variation of the camel spin.

In ice figure skating competition, the compulsory figures comprise 40 per cent of the total marks. In the prescribed free skating movements another 20 per cent and the skater freestyle performance comprises the remaining 40 per cent.

Pair Skating

Pair skating is divided into compulsory and freestyle sections. In the compulsory section, the pair is required to demonstrate six specified sequences. In the freestyle section, the two partners must perform movements giving a homogeneous impression and must fill the rink during a display. The following are the best known pair skating movements:

Pair Skating

1. **Death Spiral:** The man swings his partner at a great speed.

2. **The Single Lane Lift:** The woman is lifted overhead in an outside forward take off.

3. **The Axel Lift:** The woman is turned one and a half times completely over her partner's head.

4. **The Split Lutz Lift:** The woman is lifted from an outside back edge.

5. **The Catch Waist Camel Spin:** This is performed with the free leg pointing in the opposite direction.

Ice Dancing

There is a great difference between pair skating and ice dancing. In ice dancing lifts are not permitted. Free dancing consists of a non-repetitive performance of novel movements. Certain free skating movements which are in keeping with the character of the dances are allowed. However, the following limitations are imposed on the pair:

Ice Dancing

1. Separation of partners must not exceed the time necessary to change position.
2. Pivots must not exceed in duration.
3. Spins must not exceed one and a half revolution.
4. Maintenance of one position should not be prolonged.

A few movements of ice dancing are explained below:

(a) **The Chasse**: This is a sequence in which the free foot, during the process of becoming the skating foot, should not pass the original skating foot.

(b) **Choctaw:** A turn from forward to backward or vice versa.

(c) **Mohawk**: A half turn from forward to backward or *vice versa*.

(d) **Twizzle:** A rotation through a complete revolution performed rapidly to take place on one spot.

(e) **European Waltz:** This is the most popular of all the ice dances.

(*f*) **Fourteen-Step Dance:** The fourteen-step dance with a lively military style tempo is also popular.

(g) **American Waltz:** A series of half circles or lobes are skated along each side of the rink and joined at the ends by six best outside edges. Apart from the above, Foxtrot, Popular Blues, Argentine Tango, Rocker Foxtrot, Rumba Silver Samba, Vieanese Waltz, West Waltz and Starlight Waltz are also popular and pleasing to the eye.

Championships are in two phases—Compulsory dances and Freestyle, each carrying half of the total marks.

Championships

First world championship in figure skating was held in 1896, at St. Petersburg. First women's world championship was held at Davos (Switzerland). First world pair skating championship was held in 1908, at St. Petersburg. First world ice dancing championship was held in Paris in 1952. First international speed-skating competition. was held in Hamburg (Germany) in 1885.

Olympics: Men's speed skating was included in 1924, in Chamonix, France and women's speed skating gained Olympic status in 1960, at Squaw Valley, California. The Ice-figure skating for men, women and pairs was included in the 1908, London Olympics.

Names to Remember

Captain Robert Jones: He wrote the first book on skating in 1772, which was published in London.

Axel Paulsen (Norway): A figure and speed skater from Norway. He was the originator of the Axel jump.

Ulrich Salchow (1877-1949): Ice figure skater from Sweden and originator of the Salchow jump. He was the first man to win the Olympic figure skating gold medal in 1908. He was also ten times world champion, from 1901 to 1911 except 1906, and nine times European title holder.

Brian Orsen (Canada): A former world champion in figure skating, he was Olympic runner up in 1980, and a silver medallist in the 1984 Olympics. He was beaten by Brian Boitano of the USA to the top place.

Jin Sun-Yu (born December 17, 1988 in Daegu, South Korea): She is a Korean short-track speed skater. She was the winner of the gold medal in the 1500 meters and the silver medal in the 1000 meters at the 2005 World Championships, as she ended up as the overall champion. At the 2006 World Championships, Jin won the 100C, 1500, and 3000 meters on her way to a second consecutive overall championship. She also finished first in the overall World Cup standings for the 2005-2006 season.

At the 2006 Winter Olympics, she won three gold medals, winning women's individual 1000 meters, and 1500 meters events, and as a member of the South Korean women's victorious 3000 meter relay team. In doing so, Jin became the first athlete (by less than half an hour) from Korea to win three gold medals in one Olympics. Ahn

Hyun-Soo matched Jin's achievement later by helping Korea to win men's 5000 meters relay.

Ahn Hyun-Soo (born November 23, 1985 in Seoul): He is a Short track speed skating athlete from South Korea and is a three-time gold-medalist in the Winter Olympics. Ahn has won four Olympic medals in his career; he is one of only two Koreans to ever win three medals in one Olympics, and is the first Korean man to win at least three. Ahn is the first five-time world champion, having won five consecutive overall titles from 2003 to 2007.

Evgeni Viktorovich Plushenko, or Yevgeny Viktorovich Plyushchenko (b. November 3, 1982 in Solnechny, Khabarovsk Krai, Soviet Union, Russia): Evgeni is a Russian figure skater, the seven-time National Champion, five-time European Champion, three-time World Champion, 2006 Winter Olympics gold medalist, and four-time Grand Prix Final gold medalist.

Shizuka Arakawa (born December 29, 1981): She is a Japanese figure skater who won the gold medal at the 2006 Winter Olympics in the Ladies Singles event in Turin, Italy on February 23, 2006, and the 2004 World Figure Skating Championship. She is the first female skater who was born in Asia to win the Olympic gold medal in figure skating. She is the second oldest woman to win the Olympic figure skating gold (Yahoo, 2006 and NBC Olympics, 2006).

Tatiana Totmianina : (born November 2, 1981): In Perm, Russia, Tatiana is a pairs figure skater and Olympic Champion. Tatiana Totmianina and her skating partner Maxim Marinin began skating together in 1997. Both began their careers as singles skaters, and they were always noted for their superb single elements. Coached by 1984 Olympic Pairs Champion Oleg Vasiliev, Totmianina and Marinin made consistent progress on the world scene through the late 90's. They won their first major title at the 2002 European Championships, and went on to finish 4th at the 2002 Winter Olympics in Salt Lake City.

■

JUDO

Chapter - 30

An unarmed form of combat, Judo was developed by Dr. Kano in Japan.

History

Judo a form of martial art means the "easy way" in Japanese. Dr. Kano may be named as the pioneer to bring judo to the modern world in the late 19th century. He developed the art from the ancient schools of Jujutsu. Kano came to Britain in 1885, to spread judo in the Western world. One of his outstanding pupils Yamashita began teaching judo in the USA in 1902. By 1905, judo had reached France where it was first taught to the Paris police. Later in Europe Koizumi founded the Bondukwai in London in 1918, which helped to spread popularity of the martial art. The International Judo Federation was founded in 1951.

Judo Grading

Judo grades are divided as follows:

		Japan	*Others*
1.	5th Kyu	White belt	Yellow belt
2.	4th Kyu	White belt	Orange belt
3.	3rd Kyu	Brown belt	Green belt
4.	2nd Kyu	Brown belt	Blue belt
5.	1st Kyu	Brown belt	Brown belt
6.	1st Dan	Black belt	
7.	2nd Dan	Black belt	
8.	3rd-5th Dan	Black belt	
9.	6th-8th Dan	Red and White be	
10.	9th-11th Dan	Red belt	
11.	12th Dan	White belt	

Note: "Kyu" means pupil and "Dan" means degree.

Fighting ability and technical knowledge advances a judoka (participant) to 5th Dan. After this, advancement depends upon service to the sport and not on to fight. Theoretically advancement to 13th Dan is possible but the highest grade ever awarded so far was 10th Dan by Kodokan.

Judo is played by both men and women. The weight categories for both are as follows:

Men

1. Extra Lightweight	Upto and including 60 kg
2. Half Lightweight	Over 60 kg upto and including 65 kg
3. Lightweight	Over 65 kg upto and including 71 kg
4. Half Middleweight	Over 71 kg upto and including 78 kg
5. Middleweight	Over 78 kg upto and including 86 kg
6. Half Heavyweight	Over 86 kg upto and including 95 kg
7. Heavyweight	Over 95 kg
8. Open Category	No weight limit

Women

1. Extra Lightweight	Upto and including 48 kg
2. Half Lightweight	Over 48 kg upto and including 52 kg
3. Lightweight	Over 52 kg upto and including 56 kg
4. Half Middleweight	Over 56 kg upto and including 61 kg
5. Middleweight	Over 61 kg upto and including 66 kg
6. Half Heavyweight	Over 66 kg upto and including 72 kg
7. Heavyweight	Over 72 kg
8. Open Category	No weight limit

All judokas wear the judogi (judo suit) which is a loose suit held together at the waist. The feet are left bare.

Judo consists mainly of close fighting done in the form of throws, falls, deadlocks, etc.—some of the throws and the bow.

Shiai (contests) are conducted by a referee and two judges. The referee follows the bout 6 to 8 ft from the judokas like a boxing referee. Japanese terminology used by a referee is as follows:

1. Hajime	Begin
2. Matte	Wait

3. Sonomama	Do not move
4. Yoshi	Carry on
5. Jikan	Time out
6. Mantei	Request for decision from judges by the referee
7. Sore Made	That's all

The contest duration is five minutes for men and "men under 21" and four minutes for women. The contest can end any time if one of the contestants scores ippon or equivalent.

Scoring

An "ippon" (point) is scored when a competitor is hurled on to his back with some force. When the throw is less definite and the competitor has not landed on his back a "wazari" (7 points as against 10 for one ippon) is granted.

Competitors may also gain points by a "wazari" in "chikai waza" (5 points) or a kinsa (3 points).

The penalties are as follows:

1. Shido	3 points	note
2. Chui	5 points	caution
3. Keikoku	7 points	warning
4. Hansoku-Make	10 points	disqualification

The competition mat "tatomi" is 9 × 9 square m.

There is a periphery of one metre onto which a fighter may be thrown provided his opponent has started the movement inside the mat area.

The winner is the one who has scored most knock downs. If none has scored then the one who had been more aggressive wins. In hold downs, a competitor must trap at least one arm and hold the opponent for 30 seconds and 25 seconds for a wazari.

Championships

Many championships are held for judo at various levels. The important ones are as follows:-

1. Japan National Championships started in 1930.
2. European Championship started in 1951, in London's Royal Albert Hall.
3. World Championships (every two years) inaugurated in Tokyo in 1956.

4. Olympic Games from the 1964 Tokyo Olympics onwards.
5. Women's World championships were first held in New York.

Names to Remember

Tadahiro Nomura (born December 10, 1974 in Nara, Japan): He is one of the most famous Judo competitors in Japan. He won Gold medals in 60 Kg clas in Atlanta 1996, Sydney 2000 and Athens 2004.

Masae Ueno is a Japanese athlete who competed in the Athens 2004 Olympics. Masae Ueno was born January 17, 1979. She earned Japan's fifth Olympic Gold Medal in ten events, taking the 70kg women's judo event.

Ryoko Tani (Born September 6, 1975) is one of the most famous female Judo competitors in Japan. She has a record six world titles and she brought home the 48kg-category gold medal from Sydney Olympics in 2000 and the Athens Olympics in 2004. Tani has been very popular in Japan.

Masato Uchishiba: Masato is a Japanese judoka who won the gold medal in the men's under 66 kg division at the 2004 Olympics in Athens, Greece.

■

KABADDI

Chapter - 31

A popular no implement game of India.

History

Kabaddi had been one of the most ancient forms of outdoor sports in India. Kabaddi is popularly known as "Hututu" (Maharashtra and Madhya Pradesh), "Chadu-Gudu" (Tamil Nadu and Karnataka), "Bhadi bhadi" (Kathiawad and Kutch), "Wandikali" (Kerala), "Zabar-Gagane" (Punjab), "Do-do" (Bengal). The game was not played in the organised form until 1923, when rules were framed in Baroda. The rules were again amended in 1931, and they were implemented in 1934.

The Hanuman Vyayam Prasarak Mandal, Amravati, gave a demonstration of kabaddi in the Berlin Olympic Games in 1936. Kabaddi as a national game in the India got recognition in 1938, at Calcutta.

It was selected as a demonstration game in the 1982 Asiad in Delhi and as a medal event in the 1990 Beijing Asian Games.

No Equipment Game

It is one of the few games where no equipment is needed. The team winning the toss has a choice of raid or court. When a team sends a player into the opponents' court, he is called a raider and the opponents are called antiraiders or antis. The raider before crossing the centre line should begin to say loudly "kabaddi" which is known as cant. He has to repeat the same rapidly without taking breath until the raid is complete.

While in the opponents' court, the raider tries to touch one or more antis before retreating. If the raider touches the antis, they are declared out. The raider is out if he loses his "cant" while still in the enemy court or if he does not cross the baulk line during the raid.

Kabaddi Court

A diagram of the kabaddi court is shown below :

For men below 57 kg of weight it shall be 12.5 × 10 m divided by a middle line into two halves. For women it shall be 11 × 8 m divided by a middle line into two halves. The side lobby should be 1 m in width. The baulk line shall be drawn at a distance of 3.25 m for men and 2.25 m for women.

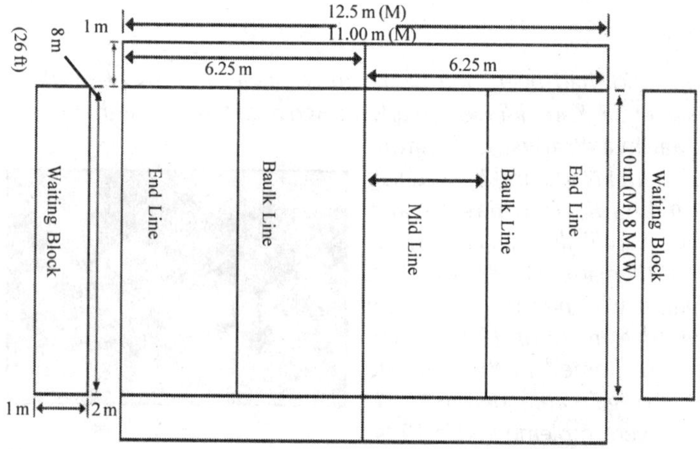

Kabaddi Court

Kabaddi Rules

1. The antis cannot resort to unfair means such as trying to still the raider's cant by shutting his mouth or wilfully pushing him over the boundary line.

2. A raider is not compelled to touch an anti. If he returns without touching anybody, neither side loses a player.

3. As long as a raider is in the court of the antis, none of them can touch the ground of the raider's court. If he does so, he will be out.

4. A player re-enters when an opponent is out.

5. **Scoring:** A team scores one point for each player put out by them. A bonus of two points if they put out the entire opposition (Lona) when only one or two players of a team are left during the game and the captain of the team declares them out in order to bring in the full team, the opponents shall score as many points as there were players just before declaring as well as two points for Lona.

6. When a raid is in progress all the antis must remain within their own court. If an anti goes over the boundary line or steps into the other half, he is out.

7. The raiders'captain or team mates cannot shout advice when their raider is away.

8. **Duration.** Two halves of 20 minutes for men and 15 minutes for women and juniors. Between two halves 5 minutes' rest is allowed. In the event of a tie an extra ten minutes, 2 periods of 5 minutes each are allowed. Should it be a deadlock again, the side scoring the first point wins the game. If there is no score at the end of the complete game of 50 minutes for men and men players below 57 kg and 40 minutes for women then the team which has won the toss before the match shall be declared the winner.

9. **Time-out:** Time-out may be called by the captain of the team in the event of an injury to a player. Time-out period should not exceed two minutes.

Officials

The officials consist of a referee, two umpires, a scorer and two assistant scorers.

1. Referee: The referee has the power to warn, declare point against or disqualify a player from the match. He may also overrule the decision of the umpire.

2. Umpire: Generally the decision of the umpire shall be final.

3. Scorer: The scorer is to fill in the score sheet, keep and note the timings, time-outs. Record team scoring first point in the first game.

4. Assistant Scorers: They keep record of those who are out. They also keep record of those who are revived.

■

KARATE

Chapter - 32

Okinawa in Japan is the birth place of Karate. In Karate, all the body parts are used as weapons.

History

Okinawa in Japan may be considered as the place of birth of karate. An early form of karate evolved during the 15th century. At first the new technique became known as Tang Hand to indicate its Chinese origin. During 1922 Funokoshi Gichin, an Okinawan, first introduced Tang Hand or Okenawa to Japan and incorporated certain aspects of Jujutsu which finally acquired the name karate. Michin wrote: As a mirror polished surface reflects whatever stands before it, so must the student of karate render his mind empty of selfishness and wickedness in an effort to react appropriately towards anything he might encounter. This is the meaning of Kara in karate. Karate ensures a state of mental calm and to facilitate maximum explosiveness. In karate the whole of the body and in particular all the body parts are used as weapons. An experienced karateka can utilise even a single finger as a highly specialised weapon."

Following Gichin's arrival in Japan other styles of karate were also developed. Each style places different emphasis on speed and power. Mabuni founded Shitoryu style, Mujagi established Goju style, Otsuka founded Wadoryu (way of peace), and Shukukai (way for all) was founded by Tani and Kyokushinkai (the peak of truth) by Oyama. Each group practised secretly and respective katas were closely guarded secrets. This group rivalry was the main cause of disunity within karate. In order to unify these various groups and with the Government backing

the Federation of All Japan Karate Organisation was formed and most of the schools were affiliated to it. FAJKO organised the first multi-style World Karate Championship in 1970, in Tokyo.

Dress

The dress for karate is known as karatege; it consists of loose white trousers and jacket. The jacket is fastened by a coloured belt indicating the grade of the karateka. Sweat band or Hichimaki may be worn around the head.

Different Forms of Karate

Jiu-Kumite: Jiu-Kumite or freestyle fighting 'contests are between two individuals irrespective of grade. Team contests are of a series of individual contests. Each team normally consists of five karatekas. The contest is controlled by one referee who is assisted by four judges. Each judge has a red flag, a white flag and a whistle. A controller is posted outside the area.

All technical terms in karate are in Japanese. They are as follows:

1.	Rei	Bow
2.	Hajime	Begin
3.	Yoi	Ready
4.	Yame	Stop
5.	Seremade	Stop (when time is up)
6.	Hantei	Decision
7.	Ippon	Full point
8.	Wazari	Half point
9.	Yjogi	Outside the area
10.	Hanteigachi	Win by decision
11.	Honsukumake	Loss by disqualification
12.	Hikiwake	Draw

In jiu-kumite attacks are stopped just before contact. Test of proficiency is also judged by the ability to stop fully focussed attack just short of contact. In "most cases to strike an opponent would result in disqualification. Only contact blow is permitted in sweeping the opponent's leg to knock him to the ground. This form of karate is the most popular and originated in Japan.

Two teams take up their position on opposite sides of the contest area which is 8 m to 10m square. The centre is marked with a cross. Initial distance between the contestants is 2 m.

Kata Training Dance: Kata is a fixed sequence of basic defence and attacking techniques designed for practice and takes the form of imaginary fighting with several attackers approaching from different directions. There are approximately 30 different katas.

Tamashiwara (Wood Breaking): This is showmanship and has got controversial reception among karatekas. However, Tamashiwara includes breaking a stack of twenty roofing tiles or three or four one inch boards with hand, foot, elbow or head. Other demonstrations may include throwing a water melon in the air and thrusting the finger through it as it descends or chopping off the top of a bottle with the bare hand while leaving the bottle standing.

Kihon: Kihon is the basic training in numerous blocks, strikes and kicks with special emphasis on correct stance, balance, breathing and focus. Kihon may be practised individually or in group.When practised in group it is normally accompanied by semi-hypnotic chanting from a leader who controls the timing and effort involved.

Different Grades

The order of belts in ascending order is given below:

1. 6th Kyu	Red belt
2. 5th Kyu	Yellow belt
3. 4th Kyu	Orange belt
4. 3rd Kyu	Green belt
5. 2nd Kyu	Blue belt
6. 1st Kyu	Brown belt

Dan or black belts are as follows:

1. 1st Dan	Shodan
2. 2nd Dan	Nidan
3. 3rd Dan	Sandan
4. 4th Dan 5. 5th Dan	Senior experts Renshl grade
6. 6th, 7th and 8th Dans	Kyoshi grade high masters

7. Some styles also have 9th and 10th Dans.

Dans with the 8th grade are entitled to be called Sheehan (honourable processor) and they wear solid red belt, but in most cases they continue to wear a black belt.

Contest and Scoring

A karate contest consists of free exchange of blocks, counter blocks, and blows till such time when one player receives a full blow

to anyone of the numbered defined areas on his opponent's body. If the blow has been delivered correctly an ippon (full point) will be awarded and the contest will be over.

If both contestants score simultaneously, that will cancel each other's point.

If a half point is gained, the contest will continue till such time when one player scores a full point or two half points.

Other means of determining a contest are as follows:

1. Hanteigachi (win by decision)
2. Hansokumake (loss by disqualification)
3. Hikiwake (draw)

Competitions

Karate has become an international sport, and the world championship, first organised in 1970, is held regularly.

Names to Remember

Chojun Miyagi (1888-1953): The Okinawan karate expert who founded go-ju style of karate.

Masatoshi Nakayama (1913-): Japanese karateka trained under Gichin. He was appointed chief instructor to the Japan Karate Association in 1955, and was awarded his 8th Dan black belt in 1961.

Tetsuo Suzuki (UK, b. 29 April, 1928): He is a 8th Dan of Wodo-ryu style. He is the chief instructor of the European Karate to Wadoki.

Funakoshi Gichin (1870-1957): Karate exponent from Okinawa. He combined Okinawan hand fighting with Japanese Ju-Jutsu and renamed it as karate. He is the founder of Shotokai style of karate.

Kenwa Mabuni (1880-1950): Mabuni arrived in Japan in 1930, from Okinawa and founded the Shitoryu style of karate.

Keinosuke Enocda (8th Dan, Shotokai style):He is the resident instructor of the Karate Union in the UK.

■

KHO KHO

Chapter - 33

A no implement Indian game played by nine players in each team.

History

The game of Kho-Kho has been extremely popular in all the Marathi-speaking areas. For many years this game used to be played in an informal manner. In 1919, the Deccan *Gymkhana club of Poona tried to formalise the game and helped to increase its popularity. The first edition of rules, of Atyapatya Kho-Kho and Hu-Tu-Tu, was published in 1935, by the newly founded Akhil Maharashtra Shareerika Shikshan Mandal. Some amendments of the rules have been made thereafter to suite the playing conditions.*

Kho-Kho Field

Diagram of a kho-kho field is given on the next page.

The overall dimension of the kho-kho court is 31 mtr × 16 mtr.

Note: The strong wooden posts are fixed at point *M* and *N*. The height above the ground is 120 cm with a circumference between 30 and 40 cm.

Rules of Kho Kho

This is a no-implement game. The rules of the game are:

1. **Duration:** (a) Each side consists of 9 players.

(b) An innings will consist of chasing and running turns which will be of seven minutes duration. Each match will consist of two innings.

(c) An interval of 5 minutes is allowed after an inning and 2 minutes between two turns.

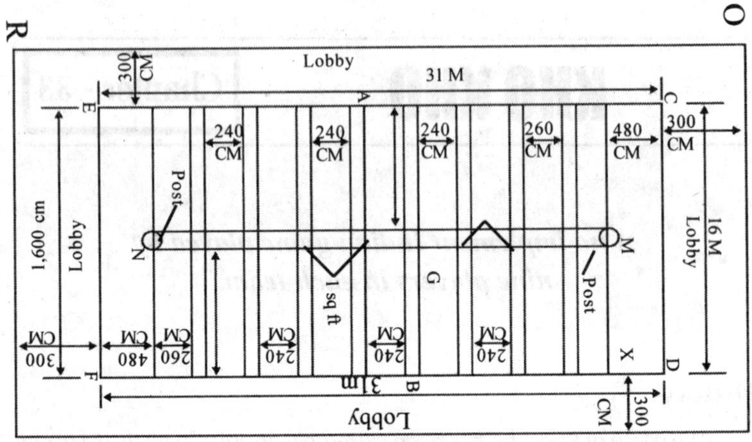

Kho Kho Court

2. The side of the chasers scores one point for putting out each runner.

3. The chaser or runner has the option to end the turn before the expiry of the allotted time.

4. The captain of the toss winning team will have the choice of chasing or running.

5. At the commencement of the game the eight chasers (players sitting in the squares) will sit in the squares facing opposite directions. No adjacent chasers should face in the same direction. The 9th chaser will stand at either of the posts.

6. The runners will fix their entry serially with the scorer.

7. At the commencement of the game three runners are to get inside the court. As soon as a runner is put out the next three runners must enter the field before "kho" is given. If a runner fails to enter the field, he is given out.

8. A runner goes out by the following means:

(a) If touched by a chaser.

(b) Fails to enter the field when a runner is given out.

(c) If he touches the seated chasers twice or after receiving a warning for similar infringement.

9. Rules for the chasers: (a) "Kho" is to be given from behind a sitting chaser and loudly.

(b) The seated chaser shall not get up without getting "kho".
(c) An active chaser shall not recede to give "kho".
(d) An active chaser shall sit down immediately after giving "kho".
(e) After getting "kho" the sitting chaser becomes active and follows the direction he is facing.
(*l*) An active chaser is not to cross the centre line.
(g) He is to take the direction that he has initially taken to the *M* or *N* posts.
(h) When an active chaser leaves a post, he shall go in the direction of other post remaining on the side of the centre line which he was facing before leaving the post.
(i) Chasers are not to obstruct runners while being seated.
(j) The face (shoulder line) of an active chaser must be in a direction he has taken. He shall not turn his face. He is only allowed to turn his face parallel to the centre line.
(k) If a foul is committed by an active chaser he will be directed to go in the opposite direction of his chaser as indicated by the umpire and if a runner is put out by this act he will not be given out.
(l) When an active chaser lets go his hold of the post or goes beyond the rectangles he is known as leaving the post.

Scoring

The side of the chasers scores 1 point for putting out each runner. If one team scores 9 points more than the other team, the winning team may ask the losers to chase without losing their option to chase afterwards.

A substitute shall be allowed to replace an injured player at the discretion of the referee.

Game Officials

Two Umpires: They supervise the game in their respective halves, divided by the centre line. A foul is indicated by continuous short whistles till the foul is corrected. An "out" is declared by a short whistle.

Referee: The referee helps the umpires and gives the final decision in case of any difference between them.

Time-keeper: He keeps the record of time and hands it over to the scorer at the end of an innings. He starts the turn by blowing a whistle: one long and one short. The end of the turn is indicated by a long whistle.

Scorer: Keeps a record of runners who are out and makes them sit.

Assistant Scorer: He helps the scorer.

■

LAWN TENNIS

Chapter - 34

Wimbledon men's championship was instituted in 1877. In 1884, the women's championship was also included.

History

Originating in England and France, Lawn Tennis was initially an aristocratic pursuit. Slowly and gradually it evolved into a worthwhile physical diversion for the middle class English men. By the time of Queen Victoria's reign, (1837-1901), it became one of the most popular games in England. Instituted in 1877, the All England Tennis Championship or Wimbledon is still the most prestigious individual championship. In course of time its popularity spread to other parts of globe. In 1887, the US Lawn Tennis Association was formed in New York.

Tennis Court

Diagram of a tennis court is given below:

There are four main types of tennis court surface:

1. **Grass:** This was the surface on which the game originated and Wimbledon, the only grand slam tournament played on grass, is rated the best today. It demands considerable time, skill and money to maintain but produces the best stroke play and players with patience, accuracy and endurance as well as techniques.

2. **Clay:** The next best to grass courts. These are made of beaten or rolled earth with gravel to bind it. Paris and Rome have the best clay courts of the world. This is a slow surface.

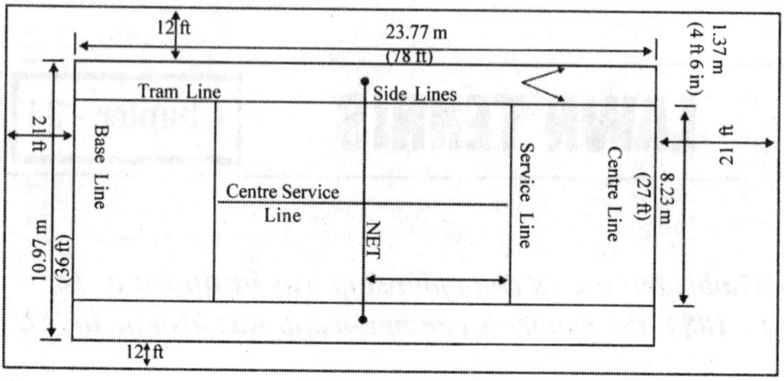

Lawn tennis court

3. **Cement:.** Also termed hard courts, these produce the service and volley game and players with speed, strength, and sharp reflexes. California in the USA has the best such surfaces.

4. **Synthetic:** Synthetic surfaces are also being used in greater numbers.

Dress

Men wear shirts and shorts. Women wear tops with skirts or short dresses. The players also wear white rubber-soled shoes. For all top class matches, the dress has to be in accordance with the dress code as specified by the International Tennis Federation.

The Net

The height of the net at the post is 3 ft 6 in and at the centre 3 ft. The net extends 3 ft outside the centre of the doubles sidelines. The side limits of the singles court may be indicated at the net by vertical sticks.

The Racket

1. The rackets are generally 32 in long and 12½ in wide. Maximum strung hitting surface is 15½ in long and 11½ inch wide.The rackets are made of wood and metal. But the best rackets nowadays are made of graphite and their size is bigger than those of the normal rackets.

2. Sheep-gut, beef-gut, natural-gut, hog-gut, and nylon-gut are used for the string. Sheep-gut has the greatest elasticity, but is the most expensive. In graphite racket, nylon-gut is used.

The Ball

The ball must have a uniform outer surface (usually 70 per cent wool and 30 per cent nylon) with stitchless seams and when dropped from a height of 100 in onto a concrete base, must bounce to more than 53 in but less than 58 in.

Diameter: More than 2½ in (6.35 cm) but less than 2 5/8 in (6.67 cm).

Weight: More than 2 oz (56.7 gm) but less than 21/16 oz (58.5 gm).

The *basic strokes* which a player should know are:

(a) Service
(b) Forehand drive
(c) Backhand drive
(d) Volley
(e) Smash
(f) Lob
(g) Drop shot.

The Game Set and Match

1. The service line is 21 ft from the net. The right half is called the "forehand court" and the left half the "backhand court". The service area remains constant for singles and doubles play. Maximum of two services are allowed, and a "double fault" costs the server 1 point. The ball is served overhand from the baseline diagonally across the net, 3 ft high at the centre and 3 ft 6 in high at the side posts. A service which the opponent cannot touch is called an "ace".

2. After the service, the receiver must return the ball on its first bounce. If it lands in the opposite court then shots are exchanged till the point is won by either of the players. This is called a rally. If a service touches the net and lands in the correct area a "let" or re-service is awarded to the server without any penalty.

3. The volley is a shot taken without any bounce on the ground at a height not more than shoulder level and a smash is hit from above the head with the arm fully stretched.

4. The game may be won by winning four points.The odd system is based on using the face of a clock to record points in the royal days of tennis. The term for zero is "love", a corruption of French 'l' ocuf' (the egg) and is thus also related to "duck" in cricket. A game in which

one of the players could not score any points is called "love-game" and accordingly a "love-set".

5. The score is given with the server's score being given first. If both the opponents win 3 points and a situation of 40-all is reached then it is called "deuce" from the French *deux* meaning "two more to win". Whenever one of them wins one point it is called "advantage" for that player and he wins the game on winning the next point. If, however, the opponent player wins the second point then it is again a "deuce".

6. The minimum number of games for a set is 6 and a lead of one was a must till the beginning of the seventies. Thereafter, the International Lawn Tennis Federation allowed a limited number of points to be played at 6-6 (6 games to each player) to settle the set. This is what is called a "tiebreak" (except in the third or fifth game).

7. The following system shall be used in a tie-break game.

(a) **Singles:** A player who first wins seven points shall win the game and the set provided he leads by a margin of two points. If the score reaches six points all the game shall be extended until this margin has been achieved. Numerical scoring shall be used throughout the tie-break game. The player whose turn it is to serve shall be the server for the first point from the right court. His opponent shall be the server for the second and third points starting from the left court, and thereafter each player shall serve alternately for two consecutive points until the winner of the game and set has been decided. When the total points become six or multiple of six, the player shall change the ends.

(b) **Doubles:** In doubles the procedure for singles shall apply. The player whose turn it is to serve shall be the server for the first point. Thereafter each player shall serve in rotation for two points.

Officials

Top class matches use the following umpires:

1. One chair umpire who shall sit on a 8 ft high chair, having a writing platform on a side. This chair will be located 4 ft away from the net post.

2. Full complements of line umpires shall be as under:

(a) Two for base lines
(b) Two for service lines
(c) Two for centre service lines
(d) Two for far side lines
(e) Two for near side lines
(*f*) One for net cord
(g) One for foot-fault (optional)
(Total: 12)

Note: For ordinary/unofficial games, the number may vary depending upon availability of line umpires.

Championships

Australian Open: The Australian Tennis Association was formed in 1904 though tennis started in this country around 1880. The women's championship started in 1923.

French Open: French national clay court championship started in 1891. But it was not open to other nations till 1925.

Wimbledon: Men's Wimbledon championships started as early as 1877 whereas the women's championships were instituted in 1884.

The US Open: The first American championship of national interest was held in 1880, at the States Island Cricket and Baseball Club. The US Open was later shifted from Forest Hills to its present venue at Flushing Meadow.

WCT Masters' (Grand Prix Masters') Championship. This tennis championship was first staged at Tokyo in 1971. It is held now in New York annually from 1977. Qualification to participate in this event is by relative successes in the preceding year's Grand Prix tournaments.

Wightman Cup: The Cup was donated by Mrs Hazal Hotchkins, US Women's Champion in 1909, 1910, 1911 and 1919, and was inaugurated in 1923. This is an annual lawn tennis competition between women players of USA and Britain.

Federation Cup: Women's Davis Cup equivalent started in 1963, and is played annually during the spring.

King's Cup: The Cup was instituted by King Gustav of Sweden in 1936. This is a competition between European nations in indoor courts.

Olympic Tennis: Tennis was a part of the Olympics till 1924. It was a demonstration sport in Mexico Olympics in 1968, and Los Angeles Olympics, in 1984. It was first included as a medal event in the 1988 Olympic Games at Seoul (South Korea). Maximum number of gold and other medals have been won in Olympics by Max Docugis (France). He won four golds, one silver and one bronze in 1900, 1906 and 1920.

Davis Cup: A gift from a leading American player Dwight F. Davis, instituted in 1900. The competition is organised by the Davis Cup National Committee. Davis Cup has been played every year except in 1901 and 1910.The men's international championships have been won by the USA 28 times.

Names to Remember

Margaret Smith (Margaret Court) (1942-):The first Australian woman to win the Wimbledon and the second woman to achieve Grand Slam. She won Australian Open from 1960 to 1966; Wimbledon in 1963, 1965 and 1970; Forest Hills 1962, 1965, 1969, 1970, 1973; French Open in 1962, 1964, 1969, 1970 and 1973. She married Barry Court. She remained undefeated in Italy from 1962 to 1966.

Billie Jean King (1943-): American tennis player from California. She won her first Wimbledon title at the age of 17 along with Karen Hantze, another American. She has created an all time world record by winning 20 Wimbledon titles. She won Wimbledon in 1966, 1967, 1968, 1972 and 1973; Forest Hills in 1967, 1971, 1972; French Open in 1972; Australian Open in 1970. At the age of 30, she was challenged by Riggs, the men's Wimbledon Champion of 1939 at Houston in 1973. She defeated Riggs easily. She married Larry King, a Californian lawyer, in 1965.

Ivan Lendl (b. 7 March 1960): A Czechoslovak player and world No.1 consecutively for four years from 1985 to 1988. He came to the USA at the age of 20. He first won French Open in 1984, and first Grand Slam title in 1985. He won French Open twice, US Open twice and WCT Championship twice. Even as a junior he was one of the most outstanding players because in 1978 he won Orange Bowl (Italy), French, US and Wimbledon junior championships.

Rodney George Laver (1938-): All time great Australian lawn tennis player who achieved Grand Slam both as an amateur and as professional. From 1959 to 1970, he almost dominated lawn tennis. During this period he won all the great titles as an amateur and professional.

Jimmy Connors (1953-): Lawn tennis player from the USA. Connors was world No.1 for 159 weeks between 29 July, 1974, to 16 August 1977. He won Wimbledon twice, US Open five times and

Australian Open once. He was in seven finals during 1986-87. Still at the age of 35 in 1988, he was ranked world No. 4. He won so far a total of 105 singles titles.

John Albert Krammer (1921-): One of the most effective post-war lawn tennis champions from America, Jack Krammer was the leader and organiser of the professional circuit for several years. He fought a long and primarily lonely battle with ILTF over Open championship and finally, in 1968, ILTF accepted Open championship. He became one of the game's best known TV commentators.

Ramesh Krishnan (India, b.5 June, 1961): Son of Ramanathan Krishnan, Ramesh was the world's best junior tennis player in 1979. He won French and Wimbledon junior crowns. He reached upto the quarter final of US Open in 1987.

Pancho Gonzales (1928-): American lawn tennis player who turned professional in 1949, after winning US Open for the second successive year. He was considered the most competent player of all times. At the age of 40, he reached semi-finals of the French Open and in 1969, beat Charlie Pasarrell (USA) in a match lasting 5 hours 20 minutes.

Vijay Amritraj (India, b.14 December, 1953): In 1985, at the Wimbledon he reached the last 16. In 1984, he won his first GP tournament defeating Tim Mayotte followed by a stunning victory over John McEnroe. He acted in James Bond film *Octopussy* with Roger Moore. He was former team captain of India's Davis Cup. Currently, he is President of the Association of Tennis Professionals (ATP).

Chris Evert Lloyd (USA, b. 21 December, 1954): Coached by her father and Dennis Ralston. Married John Lloyd on 17 April, 1979. She won the following championships:

Singles:

French Open	1974, 1975, 1979, 1980, 1983 and 1985
Wimbledon	1974, 1976 and 1981
US Open	1975, 1976, 1977, 1978, 1980 and 1982
Australian Open	1982 and 1984
Italian Open	1974, 1975, 1980, 1981 and 1982
Grand Slam	1977 and 1978
US Indoors	1978

Doubles:

Wimbledon	1976 with Navratilova
French	1974 and 1975
Italian Open	1974 and 1975

Martina Navratilova (USA). (Prague, b.18 October, 1956): After leading Czechoslovakia to victory in the Federation Cup in 1975, she defected to the USA that autumn and became an American citizen in 1981. She first became world No.1 in 1980. Combined 1982-1983 results are — 176 wins; 4 defeats and 31 tournament victories out of 35 she played. In 1984, won 78 out of 80 matches. She won a record 74 consecutive matches to eclipse Evert Lloyd's 55. She won a bonus $1 million from ITF for achieving a modern GS in 1983-84. She won six successive GS singles titles in 1983-84 and with Pam Shriver (USA) won eight successive GS tournament doubles and 109 successive matches in all events from April 1983 to July 1985.

Martina Navratilova

Bjorn Borg (Sweden, 6 June, 1956): One of the coolest players the game has ever known. He won his first Italian Open in 1974, shortly before his 18th birthday and won the French Open shortly after that. Between 1974 and 1981, he won the French Open-1974, 1975, 1978,1979,1980 and 1981. He won the Italian Open in 1974 and 1978. He created a record by winning Wimbledon five times from 1976 to 1980. Four times he was beaten in the US Open final twice by Connors in 1978 and 1979, and twice by McEnroe in 1980 and 1981. This great champion felt burnt out and retired from the mainstream restricting his play to exhibitions and special events. His errorless style, counter attacking top spin inspired a whole generation of players around the world.

Leander Adrian Paes (born June 17, 1973): Leander is currently one of the most successful professional Indian tennis players on the men's doubles and mixed doubles circuits. Most recently, partnering with Martin Damm he won 2006 US Open Men's Doubles championship in September 2006. Leander Paes was born in Goa and brought up in Kolkata (then Calcutta). His mother, Jennifer Paes, was a renowned basketball player and captain of the Indian team in the

1980 Asian Basketball Championships. His father, Vece Paes, was a hockey midfielder representing the Indian team in the 1972 Munich Olympics that won the bronze medal.

He joined the Britannia Tennis Academy in Madras (now known as Chennai) in 1985 where he was coached by Dave O'Meara. Leander shot into international fame when he won the 1990 Wimbledon Junior and 1991 U.S. Open titles and rose to No.1 in the junior world-rankings.

He turned professional in 1991 and in 1996 won a bronze medal at the Atlanta Olympics becoming the first Indian in more than 4 decades to win an individual medal. The previous individual medalist for India was K.D. Jadhav who won a bronze in 1952.

He was ranked number 1 in doubles along with his partner Mahesh Bhupathi. He was a joint winner of India's highest sporting honour, the Rajiv Gandhi Khel Ratna award in the year 1996-1997 along with Nameirakpam Kunjarani. In 2001, he was awarded the Padma Shri.

■

LACROSSE

Chapter - 35

The game is a combination of basketball, soccer and hockey. Anyone can play lacrosse--the big or the small.

History

Lacrosse is the oldest sport in North America. Rooted in Native American religion, lacrosse was often played to resolve conflicts, heal the sick, and develop strong, virile men. To Native Americans, lacrosse is still referred to as "The Creator's Game."

The evolution of the Native American game into modern lacrosse began in 1636 when Jean de Brebeuf, a Jesuit missionary, documented a Huron contest in what is now southeast Ontario, Canada. At that time, some type of lacrosse was played by at least 48 Native American tribes scattered throughout what is now southern Canada and all parts of the United States. French pioneers began playing the game avidly in the 1800s. Canadian dentist W. George Beers standardized the game in 1867 with the adoption of set field dimensions, limits to the number of players per team and other basic rules.

New York University fielded the nation's first college team in 1877. The first women's lacrosse game was played in 1890 at the St. Leonard's School in Scotland. Although an attempt was made to start women's lacrosse at Sweet Briar College in Virginia in 1914, it was not until 1926 that Miss Rosabelle Sinclair established the first women's lacrosse team in the United States at the Bryn Mawr School in Baltimore, Maryland.

Men's and women's lacrosse were played under virtually the same rules, with no protective equipment, until the mid-1930s. At that time, men's lacrosse began evolving dramatically, while women's lacrosse continued to remain true to the game's original rules. Men's and women's lacrosse remain derivations of the same game today, but are played under different rules. Women's rules limit stick contact, prohibit body contact and, therefore, require little protective equipment. Men's lacrosse rules allow some degree of stick and body contact, although violence is neither condoned nor allowed.

Field lacrosse is sometimes perceived to be a violent and dangerous game, however, injury statistics prove otherwise.

The object of a lacrosse game is to put a 5 oz. hard-rubber ball to the opponent's net using a long-handled stick with a triangular pocket at the end – while keeping one's opponent from doing the same. A lacrosse team has 10 positions, which includes: one goalie, three attackmen, three midfielders, and three defensemen.

The game is a combination of basketball, soccer and hockey. Anyone can play lacrosse--the big or the small. The game requires and rewards coordination and agility. Quickness and speed are two highly prized qualities in lacrosse. Lacrosse is played with a stick, the crosse, which must be mastered by the player to throw, catch and scoop the ball.

Face-off Lacrosse

Lacrosse is one of the fastest growing team sports in the United States. There are more than 500 college club programs, the majority of which compete under the umbrella of US Lacrosse and its "intercollegiate associates" level.

Men's Lacrosse Positions

Attack: The attackman's responsibility is to score goals. The attackman generally restricts his play to the offensive end of the field. Each team should have three attackmen on the field during play.

Midfield: The midfielder's responsibility is to cover the entire field, playing both offense and defense. The midfielder is often called upon to clear the ball from defense to offense. Speed and stamina are essential. Each team should have three midfielders on the field.

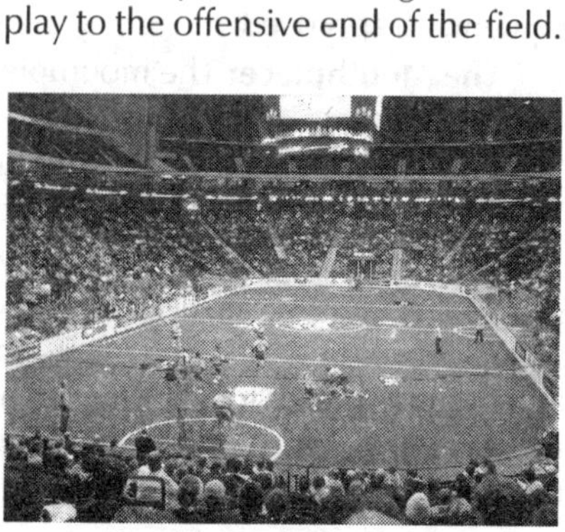

Swarm Lacrosse Ground

Defense: The defenseman's responsibility is to defend the goal. The defenseman generally restricts his play to the defensive end of the field. Each team should have three defensemen on the field.

Goal: The goalie's responsibility is to protect the goal and stop the opposing team from scoring. Each team has one goalie in the goal during play.

Lacrosse Equipment

The Crosse:

- The crosse (lacrosse stick) is made of wood, laminated wood or synthetic material, with a shaped net pocket at the end. The crosse must be an overall length of 40 – 42 inches for attackmen and midfielders, or 52 – 72 inches for defensemen.
- The head of the crosse must be 6.5 – 10 inches wide, except a goalie's crosse which may be 10 – 12 inches wide.
- The pocket of a crosse shall be deemed illegal if the top surface of a lacrosse ball, when placed in the head of the crosse, is below the bottom edge of the side wall.

The Ball: The ball is made of solid rubber and can be yellow, white, or orange. The ball is 7.75 – 8 inches in circumference and 5-5.25 ounces.

The Helmet: A protective helmet, equipped with face mask, chin pad and a cupped four-point chin strap fastened to all four hookups, must be worn by all men's players. All helmets and face masks must be NOCSAE (National Operating Committee on Standards for Athletic Equipment) approved.

The Mouthpiece: The mouthpiece must be a highly visible color and is mandatory.

The Glove: All players are required to wear protective gloves. The cutting or altering of gloves is prohibited.

Protective Equipment: All players, with the exception of the goalkeeper, must wear shoulder pads. Arm pads and rib pads are also strongly recommended and often required, as are athletic supporters and protective cups for all players. The goalkeeper is required to wear a throat protector and chest protector, in addition to a helmet, mouthpiece and gloves.

Rules of Lacross

Men's lacrosse is a contact game. The object of the game is to shoot the ball into the opponent's goal. The team scoring the most goals wins.

Each team must keep at least four players, including the goalie, in its defensive half of the field and three in its offensive half. Three players (midfielders) may roam the entire field.

Lacrosse

Men's lacrosse begins with a face-off. The ball is placed between the sticks of two squatting players at the center of the field. The official blows the whistle to begin play. Each face-off player tries to control the ball. The players in the wing areas can run after the ball when the whistle sounds. The other players must wait until one player has gained possession of the ball, or the ball has crossed a goal area line, before they can release.

Center face-offs are also used at the start of each quarter and after a goal is scored. Field players must use their crosses to pass, catch and run with the ball. Only the goalkeeper may touch the ball with his hands. A player may gain possession of the ball by dislodging it from an opponent's crosse with a stick check. A stick check is the controlled poking and slapping of the stick and gloved hands of the player in possession of the ball.

Behind Lacrosse

If the ball or a player in possession of the ball goes out of bounds, the other team is awarded possession. If the ball goes out of bounds after an unsuccessful shot, the player nearest to the ball when and where it goes out of bounds is awarded possession.

An attacking player cannot enter the crease around the goal, but may reach in with his stick to scoop a loose ball.

Officials

A referee, umpire and field judge supervise field play. A chief bench official, timekeepers and scorers assist.

Duration of the Game

Collegiate games are 60 minutes long, with 15-minute quarters. Generally, high school games are 48 minutes long, with 12-minute quarters. Likewise, youth games are 32 minutes long, with eight-minute quarters. Each team is given a two-minute break between the first and second quarters, and the third and fourth quarters. Halftime is ten minutes long.

Teams change sides between periods. Each team is permitted two timeouts each half. The team winning the coin toss chooses the end of the field it wants to defend first.

Lacrosse Personal & Technical Fouls

There are personal fouls and technical fouls in boys' lacrosse. The penalty for a personal foul results in a one to three-minute suspension from play and possession to the team that was fouled. Players with five personal fouls are ejected from the game. The penalty for a technical foul is a thirty-second suspension if a team is in possession of the ball when the foul is committed, or possession of the ball to the team that was fouled if there was no possession when the foul was committed.

Personal Fouls

Slashing: Occurs when a player's stick viciously contacts an opponent in any area other than the stick or gloved hand on the stick.

Tripping: Occurs when a player obstructs his opponent at or below the waist with the crosse, hands, arms, feet or legs.

Cross Checking: Occurs when a player uses the handle of his crosse between his hands to make contact with an opponent.

Unsportsmanlike Conduct: Occurs when any player or coach commits an act which is considered unsportsmanlike by an official, including taunting, arguing, or obscene language or gestures.

Unnecessary Roughness: Occurs when a player strikes an opponent with his stick or body using excessive or violent force.

Illegal Crosse: Occurs when a player uses a crosse that does not conform to required specifications. A crosse may be found illegal if the pocket is too deep or if any other part of the crosse was altered to gain an advantage.

Illegal Body Checking: Occurs when any of the following actions takes place:

a. body checking an opponent who is not in possession of the ball or within five yards of a loose ball.

b. avoidable body check of an opponent after he has passed or shot the ball;

c. body checking an opponent from the rear or at or below the waist; and

d. body checking an opponent above the shoulders. A body check must be below the shoulders and above the waist, and both hands of the player applying the body check must remain in contact with his crosse.

Illegal Gloves: Occurs when a player uses gloves that do not conform to required specifications. A glove will be found illegal if the fingers and palms are cut out of the gloves, or if the glove has been altered in a way that compromises its protective features.

Technical Fouls

Holding: Occurs when a player impedes the movement of an opponent or an opponent's crosse.

Interference: Occurs when a player interferes in any manner with the free movement of an opponent, except when that opponent has possession of the ball, the ball is in flight and within five yards of the player, or both players are within five yards of a loose ball.

Offsides: Occurs when a team does not have at least four players on its defensive side of the midfield line or at least three players on its offensive side of the midfield line.

Pushing: Occurs when a player thrusts or shoves a player from behind.

Screening: Occurs when an offensive player moves into and makes contact with a defensive player with the purpose of blocking him from the man he is defending.

Stalling: Occurs when a team intentionally holds the ball, without conducting normal offensive play, with the intent of running time off the clock.

Warding Off: Occurs when a player in possession of the ball uses his free hand or arm to hold, push or control the direction of an opponent's stick check.

Lacrosse Skills

Catching: The act of receiving a passed ball with the crosse.

Checking: The act of attempting to dislodge the ball from an opponent's stick.

Poke Check: A stick check in which the player pokes the head of his stick at an opponent's stick through the top hand by pushing with the bottom hand.

Slap Check: A stick check in which a player slaps the head of his stick against his opponent's stick.

Wrap Check: A one-handed check in which the defender swings his stick around his opponent's body to dislodge the ball. (This check is only legal at the highest level of play.)

Cradling: The coordinated motion of the arms and wrists that keeps the ball secure in the pocket and ready to be passed or shot when running.

Cutting: A movement by an offensive player without the ball, toward the opponent's goal, in anticipation of a feed and shot.

Womens' Lacrosse

Feeding: Passing the ball to a teammate who is in position for a shot on goal.

Passing: The act of throwing the ball to a teammate with the crosse.

Scooping: The act of picking up a loose ball with the crosse.

Screening: An offensive tactic in which a player near the crease positions himself so as to block the goalkeeper's view of the ball.

Shooting: The act of throwing the ball with the crosse toward the goal in an attempt to score.

■

MOTORCYCLE RACING

Chapter - 36

It is a sport that tests the speed, skill, endurance etc., of the competitor. The machines are classified into different groups.

History

The initial motorcycle races were completely unspecialized. Motorcycle racing began in Europe with events in which both cars and motorcycles participated, racing between two cities on ordinary roads. But the inter-city races were abandoned after the Paris-Madrid race disaster that took place in 1903. The Auto Club of France organised the close circuit race exclusively for motorcycles. This event was also undisciplined. However, the race for international cup held in France in the year 1905, was much more orderly. But in 1906, the International Cup Series came to an end due to a general boycott. In 1907, the famous banked oval circuit was opened at Brooklands, UK, and racing was held regularly at this place till the outbreak of the Second World War. In 1907, the first Tourist Trophy race in the Isle of Man was inaugurated but restricted to shorter lap. In 1911, the Tourist Trophy Race (TTR) was revised to include the full length circuit.

The Federation Internationale Motorcycliste (FIM) is an international body responsible for the regulation of the sport. Delegates from affiliated nations and clubs are appointed to this body. The body in turn is responsible for monitoring activities of many motorcycling clubs.

The term of the license of a beginner is limited to the events restricted to members of his own club. After gaining some experience, he may be given a national license to permit participation in national level races and finally a rider may apply for international license which will allow him to participate in international races.

Distances

Motorcycle races are held on roads and on specially built tracks. The distances may vary in each case. The oldest motorcycle racing circuit is the mountain course over which the Isle of Man Tourist Trophy races are held. Each lap measures 60.6 km (37 ¾ miles).

Belgium circuit is composed of ordinary roads with a distance covering only 14.5 km (9 miles) at Francer Champs near Spain.

The circuit at Assen, where the Dutch Grand Prix is held, is composed of both private and public roads and covers a distance of 7.6 km (4 ¾ miles).

Among the artificially built tracks where the major international races are held, the 5.6 km(3 ½ mile) circuit at Monza near Milan and the track at Daytina, Florida, USA, are famous. At Florida, American Motorcycle Association organises a 324 km (200 miles) race every year.

Motorcycle Classes

Races are held in the following classes:

1. Upto 60 cc
2. Upto 110 cc
3. Above 110 upto 160 cc — Scooters
4. Above 160 upto 185 cc
5. Upto 60 cc
6. Above 60 cc upto 80 cc
7. Above 80 cc upto 110 cc
8. Above 110 cc upto 185 cc
9. Above 185 cc upto 265 cc
10. Above 265 cc upto 360 cc

11. Above 360 cc upto 750 cc
12. Above 750 cc upto 1111 cc. Motor bulbs

The Machine

Engine: There is no limit on engine design other than capacity limit. (Does not apply to production motorcycle and class and US dirt track racing.)

Clutch and Brake Levers: They must have an integral ball-end of at least ¾ inch diameter.

Brakes: Brakes must be fitted on both wheels.

Tyres: The tyres must be fitted to a rim of at least 16-inch diameter. There is no restriction on the type of tyre but must conform to specification for each class.

Handle Bars: The width is not less than 20 inches. Stops must be fitted to ensure a minimum clearance of 1¼ inch between the handle

bars and the tank to avoid trapping the rider's hand. If stream lining is fitted, there must be at least 2 clearance between it and any part of the handle bar.

The Seat: The height of the seat above the track 35½ inches.

Guard: Chain guard must be fitted.

Foot Rests: Foot rests must be fixed and riders are to keep their feet on the rest and will be penalised for any violation.

Exhaust Pipe: This must not project behind the machine. Exhaust gases must not foul the tyre/brakes or raise dust waste or oil must not be discharged on the track. They must not project behind the machine.

Oil Drain Plugs: This plug must be tightly locked in position.

Petrol: Petrol should be of standard grade as supplied from normal commercial pumps.

Dress

1. Calflength boots or ankle boots, leggings on proper protective coverings for the legs and feet must be worn.
2. Leather, cord or other tough material trousers or breeches should be worn.
3. A reasonably close fitting sleeved jacket of leather, cord or similar tough material must be worn.
4. Full leather gloves must be worn.
5. Splinter proof goggles or visors of a non-inflammable material must be worn.

Start

Starting positions are arranged by means of a grid system. Positions are allocated by the organisers according to the riders' known capability or according to the timing in the heats. Pole position i.e., position at the front of the grid on the inside of the track, is allocated to the fastest rider.

Types of Start

The start is signalled by the lowering of a flag.

1. **Clutch Start:** The riders line up on the grid with their motors running. Shortly before the lowering of the flag the first gear is engaged and the machine is held on the clutch. On dropping of the flag the clutch is released.

2. **Bump Start:** The riders begin to push their machines and when the flag drops they jump on as the engine starts.

3. **Le Mans Starts**: The rider runs to his machine parked on the opposite side of the track. They are to mount, kick, start and move.

4. **Rolling Start:** Machines are started on the move. They set off for a warm up lap and at the completion of the lap the flag is dropped to indicate start.

5. **False Start**: When a rider moves forward from his position before starting signal is given for start is a false start. Due to a false start one-minute penalty is added to the offending rider's total time for that race.

Flag Signals

Riders must comply with all flag signals. These are:

1. Flag/Club/Org-flag	Start
2. Checkered flag	Finish
3. Black flag	Rider to discontinue rider's number
4. White flag	Ambulance or other vehicle on the course
5. Yellow flag	Danger
6. Green flag	Clear
7. Blue flag	Rider behind wishes to overtake
8. Red flag	Oil on the course yellow stripes

Officials

The officials consist of:

1. Stewards who are responsible to supervise the race. May be upto 5 in number.
2. Clerk-of-the-course (COC) is the most important man. He organises the event, and supervises the starters, judges, time-keepers and scrutineers.
3. Starters, judges, time-keepers, scrutineers and marshals.

Riding Conduct

The COC will immediately exclude a rider who is in his opinion guilty of riding in a foul, unfair or dangerous manner.

Finish

As the leading rider completes his last lap, the finish is signalled by waving the checkered flag. All riders are flagged off the track at the finish line even though they have not completed the required number of laps.

Special Rules

There are special rules for conducting races in formula 750 class and production motorcycle class. Scooters and mopeds may compete in class races of their own under specific rules for them.

Types of Racing

There are various types of motorcycle races, e.g., sprint races, speedway, ice racing and motor-cross.

Sprint: Sprints are point to point races in a straight line on metalled surface. Generally the length is less than one mile. The competitions are held between two or more competitors or individuals against time. These races are held for single machines or machines with side cars.

Speedway: This is a highly specialized form of motorcycle racing, particularly popular in Great Britain. Races are conducted at specially made tracks. Speedway tracks are oval shaped, the length varies between 275 m (300 yd) and 430 m (470 yd).

Ice Racing: This type of racing is similar to speedway but held on ice tracks. Motorcycles have steel spurs attached to their rear wheels to grip the ice surface.

Motor-cross: Motor-cross or Scrambling is a specialised form of motorcycle racing in which competitors race in a closed circuit, which will consist of various obstacles like mud, gravel, grass, small humps, etc. The winner is the one who completes the prescribed numbers of laps first.

Championships

World Championship: Instituted by the FIM in 1949.

Tourist Trophy (TT): Instituted by the Autocycle Union on 28 May, 1907, in the Isle of Man. This may be the most prestigious motorcycle racing trophy in the world.

Grand Prix Series: These are the most important international races. The Grand Prix of Austria, Belgium, France, Germany, Italy,

Holland and Spain are regularly included in this series. In these races, the riders earn points counting towards the world championship.

Names to Remember

Gigcomo Agostini (Italy, b.16 June,1942): He won the maximum number of world championships numbering 15 between 1968 and 1974 in 350 cc class, and 500 cc class in 1966-1972 and 1975. He is the only man to win two world championships in five consecutive years—1968 to 1972—in 350 and 500 cc classes.

Nicholas "Nicky" Patrick Hayden (born July 30, 1981 in Owensboro, Kentucky): Nicholas is known as The Kentucky Kid. He is an American professional motorcycle racer and 2006 MotoGP World Champion. The 2002 season, however, would see Hayden answering the bell: he won the Daytona 200 on a Honda Superbike en route to becoming the youngest ever AMA Superbike Champion, defeating reigning treble champion Mat Mladin, among others. He won the 2006 championship, beating Rossi 252 points to 247. On September 22, 2006, Hayden signed a two-year agreement that would allow him to race for and develop with the factory Honda Racing Corporation (HRC) team for the 2007 and 2008 MotoGP seasons.

Valentino Rossi (born February 16, 1979): Valentino is an Italian professional motorcycle racer and multiple MotoGP World Champion. He is widely considered one of the best motorcycle racers of all time, with 7 Grand Prix World Championships to his name. In 2006, he narrowly missed an 8th title by scoring a second place in the Championship, and now continues in the 2007 season as one of the title favourites. According to Sports Illustrated, Rossi is the 7th highest earning sports personality in the world (2nd outside the United States), earning an estimated $30 million a year.

Daniel "Dani" Pedrosa (born September 29, 1985 in Sabadell, Spain), is a Grand Prix motorcycle racer [1]. Pedrosa grew up in a village near Sabadell called Castellar del Vallès. He is the youngest world champion in 125cc and 250cc Grands Prix. Pedrosa stands 1.58m (5ft, 2in) tall and weighs 51kg (112.4lbs).

Jorge Lorenzo (born 4 May 1987 in Palma de Mallorca, Balearic Islands): Lorenzo is a Spanish motorcycle racer who currently runs in 250cc in the Motorcycle World Championship for the Fortuna Aprilia team. On his 15th birthday he became the youngest rider ever to compete in a grand prix on the second day of qualifying at Circuito Permante de Jerez on his professional debut in 2002. In 2006 he become the 2nd youngest World Champion in the 250cc Motorcycle World Championship.

Álvaro Bautista (born 21 November 1984 in Talavera de la Reina, Castile-La Mancha): Bautista is a Spanish motorcycle racer who currently competes in the 125cc class of the Grand Prix Motorcycle World Championship for the MVA Aspar Aprilia team. In 2006 he won the 125cc World Championship, and will go on to compete in the 250cc class in the 2007 Grand Prix season, again with the MVA Aspar Aprilia team.

■

MOTOR RACING

Chapter - 37

Motor racing is a race between two or more than two vehicles on a fixed path or point to point on a road.

History

There are conflicting views regarding the first automobile race. But the Guinness Book of Records claims that the first motor race was the 201 mile (323 km) Green Bay to Madison, Wisconsin, USA, held in 1878. In 1887 Comte de Dion won the La Velocipede 19.3 mile (31 km) race in Paris. However, there are people who claim that de Dion won a race in 1894 which was from Paris to Rouen covering a distance of 79 miles (127 km) at an average speed of 11.6 mph. In June 1895, a French Panahard Lavassor car won the first real motor race — the Paris-Bordeau- Paris race—over 732 miles (1175 km). Emile Levassor was the champion of the race. He took 48 hrs 47mts to win the race. This car was with a 1.2 litre Daimler engine developing 3.5 hp.

By the turn of the 19th century, Panahard's technical stagnation allowed manufacturers like Fiat, Mercedes, Renault, Bugatti, Alfa Romeo, Rolland-Pitain and Delage to join this exciting competition.

At the beginning the Committee of the Association Internationale' des Automobile Clubs Reconnus was the governing body of the world motor sport. At present international motor sport is governed by the Federation Internationale 'del' Automobile (FIA).

In India the sport is governed by the Federation of Motor Sports Clubs of India (FMSCI). In

America, motor racing is governed by five major bodies and a few regional clubs. The main governing bodies are:

(1) National Hot Road Association

(2) United States Auto Club

(3) Sports Car Club of America

(4) International Motor Sports Association

(5) National Association for Stock Car Auto Racing

These clubs are affiliated to the Automobile Competition Committee for the United states. The Sports Car Club of America is the main body which regulates the road racing in America. Some of the famous road races conducted by them are Can-AM, Trans-AM and Formula 5000. Various events like rallies, hill climbs, ice races, time trial etc., are also conducted by the club.

Circuit Racing

There are various types of car races. The most popular is circuit racing around specially prepared tracks. Single seater cars specially built for racing, production sedans, sports cars, etc., have circuit racing events. These races either have a set number of laps to cover or may last in a given time.

Vehicles

All vehicles participating in circuit races must have the following:

1. Not more than four wheels.
2. Must have sound construction and mechanical condition.
3. A protective bulkhead between engine and driver's compartment.
4. A full diameter steering wheel.
5. A complete floor.
6. A roll cage according to the FIA (FISA) regulations.
7. All cars must conform to "safety requirements" of the NCR (i.e., National Competition Rules) or FISA.

8. All cars shall be fitted with a shoulder-cum-waist type safety belt which must be securely fastened. Failure to use the safety belt will mean exclusion from the event.
9. Crash helmets approved by the organisers must be worn by the driver/ rider at all times on the track.
10. Fire extinguishers of the dry powder or foam type of minimum 0.9 kg or 1.14 litres content respectively must be securely fixed on all cars, which is mandatory.

Note: Every car is checked by the race officials before a race.

Circuits

As per FIA, tracks must be 30 ft wide with starting grid space of 2 × 8 m for each car. Circuits must comply with the strict safety regulations to obtain racing licence. Circuits length may vary from 1/2 mile (804.6 m) to 2½ miles (4 km). Oval tracks are generally paved with asphalt compound and the turns are banked upto 33° (high speed stock car tracks).

Officials

The following officials are generally present for a race:

1. Secretary of the meet
2. Clerk-of-the course
3. Time-keepers
4. Stewards
5. Pit marshals
6. Track marshals
7. Flag marshals
8. Finishing judges
9. Starters
10. Handicappers
11. Lap recorders.

Competitors

Competitors must have appropriate licence. They must wear approved crash helmet, protective clothing covering arms, legs and torso and goggles or visors, if necessary.

Practice

Before a race starts, cars are tested on the circuit. Each lap is officially timed to determine the car's starting position.

Starting and Duration

All cars start together. Their positions on the starting grid are determined by their performance during the practice run. As explained earlier, circuit races may consist of a set number of laps or length of time. The race at Le Mans is a 24-hour race. The Formula One races are approximately for 2 hours or 322 km (200 miles) or little less in length.

Flag Signals

1.	Club or organisation's	Signal to start the race flag
2.	Blue (motionless)	Another car following
3.	Blue (waved)	Another car trying to overtake
4.	Yellow	Danger
5.	Yellow with red stripes	Slippery surface
6.	White	Official car on the circuit
7.	Red	Stop race
8.	Green	Disappearance of a danger previously notified
9.	Black and white chequered	End of race.

The main racing car formulae officially recognised are as follows:

Formula One: Upto 3000 cc unsupercharged or 1500 cc super charged. This is considered instrumental to encourage technical advancement and to ensure control over the safety of the driver. These cars compete for the world driver's championship and the world manufactures' championship. Maximum-12 cylinders.

Formula Two: Upto 2000 cc.

Formula Three: Minimum wheel base 200 cm. Minimum track 120 cm. Maximum capacity 1600cc (valid between 1, Jan 1971, and 31 December, 1974) Four cylinders.

Formula Ford: This is also known as Formula F.

Formula B: US formula for single seater racing cars between 1100 and 1600 cc.

Formula C: US formula for 1100 cc cars.

Formula Vee: European and US formula similar to Formula Ford.

Formula Super Vee: Same as Formula Vee but uses 1600 cc Volkswagen engines.

Group 9 USAC: Indianapolis type cars–supercharged upto 2999cc or unsupercharged 4490 cc. 280.

Road Racing

Racing on public roads has almost stopped. Such races are held in former airports or in airports closed temporarily. Leading professional series are the Can-AM for Group 7 racing cars, Formula 5000 and three of the manufacturers' endurance events. The most important road race of the world is the US Grand Prix which was first held in 1959.

Club Racing

The Sports Car Club of America organises a series of road races. The drivers may be amateur or professional. The American Road Race Championship is a major event, held on the course of Road Atlanta in Georgia.

Stock Car Racing

Stock cars with engines upto 7 litres are specially made for racing. They are generally steel bodied. Stock car racing is extremely popular in rural areas of America: These races are held on oval tracks ranging from 402 to 805 m in length to super speedways 1 to 2.6 miles (4 km). The resemblance between a stock car and a passenger car is only superficial. However, for the racing car every part of the car is reinforced.

Drag Racing

Basically originated in the USA but is also practised in Australia, Canada, England, Germany, Italy, Japan, New Zealand and Sweden.

This is only a test of acceleration and run in a series of 1/4 mile (402.3 m) straight line from standing start. Usually held on specially built drag pathways. The race meetings are held on an elimination basis in a number of car classes. An electronic time device is set up near the finish line extending 20 m on either side. The timing device records elapsed time of each car and its terminal velocity. However, the winner of each race is the one who crosses the finishing line first.

Rallies

Motor rallies differ from motor car racing. In this competition the competitors cover limited stages and the entire rally is divided into several stages. Penalty points are deducted from a total number of points for each stage. A competitor with least penalty points wins the motor rally.

Elaborate penalty point system is there for a rally. Some penalty points are given below to understand the progress of rally:

		Penalty points
1.	Not complying with the route card	Disqualification
2.	Not obeying official instruction	Disqualification
3.	Not reporting at a control	Disqualification
4.	Not reporting at a check	Disqualification
5.	Stopping in a non-stop section	Disqualification
6.	Covering a stage in less than 3/4 of the specified time	Not any more, now it is "flying finish"
7.	Breach of lighting regulation	Now a monetary penalty
8.	Leaving a check point before time	Discretion of the organiser or disqualification
9.	Arriving at a control after a specified time	I point to every minute late time
10.	Breach of driving	Discretion of the organisers

There is a now Ladies' Cup in the World Rally Championship. The driver must participate (in an all-ladies' crew) in seven of the rallies counting for the driver's rounds of the world series (including one outside Europe) but they can only score points if they finish in the top 20 places. Power limitation rules apply. Turbocharged cars must be fitted with a restrictor of 40 mm if the inlet to the turbo is larger in standard form. Normally aspirated cars are now restricted by engine capacity size-3 Litres for two valve cars and 2.5 litres for multivalve cars. Popular rally cars are now blacklisted including Toyota Supra 3.01 and the Range Rover.

Other Races

Motor car racing also takes place in the following categories:

Slalom: Slalom is a competition where manoeuverability test is being carried out. Cars attempt the course one by one.

Each car starts with a point and receives one point for each second taken and 10 points for touching each marker. Winner is the one who collects the least number of points.

Hill Climb: Each car competes singly. Two attempts are allowed to complete the course in the fastest time.There is an overall winner and individual claim winner.

Autocross: Against the clock race over courses which may be made of grass or any rough surface. Length of the course generally 500-800 yd.

Hill Trials: In this competition cars attempt to climb farthest up a steep hill. The racing course is marked out on a rough, steep hilly track.

Championships

Himalayan Car Rally: Instituted in India and is supposed to be one of the toughest rallies in the world. Inaugurated in 1980.

World Drivers' Championship: This was inaugurated in 1950. The championship encompasses specified international Formula One races, under a point system.

British Grand Prix: It was inaugurated in 1926, and is held annually since 1949.

Manufacturers' World Championship: Ferrari has won this championship eight times since 1961.

French Grand Prix: Started in 1906.

Other Grand Prix: These are held in Austria, Belgium, Canada, France, Germany, Italy, Mexico, Monaco, The Netherlands, Spain, USA, Australia and Japan.

Le Mans: The 24-hour Grand Prix d'Endurance was first held on 26-27 May 1923 on the old Sarthe circuit at Le Mans, France.

Indianapolis 500: Indianapolis 500 mile (804 km) race was inaugurated in the USA on 30 May 1911.

World Rally Championship: This was instituted in 1979.

Monte Carlo Rally: This rally was inaugurated in 1911.

RAC Rally in Britain: This championship was first held in 1932.

Names to Remember

Michael Schumacher (born January 3, 1969, in Hürth Hermülheim, Germany): Michael is a former Formula One driver, and seven-time world champion. According to the official Formula One website, he is "statistically the greatest driver the sport has ever seen".Schumacher earned as much as US$100 million annually and was identified by Eurobusiness magazine as the world's first billionaire athlete in 2005. He is the first German to win the Formula 1 World championship and is credited with popularising Formula One in Germany. In a 2006 FIA survey Michael Schumacher was voted the most popular driver with F1 fans. On September 10, 2006, Schumacher announced his retirement as a driver.[10] It was revealed on 29 October 2006 that Schumacher will act as assistant to the newly appointed Scuderia Ferrari CEO Jean Todt for the 2007 Formula One Season,

Sébastien Bourdais (born February 28, 1979): Sebastien Le Mans, France) is a race car driver and three-time Champ Car (an abbreviation of "Championship Car", has been the name for a class and specification of cars used in American Championship Car Racing for many decades) series champion.

Nigel Ernest James Mansell OBE (born August 8, 1953 in Upton-upon-Severn, Worcestershire) is a British racing driver from England who won world championships in both Formula One (1992) and CART (1993). He is the only person in history to hold both titles simultaneously, and was the first person to win the CART title in his rookie season.

■

NETBALL

Chapter - 38

Netball is a seven-a-side ball game. Similar to basketball, the game is played mostly by women.

History

Netball was introduced in England from the USA as indoor basketball, played by both women and men.It is of a recent origin and it involves throwing and catching of a ball. In this connection three games of Roman and Greek origin can be named which are still in use for beginners and for experienced players to improve their footwork and ball control. Trugon was a Roman game for three players. Harpastum (Roman) and Phainmide (Greek) were extremely useful for ball control and footwork.

Following the invention of basketball in 1891, by Dr. Naismith, Dr. Toles, an American, taught the young lady students of Madam Osterberg's College of Physical Training at Hamstead in North London how to play indoor basketball. It is estimated that these English rules came to India between 1908 and 1920.

On February 12, 1926, under the chairmanship of Ms. E.Thompson, the All England Women's Netball association was formed. And finally, the International Federationn of Women's Basketball and Netball Association was inaugurated in 1960, at a conference held in Colombo, Sri Lanka, and the first world championship was held in 1963.

Netball Court

The surface of a netball court may be made of concrete, or tarmacadam firmly rolled. However earth surface for outdoor and wooden surface for indoor games may be used. The dimension of the court is 30.5 m × 15.25 m.

The court is divided into three equal areas, known as goal third, centre third and another goal third. The semi circles at either end facing the goal lane are the shooting circles. The centre circle is in the centre of the court.

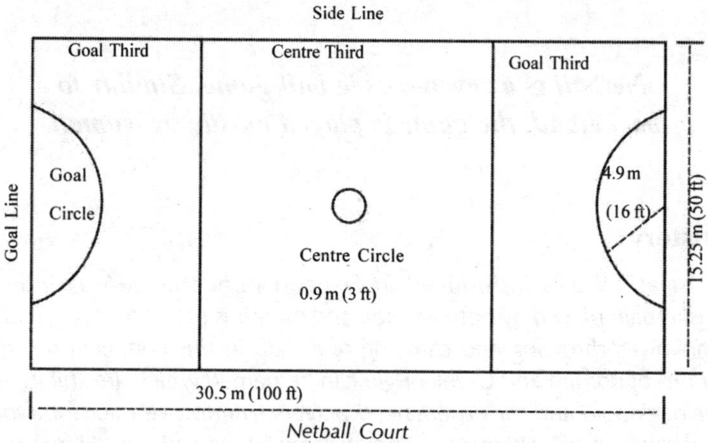

Netball Court

Goal Post

1. It is made of either wood or steel: thickness between 65 and 100 mm (2.5-4 in).
2. Height 3.05 m (10 ft).
3. Metal ring projecting 152 mm (6 in) horizontally from the post. Thickness of the ring is 15 mm (5/8 in).
4. Diameter of the ring 381 mm (15 in).

Ball

Circumference	690 - 710 mm (27-28 in)
Weight	397-454 gm (14-16 oz)

Ball may be made of leather, rubber or similar material.

Players

This is a seven-a-side game. Each side consists of the following players:

1. Goal Shooter
2. Goal Attack
3. Wing Attack

4. Centre
5. Wing Defence
6. Goal Defence
7. Goalkeeper

Each player plays within a limited area of the court as indicated in following chart.

Goal Post

Numbered Playing Areas

For the team denoted in gray letters, attacking the bottom goal:

Goal Shooter (GS)	plays in area 1 and 2
Goal Attack (GA)	plays in area 1, 2 and 3
Wing Attack (WA)	plays in area 2 and 3
Centre	plays in area 2, 3 and 4
Wing Defence (WD)	plays in area 3 and 4
Goal Defence (GD)	plays in area 3, 4 and 5
Goalkeeper (G)	plays in area 4 and 5

For the team denoted in black and attacking the top goal, the numbered areas are reversed.

Duration

Four quarters of 15 minutes each, with an interval of three minutes between the first-second and third-fourth quarters and with a maximum of 10 minutes of half time.

Teams change ends after each quarter.

In certain climatic conditions the duration of the game shall be pre-determined by the countries concerned.

Rules of Netball

1. The team scoring most goals wins the game.

2. Player's position at the beginning: Centre in possession of the ball, stand in the centre circle, the opposing centre shall be in the centre third and free to move. Other players shall be in the goal third in their respective playing area as explained above.

3. **Offside:** A player is offside if she enters any area other than that assigned to her position, whether she holds the ball or not, the penalty for such infringement is free pass from the place where it

occurred. When two opposing players commit offside at the same time, they are not penalized unless both or either of them touch the ball. The penalty is a toss up between them.

4. The umpire blows the whistle to start the game when the centre passes the ball. The opposing teams alternate in making the centre pass that follows each goal and each interval.

5. The ball is thrown from player to player, at least two passes must be made before a goal can be scored.

6. A goal is scored by throwing the ball from above and through the ring only from any spot within the shooting circle.

7. As goal shooting and goal attack players are allowed in the shooting circle, they can only score.

8. Carrying, dribling, kicking, rolling, striking, throwing or tossing the ball to oneself for a double catch not permitted.

9. Throw the ball within three seconds after catching.

10. **Footwork Rule:** Stringest footwork rule is the basis of this game. A player may jump to catch the ball and land on one foot or she may receive the ball with one foot on the ground. The following rules will apply:

(a) Step with other foot in any direction, lift the landing foot and throw the ball before she places that foot again on the ground.

(b) Step with the other foot in any direction any number of times, pivoting on the landing foot. The pivoting foot may be lifted but the player must throw or shoot before regrounding it.

(c) Jump from both feet on to either foot, but must throw or shoot before regrounding the other foot.

(d) Step with the other foot and jump but must throw the ball or shoot before regrounding either foot.

11. No personal contact with an opponent which may interfere with her play is allowed.

12. **Defending a Player Holding the Ball:** Defender must place herself at a distance of at least 914 mm (3 ft) from the player with the ball. She may thus make it difficult for the player to throw the ball in the right direction.

13. **Defending a Player who does not Hold the Ball:** The defender may stand close to the player, but not so close that she cannot move. But the defender is not allowed to raise her arm. Any infringement of this rule will give a penalty pass or if against a goal shooter in the shooting, circle, the choice between a penalty pass and a penalty shot is allowed.

14. The following are the penalties for breaking rules:

(a) **Free Pass:** Free pass is awarded for infringements of rules on the court, other than obstruction and contract.

(b) **Penalty Pass/Shot:** This is awarded for infringement of the rules of obstruction and contact.

(c) **Throw-in:** When the ball goes out of the court, it shall be put into play by a member of either of the team.

(d) **Toss-up:** The toss-up is awarded when opposing players gain simultaneous possession of the ball or opposing players simultaneously knock the ball out of court, or opposing players are offside simultaneously and one is in possession of the ball, etc.

15. **Substitution:** Substitution is allowed upto 3 players only in case of injury or illness.

16. No extra time is allowed except to take or complete a penalty shot.

17. **Advantage Rule:** An umpire may not penalise a player for an infringement, when by doing so, the umpire would place the non-offending team at a disadvantage.

Game Officials

1. **Umpires:** There are two umpires who refer the match. Each of the umpire is responsible for play in his half of the court. For this purpose the length of the court is divided across the centre. Neither umpire gives decision in the other's half.

2. **Scorers:** There are two scorers, who keep the score together with a record of the centre pass.

3. **Time-keeper:** There is a time-keeper who takes time when the game is started by the umpire and signals the end of each quarter. He is also to take time when instructed by the umpire who shall blow the whistle to stop the play and restart the same.

Championships

All England Inter-County Tournament: This tournament was started in 1932.

World Championship: In England world championship was held for the first time in 1963, when 12 countries except Nigeria represented in the council participated (Australia, Sri Lanka, England, Jamaica, New Zealand, Northern Ireland, Scotland, South Africa, Trinidad and Tobago,

Wales, West Indies). Subsequently second world tournament was held in 1967, at Perth, and third in 1971, at Jamaica. This is a four-yearly tournament held between Olympic and Commonwealth Games.

English National Club's Championship: This championship was instituted in 1966, in England.

Names to Remember

Judith Heath (GB, b. 1942): She scored a maximum number of goals in the World Tournament in 1971. She scored a total of 402 goals.

June Weightman (Northern Ireland, b. 28 June, 1946): She represented Northern Ireland at the age of 18 and played in 90 international matches.

Jillean Hipsey (England): Between 1978 and 1987 she played 100 games for England, which is a record for that country.

■

POLO

Chapter - 39

Polo is a game similar to hockey. There are four horsemen each side who use wooden mallets to strike a plastic ball to score goals.

History

We find the first trace of Polo as early as in 600 BC when the game took place between the Turkomans and Persians and the Turkomans won the game.

Thereafter the historians claimed that in 16th century AD. a polo ground (300 yards long and with goal posts 8 yards apart) was built at Ispahan, the capital, of Shah Abbas the Great. The Moguls were largely responsible for taking the game from Persia to the east. and by the 16th century the Emperor Babur had established it in India.

British tea planters introduced the game in Manipur on the Burmese border with India in 1850s. And the first polo club in the world was formed by British tea planters at Silchar, west of Manipur. Calcutta Polo Club, the oldest existing polo club, was founded in 1862. Six years later in 1868, Malta Polo Club was founded for army and naval officers stopping off there on their way home from India. A year later in 1869, Edward Hartopp of 10th Hussars, read an account of the game in The Field*, while stationed at Aldershot, and, with brother officers, organised the first game—known then as "hockey on horseback"—on a hastily-rolled Hounslow Heath against The 9th Lancers. The 1st Life Guards and the Royal Horse Guards were quick to follow suit on grounds at Hounslow and in Richmond Park; and then on a small ground near Earl's Court known as Lillie Bridge.*

The first polo club in England was Monmouthshire, founded by Capt. Francis Herbert in 1872 of 7th Lancers, at Clytha Park, near Abergavenny. All Ireland Polo Club was also founded in same year by Horace Rochfort of Clogrenane.

The first official match in Argentina took place on 3rd September 1875, where the game had been taken by English and Irish engineers and ranchers.

Lt. Col. Thomas St. Quintin of 10th Hussars, introduced the game to Australia in 1876. He was the "Father of Australian Polo" and two of his brothers stayed on there as ranchers and helped the game to develop. In the same year, polo was introduced to the U.S.A. by James Gordon Bennett Jr, who had seen the game at Hurlingham while on a visit to England. Handicaps were introduced in America 1888. In 1895, the height for polo ponies was raised from 14 hands to 14.2. In 1910, Handicaps were also introduced in England and India. In 1919, Height restriction on polo ponies was abolished.

Today, more than 77 countries play polo. It was an Olympic sport from 1900 to 1939 and has now been recognised again by the International Olympic Committee.

Polo Ground

Dimensions of full size ground must include the safety area, which should be at least 4.5 m beyond the touch lines and 18.3 m at either end.

Size of the polo ground is 274.32 m long, 182.88 m wide. At times boards are used on the side lines to keep the ball in play.

There must be considerable safety zones behind the goal lines and outside the touch lines, so that players may cross these at full speed and at any angle.

The goal posts which are 8 yards apart are about 10 ft (3 m) high and about 10 in diameter. They are usually of wicker or lath covered with cloth, fixed around a central pole of about 38 mm diameter which fits into a slot in the ground.

Sticks

The players use mallet headed sticks to strike the ball. The stick consists of handle fitted with a grip. The shaft is made of cane. This is about 19 mm thick and 1.2–1.4 m long. The mallet is made of wood which is 229 mm long and has a diameter of 51mm at the centre. It can be cylindrical, oval, or rectangular.

The Ball

It is usually made of willow, bamboo root, or plastic. It must not exceed 82.5 mm in diameter and must be between 120-135 gm in weight. Its life is not long. Therefore, many are used in each game.

Dress

The players must wear helmets, white breeches and brown leather top boots with a shirt and jersy of the team. Spurs may be worn but sharp spurs are not permitted. The horses must wear gaiter and bandages at the lower leg for protection against blows from mallet or ball.

Officials

The game is controlled by two mounted umpires. One umpire remains off the field in a central position.

Rules of Polo

The important rules of this game are explained as follows:

1. Any type of horse or pony may participate.There is no limit to size, age or sex. The horse must, however, be sufficiently well behaved so that it does not cause a danger to other horses and players. It may be sent off the ground by the umpires if it fails in this respect. The stick must be held in the right hand only.

2. **Starting the Game:** Before commencement of the play and after a goal, opposing teams line up facing the umpire in the centre of the field play. The umpire rolls the ball under arm, between the lines of players from a distance of about 5 yd. The players cannot move till the ball has left the umpire's hand. The game will restart in the following manner:
   - (a) Teams must change ends after each goal except a goal from penalty.
   - (b) After an interval between periods, the game is restarted from where the play was stopped.

(c) If a game is stopped for any other reasons without the ball going out, the play restarts at the place where the incident occurred with a line up like at the start of play.

3. The game is divided into periods or "chukkers"of 7 minutes each. The full game is normally of six periods but could be reduced to four periods.There are intervals of 3 minutes between periods and of 5 minutes at half time. Some open tournaments are of eight chukkers.

4. A bell is rung at 7 minutes and the chukker ends on a second bell at 7 ½ minutes.

5. Ends are changed after each goal.

6. The teams are drawn parallel in the following cases:

(a) After a goal and game is to be restarted.

(b) After each period.

(c) Whenever game stops, other than in the event of a foul.

7. Four players in each side are numbered 1, 2, 3 and 4. Traditionally 1 and 2 should be forwards and 3 and 4 should act as defence.

8. A player following the ball on the right of its exact line has the right of way over all other players. Any player, who crosses or enters the right of way close enough in front to be dangerous, commits a foul.

9. No player may hook an opponent's stick unless he is on the same side of the opponent's as the ball.

10. Dangerous riding or stick work is not allowed. A player may ride off fairly but must not charge an opponent at an angle of more than 30.

11. There is no offside rule.

12. The severity of penalty depends on the degree of foul.

(a) **Penalty** 1. A goal is awarded to the side fouled.

(b) Penalty 2. A free hit from 30 yd.

(c) Penalty 3. A free hit from 40 yd.

(d) Penalty 4. A free hit from 60 yd.

(e) Penalty 5. A free hit from place of foul or from the centre of the ground.

Handicap System

Except international and open tournaments, the game is played on handicap basis. The official handicap is expressed in terms of goals from – 2 to + 10. In some countries this may start from 0 instead of – 2.

Total handicap for the team is the aggregate of four players in the team. In handicap tournament, the number of goal start awarded to the weaker team is derived by multiplying the difference between the handicaps of two teams by the number of periods and dividing by 6. The fraction will be counted as half a goal.

Scoring

A goal is scored when the ball passes over the end line and between the goal posts. A match is won by a team scoring higher number of goals. Team handicap and number of goals are taken into account to decide the result.

Championships

Argentinian Open: It is the most competitive of all tournaments.

Indian Championship: It is held at Calcutta.

Cowdray Park Gold Cup: This is the English championship for polo.

Westchester Cup: Introduced in 1886. The competition is held between the USA and England.

Cup of the Americas: Instituted in 1928, for the competition between the USA and Argentina.

Olympics: Polo was part of the 1900, 1908, 1920, 1924 and 1936 Olympics.

Names to Remember

Juan Carlos Barriot (1939-): Famous Argentinian polo player. He was the captain of the Argentinian team which defeated the USA in Cup of the Americas in 1966 and 1969. Handicap 10.

Robert Cavanagh (1916-): Argentinian polo player. He was a heavyweight and was a member of the Argentina team that defeated the USA in 1936 and 1950.

Leslie Cheape (1882-1916): Famous English polo player from the 1914 winning team of Westchester Cup. Handicap 10.

Manuel Andrada (1900-): A back from Argentina who was in the losing team of 1932 and winning team of 1936 in the Cup of the Americas. Handicap 10.

Lewis Lacey (1887-1966): A polo player who represented both England and Argentina. Handicap 10.

Devereux Milburn (1885-1942): American polo player who played in all American international tournaments between1909 and 1927. Handicap 10.

C. Menditeguy (1913-): A racing driver, golfer and a polo player from Argentina. Handicap10.

Rao Raja Hanut Singh (India,1900-1982): He became the famous No. 4 of Jaipur team. He captained Jodhpur team and won Indian championship from 1932 to 1938 and English championship in 1964 and 1965. Handicap 9.

■

RACE WALKING

Chapter - 40

Race Walking is a progression by steps so taken that there is unbroken contact with the ground throughout the race. It is unlike running where the contact with the ground is broken.

History

In the 18th and 19th centuries when horse racing and boxing were the only other popular games, walking or "pedestrians", as it was called, was highly popular. The game was included in the Olympics in 1908, and in the Commonwealth Games in 1966.

A participant using the correct method attains his speed by making the fullest use of the mobility of the hips in a lateral rhythm.

Walking

1. Walking is defined as a progress of steps so taken that unbroken contact with the ground is maintained and one of the feet must be on the ground.

2. A competitor using the correct method attains his speed by making the fullest use of the mobility of the hips in a lateral rhythm. The best use of this momentum gives a stride of 40-50 in, which his arms acting as a balance are carried straight angles to the body.

Rules of Race Walking

1. Open violation of the definition by means of overstriding or a bentlegged shuffle can be clearly detected. Competitors not complying with the correct definition are warned, by means of a white flag. Only two warnings are permitted, thereafter the competitor may be disqualified. In Britain, there are no warnings and an instant disqualification is effected.

2. An attendent is permitted for each competitor to look after his personal needs while the event is on.

3. In a race of more than 20 km, drinks and spongs are supplied to the competitors at feeding stations, placed at every 5 km all along the route.

Competitions

1. Standard distances for race walking in international and national championships are as follows:

(a) 3 km
(b) 5 km
(c) 10 km
(d) 20 km
(e) 25 km
(f) 30 km
(g) 50 km
(h) 100 km

2. In Olympic games the races are for 20 and 50 km only.

3. The world records are recognised for 20 km, 30 km, 50 km and two hours by International Amateur Athletic Federation (IAAF).

1. Lugano Cup: This is regarded as the world championship for race walking and was first held in Lugano (Switzerland) in the year 1961.

2. Lugano 100 km: Another Swiss event in race walking which finishes in Lugano is generally held in late October and was inagurated in 1965.

3. Manchester Blackpool Race: A 83 km English road race walking event held annually since 1909, except during the First and Second World Wars. This is organised by the Lancashire Walking Club.

4. Three international road races are held in Italy annually:

(a) San Sesto Giovanio: A 30 km road race held at Milan annually on the last day of May, started in 1958.

(b) Roma-Castel Gandolfo: A 32 km road race, started in 1949, is held annually in September.

(c) Giro of Rome

5. Strabourg-Paris Race: This race covers a distance of 513.5 km and is the world's longest annual race walk.

Names to Remember

Jefferson Leonardo Pérez Quezada (born on July 1, 1974 in Cuenca): Jefferson is an Ecuadorian track and field athlete. He has specialised in 20 km race walk. His medal at the 1996 Olympics was the first olympic medal ever for Ecuador. In the 2003 World Championships in Paris, France, Pérez also set the world best performance (as there are no world records in race walking) with 1:17:21. Pérez also had 4th place finishes in the 20 km walk at the 2000 Summer Olympics in Sydney, Australia and the 2004 Summer Olympics in Athens, Greece.

Francisco Javier ("Paquillo") Fernández Peláez (born March 6, 1977 in Guadix, Granada): Francisco is a Spanish race walker. 1998 European Championships Budapest, Hungary 3rd. 20 km 2002 European Championships Munich, Germany 1st. 20 km 2003 World Championships Paris, France 1st. 10 km World Championships Paris, France 2nd. 20 km 2004 Olympic Games Athens, Greece 2nd. 20 km 2005 World Championships Helsinki, Finland 2nd. 20 km 2006 European Championships Göteborg, Sweden 1st.

Denis Nizhegorodov (born July 26, 1980): Denis is a Russian race walker.

His personal best time over 50 kilometres is 3:35:29, the current world leading time. 2003 World Championships Paris, France 5th. 50 km 2004 Olympic Games Athens, Greece 2nd. 50 km 2006World Race Walking Cup La Coruña, Spain 1st.

Olimpiada Ivanova (born August 26, 1970 in Munsjuty, Chuvashia): Olimpiada Ivanova is a Russian track and field athlete who competes in race walking. She has 4 medals from the major events.

Her first gold medal was won in the 2001—Edmonton World Championships—where she beat the rest of the world with the time 1.27:48. A year later, in 2002, she won another gold medal at the 2002 European Championship in Munich.

The next major sporting event she took part in was the 2004 Athens Olympics where she finished second. The winner was the home hero Athanasia Tsoumeleka, who deeply moved the ecstatic Greek crowd by getting her country's first ever medal in the event (time 1:29:12). Ivanova finished four seconds later and could not hide her disappointment. She did, however, win the gold for the 20m walk in the 2005 Helsinki World Championships.

Robert Korzeniowski (born July 30, 1968 in Lubaczów, Poland): Korzeniowski is a former Polish racewalker. He has won four gold medals at the Summer Olympics and has won three world championships.

Korzeniowski is a three-peat winner of the 50 km walk at the Summer Olympics. He won 1996 in Atlanta, 2000 in Sydney, and 2004 in Athens. In addition, he became the first athlete to claim both the long distance and the short distance crown, when he won the 20 km title at the 2000 games. He won world championship titles in 1997, 2001, and 2003. He won two times a European Championship in Budapest 1998 and in Munich 2002. He is also the world record holder in the 50 kilometers race.

Athanasia Tsoumeleka (born January 2, 1982): Athanasia is a Greek race walker who won a gold medal at the 2004 Summer Olympics in Athens.

Until 2003 Tsoumeleka was a largely unknown athlete, and she only finished seventh at the World Championships that year. To a great surprise, she won the Olympic gold medal race held in her own country ahead of Russian Olimpiada Ivanova (silver) and Australian Jane Saville (bronze).

■

ROWING

Chapter - 41

Rowing is the game of propelling a boat through water to cover a specific distance in the quickest possible time. Wooden sticks are used as oars by one or more people.

History

The earliest record of rowing as a sport can be traced back to Egyptian civilisation to about 1425 BC. This game was popular during the Roman period also. Rowing regattas were held for the first time in Venice around 300 AD. The oldest annual recorded race was from London Bridge to Chelsea held on 1 August, 1716.

Modern rowing began around the beginning of the 19th century simultaneously in England, the USA and Australia. Founded in 1892, Federation of Internationale Des Societies D' Aviron (FISA) is the world governing body of rowing.

The first major international tournament, European Championship, was organised in 1893, by the FISA. As a competitive game, rowing can be held in lakes, rivers, tidal waters or in coastal waters. Women's rowing events have also become a part of the Olympic games. Women's European championship was inaugurated in 1954.

Oars

A racing oar is either made of timber by joining two hollow half sections to provide it lightness which can be reinforced with carbon fibre or a composite material to improve its strength. Modern oars have the following specifications:

(a) Weight 2.5-3.5 kg

(b) Length 3.6-3.9 m

The blades are 56-60 cm long, 18 cm wide at the tip, 20-21 cm wide at a point and 20 cm from the tip. However there are variations in the shape of blades.

Boats

Different types of boats used in rowing are described below:

1. A sculling boat meant for only one is 25 ft long and 12 in wide.

2. A boat meant for eight is 55 to 60 ft long but only about 24 in in beam and 13 in deep.

3. Boats for four and two are correspondingly shorter. Certain weight restrictions do exist. For a fours minimum weight of the boat should be 51 kg.

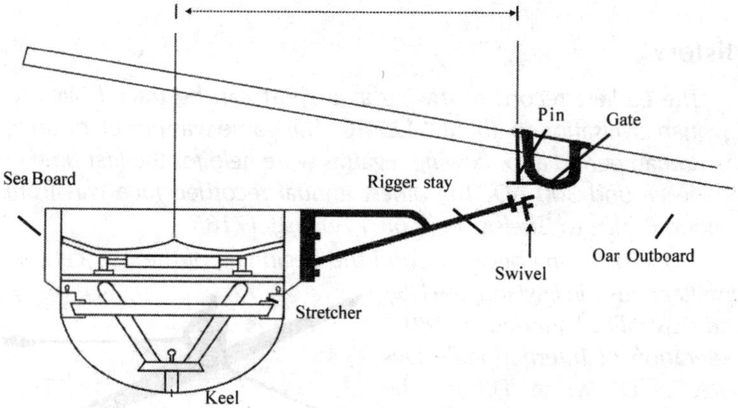

Cross section of a racing boat (oar pivots from the vertical pin attached to the end of the out rigger).

4. The skin of a racing boat is very light and thin, seldom more than 1/8 in (3.1 mm) thick. The thickness is even lesser for a sculling boat.

5. The boat builders endeavour to keep the wetted surface of the boat down to minimum for the least friction. But it has to be stable enough for the crew to row efficiently. So a compromise of the two facts is the governing factor in the making of a boat.

6. Most of the modern boats are made of honey-combed fibre glass.

Dress

The scullers and oarsmen wear shorts and shirts, which should be uniform within a crew. The shirts bear national or club colours.

Officials

Rowing championship is controlled by a Race Committee. There are supervisors at embarking and disembarking points who check the crew composition. Umpires follow the race in a motor boat. There are separate starters and aligners. The judges decide the order of finish.

Techniques in Brief

1. A team of powerful crew, rowing a long stroke with a long swing and relatively weaker crew, rowing a shorter stroke with a shorter swing, but at a faster pace can achieve the same results.

2. The best results are achieved by finding the optimum length of stroke and rate of striking and by gearing the leverage of the oars correctly for each team specially.

3. Coordination among the crew members is undoubtedly of utmost importance.

4. The rate of striking is also governed by the distance to be rowed, as in any of the track events in athletics — 100 m is sprint while 5000 m is a run.

5. Balancing the boat in water and handling the oars requires a great amount of skill; more so in smaller boats. One wrong move can throw the boat off balance and overturn the boat.

6. In boat racing, a cox-swain slots in the stem part of the boat to maintain rhythm in the crew's efforts and the directions. Quite a few modern boats have slot for cox in the bow end.

Rules of Rowing

1. The game is an infringement-less game to a very large extent. The main rules are about fouling and interference. The crew may be disqualified for touching the other boat's crew when tbey are out of their lane. Same goes for washing the other boat either by cutting through their path; or with "puddles" which are the swirls of water left by the blades after a stroke. A crew may be disqualified for merely obstructing the other boat. Touch is not necessary. However the ruling of umpire would be final.

2. At the beginning of the race, the boats line-up with their bows (fronts) on the starting line and the starter says in French *Etes vous Pret?* (Are you ready?) and *Partez* (go). The first boat to complete the race is the winner.

3. The weight restriction for coxes is 40 kg for juniors and 50 kg for seniors. Coxes below this limit are required to carry weight in the boat.

4. **Weight of the crew:** The crew are divided in open and light weight class. For lightweight class the following rules apply:

(a) The average weight of all the crew members should not exceed 70 kg.

(b) No crew member should be more than 72.5 kg.

5. International championships are held in inland waters covering a distance of 2000 m for men/women, 1500 m for juniors.

6. All championships are held in six lane courses based on availability of course but the minimum number of lanes required to conduct an international regatta and FISA rules is four.

Competitions

Rowing is in the Olympics since 1900. The following races in the World and Olympic championships are held:

	Men	Women
(a)	Single sculls	Single sculls
(b)	Double sculls	Double sculls
(c)	Coxless quadruple sculls	Coxless pairs
(d)	Coxless pairs	Coxed quadruplesculls
(e)	Coxed pairs	Coxed fours
(f)	Coxless fours	Eights
(g)	Eights	—

Pairs, fours and eights refer to the number of crew in the boat.

Sculling: The event is very popular. Sculling differs from rowing technically. Sculler holds a scull (smaller oar) in each hand rather than pulling one oar with both the hands. Sculling boats are very light and narrow. A good sculler can become a-very good oarsman but a good oarsman may not be a good sculler.

Skiff Racing: This is mostly confined to England and is a special form of sculling which operates under their own set of rules.

Sea Rowing: Sea rowing does not form a part of the sport but has considerable following in a number of countries.

Championships

World Championship: Started in 1962, this championship is a four-yearly event. In 1974, this competition superseded European championship and became an annual event except in the Olympic year.

Olympic Games: Rowing was an unofficial event in the 1900 and 1904 Olympics. In 1908, it was officially included. The first Olympic regatta was held at Henley with only four events. By 1924, all seven events became a part of the Olympics. Women's rowing championship has also become an Olympic sport.

Asian Games: Rowing was included in the Asian Games in 1982, and the Asian Rowing Federation (ARF) was also formed during the same year. The ARF conducts their championship every alternate year.

Henley Royal Regatta: This annual regatta was inaugurated on 26 March 1839, and is an annual event.

Wingfield Sculls: This was instituted in 1830, a race from Putney to Mortlake. Jack Beresford won the race a record seven times from 1920 to 1926.

Head of the River: A professional race for eight was inaugurated in 1926.

Boat Race: The annual rowing competition in London between Oxford and Cambridge Universities is known as the Boat Race.

It was first held on 10 June, 1829, from Hambledon Lock to Henley Bridge.

Names to Remember

Elisabeta Lipa (born October 26, 1964 in Siret): Lipa is a retired rower from Romania, who was born under the name of Elisabeta Oleniuc. She is the most decorated rower in the history of the Olympics, winning five golds, two silvers and one bronze. She holds the record for the most years between gold medals, at 20 years.

Sir Matthew Clive Pinsent CBE (born 10 October 1970): Pinsent is an English rowing champion, four-time Olympic gold medallist and broadcaster. In 2000 he won Olympic gold again as part of a coxless four with Redgrave, James Cracknell and Tim Foster. And was made a Knight Bachelor in the New Year's Honours list announced on 31 December 2004.

Olaf Karl Tufte (born 27 April 1976 in Tønsberg): Tufte is a Norwegian competition rower. At the 2004 Summer Olympics he won the gold medal in the men's single sculls. He won silver in the men's double sculls at the 2000 Summer Olympics together with Fredrik Bekken. He has also won two World Championships in the single sculls, in 2001 and 2003. When not rowing, Tufte earns a living growing cereals at the family farm in the Nykirke part of Horten.

Sébastien Vieilledent (born August 26, 1976 in Cannes): Sébastien is a 2004 French rowing gold medallist, who is married to Australian rower Julia Wilson. They were married in Australia and currently reside in Paris, France.

■

RUGBY

Chapter - 42

While playing soccer at Rugby School of England in 1823, William Webb Ellis picked up the ball in his hands and ran with it. This sparked an interest, leading to the creation of rugby.

History

While playing soccer at Rugby School of England in 1823, William Webb Ellis picked up the ball in his hands and ran with it. This sparked an interest, leading to the creation of rugby. Cambridge University immediately adopted the game, popularized it and made local rules. The game grew popular in area schools and in 1871, ten years after the common rules of soccer were set, the first Rugby Union was founded in London and firm rules of the game were established.

In 1895 rugby clubs in northern England called for compensation of lost wages for players. The Rugby League was founded as a result and a 13-player game with altered rules were created for professionals.

Rugby spread across the globe and competition emerged between countries. In the United States, the game emerged primarily on the West Coast. The lack of precise rules, ambiguities in the game and complexity of the sport drew a lot of United States players away from the game and major changes were invoked. In 1880 the scrum was replaced by a line of scrimmage, drawing emphasis from the free-running characteristic of the game. The game continued to play with rugby rules until 1905 when the publication of photographs of a harsh game between Sarthmore and Pennsylvania created a stir. President Theodore Roosevelt insisted on reform of the game to lower the brutality with threat of abolishing the game by edict. In 1906 the forward pass was introduced to the United States game. The rules of rugby died and the game of American football was born.

Rugby continued to flourish elsewhere, with especial regard to Britain, New Zealand, Australia and South Africa. Although a handful of clubs remained in the United States, rugby did not re-emerge until the 1960's. College campuses turned to the sport because it was one where many could play and escape the rigid discipline and professionalism inherent in college football. Minimal costs, constant action and the opportunity for frequent play with a primary emphasis on fun also attracted many. The number of clubs grew from about 80 to over 1,000 between 1964 and 1980. The United States of America Rugby Football Union (USARFU) was formed in 1975, creating added recognition and a measure of organization.

The sport continues to grow and is now played in over 80 countries worldwide. The rules of rugby continue to evolve and amateurism remains as dominant characteristic.

Pitch

This pitch is rectangular and measures 66 to 70 metres wide by 95 to 100 metres long. It is divided into 2 equal halves, separated by a line. Inside each of the halves an unbroken line is marked 22 meters from the in-goal, parallel to the half-way line.

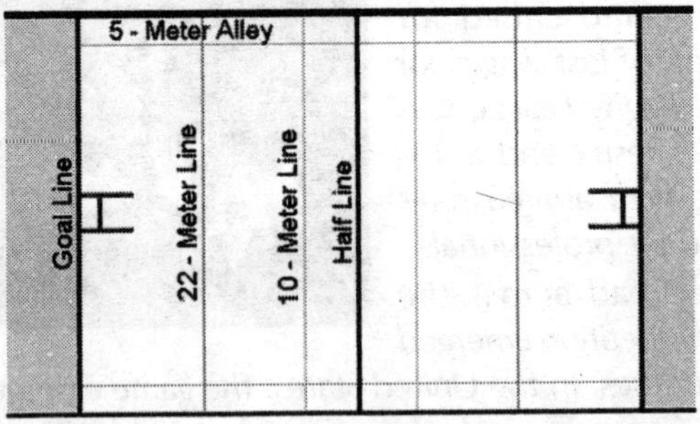

The field used is grass with the usual exception of mud. The length of the field cannot exceed 100 meters (110 yards) and the width cannot exceed 69 meters (75 yards). Each try zone cannot exceed 22 meters (25 yards) in length. Goal posts similar to those used in American football and shaped in the form of an "H" stand on the goal line at opposite ends of the field, at the beginning of each try zone. The lines usually drawn inside the field are 22 meters (25 yards) off goal, 10 meters (10 yards) off halfway and the halfway line. Also, a 5 meter (5 yard) alley is drawn along the lengths of the field measured off the touch line (out of bounds).

Players

Fifteen people play at a time per side, each of which have specific duties as a player. Players are usually talked about in respect to two categories. Members of the first group are called the forwards, or the pack, and consist of the first eight players. Members of the second group are called the backs, and consist of the remaining players. Sometimes the scrum half, number 9, is considered part of either group.

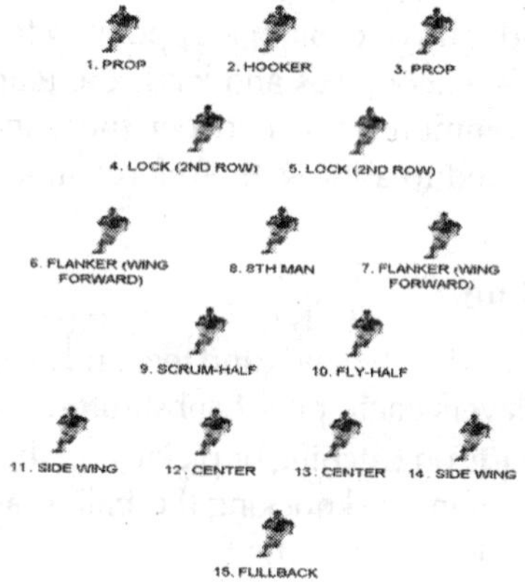

Equipment

Players do not wear any padding or protection except for a mouth guard. The traditional uniform consists of a long sleeve cotton shirt with a collar. Shorts are usually cotton and rise to about mid-thigh. Knee-length socks with turnover tops are worn along with boots similar to soccer cleats. There are strict rules governing the kinds of cleats used. An optional piece of equipment is the scrum cap worn by some forwards, made from leather or cloth and worn as protection for the ears. Any other item than what is listed is usually not allowed in play with the inclusion of jewelry. The ball comes in many sizes. It is shaped like an American football, but is larger. The standard length is about 285 mm (11 inches) and the standard center circumference is about 630 mm (24 inches).

Officials

The referee controls the game and sees that the players maintain good conduct and obey the laws of rugby. There is only one referee and that person is the only judge, timekeeper and score-keeper.

There are two touch judges, one appointed by each team. They stand outside the touch line and follow the play. If the ball is kicked out of touch, the touch judge on that side lifts the flag and stands perpendicular to where the ball went out to mark it. The touch judges also determine if a goal kick is successful. The referee still has absolute authority and makes the end decision even if both touch judges disagree.

The team coaches are not allowed to influence the team once they are on the field. Thus a captain is appointed for each team. The captain makes plays, encourages and leads the team. This person is the only means of communication between the team and the referee. Players are not allowed to address the referee unless they are called upon.

Rules of the Game

The game is played with hands and feet and an oval ball between two teams of 15 players each, plus 7 substitutes.

The game consists on catching or picking up the ball and running with it, passing, throwing or knocking the ball to another player for scoring points, as well as kicking the ball.

To take the ball from the other team, it's also possible to push or shoulder an opponent holding the ball.

The specificity of the game is that passes to another team member are always in the back.

The duration of the game is 2 h 40 min with a half-time of 10 min.

Scoring

The aim of rugby union is to score more points than the opposition. Teams score in several ways:

- Touching the ground over the opponents' goal line with the ball using the hand, hands, arm or arms.. The opponents' goal line includes the base of the posts, which is considered to be part of the goal line. Doing either of these results in a try, worth 5 points. The try got its name because originally the touching down of the ball only gave you a "try" at scoring by successfully kicking for goal, which were the only points scored if the kick was good.

- After scoring a try, the scoring team attempts a conversion: a player takes a kick at goal in line with where the touch-down occurred. Scoring the goal earns 2 points.
- Kicking the ball above the crossbar and between the uprights of a large 'H'-shaped set of posts. Goal kicking is a major part of the game, with games being won and lost at these situations. Therefore the points will be scored as such:
- **Try:** 5 points
- **Conversion:** 2 points
- This may be attempted either by a place-kick or a drop kick (commonly called a drop-goal).
- **Penalty:** 3 points
- Defenders must be static and at least 10 meters from the spot where the penalty kick has been awarded.
- The kickers team-mates remain behind the line of the ball.
- This may be attempted either by a place-kick or a drop kick (commonly called a drop-goal).
- Drop-goal: 3 points

The Kick Off

A kick-off occurs:

- at the start of each half
- after a team scores

The ball is kicked from the half way line into the opponent's half and must travel at least 10 metres. The ball is place-kicked for the start of each half and drop kicked to restart after the opposing side has scored.

The kicker's team-mates must be behind the halfway line at the moment the ball is kicked. The opposing players must be on or behind their 10 metres line.

The Scrummage

This results from a foul.

It must be composed of eight players from each team (3 front row players, 2 second row and 3 from the back row) who must remain linked together for as long as the scrum continues.

Generally, each front row player puts his head to the left of that of his opponent, and his shoulders must always be higher than his waist. The ball is then introduced, on the ground, into the tunnel formed by the front row players. The hooker rucks the ball with his foot towards the rear of his scrum. The scrum-half collects the ball as soon as it leaves the scrum to restart open play.

The Ruck or Open Scrum

This results from a foul.

It must be composed of eight players from each team (3 front row players, 2 second row and 3 from the back row) who must remain linked together for as long as the scrum continues.

Generally, each front row player puts his head to the left of that of his opponent, and his shoulders must always be higher than his waist. The ball is then introduced, on the ground, into the tunnel formed by the front row players. The hooker rucks the ball with his foot towards the rear of his scrum. The scrum-half collects the ball as soons as it leaves the scrum to restart open play.

The Maul

As with the ruck, this is a situation that occurs in open play and is not the result of an infringement.

The maul is formed in the same way as the ruck but the players surround the player with the ball. At least 3 players are needed for a maul (the player in possesion of the ball plus + one team-mate and one opponent). The maul ends when the ball goes to ground or the player with the ball gets free of the maul.

If the ball is unplayable or if the maul ceases to move forward, the referee will intervene.

The Line Out

There is a line-out when the ball goes into touch.

✥ During open play:

If the ball goes directly into touch, the throw in is awarded to the opposing team at the point where the ball was played.

If the ball goes directly into touch, the throw-in is awarded to the opposing team at the point where the ball was played, unless the kicker is within his own 22 metre line. In this case the throw-in is taken at the point where the ball goes into touch.

If the ball touches the ground inside the playing area before going into touch, the throw-in is awarded to the opposing team at the point where the ball went out, wherever the player was when the ball was played.

- From a penalty kick:

The team taking the penalty kick and who kick the ball directly into touch, takes the throw-in at the point where the ball goes out.

To form a line-out, each team must form a line composed of at least two players. The two lines (one per team) must be parallel to the line of the throw-in. Players not involved in the line-out must be at least 10 metres from the line of the throw-in.

The Tackling

Tackling is a defensive action. It consists of intercepting the player in possession of the ball and holding on to him or making him fall over (with one's arms) so that he releases the ball. It is against the rules to throw oneself on top of a tackled player who is in possession of or near the ball.

The Kick in Open Play

Kicking enables a team to find touch, to gain ground or, of course, to score points. It is an essential part of the play. It consists of kicking the ball in the desired direction, though there are several different types of kick:

- The kick ahead may be collected by the kicker to make ground, or any either player behind him at the time the ball was kicked.
- The "up and under" (a kick launched high enough to enable the kicker's team-mates to position themselves to jump to collect the ball before they touch the ground).

- The centralising cross-kick (a kind of up and under allowing the ball to be sent back towards the middle of the pitch).
- The drop goal which is kicked on the half volley between the goalposts and over the cross bar. If successful, this kick scores 3 points.

The Try

A player scores a try when he touches the ball down in the opponent's in-goal.

Calling the Mark

A player may call for the mark when he catches the ball on the volley or on behind his 22 metre line. The ball must have come directly from an opposing player's kick. The player who catches the ball must call "MARK".

The Off Side

A player is offside:

- when he is in front of a team-mate who has the ball or has just played it;
- during a ruck or scrummage, if he remains or advances in front of the offside line. Only the number 8 is allowed to detach himself from the ruck or scrummage and collect the loose ball; and
- if before a line-out is completed, a non-participating player advances or remains in front of the offside line.

Unsportsman like Conduct

Unsportsmanlike conduct occurs where an action breaches the rules or spirit of the game. This includes obstruction, unfair action, dangerous play, unsporting behaviour or repeated foul play. These infringements may result in players being sent off, cautioned, or the awarding of penalty tries or penalty kicks.

The Yellow and Red Cards

In the Five Nations Tournament and in all international matches, the yellow card represents a caution. Now in the Six nations Tournament, if the referee judges a player to be guilty of an aggressive play or accidental unsportsmanlike conduct, he must temporarily exclude the guilty player without further warning. To do this, he summons the player at fault, and shows him a yellow card. The player is sent behind the opposing team's dead ball line. The minimum duration of the exclusion is 10 mins.

The red card means a player is definitively sent off. It is handed out in cases of violent conduct, dangerous play and dissent or threatening behaviour towards the referee.

The Penalty

This is a punishment for a team that has committed a foul. The penalty kick may be taken in the same way as a conversion, and in this manner is worth 3 points. It may also be taken rapidly in order to keep play moving. Finally, it can be kicked into touch, and in this case, the kicking team will take the throw-in. The team awarded the penalty kick can ask the referee to replace it with a scrummage.

Major International Tournaments

The most important tournament in rugby union is the Rugby World Cup, a men's tournament that takes place every four years between the elite national rugby union teams. The tournament is one of the top three international sporting events in the world, with the FIFA World Cup and the Summer Olympics being the largest.[England are the current world champions, winning the 2003 tournament held in Australia]. The fact that four countries have won the last five World Cups confirms the level of competition in the tournament, creating intense interest from supporters, the media and major sponsors.

The women's World Cup event takes place every four years as well. Major international competitions in the northern and southern hemisphere are the Six Nations Championship and the Tri Nations Series, respectively.

The Tri Nations Series is an annual international rugby union series held between Australia, New Zealand and South Africa. The series was initially played on a home and away basis with the three nations playing each other twice. In 2006 a new system was introduced where each nation plays the others three times rather than two. In 2007 the teams will play each other only twice, as it is a world cup year. Amidst all the rugby union competitions are also the autumn and summer Tests, which take place between September to December and June to August. These are played by the major rugby union nations on a home or away basis.

■

SAILING

Chapter - 43

Sail boat racing is popular among the sea-faring nations. It forms a part of Olympics.

History

Among the sefaring nations, Holland and England were among the pioneers to promote yachting. In 1820, England gave the sport a formal shape by forming the Royal, Yacht club or Royal Yacht Squadron. It was the International Yachting Union (IYRU) in Great Britain that drew up the rules for modern Yacht racing. Nowadays small yachts and dinghies are designed to the measurement and speciafications for greater emphasis on sailing skill. There are various types of yachts that are used for racing purposes.

Types of Yacht

Yacht: It is the collective name given to all small pleasure craft by sail or power, which afford living accommodation for their crew. These do not include half decked or fully decked racing yachts, dinghies or day sail in boats. The largest yachts built today for inshore racing are the 12-metre class. These are characterised by their two free board (hull height above the water) and raking bow and counter sections, designed to give greater water line length, and therefore greater speed potential. Off-shore yachts have a higher free-board for greater buoyance and carrying capacity.

Dinghy: It applies to all unballasted sailing craft from about 8 to 20 ft (2.34 to 6.09 m) overall length. Dinghies depend on the weight of the crew for trim and to balance the heeling effect of the wind in the sails. To maintain lateral resistance, and to be able to steer a course across the wind or close to it, a centre board is used. Much of the skill in dinghy sailing lies in the ability of the crew of two to shift their body weight from side to side, forward act to keep the boat as upright as possible.

Catamaran: This word has its origin in Tamil. It is a twin hulled craft and the fastest of all sailing boats with speed of more than 20 knots having been recorded. A catamaran's speed is made possible by its combination of weight displacement and rigidity, or resistance to the heeling force of the wind. These are affected by her two narrow canoe-shaped hulls, locked parallel to each other by a cross-bracing bridge structure. Despite several successful ocean passages, their acceptance for off-shore sailing has been limited.

Trimaran: It is a multi-hulled sailing craft, having a main central hull flanked by two smaller hulls which act as outriggers. Trimarans are fast craft but catamarans have proved more popular in small inshore racing classes. They have been used more widely for deep water sailing.

Dress

The weight of clothing or equipment worn by the competitors must not exceed 15 kg when soaked in water, unless class rules specify otherwise.

Officials

The races are controlled by a race committee. No umpires accompany the racing yachts. The competitors are to lodge protests, which are heard by a jury after the completion of the race.

Layout of a Course

Course: Most courses are triangular. There is no restriction on the size or layout of the course. Turning points in a course are indicated by marks (buoys). These marks are to be rounded or passed in a correct order.

Starting Line: The starting line may be between two marks.

Finish Line: This should be marked in similar fashion as the starting line.

Definitions

Luffing: This means altering a course until head to wind.

Gybing: A yacht is said to have started gybing when with the wind behind her, the main sail crosses her centre line. The gybe ends when the main sail has filled on the other tack.

Tacking: This means altering a course from port to starboard.

On a Tack: A yacht is on a tack except when it is gybing or tacking.

Bearing Away: This means altering a course away from the wind until the yacht begins to gybe.

Starting: Starting signals are as follows:

(a) Ten minutes before the race, the warning signal, the flag indicating the class of the race is hoisted, along with a sound signal to draw attention.

(b) Five minutes later the preparatory signal, the code flag P (Blue Peter) is hoisted.

(c) After five minutes both flags are lowered indicating commencement of the race. This is also accompanied with a sound signal.

Scoring

In the major competitions, points are awarded as follows:

	Points
(a) First place	0
(b) Second place	3
(c) Third place	5.7
(d) Fourth place	8
(e) Fifth place	10
(f) Sixth place	11.7
(g) Seventh place and below	Place of the yacht in the race plus 6 points.

(h) Yachts that do not finish, or sail the course incorrectly, score the points for a last place finish.

(i) In the Olympic Games, there are seven races for each class. Out of these, six best results are counted towards the total score. The yacht with the lowest score is the winner.

Going Round a Mark: A yacht must go round a mark on the required side. If a yacht touches the mark then it:

1. Retires from the race.
2. Protests against another yacht for causing her to do so.

3. If the mark is surrounded by navigable water, she can absolve herself by going round the mark without touching it and then re-rounding the same mark.

4. If the mark is not surrounded by navigable water the yacht should go round the mark and carry out a 3600 turn at the first available opportunity.

5. If yacht touches a finishing mark, its race is not complete till such time it has completed rounding of the mark and crossed the finishing line again.

6. If a yacht touches a starting mark, before starting the race, it must comply with any of the above alternatives after the commencement of the race.

Right of Way: Basic rules are as follows:

1. When yachts are on the same tack and one is overtaking, the yacht overtaking must keep clear from the yacht ahead.

2. Yachts on the same tack, the windward yacht keeps clear.

3. Yachts on the opposite tack, the port tack yacht keeps clear.

4. When both yachts changing tack, the yacht on the other's portside keeps clear.

Penalties

Any infringement of rules by the yacht or if it has forced any other yacht to do so, the offending yacht must retire or undergo any other penalties as given in the rules.

After completion of a race, the crew members are required to sign a declaration that all rules have been observed or lodge any protest. Before lodging a protest, the crew must fly a "protest flag" during the race and inform the offending yacht that a protest will be made.

Collision

1. If two yachts are on collision course the yacht that does not have the right of way must keep clear.

2. If there is contact between two yachts in any way, both yachts are disqualified, unless—

(a) One yacht retires.

(b) She accepts a alternative penalty.

(c) Registers a protest against the other causing her to do the offence.

Important Races

Olympics: Olympic yachting started in 1908, at London. Yachting is done in following classes:

(a) 5.5 metres (till 1968)
(b) Tempest
(c) Soling
(d) Flying Dutchman
(e) Dragon (till 1972)
(f) Star (till 1972)
(g) Tornado
(h) Finn
(i) 470

Admiral's Cup: A yachting trophy competition in ocean racing series held biennially with maximum participation. This is organised by the Royal Ocean Racing Club. Three boats are permitted from each nation. The competition comprises four races, two off-shore and two in-shore. Great Britain has won the trophy eight times.

America's Cup: The trophy is named after the yacht *America* which won the Cup in 1851. This is an ewer-shaped trophy originally presented by the Royal Yacht Squadron in 1851, for a race round the Isle of Wight. In 1857, the owner of *America,* the Stevens Syndicate, gave the Cup to the New York Yacht Club as a perpetual international challenge trophy. *America* won the Cup 77 times.

Asian Games: Yachting was introduced in the 1970 Asian Games in the following classes:

(a) Enterprise
(b) Fireball
(c) Flying Dutchman
(d) Moth
(e) OK Dinghy
(f) Windglider

Asian Regatta: The regatta was first held at Bombay in 1981, in the following classes:

(a) Enterprise
(b) OK Dinghy
(c) Windglider
(d) Seabird.

Names to Remember

Ben Ainslie MBE (born 5 February 1977 in Macclesfield) is a British sailor and two-times Olympic gold medalist. He started sailing at the age of 4 and first competed at the age of 10. Ainslie's first International competition was the Optimist (dinghy) 1989 World Championship's held in Japan where he was placed 37th.

The son of Roderick 'Roddy' Ainslie, who captained a boat that took part in the first Whitbread Round The World Race in 1973, he won a gold medal at the World Youth Championships in 1995, and was awarded the title of British Yachtsman of the Year in 1995, 1999, 2000 and 2002. He is also the holder of an MBE.

Olympic medal record

Gold 2000 Sydney Laser

Gold 2004 Athens Finn

Silver 1996 Atlanta Laser

Ainslie was a gold medalist at the 1993 Laser Radial World Championship, gold medalist at the 1993 Laser Radial European Championship, silver medalist at the 1994 IYRU World Youth Sailing Championship in Marathon, Greece and gold medalist at the 1995 IYRU World Youth Sailing Championship in Hamilton, Bermuda. Ainslie won silver at the 1996 Olympic Games and Gold in the 2000 Summer Olympics in the Laser class. He put on 40 pounds (18 kg) and moved to the larger Finn class for the 2004 Summer Olympics, where he won gold.

Americas Cup

At the beginning of 2005 he was working in the role of Tactician in the New Zealand based Team New Zealand who are preparing to compete in the challenger selection process to win the right to Challenge for the Americas Cup held by Alinghi.

Siren Sundby (born December 2, 1982, Lørenskog) is a former Norwegian sailor. She won an Olympic gold medal in the Europe-class in the 2004 Summer Olympics. She also won the world championships in the Europe-class in 2003 and 2004. Sundby was selected female sailor of the year by the International Sailing Federation in 2003.

Sundby revealed in July 2006 that she was giving up sailing. Since her sailing partner Karianne Melleby became pregnant and gave up sailing, Sundby had been looking for a new partner, but then decided that there was not enough time to prepare with a new partner before the 2008 Olympics, and still have a realistic chance of winning gold.

Robert Scheidt (born April 15, 1973) is a renowned Brazilian sailor.

Born in São Paulo, his father gave him his first boat at the age of 9 and began practising in the Guarapiranga dam. With the help of Dudu Melchert, his coach, he began winning several competitions. Currently, with three Olympic medals (2 golds and 1 silver), Scheidt is one of the most successful Brazilian olympic athletes.

Shirley Ann Robertson, OBE (born July 15, 1968, Dundee) is a Scottish sailor and Olympic gold medallist.

She won her first Olympic gold medal in the Europe class at the 2000 Summer Olympics. In the 2004 Summer Olympics, her crew in the Yngling class clinched the gold medal with one race to spare.

Robertson was named female sailor of the year by the International Sailing Federation in 2000, and was awarded an MBE in 2001 and an OBE in 2004.

■

SEPAK TAKRAW

Chapter - 44

The national game of Malaysia is a three-a-side ball game in which the players kick and head the ball back and forth across a net. The literal meaning of Sepak Takraw is "kick the ball".

History

The game is a cross between football and volleyball, played with feet and other parts of the body, except the hands. Sepak Takraw is a traditional Malaysian game which can be traced back to the days of the 15th century Malacca Sultanate.

As a modern game, with nets, it emerged in the 1930s. It was one of the games played at Seremban in 1935, for the Silver Jubilee celebrations of King George V. The first well organized Sepak Takraw competition was held in 1945, in Pulau Pinang when three teams competed for the Nyak Dan Bin Nyak Sham Trophy. Consequently, the game spread out rapidly throughout the kingdom. The Malaysian Sepak Raga / Takraw Federation was established in 1960, in Pulau Pinang with representatives from Kedah, Selangor and Negeri Sembilan as well as from Pulau Pinang itself. The first inter-state tournament was held in 1962 ,for the Khir Johari Gold Cup. The game got international recognition in 1965, when it was included in the SEAP games at Kuala Lumpur. In 1988, the International Sepak Takraw championship was held in 1988 in conjunction with World Games at Tokyo. The Federation has also amended its constitution so as to admit representatives from all the 15 states of Malaysia. The game was included in the 1990 Asian Games also.

The Court: Area 13.42 × 6.1 m, free from all obstacles up to the height of 7.32 m measured from the floor surface.

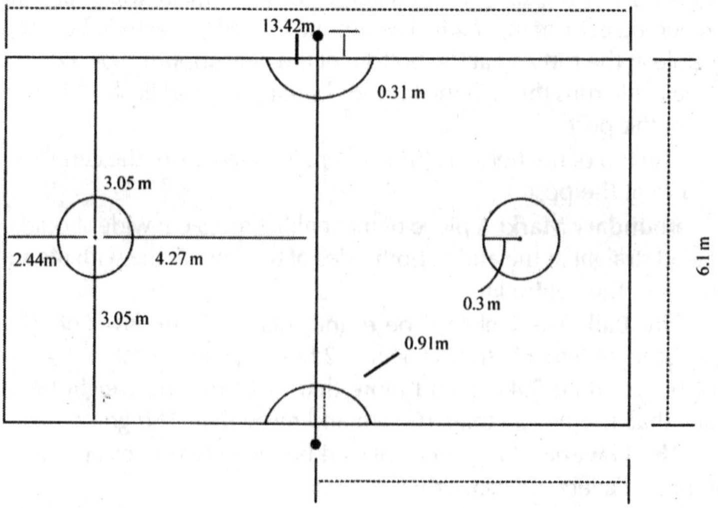

Sepak Takraw Court

Side Lines: The width of all the side lines bounding the court should not be more than 0.038 m measured from the inside. All the side lines should be drawn between 0.91 m and 1.82 m away from all obstacles.

The Centre Line: The centre line of 0.038 m should be drawn equally dividing the right and the left court.

The Quarter Circle: In the corner of each court at the centre line, the quarter circle shall be drawn, radius 0.91m measuring from the side line to the centre line. The 0.038 m line should be measured from outside the quarter circle.

The Service Circle: The service circle of 0.31 m radius shall be drawn on the left and on the right court, the centre of which is 2.44 m from the back line of the court and 3.05 m from the side line. The 0.038 m line shall be measured from the outside of the service circle.

The Post: The posts shall be 1.55 m in height from the floor and they shall be sufficiently firm to keep the net strain. They should be made from very strong material and shall not have more than 0.038 m radius.

Position of Post: The post shall be erected or placed firmly 0.31 m away from the side line and in line with the centre line.

The Net. The net shall be made of fine ordinary cord or nylon from 4-5 cm mesh. The net shall be of 0.72 m in width and not exceeding 6.71 m in length. The net shall be edged with 5.3 cm tape double at the top and at the bottom of the net supported by a cord or a fine cable runs through the tape and strain over and flushed with the top of the post.

The top of the net shall be 1.524 m in height from the centre and 1.55 m at the post.

Boundary Mark: A piece of moveable tape 5 cm wide should be placed straight at the end of both sides of the net, in line with the side lines and the centre line.

The Ball: The ball shall be round, made of one layer of rattan consisting of 9 to 11 strains having 12 holes. The circumference shall not be less than 0.41 m and more than 0.43 m. The weight before play, shall not be less than 160 gm and more than 180 gm.

The Players: The game is played between two Regus consisting of three players on each side.

One of the three players shall be at the back and he is called "back" (tekong).

The other two shall be in front, one on the left and the other on the right. The player on the left is called "left inside" and the player on the right is called "right inside".

Substitution: Substitution of á player is allowed on request by the team manager to the official referee.

Each Regu is allowed to make one substitution only.

Dress

The players must wear jerseys-shirts, shorts and rubber shoes. (The sole and the heel shall be made of rubber or imitation rubber.) It is forbidden for players to wear anything that will endanger the opponents during play. In case of cold weather, the players are permitted to use training suits. The entire apparel of a player is regarded as part of his body. Anything that helps to speed the ball or that helps the movement of a player is not allowed.

Position of Players

At the start of play, the players of both Regus must be in their respective courts.

For first service, the back shall be at the service circle while the left inside and the right inside must be in their respective quarter circles.

The opponent is free to be anywhere within his court.

The players can move anywhere in their own side when the ball is in play.

Officials

The game shall be managed by the following officials:

1 Referee

1 Umpire

1 "Centre Line" Linesman

6 Linesmen

The Toss

Before commencing play, the umpire will toss and the side winning the toss shall have the option of first service or choosing ends.

Start of Play and First Service

1. The start of play is counted as soon as the inside throws the ball to the back after the umpire has announced the points.

2. When making the first service, the back shall have one of his feet inside the circle. The other foot must be outside the circle, to kick the ball.

3. Both the insides must be in their respective quarter circle until the back has kicked the ball.

4. The side that chooses to start the game, shall start the first game.

5. The ball shall be kicked as soon as the inside throws the ball. As soon as the service is executed, all the players are allowed to move about in their respective courts.

6. The first service is considered good if the ball passes over the net, whether it touches the net or not and within the two boundary cords.

7. The throw must be executed as soon as the umpire calls the points. If any of the inside throws before the umpire calls the score, it

must be a rethrow and a warning will be given to the side making the throw.

8. The execution of the service by the back can be kicked in any manner.

Faults

The Serving Side during Service: 1. Anyone player steps on the quarter circle line, centre line, side line or the service circle line.

2. The ball touches the net and does not go over it.

3. The ball is kicked and goes under the net.

4. The thrower plays a bout with the ball (throwing up the ball, bumping, giving to the other inside, etc.) after the call of score has been made by the umpire.

5. The ball goes over the net but falls outside the court.

6. The ball touches his own player before crossing over the opponent's court.

7. The back does not kick the ball on the service throw.

Receiving Side during Service

1. Stand outside the court.

2. Walk about in a distracting manner or create any noise or otherwise intentionally baulk the opponent.

For Both Sides during Play

1. Stepping on the centre line.
2. The ball falls inside or outside the court.
3. The ball touches the net and does not go over to the opposite side.
4. The ball touches the hand or arm.
5. To hold the ball under the arm or between the legs.
6. Any part of the body or players' outfit touches the net or the post.
7. To play the ball more than 3 times in succession.
8. Any player's outfits e.g., shoes, head bands, etc., fall into the opponent's side.
9. The ball runs over the body.
10. The ball does not cross between the boundary tapes.
11. Any player who touches the ball on the opponent side.

12. The ball touches the ceiling, roof or the wall.
13. Any part of a player's body crossing over into his opponent court whether above or under the net except during follow through of the ball.
14. Any player who unnecessarily delays the run of play.

Change of Service

1. Change of service is given when any fault is made by the serving side.
2. Change of service is given when the receiving side kills the return.

Scoring

1. A point is given to a Regu when its opponent has made any fault.

2. The winning point for a set is 15 points.

3. After each set, both the Regus shall change side. The change of side will also occur in the final set (rubber) when one Regu has reached 8 points. However if the change is not made at this juncture in the final set (rubber), the change should be made as soon as the mistake is realized. The score shall remain.

4. If each Regu wins a set, the game shall be decided in the third set (rubber set).

5. When both teams reach the score of 13, the side which had first reached 13, has the option of setting the game to 5 and when the score is 14-all the side, which had first reached 14, has the option of setting the game to 3.

6. After the game has been "set" the score is called 0-0 and the side, which scores 5 or 3 points according to the game has been "set" at 13-all or 14-all wins the game.

7. A side rejecting the option of "setting" at the first opportunity shall thereby be barred from setting, if a second opportunity arises.

Accidents/Suspended Play

1. The umpire can 'suspend play temporarily because of obstructions, disturbances or accidents for not more than 5 minutes.

2. In the course of the suspension, all players are not allowed to leave the court, to receive either drinks or any other form of aids.

Discipline

1. Every player must abide by the rules of the game.
2. Only the captain of the Regu is allowed to approach the umpire during play.

Penalty

The following offences will be penalised:

1. To approach an official in a bad manner with regard to any decision.
2. To utter bad remarks to any official.
3. To take any improper step or action in order to influence any decision made by the officials.
4. To utter bad remarks so as to insult opponents.
5. To leave the court without the permission of the umpire (except between the second and the third set).
6. To give the ball to an opponent using legs.
7. To commit ungentlemanly conduct.
8. To disobey orders and rules of play.
9. Players disobeying rules are given a warning by the umpire. The umpire will use one of the following cards:

(a) Caution	yellow card
(b) Expulsion	red card

■

SHOOTING

Chapter - 45

Shooting is a game that tests the accuracy of target shooting. It involves the use of rifles, air rifles and pistols.

History

Clay Pigeon : *The game owes its origin to a competition held near London around the year 1790, in which live pigeons were used. Later on, it was McCasky of Scotland who invented a target made of river silt and pitch followed by the invention of the mechanised trap by Ligosky of America. The first governing body named Inanimate Bird Shooting Association was formed in 1893, in Great Britain. The Amateur Trap Shooting Association of America was formed in 1924. Then the Clay Shooting Association was formed in 1928. The game was included in the Olympics in 1900, and continued till 1924, and later on from 1952, onwards. Since 1947, the games administration has been taken over by the International Shooting Union.*

CLAY TARGET SHOOTING

Trap and Skeet

Weapon: All types of shot guns, including semi-automatic, may be used provided their gauge does not exceed 12 bore. Generally, the barrel length is 30 to 32 in and weight is upto 6.51bs. The effective range of the gun is upto 40 yd. The velocity of the shot is about 865 ft/sec.

Cartridge: Both for trap and skeet the cartridge length should not exceed 70 mm. The load of pellets must not exceed 28 gm with loading tolerance of 0.5 gm. Pellets must be spherical in shape, made of lead or lead alloy, with size not longer than 2.5 mm diameter for trap events and 2.0 mm for skeet events. Specially built cartridges like tracer, incendiary, etc., are prohibited.

Target: The colour of the clay targets may be black, white, yellow, orange or full dome may be painted white, yellow or orange or a ring may be painted around the dome in white, yellow or orange. General specifications are as follows:

Diameter	110 mm (±1 rom)
Weight	105 gm (± 5 gm)
Height	(25 -26 rom)

Trap Range: 1. The roof of the trap house must be at the same level as the surface of the shooting stations.

2. Clay Target Throwing Machine (The Traps): Each pit must have 15 traps attached to the floor or to the front wall of the pit. The traps must be divided into 5 groups of 3.

3. The trap must be released by an electrical manual or electric-microphone system.

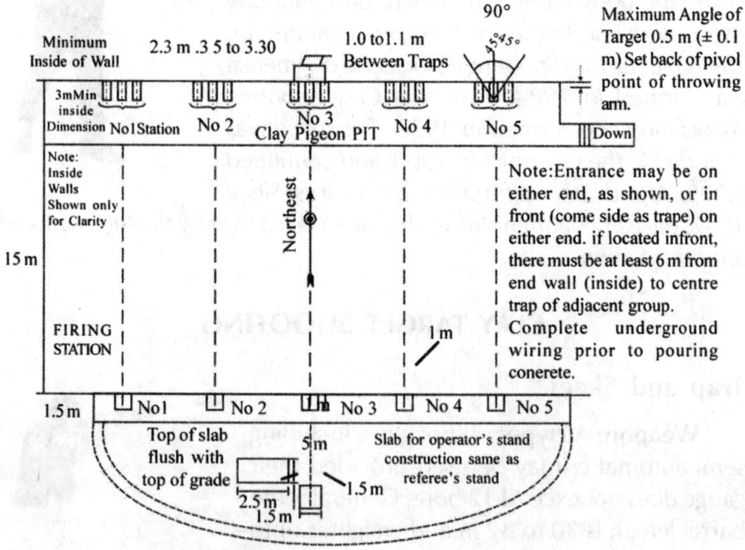

Layout of a Trap Range.

4. The five shooting stations must be arranged on a straight line at a distance of 15 m to the rear of the front edge of the trap pit. Each station is marked with a square 1× 1 m. The sixth station is marked about 2 m to the rear and slightly to the left of the station 1, where No.6 shooter takes his position. Layout of a trap range is described below:

Skeet Range: A skeet range consists of two houses — high house and low house. The size of each shooting station 1 to 7 is 91× 91 cm square. The size of station 8 is 91× 183 cm with its long side parallel to base chord. Shooting stations are arranged on a segment of a circle with a 19.20 m radius. The base chord is 36.80 m, which is 5.49 m from the centre of the circle.

The targets released from high house and low house must emerge at 3.05 m and 1.67 m above the ground level.

Trap Round: At the beginning of each round, the first five shooters must take positions on stations 1 to 5, the sixth shooter must remain behind station 1, ready to move in as soon as No.1 shooter has completed firing. No.1 shooter must move to No.2 station as soon as the shooter on that station has fired. Likewise, when the shooter on station 5 has fired, he must move around the rear of the firing line and return to station 1 (6). This rotation continues till each shooter has

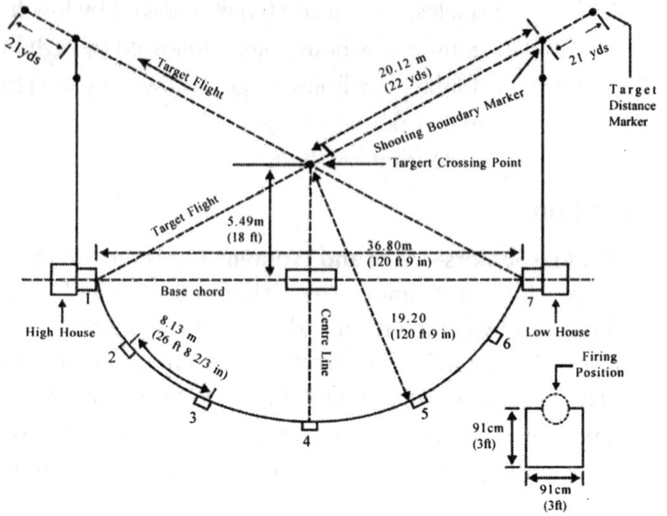

Layout of Skeet Ground.

fired at 25 targets.

Skeet Event: The following are the shooting sequences from each station:

Station	Sequence of Shots at Targets
1.	I single from high house. I double high house target followedby low house target.
2.	2 singles, high house, followed by low house. 1 double, high house target, followed by low house.
3.	2 singles, high house, followed by low house, 1 double, high house target followed by low house.
4.	2 singles, high house target followed by low house.
5.	2 singles, high house target followed by low house. I double low house target followed by high house.
6.	2 singles, high house target followed by low house. 1 double, low house target followed by high house.
7.	1 double, low house target followed by high house.
8.	I single from high house. I single from low house.

Competitions

Individual Seniors—Men and Women: This competition consists of 200 targets for UIT championships, shot in 8 rounds of 25 targets each. These may be completed in 2 days of 100 targets each day or in three days with 75 + 75 + 50 targets. The event may be completed in four days in certain circumstances by shooting at 50 targets a day.

Team: Teams consist of three shooters. The result of the team is decided by adding the totals of the results of three team members over the first 150 targets.

Scoring: Scoring is done on each field for each round of 25 targets.The winner is the one who has scored the maximum number of hits.

Tie Breaking: Perfect score ties will not be broken. Ties for the first three places of the event must be decided by a shoot off in rounds of 25 targets upto a maximum of three tie breaking rounds. If the tie is not broken, the shooters will be ranked equally.

Ranges for 300 m, 50 m, 25 m, and 10 m Rifle and Pistol Events: Ranges may be surrounded by a wall and the targets may be constructed in such a way so that the sun is behind the shooter as much as possible during the competition.

Protection against rain, sun and wind must be provided. Air gun of 10m ranges for World championship and Olympics must be installed indoors.

Sufficient space must be provided for the range officials behind the shooters.

Each range must be equipped with a large clock which can be clearly seen by all.

Targets should not have appreciable movement even in high winds.

Wind flags for 300 m and 50 m rifle and pistol events are used to indicate air movement on the range.

Target Height: The centre of the target must be within the following heights measured from the level of the floor of the firing point.

Ranges	Target Height
300 m	3.00 m
50 m	0.75 m
25 m	1.40 m
10 m	1.40 m
50 m and 10m Running Target	1.40 m

Special Range Requirements: 1. For 300 m ranges, the size of the firing point must not be less than 1.5 m wide and 2.5 m long.

2. For 50 m ranges, the size of the firing point must not be less than 1.5 m wide, and 2.5 m long if the firing point is also used for the 300 m shooting.

3. For 10 m ranges, firing point must be minimum 1 m wide.

4. For 25 m pistol ranges, roofs and screen must provide adequate

shelter from wind, rain and sun to the shooters.

The floor must be firm and not permit any vibration.

The 25 m turning target must be equipped with a target rotating or turning mechanism which permits 90 degree turning of the target on its vertical axis.

Running Target Ranges: The ranges must be arranged in such a fashion so that the target runs horizontally in both directions across an open area with a constant speed. Where the target is fired upon is called the "opening". The movement of the target across the opening is called a "run". Run or time the target are visible in the opening and will be as follows. Slow run 5.0 secs Fast run 2.5 secs.

TARGETS

1. Rifle Targets

10 m Air Rifle Target

10	Ring 0.5 mm	(± 0.1 mm)	5	Ring 25.5 mm	(±0.1 mm)
9	Ring 5.5 mm	(-)	4	Ring 30.5 mm	(-)
8	Ring 10.5 mm	(-)	3	Ring 35.5 mm	(-)
7	Ring 15.5 mm	(-)	2	Ring 40.5 mm	(-)
6	Ring 20.5 mm	(-)	1	Ring 45.5 mm	(-)

Inner ten: When the 10 Ring (dot) has been shot out completely as determined by the use of a 4.5 mm Air Rifle Scoring Gauge.

The 10 dot is white, the scoring zone from 4 to 9 is black 30.5 mm.

Ring thickness: 0.1 to 0.2 mm.

Minimum visible size of target card: 80× 80 mm.

Scoring ring values 1–8 are printed in the scoring zone, in vertical and horizontal planes, at right angles to each other. The 9 point zone is not marked with a number.

Background cards 170 × 170 mm. Similar in colour to the target material must be provided to improve the visibility of target.

50 m Rifle Target

10	Ring 10.40 mm	(± 0.1 mm)	5	Ring 90.40 mm	(± 0.5 mm)

9 Ring 26.40 mm	(± 0.2 mm)	4 Ring 106.40 mm	(± 0.5 mm)
8 Ring 42.40 mm	(± 0.2 mm)	3 Ring 122.40 mm	(± 0.5 mm)
7 Ring 58.40 mm	(± 0.5 mm)	2 Ring 138.40 mm	(± 0.5 mm)
6 Ring 74.40 mm	(± 0.5 mm)	1 Ring 154.40 mm	(± 0.5 mm)

Inner ten: 5 mm (± 0.1 mm).

Diameter of the black bull's eye: 112.4 mm (± 0.5 mm).

Ring thickness: 0.2 mm to 0.3 mm.

Minimum visible size of target card: 250 × 250 mm.

Scoring ring values 1–8 are printed in the scoring zones in vertical and horizontal planes, at right angles to each other.

The 9 and 10 point zones are not marked with a number.

300 m Rifle Target

10 Ring 100 mm	(± 0.5 mm)	5 Ring 600 mm	(± 3.0 mm)
9 Ring 200 mm	(± 1.0 mm)	4 Ring 700 mm	(± 3.0 mm)
8 Ring 300 mm	(± 1.0 mm)	3 Ring 800 mm	(± 3.0 mm)
7 Ring 400 mm	(± 3.0 mm)	2 Ring 900 mm	(± 3.0 mm)
6 Ring 500 mm	(± 3.0 mm)	1 Ring 1000 mm	(± 3.0 mm)

Inner ten: 50 mm (± 0.5 mm)

Black from 5 to 10 rings: 600 mm

Ring thickness: 1.0 mm – 2.0 mm

Minimum visible size of target card: 1300 mm × 1300 mm

Scoring ring values 1-9 are printed in the scoring zones, in diagonal planes, at right angles to each other.

The 10 point zone is not marked with a number.

2 m Pistol Target

10 Ring 11.5 mm	(± 0.1 mm)	5 Ring 91.5 mm	(± 0.5 mm)
9 Ring 27.5 mm	(± 0.2 mm)	4 Ring 107.5 mm	(± 0.5 mm)
8 Ring 43.5 mm	(± 0.2 mm)	3 Ring 123.5 mm	(± 0.5 mm)
7 Ring 59.5 mm	(± 0.5 mm)	1 Ring 155.5 mm	(± 0.5 mm)
6 Ring 500 mm	(± 3.0 mm)	1 Ring 1000 mm	(± 0.5 mm)

Inner ten: 5.0 mm (± 0.1 mm)

Black from 7 to 10 rings: 59.5 mm

Ring thickness: 0.1 mm – 0.2 mm

Minimum visible size of target card: 17 cm × 17 cm

The scoring zones are marked with numbers corresponding to the

value in points which they repesent. The scoring ring values 1 to 8 are printed in the scoring zones in vertical and horizontal planes, at right angles to each other. The ten point and the nine point zones are not marked with a number for each. The number shall be not more than 2 mm high and shall be easily read with normal spotting telescopes at the appropriate distance.

25 m Rapid Fire Pistol Target: For the Rapid Fire Pistol event and the Rapid Fire stage of the Centre Fire and Sport Pistol events:

10 Ring 100 mm	(± 0.4 mm)
9 Ring 180 mm	(± 0.6 mm)
8 Ring 260 mm	(± 1.0 mm)
7 Ring 340 mm	(± 1.0 mm)
6 Ring 420 mm	(± 1.0 mm)
5 Ring 500 mm	(± 1.0 mm)

Inner ten: 50 mm (± 0.2 mm)

Black from 5 to 10 rings: 500 mm

Ring thickness: 0.5 mm to 1.0 mm

Minimum visible size of target card: 55 × 55 cm

Scoring ring values 5-9 are printed in the scoring zones, in vertical and horizontal planes, at right angles to each other. The 10 point zone is not marked with a number. The numbers shall be approximately 10 mm high and 1 mm thick.

25 m and 50 m Precision Pistol Target: For the 50 m Free Pistol and 25 m Standard Pistol events and the Precision stage of Centre Fire and the Sport Pistol events.

10 Ring 50 mm	(± 0.2 mm)	5 Ring 300 mm	(± 1.0 mm)
9 Ring. 100 mm	(± 0.4 mm)	4 Ring 350 mm	(± 1.0 mm)
8 Ring 150 mm	(± 0.6 mm)	3 Ring 400 mm	(± 1.0 mm)
7 Ring 200 mm	(± 1.0 mm)	2 Ring 450 mm	(± 1.0 mm)
6 Ring 250 mm	(± 1.0 mm)	1 Ring 500 mm	(± 1.0 mm)

Inner ten: 25 mm (± 0.2 mm)

Black from 7 to 10 ring: 200 mm

Ring thickness: 0.2 mm to 0.5 mm

Minimum visible size of target card: 55 × 55 cm.

Scoring ring values 1-9 are printed in the scoring zones, in vertical and horizontal planes, at right angles to each other. The 10 point zone is not marked with a number. The numbers shall be approximately 10 mm high and shall be easily read with normal spotting telescopes at the appropriate distance.

Running Target

Running targets of 50 m must depict a running wild boar with scoring rings printed on the shoulder of the animal. Target must be printed in one colour only. The running target is printed to show the animal running into left and right directions. The animal must be printed on a rectangular shaped target paper. Trimming the frame to the shape of the animal is not permitted.

50 m Running Target

10 Ring	60 mm	(± 0.2 mm)	5 Ring	220 mm	(± 1.0 mm)
9 Ring	94 mm	(± 0.4 mm)	4 Ring	264 mm	(± 1.0 mm)
8 Ring	128 mm	(± 0.6 mm)	3 Ring	298 mm	(± 1.0 mm)
7 Ring	162 mm	(± 0.8 mm)	2 Ring	332 mm	(± 1.0 mm)
6 Ring	196 mm	(± 1.0 mm)	1 Ring	366 rom	(± 1.0 mm)

Inner ten: 30 mm (± 0.2 mm)

Ring thickness: 1 mm (± 1.0 mm)

The centre of the 10 ring must be 500 mm from the tip of the nose of the boar measured on a horizontal line.

Running Target

Scoring ring values 1 to 9 must be clearly printed in the appropriate scoring zones in diagonal columns.

The repair centre or half targets may be used. The repair centre must be matched to the full target. In UIT championships, the repair centre must include the nose, head and all scoring rings.

10 m Running Target

The 10 m Running Target is a single card with two scoring zones each with rings 1 to 10 on the two sides and a single aiming mark in the centre.

10 Ring	5.5 mm	(± 0.1 mm)	5 Ring	30.5 mm	(± 0.2 mm)
9 Ring	10.5 mm	(± 0.1 mm)	4 Ring	35.5 mm	(± 0.3 mm)
8 Ring	15.5 mm	(± 0.1 mm)	3 Ring	40.5 mm	(± 0.3 mm)

7 Ring	20.5 mm	(± 0.2 mm)	2 Ring	45.5 mm	(± 0.3 mm)
6 Ring	25.5 rom	(± 0.2 mm)	1 Ring	50.5 mm	(± 0.3 mm)

Inner 10 is white: 0.5 mm (± 0.1 mm)

Ring thickness: 0.1 mm to 0.2 mm

Size of target card: 26 cm × 15 cm

The centre of the 10 ring must be 70 mm from the aiming mark measured on a horizontal line. The targets will be black 10 ring through 5 ring (30.5 mm). The centre aiming point will be black with an outside diameter of 15.5 mm.

Scoring ring values 1 to 9 must be clearly printed on the target. All scoring ring values must be printed in diagonal columns.

Dress

Rifle Shooting: One shooting jacket, one pair of shooting trousers and one pair of shooting boots are allowed to be worn by the competitor. Clothing worn under the shooting jacket must not be thicker than 2.5 mm single thickness and 5 mm double thickness. Shooting gloves with thickness not exceeding 12 mm may be used. The gloves must not extend 50 mm above the wrist.

Pistol Shooting: No special garments, including shoes which support or immobilise the shooter's legs, body or arms are prohibited.

Trap and Skeet: A shooter must appear at a competition dressed appropriately for a public event.

Officials

At all championships, the jury will be composed of 3 to 7 members who in conjunction with Range Officers conduct the meet.

Rifle Events Officials:

Chief Range Officer and Range Officer

Register Keeper

Target and Pit Officers

Pistol Events Officials:

Chief Range Officer

Range Officer

Register Keeper

Target Operator

Target Officer

Scorer

The Second Register Keeper
Marker
Trap and Skeet Officials:
Referee
Three Assistant Referees

Rifles

Specifications for Smallbore, Bigbore, Standard and Air Rifles are as follows:

1.	Length of front sight tunnel	50 mm
2.	Diameter of front sight tunnel	25 mm
3.	Lowest point of pistol grip from the centre line of barrel	140 mm
4.	Heel to toe length of butt plate	53 mm
5.	Total thickness of foreend	50 mm
6.	Trigger weight smallbore standard trigger	Free. No set trigger
7.	Trigger weight bigbore standard rifle	1.5 kg
8.	Trigger weight air rifle	Free. No set triggers
9.	Weight with sights and handstop	5.5 kg
10.	The front sight may not extend beyond the muzzle of the rifle.	
11.	Calibre —	
	(a) Smallbore free rifle	.22
	(b) Small bore standard rifle	.22
	(c) Bigbore free rifle	8 mm
	(d) Bigbore standard rifle	8 mm
	(e) Air rifle	4.5 mm

Ammunition

Smallbore Ammunition: Rimfire 5.6 mm (.22 calibre) long rifle. The length of the cartridge should not exceed 28 mm. Bullets are made of lead or lead alloy, weighing approximately 40 gm. The muzzle velocity of these bullets are just below the sonic speed.

Bigbore Free and Standard Rifle Ammunition: Any type of ammunition that can be fired without any danger to shooters or range personnel may be used. Armour piercing, tracer and incendiary ammunitions are prohibited.

Air Rifle Ammunition: Projectiles made of lead or any other soft material with a maximum diameter of 4.5 mm can be used.

Rifle Events

Smallbore Rifle Prone — 50 m: Men's event Free Rifle. Women's event Standard Rifle. Firing 60 shots in prone position. Time limit 1 hour 45 minutes.

Smallbore Free Rifle Three Positions — 50 m: Fired from 3 positions at 50 m. A total of 120 shots: 40 prone, 40 standing and 40 kneeling and 10 sighting shots for each position. Shooting time-1 hour 15 minutes prone, 1 hour 45 minutes standing, and 1 hour 30 minutes kneeling.

Smallbore Standard Rifle Three Positions — 50 m: 60 shots are fired from three positions: 20 prone, 20 standing, 20 kneeling and 6 sighting shots are permitted from each position. Duration is 2 hours 30 minutes.

Bigbore Free Rifle Prone— 300 m: 60 shots are fired from prone position.Shooting time 2 hours including sighting shots.

Bigbore Free Rifle 3 Positions — 300 m: 120 shots are fired: 40 prone, 40 standing and 40 kneeling. Duration 5 hours 15 minutes.

Bigbore Standard Rifle 3 Positions: 60 shots are fired: 20 prone, 20 standing and 20 kneeling. Duration including 6 sighting shots 2 hours 30 minutes.

Air Rifle — 10 m.

Men's event includes 60 shots standing. Duration 2 hours.

Women's event includes 40 shots standing. Duration 1 hour 30 minutes.

Ammunition

Rapid Fire Pistol.: 5.6 mm (.22 calibre) rimfire cartridges are permitted. Centre Fire Pistol; 7.62 to 9.65 centre fire cartridges are allowed. High power magnum type ammunition is not allowed.

Sports Pistol and Standard Pistol: Any 5.6 mm (.22 calibre) rimfire, long rifle cartridges may be used.

Free Pistol: 5.6 mm (.22 calibre) rimfire cartridges are used.

Air Pistol: 4.5 mm projectile made of lead are used.

Pistol Shooting Competitions

Firearm	Maximum Weight	Trigger Pull	Sight Radius	Maximum Barrel Length	Measuring Box State	Other Specifications
Rapid Fire Pistol	1250 g	No Restriction	Box Restriction only	Box Size Restriction only	300×150×50 mm	Calibre5.6mm (.22cal)40mm Barrel Height Maximum
Centre Fire Pistol	1400 g	1360 g	220 rom	153 mm	300×150×50 mm	Calibre7.62mm –9.65 mm (.30-.38) No MuzzleBrake
Sport Standard Pistol	1400 g	1000 g	220 mm	153 mm	300×150×50 mm	Calibre 5. 6 mm (.22 L.R.) No MuzzleBrake
Free Pistol	No Restriction	No Restriction	No Restriction	No Restriction	Not used	Calibre 5.6 mm (.22 L.R.) Grip Size – Free Wrist
Air Pistol	1500 g	500 g	Box Size Restrition only	Box Size Restriction only	420 × 200 × 50 mm	Calibre4.5mm (.177 cal)

Pistol Events

Rapid Fire Pistol: This event is usually fired in two half courses of 30 shots making a total of 60 shots, fired in 5 shot strings, 5 practice shots are permitted at a time chosen by the competitor. Each stage is subdivided into six series of five shots each, two in 8 seconds, two in 6 seconds and two in 4 seconds. The target is revealed for 3 seconds. An elongated shot hole more than 7 mm in length for small calibre and 11 mm in length for centre fire calibre is counted as miss.

Sports Pistol and Centre Fire Pistol Event: The centre fire event started from 1952 in its present form though the centre fire pistols were already permitted in Olympic Games of 1912, 1920 and 1924. Men compete the centre fire event whereas women/juniors shoot the sports pistol event. In two stages 60 shots are fired, precision and rapid fire.

The precision stage is fired on the 25 m and 50 m precision pistol target. 30 competition shots are fired in 6 series of 5 shots. The time limit for each series, 6 minutes.

Six 5 shot strings are fired at a single target used for rapid fire.The target is exposed for 3 seconds only at an interval of 7 seconds. A maximum of 5 practice shots are allowed for each stage.

Standard Pistol: 60 shots are divided into 3 stages of 20 shots each. Each stage consists of 4 series of 5 shots. The time limit for the first stage is 150 seconds per series, for the second stage 20 seconds per series and for the third stage 10 seconds per series. Five sighting shots are permitted within a time limit of 150 seconds.

Free Pistol: The free pistol event is shot on the 25 m and 50 m precision pistol target. The event consists of 60 shots, fired in 6 series of 10 shots.Total time limit including sighting shots 2 hours and 30 minutes.

Air Pistol Event: Sixty competition shots consisting of 6 series of 10 shots in men's event. The time limit, 2 hours 30 minutes.

In women's competition, 40 shots are fired in 4 series of 10 shots each. The time limit, 1 hour 30 minutes.

Scoring

All bullet holes are scored according to the value of the target scoring zone or ring. If any part of the scoring ring is touched by the bullet, the shot will score the higher value of the two scoring zones. The value of the shots in dispute must be determined by a gauge.

Misses: 1. If a competitor fails to hit a target, the shot may be repeated with a deduction of 2 points.

2. If he fires a sighting shot on to another competition sighting target, there is no penalty; but he is not allowed another shot.

3. If he fires a competition shot to another competition target or on to his own sighting target, he is penalised 2 points.

Excess Shots: 1. If a competitor fires too many sighting shots, he is penalised two points for each shot.

2. If he fires too many competition shots, he is penalised two points for every excess shot after the first two, for which penalty points are not deducted. He must thus fire correspondingly fewer shots at the next target.

Tie-Breaking: Perfect score ties will not be broken. Ties in first three places in the 25 m pistol, skeet, trap and running target are broken by shoot offs. In all other events, in case of a tie in the first ten places, the tie is broken as such:

1. The highest score of the last ten shot series working backward by 10 shots series till the tie is broken.
2. The highest number of l0s, 9s, 8s, etc.
3. Highest number of inner tens.
4. If the tie remains, the shooters will have the same ranking.

Championships

Olympics: Shooting was included from 1896, onwards in the Olympics. Presently, the following 8 events form part of the Olympics:

1. Free pistol
2. Moving target
3. Rapid fire pistol
4. Free rifle (range 300 m)
5. Small bore rifle (prone)
6. Smallbore rifle (three positions)
7. Trap shooting
8. Skeet

World Championship: World championship in shooting started from 1897 onwards. It is more elaborate than the Olympic Games. Various events were introduced from time to time during the 20th century. Air rifle shooting championship was introduced as late as 1979. Almost all events are held for individual and team.

Asian Games: The first shooting event was instituted in the Asian Games in 1954. Since then the following 12 events have been included. Except for free rifle (300 m) all events are held for individual and team.

1. Rapid fire pistol
2. Free pistol
3. Centre fire pistol
4. Airpistol
5. Standard Pistol
6. Smallbore rifle (three positions)
7. Trap shooting
8. Skeet

World Championship: World championship in shooting started from 1897, onwards. It is more elaborate than the Olympic Games. Various events were introduced from time to time during the 20th century. Air rifle shooting championship was introduced as late as 1979.

Almost all events are held for individual and team.

Asian Games: The first shooting event was instituted in the Asian Games in 1954. Since then the following 12 events have been included. Except for free rifle (300 m) all events are held for individual and team.

1. Rapid fire pistol
2. Free pistol
3. Centre fire pistol
4. Airpistol
5. Standard pistol
6. Smallbore rifle (three positions)
7. Smallbore rifle (prone)
8. Smallbore standard rifle
9. Free rifle-300 m
10. Air rifle
11. Trap
12. Skeet

Palma Match: It was instituted in the USA in 1876. This is a team contest. The trophy was named in honour of Senator Palma. This has a unique design with a height of 7 ½ ft. The competition is held annually in the country which had won the trophy the previous year. The team consists of 20 shooters.

Kolhapore Match: In 1871, Raja of Kolhapore presented £100 to the British National Rifle Association for a challenge trophy, originally for competition between Britain and the Dominions. Now it is the major team event of the Bisley Imperial prize meeting and has been won by Britain 58 times. The team consists of 8 shooters.

Empire Match: This was promoted by Australia in 1907. It is held only when an Australian team is present, but is open to all Commonwealth countries. Teams are eight-a-side.

The Elcho Shield: The shield was presented by Lord Elcho for competition at long ranges.Teams are eight-a-side. This is the premier home countries match rifle award at the Bisley Imperial meeting.

The International Canada Match: This competition takes place in Canada at the annual prize meeting promoted by the Dominion of Canada Rifle Association. The trophy was presented by the Canada National Railway.

Bisley Imperial Prize Meeting: The first Bisley meeting was held in 1890. The Queen's Prize—The Blue Riband of British and Commonwealth target shooting, was founded by Queen Victoria in 1860, at the first Imperial Prize meeting at Wimbledon as an annual prize of £ 250. After the Great War according to the wish of King George V, the competition was opened to all who had served in the war.

World Championship: In 1947, Carlsson, a Swedish newspaper owner, promoted World Championship at Stockholm.

Names to Remember

Dr Karni Singh: Maharaja of Bikaner became Indian national clay pigeon shooting champion in 1960, and retained the title for 17 years. He represented India in the 1960 Olympics and subsequently in World and Asian championships. He won a silver medal in the 38th World Championships in Cairo in 1962. He was the only one to win all three Welsh Grand Prix in 1981. He was a qualified pilot, a golfer and a painter.

Lindsay Peden (Scotland): At Bisley for the Queen's prize maximum possible points are 300. On 24 July, 1982, Peden created history by scoring 295 out of 300. He is the record holder so far.

Arthur George Fulton (1887-1972): Belongs to the famous Fulton family. He won the Queen's (King's) prize three times. His father won this prize before him in 1898, and his son won Queen's prize in 1958.

Majorie Elaina Foster (1894-1974): She was the only woman in the history of Bisley to win the Queen's Cup. She scored a total of 280 points.

■

SKIING

Chapter - 46

Skiing is a modern competitive game in which a pair of wood, metal or plastic runners are used for gliding over snow surface.

History

The earliest reference to skiing can be traced back to the Tang dynasty of China. The first book on skiing with illustration was produced in the 16th century. But the actual credit for discovering modernn ski should be given to Southern Norwegian Nordhein who discovered the possibility of landing from a jump with a ski. In 1896, Zdarsky, an Austrian Army officer, introduced for the first time Alpine skiing and it was Arnold Lunn who invented modern slalom and first put on skies at championix in 1898. The Federation Internationale de Ski (FIS) was formed in 1924 under the presidentship of Col. Hoklmquist of Sweden.

Scandinavian skiers started the Nordic games in 1901, in which long lauf skiing and jumping played an important part. They resented bitterly the Alpine skiers. Skiing thus got divided into two groups—Nordic and Alpine. The game was included in winter Olympics in 1908. Alpine skiing is racing on ski down slope and Nordic skiing includes cross country and ski jumping.

Ski

Skis are made with strips of wood or composite wood, metal or synthetic fibre. They are upturned at the front so that they should not dig into the snow. The length of a ski varies from 180 cm (5 ft 11 in) to

210 cm (6 ft 11 in). The width is 90 mm (3½ in) in the front, narrower in the middle by about 15 mm (approx. ½ in) and slightly wider at the end part. Alpine skis are made of metal and plastic whereas Nordic skis are made of wood with as many as 32 laminations.

Ski Equipment

Downhill Ski: Downhill skis are generally longer and wider than other skis and do not turn so easily. A long ski is one which measures about 30 cm above the height of the skier. Therefore 200 cm ski would be correct for a 170 cm sKier.

Slalom Ski: This type of ski is shorter with a stiff arch and a softer tail. The ski gives great control in turn but may wander at high speeds when running straight.

Giant Slalom Ski: This is designed for controlled turning and fast running and is used by everyday skiers and learners.

Short Ski: A short ski is wider than normal and reaches up to the skier's shoulder. This is used for recreational and stunt skiing.

Waxing: Waxing means to apply wax to the sole of the ski to improve performance in both Alpine and Nordic skiing. This is a very important aspect of skiing and often mistakes are made at the highest level.

Ski Sticks: Ski sticks are also known as batons or poles. These are usually made of metal tubing with a leather or plastic handgrip at the top and a strap which is looped over the hand and a disc at the bottom with about 100 mm (4 inch) above the point to prevent the stick from sinking too deeply into the snow. The length of the stick should be upto the armpit with the point touching the ground. The sticks help a skier to move, propel, pivot, brake and to maintain balance.

Ski Boots: The ski boots are water proof and weigh about 8 1b (3.6 kg). They are made of soft leather or foam lining and have welts to which ski binding attach.

Crampons: These are a set of 12 pointed metal spikes used by ski mountaineers to negotiate ascents unclimbable by skis. These are fixed to boots by straps.

Alpine Skiing: Alpine ski races are divided into three categories:

(a) *Downhill Race:* An international downhill race requires vertical

Alpine Skiing

descent up to 1000 m for men. The length for men is 3500-4500 m (2-3 miles) and for women 1600-2500 m (1-1½ miles). These descents are termed in terms of time in the minute downhili and not in terms of length of the course. The terrain of a downhill includes bumps, rolls, gullies, sudden changes of steepqess, light and shade, etc. Gates at least 8 m (26 ft) wide are generally used to keep the speed within bounds or to keep the racer away from dangerous obstacle. The gates are marked with red flags for men and alternate red and blue flags for women.

(b) *Giant Slalom:* This was introduced in world championship in 1950.This is a test of a skier's ability to find and hold the fastest traverse on a course about 1500 m long. With a vertical drop of 450 m and through 60 to 70 gates from 4 to 8 m wide marked by alternate red and blue. Each racer has to do two legs with the aggregate time giving the winner. Women's giant slalom course is shorter in length.

(c) *Slalom:* Slalom is primarily a test of control. The racer races on two different courses usually set adjacent to each other. The winner is the one who clocks the fastest aggregate time.

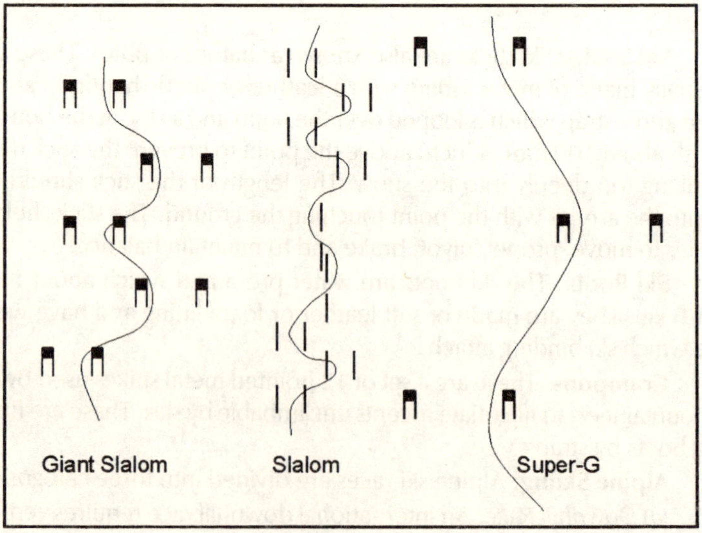

Slalom gates and combinations

The average length of the course is about 575 m with a vertical drop of 150 to 200 m. There are maximum 75 gates with a minimum width 3.2 m each and 75 cm (2 ft 6 in) apart. The gates are blue, red and yellow. There are two types of gates, open and closed. The open gate is the one in which the imaginary lines between the poles is across the fall line whereas the closed gate is down the fall line. Combination of gates are known as flushes, hairpins and gates. Observers are at every gate to ensure skiers cross all gates or to disqualify them.

Nordic Skiing: Rules of FIS Nordic ski races are given below:

(a) Races for men-l0, 15 and 50 km

(b) Races for women- 5 and 10 km

(c) Relay races: men – 3 × 10 or 4 × 10 lan, women–3 × 5 km

(d) Altitude not exceeding 1650 m

(e) Vertical drop:

10 km for men	300 to	450 m
15 km for men	450 to	500 m
30 km for men	750 to	1000 m
50 km for men	1200 to	1500 m
5 km for women	150 to 200 m	
10 km for women	250 to 350 m	

(f) Course must be clearly marked with markers of a single colour. Signs giving course distances must be put up.

Winter Biathlon: First accepted in Olympic games in 1960, it consists of 20 km cross country race in skis. During the race four firing exercises are to be carried out with five shots to be fired at each post. Competitors carry a single shot rifle. At 4,8, 12 and 16 km marks competitors fire at targets in order lying-standing-lying-standing. In lying position the target is 25 cm in circumference with a 12.5 cm inner ring. Standing targets are 50 cm in circumference with a 35 cm inner ring. Two minutes are added to competitor's total time for a complete miss. One minute is added if the competitor hits only the outer ring. Distance of each range varies between 100 m and 250 m. Longer distances are for prone shooting and shorter distances for standing position.

Biathlon Relay: Introduced at the winter Olympics at Grenoble in 1968. Each of the four runners has to fire twice during laps of 7.5 km. At the first shoot they have five targets 30 cm for a standing position and at the second 10 cm five targets for a prone position. The competitors have eight shots to hit five targets. For each target they fail to hit they must run a penalty lap of 200m.

Ski Jumping: The distance from the tip of the take off to the middle point where the jumper's feet touch the snow on landing is measured. Style and form also form a part of ski jumping which is judged by official judges.The points for distance and style of the best two rounds of jumping are added together. In ski jumping major competitions there are five judges. But the lowest or highest points are removed.

Officials

(a) Organising committee

(b) A racing committee of at least six members

(c) Jury

(d) Medical officers, Time-keepers, Start and Finish referees

(e) Controllers for cross-country races

(f) Gate judges

(g) Jumping judges

(h) Distance recorders

(i) Firing point officials

Championships

World Alpine Ski Cup: This was introduced in 1967 and helped skiing to be based on a much clearer format.

World Cup: This was sponsored by the French sporting newspaper *L'Equipe* and a mineral water firm with the support of FIS. The cup is awarded to a man or a woman with the best overall result at the end of the season.

World Championship: The FIS organises this championship every fourth year. It alternates with the winter Olympic Games. Thus a two-ye'arly championship cycle has been established.

Arlberg Kandahar Cup: The "Derby"of ski racing introduced by Arnold Lunnand Schneider at St.Anton in 1928. The success of the events in 1928, and 1929, actually established downhill and slalom racing with the FIS Congress in Oslo in 1930. The race is held at Murren, headquarters of the Kandahar Club, St.Anton, Chamonix, Sestrieve and Gramisch Parten Kirchen. The cup is awarded on the combined results of downhill and slalom race.

Names to Remember

Sir Arnold Lunn (1888-1974): Son of Sir Henry Lunn, he was one of the greatest formative personalities in skiing and mountaineering. He was knighted in 1953. He was FIS council member for 15 years and is the author of about 50 philosophical, skiing and mountaineering books. He devised rules for downhill and introduced slalom as a separate competition in the British Championship at Murren in 1923. He along with Schneider organised the first Arlberg- Kandahar races at St. Anton in 1928.

Hannes Schneider (1896-1954): Austrian by birth. He introduced Arlberg style. Schneider laid down a detailed definition of Alpine skiing techniques. It was Schneider and Sir Arnold Lunn who started and developed Arlberg-Kandahar race.

Alberto Tomba (1967-): He won the gold medal in giant slalom at Calgary in 1988. In 1988, he won seven races in giant slalom and was second in the World Cup next to Zubriggen.

Antoine Dénériaz: Born March 6, 1976 in Bonneville, Haute-Savoie, he is a French Alpine skier. He won a gold medal in the Olympic downhill competition at the 2006 Olympic Games in Turin, Italy, trailed by Austrian Michael Walchhofer and Swiss Bruno Kernen. He also participated in the men's Super-G, where he was placed 11th.[1]

Michaela Dorfmeister: Born 25 March 1973 in Vienna, she is a professional alpine skier from Austria. Her specialities are both the Downhill and Super-G disciplines, although she skis in and has had success in Giant Slalom. In 2000 she won the World Cup for Giant Slalom, and in 2002 the aggregate World Cup. She won two more speciality World Cups, in 2003 (Downhill) and 2005 (Super-G). At the 2006 Winter Olympics, she won the gold medal in the downhill and Super-G races.

Benjamin Raich: Born February 28, 1978 in Arzl im Pitztal, Tyrol, he is an Austrian skier who won gold medals in the giant slalom and slalom at the 2006 Winter Olympics in Turin, Italy. In 2001 he won the silver medal in Slalom at the World Championships, and at the end of the season he gained the Slalom World Cup. In 2002 he won two bronze medals at the Salt Lake City Olympics. In the 2005 Alpine Skiing World Championships he won a total of five medals, one for each race of the program except downhill (including also Combined, where he won a gold medal, as well as in Slalom).

Anja Sofia Tess Pärson: Born April 25, 1981 in Umeå, Sweden, she is a Swedish alpine skier, the winner of seven World Championships gold medals and two Overall Alpine Skiing World Cup titles. She is also the reigning Olympic champion in the slalom, after her victory in that event at the 2006 Winter Olympics in Turin. Pärson won the Alpine Skiing World Cup overall title in 2004 and 2005. The latter title was won by the smallest margin ever, only 3 points over her fiercest rival, Janica Kostelic. Being initially a slalom and giant slalom specialist, she won her first Super-G and downhill races in March 2005 at San Sicario, Italy, during the pre-Olympic competitions. As of February 2007, she has won a total of 34 World Cup races in four disciplines.

Julia Mancuso: Born March 9, 1984 in Reno, Nevada, he is an American alpine skier and Olympic gold medalist in the giant slalom at the 2006 Winter Olympics. The daughter of Ciro Mancuso, she resides in Olympic Valley, California. Mancuso made her debut in the alpine skiing World Cup at Copper Mountain, Colorado, on November 20, 1999, at the age of only 15. She scored her first World Cup points (top-30 finish in a race) during the 2000–2001 season. While she often struggled in World Cup races over the next few seasons, she enjoyed exceptional success at the Junior World Championships, winning a record eight medals including five golds in 2002, 2003, and 2004.

Andrus Veerpalu: Born February 8, 1971 in Pärnu, he is an Estonian cross country skier who competed from 1993 to 2006.

On February 17, 2006 he won his second Winter Olympics gold medal (in 15 km cross country skiing; his previous gold medal is from the Salt Lake City games), becoming the fourth Estonian to have won two Olympic gold medals (Kristjan Palusalu, Erika Salumäe and Kristina

Šmigun are the first three). He is the most successful Olympic athlete from Estonia with three medals.

Han Xiaopeng: Born December 13, 1982 in Peixian, Xuzhou, in Jiangsu Province of China, Han is a freestyle skiier who competed at the 2006 Winter Olympics in Turin, Italy, and won gold in the men's aerials event. He is the first Chinese man to ever win a gold medal at a Winter Olympics.

■

SNOOKER

Chapter - 47

It is a game played by two people on a Billiard Table. Fifteen red balls, 6 balls of other colours and a white cube ball are used in the game. The object is to pot them in a certain order.

History

The game was invented by British Army officers serving in India. Col. Sir Neville Francis Fitzerland Chamberlain invented the game in 1875, in India. It reached England in 1885, where modern scoring system was adopted in 1891.The game developed from two games played on a Billiard table: Pyramids which used 15 red balls and a cube ball and Life-pool which used coloured balls.

Snooker Equipment

The Balls: The game is played with 22 coloured balls.The balls must be of equal size and weight. English balls are 21/16 in and American balls are 21/8 in in diameter. Position and value of the balls are as follows:

	Scoring Value	Position
(a) One white cube ball		
(b) 15 Red balls	15	Forms a triangle with the apex close to pink but not touching it. Base, parallel to the bottom cushion.
(c) Yellow	2	Right-hand corner of "D"
(d) Green	3	Left-hand corner of "D"

(e)	Brown	4	Middle of balk line
(f)	Blue	5	Centre spot
(g)	Pink	6	Pyramid spot
(h)	Black	7	Spot

Snooker is played on an English Billiards table with the cubes as used in billiard. A frame is completed when conceded or the black is potted or fouled.

A game is an agreed number of frames and the match is an agreed number of games.

Starting Play: A toss of coin decides who will play first. The game begins with the starter playing the cube ball from within the "D" at any red ball.

Rules of Snooker

1. The initial stroke of each turn must strike the cube ball against a red, so long as any red remains on the table.

2. If the striker pockets a red ball, he scores it and continues by pocketing any non-red ball which he nominates. If he pockets it, the value is added to his score.

3. Red balls that are pocketed are not replaced on the table. But coloured balls are. The play continues with potting of one red followed by potting of non-red ball, till such time all red balls are potted.

4. Thereafter, the coloured balls must be struck by the cube ball and pocketed in strict ascending order of value. Now if they are pocketed they are not put back on the table.

5. When only the black is left the first potting of black or foul ends the frame.

6. If the scores are equal, then—
   (a) Black is spotted.
   (b) Players toss a coin to play.
   (c) Next players plays from in-hand "D".
   (d) Next score or foul ends the frame.

7. If the cube ball is pocketed the turn ends and it is next played from the "D".

8. **On ball**: The ball that is next to be struck is referred to as "on".

9. **A Snooker:** A player is snookered when a ball he must not play obstructs a straight line beween the cube ball and the ball that is "on".

10. The player is penalised for missing the "on" ball or for first hitting any other ball.

11. If he is snookered by an opportunity's foul stroke, he may play any ball that he nominates. If he pockets it, it is treated as red unless all reds are off the table; in that case it is treated as the "on" ball from which he is snookered.

12. **Ball Touching**: If the cube ball comes to rest against another ball, it must be played away from that ball without moving it or it counts ball, if shot. If it is touching the "on" ball the striker incurs no penalty for missing the "on" ball or for striking another ball.

13. A winner is the one whose aggregate score is more.

14. **Re-spotting of Balls**

(a) Red Balls are not re-spotted even if illegally pocketed.

(b) Any colour ball pocketed when there is a red on the table is re-spotted.

(c) If the appropriate spot is covered, the ball is replaced on the first available spot in descending order of value beginning with black spot.

(d) If all spots are covered any ball except the black or pink is replaced as close as possible to its own spot on the top cushion side away from "D" and touching any other ball.

(e) The pink or black is spotted as close as possible to its spot on the side towards "D" and on the centre line of the table.

15. Penalties: The following are fouls and incur penalty of four points or more as prescribed:

(a) Penalty equivalent to value of the "on" ball when striking:

- (i) Balls are not at rest.
- (ii) Cube ball more than once.
- (iii) Out of turn.
- (iv) With both feet off the floor.
- (v) Improperly from in-hand.

(b) Penalty equivalent to value of the "on" ball by causing:

- (i) The cube ball to miss all object balls.
- (ii) The cube ball to enter a pocket.
- (iii) A snooker with free ball.
- (iv) A jump shot.

(c) Penalty equivalent to the value of the ball "on" or ball concerned by causing:
   (i) A ball not "on" to enter a pocket.
   (ii) The cube ball to first hit a ball not "on".
   (iii) A push stroke.
   (iv) By striking a ball incorrectly spotted.
   (v) By touching a ball with other than the tip of the cube.
   (vi) By forcing a ball off the table.

(d) Penalty equivalent to value of the "on" ball or higher value of the two balls other than two reds or a free ball and a ball "on".

(e) A penalty of seven points is imposed if a player:
   (i) After potting a red commits a foul before nominating a colour.
   (ii) Uses a ball off the table for any purpose.
   (iii) Plays at reds in successive strokes.
   (iv) Uses any ball other than white as cube ball.

16. **Fouls:** When a foul is committed, the referee shall immediately state foul and on completion of the stroke announce the penalty. If a foul is not announced or claimed by the non-striker, it is condoned. All points scored, before the foul is awarded or claimed, are permitted. If more than one foul is committed in one stroke, maximum penalty will be imposed. The player who has committed a foul:

(a) Incurs the penalty which is added to the opponent's score.

(b) He has to play again if requested by the next player. Once such request is made it cannot be withdrawn.

17. **Free Ball:** The referee shall declare a free ball when after a foul the cue ball is snookered. In that case if the non-offending player takes the strike he may nominate any ball as "on". For this strike, this ball will be regarded as and acquire the value of the ball "on". Rules regarding free ball are:

(a) If the free ball is potted it is spotted.

(b) The value of the ball "on" is scored.

(c) If the ball "on" is potted it is scored.

(d) If both free ball and the ball "on" are potted only the value of the ball "on" is scored.

Officials

Referee: He is the sole judge of fair or foul play.

Marker: The marker shall keep the score on the score board and assist the referee to carry out his duties.

Championships

World Professional Championship instituted in 1927.

The first championship was held in 1927, and the legendary Joe Davis helped to organise the event. Matches were held at various venues, and the final took place at Camkin's Hall, Birmingham. Joe Davis won the event, beating Tom Dennis 20-11. His prize money was £6.10s. The highest break of the tournament was 60 by Albert Cope.

- The greatest number of wins is fifteen, by Joe Davis. This was in an era when there were few professional players, and is unlikely to be beaten. In the modern game, the best record is that of Stephen Hendry, who has won seven times to date. Steve Davis won six times in the 1980s, as did Ray Reardon in the 1970s.
- The first 147 in the championship was achieved by Cliff Thorburn in 1983. Ronnie O'Sullivan is the only player to achieve the feat twice, and the only player to lose a match in the World Championship after scoring a 147 (against Marco Fu in 2003). His other was in 1997 and was, at 5 minutes 20 seconds, the fastest ever recorded in the professional game. Jimmy White (1992), Stephen Hendry (1995) and Mark Williams (2005) are the other players to have made a maximum break at the world championship.
- History was further made on 14 March 2006 when Robert Milkins became the first player to make a 147 in the qualifying stages of the tournament.
- Fergal O'Brien is the only player to score a century in his first frame at the Crucible, which he did in 1994.
- The longest ever frame at the Crucible lasted 74 minutes, and was played between Graeme Dott and Peter Ebdon in the 2006 final.
- Stephen Hendry was the youngest ever champion when he won in 1990 aged 21.

- The player to reach the most World Championship finals since 1969 is Stephen Hendry with 9.
- The highest scoring frame in the Championship's history came in 2000, in the qualifying rounds at Newport, South Wales. Kristjan Helgason obtained four snookers against Rod Lawler, in levelling the score at 85-85, necessitating a re-spotted black. The resultant score, 92-85 to Helgason, is a total of 177 points.
- The so-called Crucible Curse has ensured that no first-time Crucible champion, since the event was first held there in 1977, has retained his title the following year.
- John Parrott is the only player to have recorded a whitewash in the final tournament. He beat Eddie Charlton 10-0 in the first round in 1992.

The 2006 888.com World Snooker Championship took place between 15 April and 1 May 2006. Graeme Dott beat Peter Ebdon at 00:53 GMT in the latest finish ever to a Crucible final (though not the longest final), earning him his first professional title in his 12-year career.

(From Wikipedia free encyclopaedia)

■

SQUASH

Chapter - 48

It is a racket and ball game played by two players in an enclosed court.

History

Squash is the newest of the racket and ball games that have gained much popularity. The game originated at the Harrow School, England. It is said that in 1850, boys waiting for their turn to play rackets knocked a ball about in a confined space adjoining the rackets court. The area was so small that it was necessary to use a softer and slower ball—one which could be squashed with hand — thus giving the game its name.

Initially the game was popular among the rich. The Squash Rackets Association was formed in 1929. Around the Second World War, the game became popular with the British troops. They built numerous courts in India and Egypt. Later it was the Royal Air Force which popularised the game by building courts at all its stations. The International Squash Rackets Federation's first meeting was held in 1967. The other members who participated in the meeting were England, Pakistan, Australia, South Africa, New Zealand and the United Arab Republic.

Dimensions of a Squash Court

Length: 9.75 m (32 ft)	:	Breadth: 6.40 m (21 ft)
Height to upper edge of cut line on	:	1.83 m (ft)
front wall	:	4.57 m (15 ft)
Height to lower edge of front wall line	:	2.13 m (7 ft)

Distance to nearest edge of short line from back wall	:	4.26 m (13 ft 10 in)
Height to upper edge of board from round	:	0.48 m (19 in)
Thickness of board (flat or rounded at top)	:	12.5 mm to 25 mm (1/2 to 1 in)
Height of the side wall line	:	the diagnoal line joining the front wall and the back wall.

The service boxes shall be entirely enclosed on three sides within the court by lines, the short line forming the side nearest to the front wall, the side wall bounding the fourth side.

Squash Racket Court

The internal dimensions of the service boxes shall be 1.60 m (5 ft 3 in). All dimensions in the court shall be measured from junction of the floor and front wall: 1 metre above the finished floor level.

All lines shall be 50 mm (2 in) in width. All lines shall be coloured red.

In respect of the outer boundary lines on the walls, it is suggested that the plaster should be so shaped as to produce a concave channel along such lines.

Presently the court is made of glass on four sides and the players cannot see through the side wall or the front wall. Flooring of the court is blue. In this type of court white balls are used.

Rackets

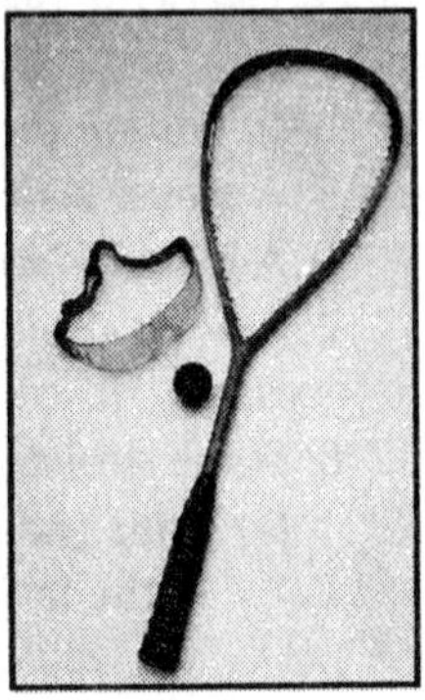

The squash racket has the following specifications:

(a) **Shape:** Circular head of wood strung with gut with a wooden handle (sometimes of metal).

(b) **Length:** Not more than 27 in.

(c) **Internal Stringing Area:** Not more than 8½ in long and 7½ in wide.

Squash Ball

The ball is hollow and squashy in nature having the following specifications:

Diameter: Just over 1 ½ in (39.5 to 41.5 mm).

Weight: 23.3-24.6 gm.

It is made of rubber or butyle or combination of both.

Dress

Squash dress should be white or light pastel colour. Shoes should have soles which will not produce scratch mark on the surface of the court.

Rules of Squash

1. The game is played between two players only. It is played in an enclosed rectangular space 32 ft long and 21 ft wide. The aim of the game is to hit the ball out of the reach of the opponent with a racket quite similar to but smaller than the Rackets' racket.

2. The server serves over the middle line and one foot inside the box while serving.

3. The player winning the toss serves the ball on to the front wall of the court from either of the two service boxes 5 ft 3 in square; halfway down each side of the court where the opponent hits it so that after hitting the front wall and before bouncing on the floor twice, it cannot be returned by the server. The rally continues till one player is unable to reach the ball and hit it before it bounces on the ground twice or the ball has been hit outside the lines denoting the boundary of the playing area. If the player winning the rally is the server he gets a point, if not, he loses the service.

4. A game is of 9 points. It may be raised to 10 depending upon the choice of the player who scores 8 first. If he decides against it, the game ends at 9. This is the British system. Nowadays most of the competitions are of 15 points.

5. A player scores only if he serves.

6. A match is won by a player who wins the first three games.

7. A point could be awarded by the referee against a player who unnecessarily obstructs his opponent's stroke.

8. Some strokes of squash are explained below:

   (a) **Die:** The drive to a length and thereby making the ball die in the far rear part of the court preferably in the corner.

(b) **The drop** in which the ball is hit softly so as to make it dead very close to the front wall.

(c) **The lob** in which the ball is lofted high above the opponent's head so as to make him go back and pick it near the back wall.

(d) **The beast** is to hit the ball on the side wall before it reaches the front wall, the object being to wrong foot of the opponent.

Championship

Open Championship: This is held annually in Britain.

World Open Championship: Instituted in 1976.

European Championship: European Squash Racket Federation holds European championship annually.

Australian Championship: Australian championship started in 1931.

Wolfe Noel Cup: Inaugurated in 1933, for women's championship, it is played between USA and England.

World Amateur Championship: Started in Melbourne, Australia, in August 1967. Now known as ISRF World individual title.

Names to Remember

Heather Pamela McKay (Australia, b.31 July, 1941): In her career from 1959 to 1980 she won 16 women's squash racket championships. She lost two games during this period in 1960 and 1962.

Fatah A.M.R. Bey (Egypt, b.14 February, 1910): He won six amateur championships (1931-1933 and 1935-1937). He was Egypt's Ambassador to London.

Mehmoud Karim (Egypt): Winner of British Open championship in 1947.

Amin (Egypt). Winner of Open championship in 1956.

Whitley (South Africa): Eight times winner of South African championship.

Jansher Khan (Pakistan): Teenager squash player from Pakistan who has finally arrived on the squash scene to end the Jahangir Khan era. He has already won Malaysian,

Hashim Khan (Pakistan, b. 1916): One of the famous Khan brothers of Pakistan. He won the Open championship seven times between 1951-1958 and the vintage title six times (1976-1983).

Geofrey B. Hunt (Australia, b. 11 March, 1947): At the age of 17, he became Australian amateur champion but could regain the championship only in 1970. He won the Open championship of the British Isles in January 1969, but was beaten in 1970, by Jonah Barrington in a match lasting two hours and 15 minutes. He was regarded as the best player in the world during the early 1970s. Hunt turned professional in 1972, Hong Kong, Singapore, Pakistan, World and US Open Championships. He has also won the Swiss Masters, PIA Masters and Alfalaji open. He has defeated the great Jahangir 7 times. But he lost to Rodney Martin of Australia in Canadian Open Championship in 1988.

Jahangir Khan (Pakistan, b, 10 December, 1963): A gifted and almost unbeatble king in the field of squash till he met his nephew, Jansher Khan. Jahangir won the most coveted British Open title for the eighth successive time in 1989.

Susan Devoy (1964–): New Zealander, she won the British Open for five successive years from 1984 to 1988.

Other famous Pakistani players are:

(a) Mohibullah

(b) Jawaid, and

(c) Qamar Zaman.

■

SWIMMING

Chapter - 49

Swimming is the act of moving the body in water with the help of arms and legs. In a swimming competition, the speed of the swimmer is tested.

History

The earliest record of swimming competitions are traced to as early as 36 BC, in Japan during the reign of Emperor Suigiu. The game was included in the modern Olympics Games in 1896, in Athens. Since the 1968, Mexico Olympic Games, 31 races (15 for men and 16 for women) have come into existence.

Swimming Pool

The following are the specifications of a swimming pool for Olympic Games:

(a) Length: 50 m.

(b) Width: 21 m minimum with two spaces for each of 50 cm between the outside lane and the bath side walls. Lane width 2.5 m, total 8 lanes.

(c) Depth: 1.8 m overall which allows water polo matches to be played in the same bath.

(d) Floats on lane ropes: Circumference 0.05 to 0.11 m.

(e) Lane markings of a contrasting dark colour are set on the floor of the pool in the centre of each lane to guide competitors.

(f) Starting platform: It may be from 0.5 to 0.75 m above the surface of water. The surface area of each platform must be 0.5 × 0.5 m with a maximum slope of not more than 10. Surface of each block must be covered with non slip material with back stroke hand grip facility.

(g) Minimum water temperature must be 24°C (75°F).

Dress

Men have to wear swimming trunks and women one-piece non-transparent swimming trunks with no open work except at the back. Caps and goggles may be worn, if desired.

Competition Judges

The regulations for international competitions for judges are as follows:

(a) Referee

(b) Two starters

(c) Chief Time-keeper

(d) Three Time-keepers per lane

(e) Chief judge

(j) Three finish judges per lane

(g) Inspector of turns (one at each end of the lane)

(h) Four stroke judges

(i) Recorder

(j) Clerk-of-course.

The referee has complete control of the races. He may even disqualify a competitor for an infringement.

It is obligatory to use electronic equipment for time-keeping at the Olympic Games.

Types of Strokes

Freestyle: Freestyle means that the swimmer may use any style he wishes to. In modern days, the competitors use the "front crawl". In front crawl the arms are carried through the air, one at a time, elbow relaxed and the hand turning palm downwards ready to catch the water as the other arm is pulled under the water. The legs are kept constantly fluttering all the while; left leg with right arm and vice versa, to maintain balance. Breathing is done by turning the face and inhaling/exhaling. Breathing is generally done once in one arm cycle.

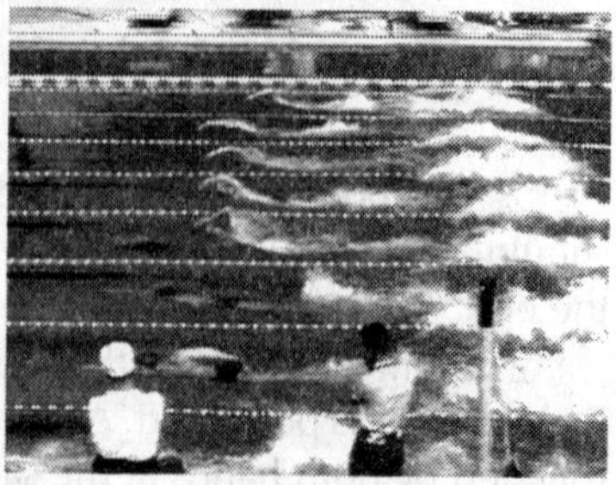

Back Stroke: Back stroke is front crawl done on the back. Since the nose is in air all the time there is no breathing problem. This makes the style very easy to perform. The arms are lifted from beside the legs, palm turned outwards, to an easy position behind the head. As the leading hand takes hold of the water to pull, the other one begins to lift from the side. This cycle is repeated while the legs are fluttered all along. Some swimmers raise and pull with both arms together.

Breast Stroke: This is the oldest and the slowest stroke and is defined by the FINA in the following manner:

1. The body shall be kept perfectly on the breast and both the shoulders shall be in line with the water surface.

2. All movements of arms and legs must be simultaneous in the same horizontal plane.

3. The hands shall be pushed forward together from the breast and must be brought back on or under the water surface.

4. In the leg kick, the feet must be turned outward in the backward movement (frog kick). A dolphin kick is not permitted.

5. At the turn/end of the race, both arms must touch the wall simultaneously.

6. During each complete arm cycle some part of the head shall break the surface of the water except during the starting dive and during each turn.

Butterfly: It was developed from the breast stroke and was declared the fourth stroke in 1952. The style, once again clearly defined by the FINA, is as follows:

1. The arms must be brought forward over the water and brought backwards in water simultaneously.

2. The body must be kept perfectly on the breast and both the shoulders in line with the surface of the water from the beginning till the end.

3. All movements of the feet must be executed simultaneously. Dolphin kick is permitted. At the turn or at the finish the wall must be touched by both hands at the same level.

4. At the start and at turns, a swimmer is permitted one leg kick and one arm pull under the water which must bring him to the surface.

Medley: This is an event where all four strokes are to be executed by swimmer. The order of strokes for individual medley is butterfly, back stroke, breast stroke, and freestyle. In team relays, the order is back stroke, breast stroke, butterfly and freestyle. In both types of medley event, the distance to be swum in each style — known as leg — is equally divided. For relay, it is 4 × 100 m while there are individual events over 200 and 400 m, i.e., for swimmer covering either 50 or 100 m in each style.

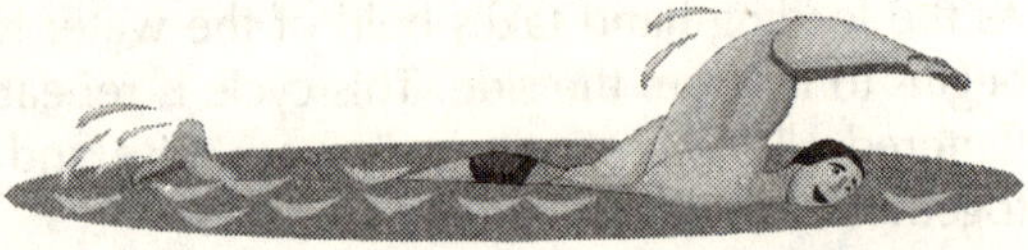

Relays: These are quite similar to athletic relays and are obviously team events. They are generally freestyle. At the change over, the previous competitors must have touched the wall before the next one leaves the diving block. Only the first swimmer can set an individual record in a relay if officially informed earlier. In medley relay each of the four swimmers executes one stroke whereas in individual medley the same swimmer executes all four strokes.

Turning at the end of the Bath: The following are the rules for turning at the end of bath:

1. In freestyle (front crawl), the touch on the wall may be made with any part of the body.

2. In back stroke, the swimmer must stay on his back till his head or the foremost part of the hand touches the wall. He may now turn beyond vertical but must come back onto his back before his feet leave the wall.

3. In breast stroke, the touch should be made with both hands simultaneously.

4. In butterfly, the breast stroke rule applies.

5. In medley he/she has to comply with the rule of the stroke he/she is doing at the particular moment.

Long distance swimming takes place in open water for distance over 1,500 m.

Synchronised Swimming: This form of swimming, ballet in the water, was recognised internationally in 1952, by the FINA and is now a part of the Olympics. There are three types of events-solo, duet and team.

Championships

Olympics: The following swimming events form part of the Olympics: *Freestyle* (Both for men and women)

(a) 50 m
(b) 100 m
(c) 200 m
(d) 400 m
(e) 800 m (only for women)
(j) 1500 m (only for men)

Breast Stroke
(a) 100 m
(b) 200 m

Back Stroke
(a) 100 m
(b) 200 m

Butterfly
(a) 100 m
(b) 200 m

Medley (Individual medley)

(a) 200 m (only in 1968 and 1972)

(b) 400 m

Relay

(a) 4 × 100 m freestyle

(b) 4 × 200 m freestyle (only for men)

(c) 4 × 100 m medley

Asian Games: Swimming was included in the first Asian Games. Gradually all Olympic swimming events became part of the Asian Games.

World Championship: World championship in swimming events, instituted in 1973, includes all the events of Olympics. World record in 50 m freestyle for men and women are also recognised. Swimming forms part of other major international games like the Commonwealth Games and European championship.

Names to Remember

Mark Spitz (b.1950): American swimmer who created history in the 1972 Olympics by winning seven gold medals. No sportsman has ever won so many gold medals in any game in the history of the Olympics. Between 1967 and 1972, he set 27 individual world records.

Dawn Fraser (b.1937): Australian swimmer and the only one to win 100 m free style during three consecutive Olympics in 1956, 1960 and 1964. She also set 27 individual world records from 1956 to 1964 which included nine successive records in 100 m.

Donald Arthur Scho Uandar (b.1946): American swimmer. He won four gold medals in 100 and 400 m in the Tokyo Olympics held in 1964 and was a member of the two freestyle relay teams.

Ambrose Gains (b.17 February 1959): American swimmer. He won the maximum swimming medals in world championship. He won five gold and three silver medals in 1978 and 1982.

Kornelia Ender (b.24 October 1958): Swimmer from East Germany who won a maximum of 8 medals in Olympics including 4 gold medals. She has also won 10 medals in world championships, instituted in 1973, which include 8 gold and two silver medals.

Murray Rose (b.1939): Australian swimmer who became the youngest triple Olympic gold medal winner in the 1956 Melbourne Olympics. He won 400 m and 1500 m freestyle and was also a member of the winning relay team. One of the finest swimmers of his time, he was awarded the Helms Foundation World Trophy in 1962.

Shirley Babashoff (USA, b.3 January 1957): She equals the record Olympic medal winning of 8 with Dawn Fraser. She won 2 gold (4 ×100 m freestyle) in 1972 and 1976, and 6 silver medals (100 m freestyle in 1972, 200 m freestyle in 1972 and 1976, 400 m and 800 m freestyle in 1976 and 4 × 100 m medley in 1976).

Matthew Biondi: Winner of maximum medals in a single world championship. He won 7 medals in 1986-three gold, one silver and three bronze.

Adrian Moorhouse (UK): Set the world record in March 1987, in 100 m breast stroke at Bonn covering the distance in 59.75 sec. It was for the first time that a swimmer broke the one minute barrier.

Sarah Hardcastle (UK, b.1969): The youngest medallist at the 1984 Olympics held in Los Angeles (USA).

■

TABLE TENNIS

Chapter - 50

It is a racket and ball game played on a table by two or four players. The ball is hit across a net placed at the centre of the table.

History

Nothing is known about the exact origin of the game, but the game might have originated from the efforts to miniaturise tennis for the home, at about the same time when efforts were on to adopt tennis for outdoor play on the lawns in England. The game assumed its present form around 1922, in Europe and England. The first international event, Swaythling Cup World Team Championship, was held in London in 1926. The first women's Corbillon Cup was inaugurated in 1934. During the initial years of the world competition, Hungary dominated both men's and women's game. But by the late 50s, the dominance shifted to far east, to Japan and China. The latter still dominates the game.

Credit for spreading table tennis in Asia may be given to Counsellor Amin Aby Heif of Egypt and T.D. Rangaramanujan of India.

The Table: It may be made of any material so long as a standard ball, dropped from a height of 30 cm, rebounds uniformly to a height, between

Table Tennis Table

22 and 25 cm. Hard wood uniformly painted or sprayed with dark paint lacquer.

The Net: The net is 183 cm long, projecting 15.25 cm outside the table each side and 15.25 cm height throughout its length. It is dark green surmounted by white tape of specified width, with a uniform mesh so that no ball passes through it.

The Ball: Early players towards the end of the last century used rubber and cork balls. Today, it is made of celluloid or similar plastic of white or yellow colour.

Diameter	:	37.2 to 38.2 mm
Weight	:	2.4 to 2.53 gm
Surface	:	Matt (not shiny) white and yellow

The Racket: The size, shape and weight are not strictly regulated but usually it has a roughly circular/elliptical blade, with a diameter of 12.5-16.5 cm and thickness of 5-9.5 mm. Weights vary between 170-200 gm and 115 gm. The specifications for the material of the blade and the surface are as follows:

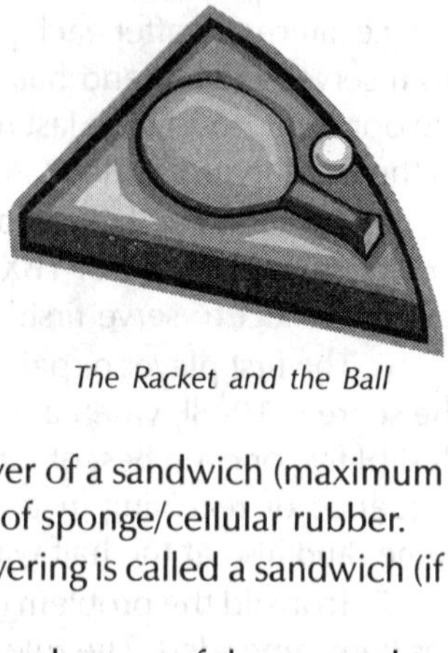

The Racket and the Ball

1. The surface must be dark in colour.

2. The blade must be of wood. It may be covered with pimpled rubber applied directly to the wood (in which case the maximum thickness is 2 mm) or with pimpled rubber as the outside layer of a sandwich (maximum thickness 4 mm), the middle layer being of sponge/cellular rubber.

3. If the pimples are outward, the covering is called a sandwich (if turned inward, it is a reverse sandwich).

4. The grip of the wooden handle may be one of the two styles, the "shakehand" or the "penholder" grip, the latter's disadvantage is that usually only one side of the blade can be used, but once perfected it has the tactical advantage of providing instant control for all shots used. Asiatics have been found preferring this penholder grip.

Space Requirement: The space requirement for championship play is an area 14 m long and 7 m wide, and clear above (to the lowest light fixture) to 4 in. This area is delineated by a canvas. The floor should be hard rigid and not slippery or shiny. No daylight source is permitted, only artificial lighting (without shadows) of prescribed intensity is allowed.

Scoring

1. The services must be delivered by striking the ball with the racket so that it strikes first the server's court and then passing over the net touches the receiver's court. At the moment of service the server must be behind the end line and between the extension of imaginary side lines.

2. During service the free hand must be held flat, fingers together and thumb free with the ball resting visibly on the palm. The ball must be projected vertically upwards and allowed to fall before being struck.

3. Scoring is very simple. Each player delivers five services. The loss to a server is a gain to his opponent. The first player or pair to reach 21" points wins the game. At "10-all" the service alternates after each point till a 2-point lead is established by a competitor or pair. Best of five or even best of three games decide the match.

4. Each player delivers two services, except at 20-all when the service alternates after each point. In doubles, service must always be from server's right hand half court, the return may be anywhere on the opposing court. The last receiver of service in doubles next serves to the last server's partner.

5. In doubles, if there are two pairs AB and XY, the order of striking must be AXBY or YBXA, depending on whom the partner "X" and "Y" select to serve first.

6. The first player or pair to reach 11 points wins the game unless the score is 10-all, when a 2-point lead is required to win the game. Best of five or even best of three decide the match. Service, as well as sequence of receiving in a doubles game, are changed after each game, and also at the half way stage (score 10) in a deciding game.

7. To avoid the problem of prolonged unnecessary rallies the rule has been amended. The rule states that if a game remains unfinished after 10 minutes, the left over part of the match will proceed as per "expedite system". In this system the service alternates point by point and the server is obliged to win each rally in 13 strokes (including his service) or else forfeit the point to his opponent.

Championships

Swaythling Cup: The Cup was presented by Hady Swaythling as the men's team championship of the world. The championship was first held in 1926.

Marcel Corbillon Cup: Marcel Corbillon Cup is awarded for women's team championship of the world for table tennis. The team consists of two single players and one pair chosen from a team of four. The result follows the best-of-five matches as in Davis Cup. The Cup was inaugurated in 1934, at Paris.

Biennial World Championships: The biennial world championships are held alternately in Europe, Africa, South America, East Asia, Balkan, Commonwealth, Caribbean and Scandinavian countries. Chinese invitation competition, European league and European club knock-out competitions are also famous tournaments.

India Cup: This was instituted in 1985 by Bajaj Company.

Asian Games: Table tennis was first included in the Asian Games in 1958.

Names to Remember

Adrianne Shirley Haydon Jones (Britain, 1938-): A lawn tennis and table tennis player who first represented England at the age of 15. She reached the final five times in world table tennis championship. She switched over to lawn tennis and won the French title in 1961 and 1966, and Wimbledon in 1969.

Zolten Machlevits (Hungary, 1892-1951): Five times captain of the successful Hungarian Swaythling Cup team. He was probably the best trainer and captain during that era.

Maria Mednyanszky (Hungary): One of the strongest women players from Hungary, she won the first five women's world championships (1926-1931). She also won seven women's doubles titles and six mixed doubles.

Victor Barna (1911-1972): Hungary-born Victor Barna, who adopted British nationality, may be called the greatest player of table tennis. His victories in various international tournaments are innumerable. He captained the England team several times including the 1953 Swaythling Cupwinning team at Bucharest.

Stellan Bengtsson (1952-): Swedish player, started playing at the age of 8. He won the following:

1970	–	European junior title
1971	–	World men's singles title
1972	–	English, French, Yugoslav and European men's singles titles
1972-73	–	Swedish
1973	–	Helped Sweden to break the Far-East monopoly in Swaythling Cup. He won all singles matches against China and Japan.

Richard Bergmann (1920–1970): Austria-born British national, he was dubbed as Mr.Table Tennis by the sporting press. Four times winner of men's singles world championship and six times winner of men's English Open championship.

Johnny Leach (England, 1922–): He partnered legendary Barna and Bergmann. He won the men's world championship in 1949 and 1951. In 1950, he won the singles, men's doubles and mixed doubles.

Chuang Tse Tung (1942 –): Chinese player, he won the world men's singles title in 1961, 1963 and 1965. He was a member of the National People's Congress in 1964.

Daimon (Japanese): Inventor of the penholder grip. Other famous Japanese players are: Ichiro Ogimura, Toshio Tanaka, Fujie Eguchi, Kimiyo Matsuzaki, Nobushiko Masegawa, Naoko Fukazu and Shigeo Ito.

Insook Bhusan (USA): A Korean by birth, represented South Korea twice, at Nagoya in 1971, and Sarajevo in 1973. She later migrated to the USA and represented the USA five times in world championship. Married an Indian, Shekhar Bhusan, in 1975.

Jiang Jialing (China): A Chinese player, he won the world men's singles championship in 1987 in New Delhi.

Jan-Ove Waldner (Sweden): World No.2 of 1987.

He Zhili (China): Women's world champion in 1987.

Yang-Young-Ja (South Korea): South Korean National Women Champion and also World No.2 in 1987.

Jiao Zhimn (China). A formidable player who won the gold medal in the tenth Asian Games at Seoul (South Korea).

Ryu Seung Min is a Korean table tennis player who won the gold medal at the 2004 Summer Olympics in the men's singles competition. His opponent was Wang Hao, a top-seeded player from Chinese national team. Along the way, he defeated many times Olympic champion Jan-Ove Waldner. Ryu is currently number eleven in the world.

Zhang Yining is a Chinese table tennis player, born October 5, 1981 in the city of Beijing, China. As of June 2005, she was ranked No 1 in the ITTF rankings, in both women's singles and women's doubles.[1] She remains a dominant figure. However, though she is No 1 in the world of Women's table tennis, she recently lost in the finals of the 2006 Women's World Cup to the No 2 women's player, Guo Yan (China).

■

TAEKWONDO

Chapter - 51

Taekwondo is a game of Korean origin. In Korean, TAE means to kick on a mark with the foot, Kwon means to strike or punch with hands and DO means an art. In short, it is a martial art of self defence.

History

It is the Korean way of self defence with the help of hands and feet. The history of this martial art goes back to the seventh century when the Silla kingdom, in the Korean Peninsula, assembled an elite corps of fighting force called HWA RANG DO. The five principal codes adopted by these soldiers–loyalty to the king, obedience to parents, honour and faith among friends, perseverance in battle and killing with justice– form the cornerstones of modern Taekwondo.

The martial art practised by these soldiers was called SOOK BAK. It consists of mainly of kicking techniques. After years of practice, several new techniques were incorporated into the game. With passage of time, using hands and feet were incorporated into SOOK BAK. This was known as TAEKON. Throughout its history, TAEKON has seen many ups and downs. But it survived all of them including the Japanese occupation of the Korean Peninsula in the 20th century. In 1955, the Korean Board renamed TAEKON as TAEKWONDO.

The World Taekwondo Federation was formed in the year 1973. It was included in the 10th Asian Games in Seoul. The International Olympic Committee recognised the game in 1980. It was a demonstration event at the 1988 and 1992 Olympic Games.

Dress

Taekwondo suit is called a tobok. It has been developed from the peasant's costume and is loose like the karate uniform. It consists of a loose shirt and tunic with baggy pants, tied together in the middle with a belt. The beginner starts with a white belt. During competition shin and instep pads, headguard, foot pads and hand mitts are worn for protection. These guards are all padded with foam or sponge.

Training

Self-discipline is an important thing through which a student learns to submerge his ego and develop the correct attitude towards his teacher and fellow students.

All instructions in taekwondo are given in the Korean language.The training place is called Dojang.

At the beginning of the training great emphasis is placed on stretching and other exercises. Initially both defensive and offensive blocking and punching are taught. This is followed by linking up these movements together in a set of logical sequences, so that a beginner can understand the continuity of the movement.

The basic kicks are:

(a) Front kick
(b) Side kick
(c) Back kick
(d) Round house kick.

In addition, special emphasis is placed on the following:

(a) Spinning hook kick
(b) Jumping front kick
(c) Jumping side kick
(d) Low spinning and sweeping kicks
(e) The drop spin kick and the drop side kick.

Similar to Karate: A beginner starts at tenth class which is called KUP in Korean. Gradually he works his way to the proficiency of an instructor or black belt or 1st Dan.

Stances

The correct posture is extremely important to perform the various techniques. That is why a student learns the basic stances which resemble the karate stances. One of the popular stances is the walking stance. The basic stances are called SEOGI.

Techniques of the Hand

Basic defensive blocks by hand are also similar to karate, like forearm downward block, the inner forearm downward block, and the rising block. In application, these are more forceful in taekwondo than in karate. In addition, taekwondo uses evasion techniques to a great extent for blocking and countering attacks.

After learning blocking a beginner learns the techniques to strike. They are:

(a) Straight fingertip thrust
(b) Reverse knife hand strike
(c) Palm heal strike
(d) Back knuckle strike
(e) Inward knife hand strike
(f) Ridge hand strike
(g) Basic punch
(h) Elbow strike.

Taekwondo Patterns

Taekwondo has various set patterns, like katas in karate. But unlike karate, it stipulates that the students must master all the techniques before they graduate to practise the patterns. A pattern is a set series of combinations of techniques performed in a sequential order and it is designed to teach a beginner to perform movements in all directions. All patterns begin and end at the same spot. That is why it is said that to understand taekwondo, it is essential to understand the patterns. The name of the first pattern is POOMSE. TAEGUEK means the origin of all things in universe and POOMSE means a pattern. The first pattern has 18 movements.

Free Sparring

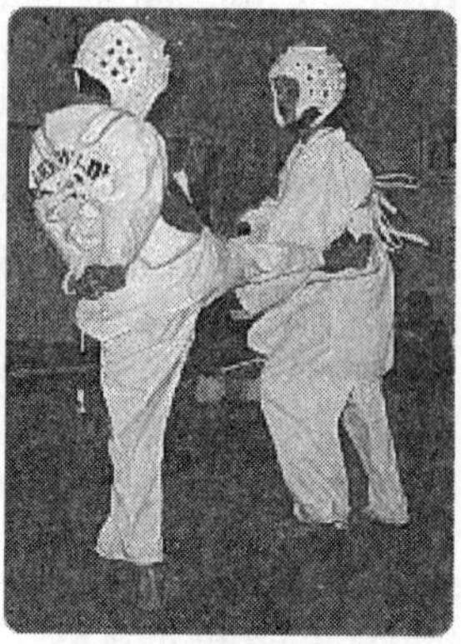

Free fighting is generally permitted after a student has achieved certain amount of proficiency at all levels. A fighter must be in a position to exploit the full range of fighting techiniques.

Techniques of Destruction in Taekwondo

Taekwondo places special emphasis on destruction techniques. Testing the efficiency of strikes, punches and kicks by directing them at roofing tiles, bricks, etc., are standard requirements to pass a grade and to get promoted to the proficiency level. Taekwondo advocates use of these techniques in a life and death situation.

Competition

1. Competition fights generally consist of 3 rounds of three minutes with one minute interval between each round.

2. In Individual fight categories, there are 10 weight divisions for men and 8 for women. During the 10th Asiad only 8 weight divisions were there for men.

3. Tournament competitors have to be of black belt standard.

4. The competitors try to score maximum points by using techniques which involve body contact.

5. The kicks score more points.

6. Knock outs are possible.

Championships

Asian Games: In 1986, at the 10th Asiad, taekwondo was included for the first time. There were contests in eight weight divisions. Korea won 7 gold medals.

World Championship: World championship began in South Korea in 1974.

Names to Remember

Hadi Saei Bonehkohal (born June 10, 1976 in Tehran, Iran) is an Iranian Taekwondo athlete who competed in the Men's 68 kg (featherweight) at the 2004 Summer Olympics and won the gold medal. In the 2000 Summer Olympics in Sydney, he won bronze. Having previously competed in Lightweight (67-72 kg), he is the 1999 World

Champion and 2003 World Championship silver medallist. When his home town of Bam was devastated in the 2003 earthquake, Saei put his medals on auction to raise money for the victims. He has been World Champion in the Tae Kwon Do World Championships 7 times and was recently awarded the title of 'Best Tae Kwon Do Player of all Time' by the International Board.

Steven Lopez (born November 9, 1978) is the 2000 and 2004 Olympic gold medalist in Taekwondo at the Olympics. in the 80 Kg category. Lopez is a 1997 graduate of Kempner High School in Sugar Land, Texas. Steven's siblings, Mark, Diana, and Jean Lopez were all USA National Team Members in the sport of Taekwondo. His dream is to have his two younger siblings, Mark and Diana on the same Olympic team one day. He is also 2005 World Taekwondo Championships (Welter): GOLD and 2005 Sullivan Award Finalist.

Chu Mu-Yen born March 14, 1982) is a Taekwondo athlete from Taiwan. He is the second Taiwanese athlete and first male to win a gold medal at the Olympics, winning in men's under 58-kilogram class in Taekwondo at the Athens 2004 Games. Later he got involved in some scandal and apologised publicly.

■

TENIKOIT

Chapter - 52

Tenikoit is played with a rubber ring across a net in a rectangular court. Also known as 'ring tennis', it is played by two or four players.

History

Tenikoit, also known as ring tennis, is a combination of tennis and quoits. Quoits is also an outdoor game in which a ring is thrown at a peg target.

Tenikoit, which closely resembles Deck Tennis, can be played by two or four players in either singles or doubles and like Deck Tennis it can be played in a much smaller area than tennis.

Court Dimensions

Dimensions of a tenikoit court are described here:

Net

Length of net	:	18 to 20 ft
Width of the net	:	18 in
Top of the net	:	5 ft high
Net height at the	:	Height 5 ft.

Ring

Material	:	Rubber
Diameter	:	7 in
Thickness	:	1½ in
Weight	:	7-9 oz

Rules of Tenikoit

Rules are explained briefly as under:

1. It is played by either one or two players on each side. They throw the ring from one side to the other by hand over a net.

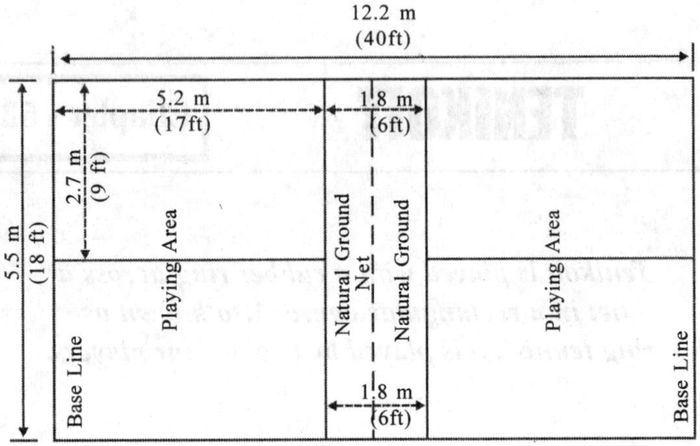

Tenikoit Court

2. It consists of 15 points. If the score is 14-all, the play is continued till one side has a lead of two points.
3. A Rubber is the best of three games.
4. Players are to change ends at the end of each game.
5. In doubles, the person who is serving should stand behind the back line of the right hand court. He serves the ring diagonally over the net to the opponent. The side serving is called "in" and the side receiving the service is called "out".
6. The ring is returned by the receiver only.
7. The ring must be returned by the same hand with which it was caught.
8. The ring must be returned immediately as holding the ring is considered baulking.
9. The ring must be caught with only one hand. Either hand is permitted.
10. After the serve, the players can take any position.
11. The ring must be played over the net.
12. Over-hand delivery is not allowed.
13. Baulking is not allowed.
14. Walking with the ring is not allowed.
15. **Let:** A service which is good but touches the net is called let. Reservice is allowed. It is not allowed if the ring falls untouched in the wrong court or in the out of bound area.

16. The ring touching the boundary line in any way is in play.
17. After losing the service in doubles, the player who has been serving occupies the right hand court.
18. If the "in" side scores a point then the server next time serves from the back of the left hand court.
19. If the point is scored by the opponent then the service change takes place.
20. No player may stand within the neutral ground on either side of the net and if the ring falls within the neutral ground even though it has crossed the net in service, it is a fault against the serving side which loses a point.

Scoring

The play becomes dead on the following occasions:

(a) The ring is not caught and falls to the ground within the playing area.

(b) The ring is touched but not caught by a player.

(c) The ring is caught but not thrown back correctly within the playing area.

(d) The ring is caught with both hands.

■

TUG OF WAR

Chapter - 53

This is a contest of stength and skill between two teams using a rope for test.

History

It is said to have originated in harvest gathering in ancient China, or in training slaves to lift stones up the Sphinx. It might have developed from hoisting sails by sailors or hauling guns by soldiers up the mountains of India's North-West frontier. It also has deep roots in England in inter-village competitions in the 18th century. By 1880 , it became an approved event at athletic meetings and in 1900, it was included for the first time in the Olympic Games. At the 1920 Olympics, it was included for the last time and was won by Britain. In 1958, the Tug of War Association was formed in England, followed by the formation of the seven-nation International Tug of War Federation.

The Game

It is a contest of strength and skill between two teams of eight men each, pulling from opposite ends of a long thick rope. The rope is between 4 in and 5 in (10-12.5 cm) in circumference and 32 m (35 yd) long. A coloured tape is fixed at the centre of the rope. On either side of this mark, at a distance of 6 ft 6 in (2 m) are fixed two white tapes. The ground is marked by three parallel lines corresponding exactly to the three markings on the rope.

Rules of Tug of War

1. The hands of the nearest member of each team must be within 12 in (30 cm) of the outside coloured tapes on the rope but should not touch them.

2. Contestants are weighed just before the competition begins, wearing the kit such as boots without studs, jerseys, shorts and socks.

3. Total team weight must be under the limit of the class for which they are entered, usually 559 kg to 711.2 kg, plus the most popular open catch weight class.

4. Each team is allotted one coach, who controls the effort of the team to catch the opponents off balance.

5. The anchorman may have the rope under one arm and over the other shoulder, but the end must hang free and may not at any point cross the rope.

6. Any two infringements as described below may lead to disqualification:

(a) Persistent sitting on the ground.

(b) Deliberate sitting on a foot.

(c) Failure to return immediately to the pulling position after slipping. The offending team is disqualified for that game only.

7. For indoor events the rules are slightly amended.

8. The centre mark for the indoor rope is a white tape.

9. On the floor the outside marks are 13 ft 1/2 in. (4 m) from the centre mark. The centre tape on the rope must pass over one of the outside marks to denote a win.

Championships

National outdoor championships, first organised in 1958, with three and later with four weight classes, are held annually. Indoor championship began in 1966. European championship was first held in 1965, and from 1968, it has become an annual event in two weight classes only, i.e., 640 kg and 720 kg. World championships started in 1975. Women's event started in 1986.

■

VOLLEYBALL

Chapter - 54

Volleyball is a six-a-side team game played indoor or outdoor on a rectangular field which is divided into equal square courts. The two teams hit a large ball back and forth over a horizontal net with their hands.

History

In 1995, the sport of Volleyball was 100 years old! The sport originated in the United States, and is now played all over the world. It ranks behind only soccer in popularity among participation sports. Today there are more than 800 million players worldwide who play Volleyball at least once a week.

In 1895, William G. Morgan, an instructor at the Young Men's Christian Association (YMCA) in Holyoke, Mass., decided to blend elements of basketball, baseball, tennis, and handball to create a game for his classes of businessmen which would demand less physical contact than basketball. He created the game of Volleyball (at that time called mintonette). Morgan borrowed the net from tennis, and raised it 6 feet 6 inches above the floor, just above the average man's head.

During a demonstration game, someone remarked to Morgan that the players seemed to be volleying the ball back and forth over the net, and perhaps "volleyball" would be a more descriptive name for the sport. On July 7, 1896, at Springfield College the first game of "volleyball" was played.

Playing Area

The playing area includes the playing court and the free zone. It is rectangular and symmetrical.

Dimensions

The playing court is a rectangle measuring 18 x 9 m, surrounded by a free zone which is a minimum of 3 m wide on all sides.

The free playing space is the space above the playing area which is free from any obstructions. The free playing space shall measure a minimum of 7 m in height from the playing surface.

Playing Surface

The surface must be flat, horizontal and uniform. It must not present any danger of injury to the players. It is forbidden to play on rough or slippery surfaces.

Lines on the Court

All lines are 5 cm wide. They must be of a light colour which is different from the colour of the floor and from any other lines.

Boundary lines

Two sidelines and two end lines mark the playing court. Both sidelines and end lines are drawn inside the dimensions of the playing court.

Centre line

The axis of the centre line divides the playing court into two equal courts measuring 9 x 9 m each; however the entire width of the line is considered to belong to both courts equally. This line extends beneath the net from sideline to sideline.

Attack line

On each court, an attack line, whose rear edge is drawn 3 m back from the axis of the centre line, marks the front zone.

Zones and Areas

Penalty area: A penalty area, sized approximately 1 x 1 m and equipped with two chairs, is located in the control area, outside the prolongation of each end line. They may be limited by a 5 cm wide red line.

Net and Posts

Height of the Net: Placed vertically over the centre line there is a net whose top is set at the height of 2.43 m for men and 2.24 m for women. Its height is measured from the centre of the playing court. The net height (over the two sidelines) must be exactly the same and must not exceed the official height by more than 2 cm.

Structure: The net is 1 m wide and 9.50 to 10 metres long (with 25 to 50 cm on each side of the side bands), made of 10 cm square black mesh. At its top a horizontal band, 7 cm wide, made of two-fold white canvas, is sewn along its full length. Each extreme end of the band has a hole, through which passes a cord, fastening the band to the posts for keeping its top taut. Within the band, a flexible cable fastens the net to the posts and keeps its top taut.

At the bottom of the net there is another horizontal band, 5cm wide, similar to the top band, through which is threaded a rope. This rope fastens the net to the posts and keeps its lower part taut.

Side Bands: Two white bands are fastened vertically to the net and placed directly above each sideline. They are 5 cm wide and 1 m long, and are considered as part of the net.

Antennae: An antenna is a flexible rod, 1.80 m long and 10 mm in diameter, made of fiberglass or similar material. An antenna is fastened at the outer edge of each side band. The antennae are placed on opposite sides of the net. The top 80 cm of each antenna extends above the net and is marked with 10 cm stripes of contrasting colour, preferably red and white. The antennae are considered as part of the net and laterally delimit the crossing space.

Posts

The posts supporting the net are placed at a distance of 0.50-1.00 m outside the sidelines. They are 2.55 m high and preferably adjustable.

Balls

The ball shall be spherical, made of a flexible leather or synthetic leather case with a bladder inside made of rubber or a similar material. Its colour may be a uniform light colour, or a combination of colours. Synthetic leather material and colour combinations of balls used in International Official competitions should comply with FIVB standards. Its circumference is 65-67 cm and its weight is 260-280 g. Its inside pressure shall be 0.30 to 0.325 kg/cm2 (4.26 to 4.61 psi) (294.3 to 318.82 mbar or hPa).

TEAMS

A team may consist of a maximum of 12 players, one coach, one assistant coach, one trainer and one medical doctor. For FIVB World and Official Competitions, the medical doctor must be accredited beforehand by the FIVB.

One of the players, other than the Libero, is the team captain, who shall be indicated on the scoresheet.

Equipment

A player's equipment consists of a jersey, shorts, socks (the uniform) and sport shoes. The colour and the design for the jerseys, shorts and socks must be uniform for the team (except for the Libero). The uniforms must be clean. The shoes must be light and pliable with rubber or leather soles without heels.

Team Leaders

Both the team captain and the coach are responsible for the conduct and discipline of their team members. The Libero cannot be the team captain.

To Score a Point, to win a set and the Match

To Score a Point

Point: A team scores a point:

- By successfully grounding the ball on the opponent's court;
- When the opponent team commits a fault;
- When the opponent team receives a penalty.

Fault: A team commits a fault by making a playing action contrary to the rules (or by violating them in some other way). The referees judge the faults and determine the consequences according to the rules:

- If two or more faults are committed successively, only the first one is counted.
- If two or more faults are committed by opponents simultaneously, a DOUBLE FAULT is called and the rally is replayed.

Consequences of winning a rally

A rally is the sequence of playing actions from the moment of the service hit by the server until the ball is out of play.

If the serving team wins a rally, it scores a point and continues to serve;

If the receiving team wins a rally, it scores a point and it must serve next.

To Win a Set

A set (except the deciding, 5th set) is won by the team which first scores 25 points with a minimum lead of two points. In the case of a 24-24 tie, play is continued until a two-point lead is achieved (26-24; 27-25; ...).

To Win the Match

The match is won by the team that wins three sets.

In the case of a 2-2 tie, the deciding set (the 5th) is played to 15 points with a minimum lead of 2 points.

Positions

At the moment the ball is hit by the server, each team must be positioned within its own court in the rotational order (except the server).

The positions of the players are numbered as follows:

The three players along the net are front-row players and occupy positions 4 (front-left), 3 (front-centre) and 2 (front-right);

The other three are back-row players occupying positions 5 (back-left), 6 (back-centre) and 1 (back-right).

Rotation

Rotational order is determined by the team's starting line-up, and controlled with the service order, and players' positions, throughout the set.

When the receiving team has gained the right to serve, its players rotate one position clock-wise: the player in position 2 rotates to position 1 to serve, the player in position 1 rotates to position 6, etc.

States of Play

Ball in Play: The ball is in play from the moment of the hit of the service authorized by the first referee.

Ball out of Play: The ball is out of play at the moment of the fault which is whistled by one of the referees; in the absence of a fault, at the moment of the whistle.

Ball "In": The ball is "in" when it touches the floor of the playing court including the boundary lines.

Ball "Out": The ball is "out" when:

- The part of the ball which contacts the floor is completely outside the boundary lines;
- It touches an object outside the court, the ceiling or a person out of play;
- It touches the antennae, ropes, posts or the net itself outside the side bands;
- It crosses the vertical plane of the net either partially or totally outside the crossing space.
- It crosses completely the lower space under the net.

Playing the Ball

Each team must play within its own playing area and space. The ball may, however, be retrieved from beyond the free zone.

The team is entitled to a maximum of three hits (in addition to blocking, for returning the ball. If more are used, the team commits the fault of: "FOUR HITS".

Consecutive Contacts

A player may not hit the ball two times consecutively.

Faults in Playing the Ball

Four Hits: a team hits the ball four times before returning it.

Assisted Hit: a player takes support from a team-mate or any structure/object in order to reach the ball within the playing area.

Catch: the ball is caught and/or thrown; it does not rebound from the hit

Double Contact : a player hits the ball twice in succession or the ball contacts various parts of his/her body in succession.

Ball at the Net

Ball Crossing the Net

The ball sent to the opponent's court must go over the net within the crossing space. The crossing space is the part of the vertical plane of the net limited as follows:

- Below, by the top of the net;
- At the sides, by the antennae, and their imaginary extension;
- Above, by the ceiling.

Ball Touching the Net

While crossing the net, the ball may touch it.

Ball in the Net

A ball driven into the net may be recovered within the limits of the three team hits.

If the ball rips the mesh of the net or tears it down, the rally is cancelled and replayed.

Player at the Net

Reaching Beyond the Net

In blocking, a blocker may touch the ball beyond the net, provided that he/she does not interfere with the opponents' play before or during the latter's attack hit.

After an attack hit, a player is permitted to pass his/her hand beyond the net, provided that the contact has been made within his/her own playing space.

Contact with the Net

Contact with the net by a player is not a fault, unless it is made during the action of playing the ball, or it interferes with the play.

A player penetrates into the opponents' court.

A player touches the net or the antenna during his/her action of playing the ball or interferes with the play.

Service

The service is the act of putting the ball into play, by the back right player, placed in the service zone.

First Service in Set

The first service of the first set, as well as that of the deciding set (the 5th) is executed by the team determined by the toss.

The other sets will be started with the service of the team that did not serve first in the previous set.

Service Order

The players must follow the service order recorded on the line-up sheet.

After the first service in a set, the player to serve is determined as follows:

- when the serving team wins the rally, the player (or his/her substitute) who served before, serves again;
- when the receiving team wins the rally, it gains the right to serve and rotates before actually serving. The player who moves from the front right position to the back-right position will serve.

Blocking: Blocking is the action of players close to the net to intercept the ball coming from the opponents by reaching higher than the top of the net. Only front-row players are permitted to complete a block.

Time-out and Technical Time-outs

All time-outs that are requested last for 30 seconds.

For FIVB World and Official Competitions, in sets 1-4, two additional 60-second "Technical Time-Outs" are applied automatically when the leading team reaches the 8th and 16th points.

In the deciding (5th) set, there are no "Technical Time-Outs"; only two time-outs of 30 seconds duration may be requested by each team.

During all time-outs, the players in play must go to the free zone near their bench.

Substitution of Players

A substitution is the act by which a player, other than the Libero or his/her replacement player, after being recorded by the scorer, enters the game to occupy the position of another player, who must leave the court at that moment. Substitution requires the referee's authorization.

Six substitutions is the maximum permitted per team per set. One or more players may be substituted at the same time.

Intervals and Change of Courts

Intervals

All intervals between sets last three minutes.

During this period of time, the change of courts and line-up registrations of the teams on the scoresheet are made.

The interval between the second and the third sets can be extended up to 10 minutes by the competent body at the request of the organizer.

Change of Courts

After each set, the teams change courts, with the exception of the deciding set.

In the deciding set, once the leading team reaches 8 points, the teams change courts without delay and the player positions remain the same.

The Liber Player

Designation of the Libero

Each team has the right to designate among the list of 12 players one (1) specialised defensive player "Libero". The Libero must be recorded on the scoresheet before the match in the special line reserved for this. The Libero is allowed to replace any player in a back row position.

Line Judges

If only two line judges are used, they stand at the corners of the court closest to the right hand of each referee, diagonally at 1 to 2 m from the corner.

Championships

World Championship. This was instituted in 1949. The USSR has won the maximum men's titles so far (1949, 1952, 1960, 1962, 1978 and 1982). It also won the women's championships in 1952, 1956, 1960 and 1970 which was instituted in 1952. Japan has also won women's 4 titles (1962, 1967, 1974 and 1987).

Olympics. Volleyball for both men and women was introduced in the 1964 Olympics. The USSR won the men's competition in 1964, 1968 and 1980. Japan won the women's competition in 1964 and 1976. The USSR won 4 women's championship in 1968, 1972, 1980 and 1988.

Names to Remember

Dante Guimaraes Santos do Amaral, mostly known as Dante(Born 30 September 1980 in Itumbiara) is a Brazilian professional volleyball player. Dante, who is 2,01 m and 86 kg, plays in the position of wing-spiker. He won the Gold for Brazil in 2004 Olympic games.Since 2005 he plays to the Greek giants Panathinaikos, aiming to win the Champions League. Up to now he has won the Greek championship in 2006 and the Greek cup and supercup in 2007.

Gilberto Amaury de Godoy Filho, known as Giba (born December 23, 1976 in Londrina) is a Brazilian professional volleyball player. Giba is 194 cm and plays as passer-attacker. He had leukemia in the childhood. He was a team memebr of the 2004 Olympic Gold Champion of Brazil.

■

WATER POLO

Chapter - 55

The game is played in water in which each side tries to throw or propel an inflated ball into the opponent's goal. There are seven players each side.

History

There is little documentation as to the origins of water polo. It is known, however, that the sport originated in the rivers and lakes of mid-19th century England as an aquatic version of rugby. Early games used an inflated, vulcanized rubber ball imported from India known as a "pulu" (the single Indian word for all "balls"). Pronounced "polo" by the English, both the ball and the game became known as "water polo."

To attract more spectators to swimming exhibitions, the London Swimming Association developed a set of water polo rules for indoor swimming pools in 1870.

At first, players scored by planting the ball at the end of the pool with both hands. A favorite trick of the players was to place the five-to-nine inch rubber ball inside their swimming suit and dive under the murky water, then appear again as near the goal as possible.

If the player came up too near the goal, he was promptly jumped on by the goalie, who was permitted to stand on the pool deck. Games were often nothing more than gang fights in the water as players ignored the ball, preferring underwater wrestling matches that usually ended with one man floating to the surface unconscious.

The introduction of the "Trudgeon stroke" by Scottish players changed the nature of water polo. It became a game that emphasized swimming, speed and passing. Scottish rules moved from a rugby variant to a soccer style of play. Goals became a cage of 10 x 3 feet and a goal could be scored by being thrown. Players could only be tackled when they "held" the ball and the ball could no longer be taken under water. The small rubber ball was replaced by a leather soccer ball.

Water polo was first played in the United States in 1888. The game featured the old rugby style of play which resembled American football in the water. "American style" water polo became very popular and by the late 1890's was played in venues like Madison Square Garden and Boston's Mechanics Hall, attracting large number of spectators to national championship games.

The game of the day featured plays like the "flying salmon," where the player with the ball leapt through the air from the backs of his teammates to score a goal. Violence was the game's main attraction.

Meanwhile, the rest of the world adopted the Scottish rules: Hungary in 1889, Belgium in 1900, Austria and Germany in 1894 and France in 1895. By 1900, water polo was so popular it became the first team sport added to the Olympic program.

In 1911, the Federation International de Natation Amateur (FINA), the international governing body for all amateur aquatic sports, adopted the Scottish rules for all international events.

However, the Americans continued to play by their own rules until 1912, but by 1914 American clubs agreed to play under the international rules.

Internationally, European teams have dominated the sport. The United States is the only non-European team to win Olympic medals.

Water Polo Field

The dimensions of a water polo field are 30 × 20 m.

(a) Minimum depth of water for the Olympic and international tour-naments is not less than 1.8 m (5 ft 11 in).

(b) Distinctive marks are provided on both sides of the field to denote the goal line, 2 m and 4 m line, and the half distance line.

(c) The goal posts and cross bars are made of wood or metal or synthetic, with rectangular sections of 0.075 m (3 in) square with the goal line and painted white.

(d) The goal posts are fixed rigid and perpendicular and equidistant from the sides and at least 0.30 m (11¾ in) in front of the ends of the field of play.

(e) The inner sides of the goal posts are 3 m (9 ft 10¼ in) apart. The underside of the crossbar is 0.90 m (2 ft 11½ in) above the surface of water where the water is 1.5 m (4 ft 11 in) deep, and 2.40 m (7 ft 10½ in) from the bottom of the bath when the depth of the water is less than 1.50 m.

(f) Limp nets are attached to the goal fixtures to enclose the entire goal space, securely fastened to the goal posts and cross bar and allowing not less than 0.30 m (11¾ in) clear space behind the goal line everywhere within the goal area.

The Ball

The circumference must not be less than 0.68 m (2 ft 2¾ in) and more than 0.71 m (2 ft 4 in). Its weight should be between 400 g (14 oz) and 450 g (15 oz).

Dress

Swimming trunks with strips underneath. Grease or oil cannot be used on the body.

Rules of Water Polo

1. The officials are: two referees, two time-keepers, two secretaries, and two goal judges, with specified duties and powers.

2. The referees are in absolute control of the game. All decisions of the referee are final and his interpretation of the rules must be obeyed during the game.

3. The time-keepers must have water polo stop watches.

4. The goal judges signal with a white flag for a goal throw (i.e., when the entire ball has passed over the goal line, excluding the goal post area last touched by one of the attacking teams) and with a red flag (when the last player to touch the ball was a defender). The judges signal with both the flags when a goal is scored.

5. The game consists of four quarters of seven minutes each of actual play. The team changes position before the start of each quarter. There are intervals of two minutes between each quarter.

6. Extra time, if required, is played after a five-minute interval. The extra play is two parts of three minutes of actual play each with an interval of one minute.

7. A team consists of seven players and six reserves or substitutes.

8. Each side wears caps, one side white and the other dark blue, which are numbered on both sides. The goalkeeper wears a red cap numbered 1. If change of the goal keeper takes place then the substitute must wear his cap.

9. Before a match begins the players must discard all articles like rings and they must wear trunks with separate drawers underneath.

10. At the beginning of each quarter of the play, the players take up positions on their respective goal lines about one metre apart. Not more than two are permitted between the goal posts.

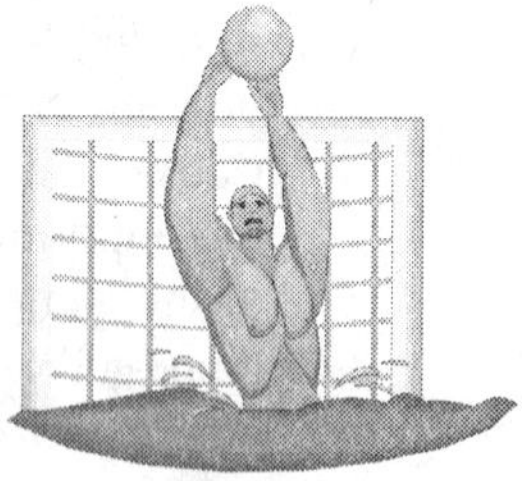

11. The ball is held in saucer on the surface at the centre of the pool and released accurately into the centre of both or the referee throws the ball in the centre of the field.

12. The goal may be scored by any part of the body, except the clenched fist, provided that at the start or re-start of the game, the ball has been played by two or more players of either side.

13. The goalkeeper has certain privileges, not given to other members of the team, but also certain limitations within the 4 m area. The goalkeeper may stand and walk, strike the ball with clenched fist, jump from the floor and touch the ball with both hands at the same time.

14. **Rules for Penalty:** (a) The penalty for an ordinary foul is a free throw to the opposing team. Ordinary fouls are:

(i) Moving beyond the goal line at the start or restart, before the referee's signal.

(ii) Holding on to or pushing off from the goal posts, fixtures, sides of the pool, etc., during play.

(iii) Taking an active part in the game when standing on the floor of the pool, walking when the play is in progress, jumping from the floor of the bath to play the ball or tackle an opponent.

(iv) Deliberately impeding or preventing the free limb movement of an opponent unless he is holding the ball.

(v) Touching the ball with both hands at the same time, pushing off from an opponent, wasting time in order to hold the normal progress of the game.

(b) Penalties for major fouls are heavier than for ordinary fouls. Major fouls are:

(i) Holding, sinking or pulling back an opponent not holding the ball.

(ii) Kicking or striking an opponent or making excessive movements with that intent.

(iii) The same player persisting in an ordinary foul.

(iv) Refusing to obey the referee: the offending player is ordered out for the rest of the game.

(v) Causing an act of brutality. A free throw is awarded to the opposing team and the offending player ordered out of the game.

(vi) Being guilty of misconduct such as violence, bad language, persistent fouling, etc.

(vii) Interfering with the taking of a free throw, penalty throw, corner throw or goal throw.

(c) A penalty throw, which is a direct shot at the goal, is the ultimate punishment. Penalty throws are awarded for a number of major fouls on an attacking player within 4 m (13 ft 1 in) of the defender's goal line.

(d) A free throw is awarded for an ordinary foul committed within the 2 metres area and must be taken from the 2 metres line. Other than this, free throws are taken from the point where the foul occurs.

Championship

Amateur Swimming Association's Club Championship: Instituted in 1888, in Britain. The London Polytechnic has won this title 14 times between 1956 and 1982.

World Championship: Instituted in 1973, at Belgrade, Hungary won this championship. Silver and bronze medallists were the USSR and Yugoslavia. A women's competition was introduced in 1986, and Australia won this competition.

Olympic Games: Instituted in 1900, at the Paris Olympics.

Names to Remember

Tibor Benedek (born July 12, 1972 in Budapest) is a Hungarian water polo player, who played in the gold medal squads at the 2000 Summer Olympics and 2004 Summer Olympics. Benedek also competed at the 1996 Summer Olympics, where the Hungarian team was placed 4th. Benedek was named Hungarian Water Polo Player of the Year in 1992, 1993 and 1994. He made his debut for the national side in 1990. His father, Miklos Benedek, is a famous actor.

Peter Biros (born April 5, 1976 in Miskolc) is a Hungarian water polo player, who played on the gold medal squads at the 2000 Summer Olympics and 2004 Summer Olympics. He is nicknamed Facan, meaning 'pheasant', and made his debut for the national side in 1997, during an international tournament in Seville, Spain.

Aleksandar Ciric (born December 30, 1977) is a Serbian water polo player who played on the bronze medal squad (of FR Yugoslavia) at the 2000 Summer Olympics and the silver medal squad (of Serbia and Montenegro) at the 2004 Summer Olympics and he is a great boxing player in the pool.

■

WEIGHTLIFTING

Chapter - 56

The aim of the game is to lift weight in a specified manner.

History

The origin of weightlifting dates back to the early days of human civilization. Initially lifting heavy stones had been a pastime and a number of competitions were held. Even today in Greece huge boulders can be found with names of the lifters. Stone-lifting is still popular in Spain and France. Modern weightlifting with barbells became popular towards the end of the 19th century. The International Weightlifting Federation was formed in 1920, in Paris by Jule Russet of France. It was included in the Olympic games for the first time in 1896.

In 1935, the Indian Weightlifting Federation was formed . Sir Bijoy Chand Mahatab of Burdwan was its first president and N.N. Bose, Barristar-at-Law, was the first honorary secretary. In the same year it got affiliated with the Indian Olympic Association and International Weightlifting Federation. In the 1936 Berlin Olympic games, Indian weightlifting team participated for the first time. Similarly, in the Asian games India participated in 1951 games held in Delhi and in the Commonwealth Games in 1966, at Kington.

Initially, five body-weight categories were established for the Olympic games. They were Feather Weight (60 kg), Light Weight (67.5 kg), Middle Weight (75 kg) Light-Heavy weight (82.5 kg) and Heavy weight (90 kg) and in 1972 Fly weight (52) and Super heavy weight (over 110 kg). A new category (100 kg) was added again in the year 1980. At present the following are the weight categories:

For Women

1. Upto 52 kg
2. Upto 56 kg
3. Upto 60 kg
4. Upto 67.5 kg
5. Upto 75 kg
6. Over 82.5 kg
7. Over 90 kg
8. Over 100 kg
9. Over 110 kg
10. Over 110 kg

For Men

1. Upto 44 kg
2. Upto 48 kg
3. Upto 52 kg
4. Upto 56 kg
5. Over 60 kg
6. Over 67.5 kg
7. Over 72 kg
8. Over 82.5 kg
9. Over 82.5 kg

Barbells

Barbells used in international competitions must conform to the following measurements:

(a) Length of the bar 2200 m with tolerance of ± 1 mm.
(b) Diameter of the bar 28 mm (± 0.03 mm) on smooth part of the bar.
(c) Diameter of the sleeve 50 mm (± 0.2 mm).
(d) Distance between inside collars 1310 mm (± 0.5 mm).
(e) Width of the inside collar including the collar of the sleeve 30 mm (± 1 mm).
(f) Weight of the bar with sleeves 20 kg.
(g) Weight of the collar 2.5 kg each.
(h) Diameter of the largest disc 450 mm.
(i) Weight of the largest disc 25 kg. U). The discs must be of the following range:

25 kg — red
20 kg — blue
15 kg — yellow
10 kg — green
5 kg — white
2.5 kg — black
1.25 kg — chrome
0.5 kg — chrome
0.25 kg — chrome

450 mm dia discs must be covered with rubber or plastic.

Competition Platform

The platform must be square, measuring 4 metres on each side, the top edge of the platform must have a different coloured line at least 5 cm. The platform may be of wood or plastic and may be covered with a non-slippery material. Height must be between 50 mm and 150 mm.

Referees' Light

Three white and 3 red lights are arranged horizontally to coincide with the position of three referees, each of them has switches of one white and one red lights. White light indicates "good lift" and red light "no lift." For a decision, two or three white lights and two or three red lights are used.

Timing Clock

The timing device must have the following characteristics:

(a) Operate continuously upto a minimum of 3 minutes.

(b) Indicate intervals of minimum ten seconds.

(c) Give an automatic audible signal one minute before the end of the lifter's allocated time.

(d) The elapsed time has to be well displayed simultaneously both in competition and warm-up areas.

Attempt Board

A visible board has to be put up on which must appear the name of the lifter, the weight to be attempted and the number of the attempt.

Score Board

A score board has to be set up in the competition arena in order to record and display the results.

Warm-up Room

The competitors must be provided with a warm-up area located close to the competition platform.This area has to be equipped with an appropriate number of platforms, barbells, etc., in relation to the number of competitors. In addition, it has to be equipped with a loudspeaker linked with the microphone of the announcer, a score board showing names of the competitors, lot number, body-weight and the weights they have requested before being called to the platform.

Dress of Competitors

Costume: It consists of a one-piece costume (leotard type). A collarless Tshirt may be worn under the costume, its sleeves cannot extend further than halfway on the upper arm. Trunks may be worn over the costume. Socks may be worn but they cannot go above the knees and cannot cover the bandages.

Belt: The maximum width of the belt may be 120 mm at its widest part. No belt can be worn under the competitor's costume.

Bandages and Plasters: Bandages may be worn on the wrists, knees, hands, fingers and thumbs. They may be made of gauze, medical crap or leather. A one-piece elastic bandage may be worn on the knee. Plasters on fingers are allowed but cannot cover the tip of the fingers. There are specific rules for the size of bandages.

No bandages or substitute of bandages are allowed on the elbow, the torso, the thighs and the shins.

Weightlifting Shoes: A competitor must wear shoes. The shoes must be made in such a way as not to give the athlete an unfair advantage or additional support. Maximum height permitted on the upper part of the shoe, measured from the top of the sole, is 130 mm. The sole cannot project from the shoe by more than 5 mm at any point. The heel of the shoes must not be tapered.

The Two Lifts

The international body recognises the following two lifts:

(a) The snatch

(b) The clean and jerk

These lifts must be executed with both the hands and only three attempts are allowed in each type of lift.

Snatch

The bar is placed horizontally in front of the lifter's legs. It is gripped palms downwards and pulled in a single movement from the ground to the full extent of both arms above the head, while either splitting or bending the legs. The bar passes with a continuous movement along the body. No part other than the feet may touch the ground during the execution of the lift. The weight which has been lifted must be maintained in the final motionless position, arms and legs extended, the feet on the same line, until the referee gives the signal to replace the bar on the platform.

Incorrect movements are — pulling from the hang, uneven or incomplete extension of arms, pausing during execution of arms, finishing with a press out, bending and extending arms during recovery, leaving the platform or touching the area outside the platform, replacing the bar on the platform before the referee's signal, dropping the bar from behind after the referee's signal, failing to bring the feet and the barbell in the same line and failing to replace the complete barbell on the platform.

Clean and Jerk

The Clean: The bar is placed horizontally in front of the lifter's legs. It is gripped, palms downwards and pulled in a single movement from ground to the shoulders, while either splitting or bending the legs. During this continuous movement, the bar may slide along the thighs and the lap.The bar must not touch the chest before the final position. It then rests on the clavicles (collar bones) or on the chest above the nipples or on the arms fully bent. The feet return to the same line, legs straight, before performing the Jerk.

The Jerk: The lifter bends the legs and extends them as well as the arms so as to bring the bar to the full stretch of the arms vertically extended. He returns the feet to the same line, arms and legs extended, and wait for the referee's signal to replace the bar to the platform.

Incorrect movements are — any unfinished attempt in which the bar has reached the height of the knees, pulling from the hang, touching the ground with any part of the body other than the feet, uneven or incomplete extension of arms, pause during extension of arms, finish with a press out, bending and extending arms during recovery, leaving the platform or touching the area outside the platform during the lift, replacing the bar on the platform before the referee's signal, dropping the bar before the referee's signal, dropping the bar from behind, failing

to finish with feet and barbell in the same line and failing to replace the complete barbell on the platform, touching the elbow or upper arm with knee or thigh, apparent effort of jerking which is not completed and any deliberate oscillation of the bar to gain advantage.

Other Important Rules

1. Draw of lot : At the technical meeting a number is drawn for each lifter. This number is retained throughout the competition even if a lifter moves to a higher category. It decides the order of weigh-in and the order of lifting.

2. Weigh-in begins 2 hours before the start of the competition of a particular category and lasts for one hour. They have one hour from the start of the weigh-in to make the required limit. A lifter heavier than his category may move to the next higher category if there is a vacancy. Lifters are weighed nude or in underwear.

3. Weight of the barbell must always be multiple of 2.5 kg. The progression must be of a minimum of 2.5 kg in the 2nd or 3rd attempt.

4. A minute and a half is allowed to a lifter between calling of his/her name and beginning of the attempt. Within this time the lifter must raise the bar from the platform to make the attempt. When a lifter attempts 2 lifts in succession he/she is allowed 3 minutes for the succeeding attempt.

5. The barbell is loaded in progression, a lifter taking lowest weight lifting first. Under no circumstances may the barbell be reduced to a lighter weight when a competitor has performed a lift with the weight announced.

6. The highest weight lifted in the two styles are added together and the lifter with the highest total is the winner.

7. In case of a tie a lighter competitor is classified before the heavier one.

8. When two or more competitors obtain the same result where they registered the same body-weight, the competitor who reaches the result earlier in the course of the competition is classified before the other one (s).

9. A jury is selected which ensures that the technical rules are followed and the referees work correctly.

10. The referees check up all equipment, control the competition, judge every lift and indicate their decision by light signals.

Names to Remember

Taner Sagir (born on March 13, 1985 in Kircaali, Bulgaria) is a Turkish word and Sagir is an Olympic weightlifting champion. Coming to Athens as holder of all the junior world records, he broke, at the age of 19 only, Olympic records in the category 77 kg snatch, clean and jerk and total, and became so the youngest Olympic champion in the weightlifting history. He is seen as a great talent by authorities.

Zhang Guozheng (b. September 14, 1974 in Xian You, Fujiang Province, China) is a weightlifter. He began his current career of weightlifting when he started Nanping Sport School in March 1983. During college, Guozheng was in the Yunnan Provincial Team. By 1999, he was on the national team for China. Zhang is a World champion, an Olympic champion and World Record holder. His impressive feats include a 197.5kg Clean and Jerk at 69kg BW (286% BW). He uses the unconventional squat-jerk style, where one carries the squat jerk into the hole prior to recovery.

Hossein Reza Zadeh (born May 12, 1978 in Ardabil, Iran) is an Iranian weightlifter and the current world record holder in the sport. He is the first Iranian athlete to have won two Olympic gold medals. In 2002 he was voted the "Champion of Champions" of Iran and was one of 16 Iranian athletes granted a badge of courage from Iranian President Mohammad Khatami. As a reward for setting a world record at the 2003 World Weightlifting Championships in Vancouver, Canada, Mohammad Khatami awarded him 600 million rials.

He surprised many at the 2000 Summer Olympics, earning a gold medal and breaking the decades-old monopoly on the gold by the Soviet Union and then Russia. He has since broken his own records on a number of occasions leading up to his world record 263.5 kg (580.9 pounds) lift in the clean and jerk at the 2004 Summer Olympics.

Nameirakpam Kunjarani Devi (born March 1, 1968) is an Indian sportswoman in weightlifting. She is a recipient of Arjuna award in 1990 and shared the Rajiv Gandhi Khel Ratna award year 1996-1997. She has more than fifty international medals to her credit. She also won a gold medal at the 2006 Commonwealth Games.

Karnam Malleswari (born June 1, 1975) is an Indian Weightlifter. She won a bronze medal in the 2000 Summer Olympics at Sydney.

■

WRESTLING

Chapter - 57

Wrestling, an ancient form of sport, is in vogue in different forms and shapes in different countries. It is a part of the modern Olympics.

History

The ancient Greek Olympics put wrestling on the map. Wrestling made it's Olympic debut in the Games of 708 B.C. It was apparently a much more violent, punishing sport in those early days. Wrestling was highly valued as a form of military exercise without weapons. There were two distinct versions of the game, differing according to the holds and the methods of deciding the victor.

Orthia pale (Upright and Proper Wrestling): The object of this type of wrestling was simply to throw the opponent to the ground. Three falls constituted a loss for that opponent, and the winner was called the "triakter". The match continued without stops until one man emerged victorious.

Kato pale (Ground Wrestling) :Victory in this competition depended on one competitor acknowledging defeat. Defeat was indicated by raising one's right hand with the index finger pointed.

Wrestling spread through the Roman world, as well as other early civilizations in India, China, Japan and the Middle East.

Wrestling died out with the Olympic Games in the Dark Ages, but it was natural that when organizers of the 1896 Olympics searched for sports with roots in antiquity, they looked to wrestling. It was the showpiece event of those Olympics, much as the 100-metre final is in the present day Games.

Modern Greco-Roman wrestling was first made popular in France. At the same time, a less restrictive brand of wrestling made inroads in the Western world. Unlike Greco-Roman wrestlers, who tried to throw or otherwise force their opponents to the mat with holds around the upper body, freestyle wrestlers had more options. They could trip their opponents, grab their legs and use their own legs in holds and take-downs. Fittingly, freestyle wrestling also became known as "catch as catch can" and proved to be popular entertainment in the 19th Century.

And here's where the history gets a little confusing. Despite being a revival of the Olympic tradition, it seems the wrestling showcased at the 1896 Games was closer to freestyle than classical Greco-Roman. The toast of the 1896 competition was Germany's Carl Schumann in the heavyweight class – not so much for his wrestling victory, but for the fact that he was also a gold medalist in gymnastics.

After a hiatus in 1900, wrestling was back as freestyle wrestling in 1904. Four years later, Olympic organizers resurrected Greco-Roman wrestling, in which use of the legs is forbidden, a style they believed to be a direct carryover from the Greek and Roman wrestlers of old.

Wrestling Mat

A mat having a diameter of 9 metres and surrounded by a border of the same thickness between 1.20 and 1.50 m wide is required in all contests.

A red band, 1 m wide and forming an integral part of the wrestling surface, is drawn on the inside of the circle-9 m in diameter—and running along its entire circumference.

A mat 10 m in diameter, including the 1m wide passivity zone, may be used, as long as the protection surface is 1.20 m wide throughout.

A circle must be traced in the middle of the mat with a diameter of 1m and a surrounding band of 10 cm width.

Dress

The contestants must present themselves at the edge of the mat in a one piece costume with a colour assigned to them (red or blue). Under this dress they must wear a protective genital supporter, and shorts or similar undergarments.

Contestants are not permitted to wear protective head gear.This must be of a type which will not cause any injury to the opponent. Light knee pads and suitable sports shoes may be worn. These shoes must be worn on the mat only.

Weigh-in

For all competitions the weigh-in starts a day before the competition between 6 p.m.and 8 p.m. at the organisers' discretion and lasts for 30 minutes. Six weighings take place everyday.

Second and Third Weigh-in

Immediately after the end of the last bout of the day in each weight class. Duration of weigh-in: 1 hour 30 minutes. Generally big competitions are spread over 5 days per style and finals of each category are over within 3 days.

Wrestling Rules

Wrestling rules, in a nutshell, are given below:

1. **Duration.:** Duration of the bout is 5 minutes of actual wrestling without rest.

2. Competitors are called for the contest. If any competitor fails to respond he will be considered defeated by fall and eliminated. A delay of 5 minutes in this respect may be accepted only for the contestant's first bout in the first round.

3. The time-keeper indicates the end of a bout by striking the gong.

4. A bout may be stopped for a maximum of 2 minutes by the referee for injury or any other reason beyond the control of the wrestler in each bout.

5. The coach during a bout can remain at the foot of the platform or at a minimum distance of 4 m from the edge of the mat.

6. **Danger Position:** A wrestler is considered in a danger position when the line of his back or the line of his shoulder vertically or in parallel with the mat forms an angle of less than 90° with the said mat. Also when he resists to avoid a fall. The following positions are considered danger positions:

(a) A defending wrestler assumes the bridge position to keep him from being pinned.
(b) A defending wrestler with his back towards the mat supports on one or both elbows in order to avoid having his shoulders forced to the mat or when he is blocked in this position on both hands.
(c) When a wrestler has shoulder in contact with the mat and at the same time exceeds the 90 deg. vertical line with the other shoulder.
(d) A wrestler finds himself in an instantaneous fall position.

7. In the event of a danger position 2, 3 or 5 points may be scored.

8. **Fall:** When the defending wrestler is held by his opponent with his two shoulders or base of his scapulae against the mat, and allows the referee to count ONE or pronounce mentally TOMBER, it is considered a fall.

9. **Technical Superiority:** A bout must be terminated when there is a difference of 15 points between the wrestlers. Difference of 14 points is called great superiority.

10. **Passivity:** If a wrestler continues to be passive even after the second warning, he can be awarded the third caution after which he will be declared as loser of the bout.

11. **"Par Terre" Position:** Each wrestler can be placed in the "par terre" position. The wrestler who is put in the "par terre" position should fall on his knees with his hands on the mat, hands and elbows spread at a distance of 20 cm from his knees. The attacking wrestler may take any position which he considers suitable for attacking but he must touch the back of the defending wrestler before the attack from behind.

12. **Situation:** If a wrestler is fleeing from the mat a second or third time, the "par terre" position is given. Also, if a wrestler is fleeing from a danger position, the "par terre" position is given.

13. **Wrestling at the edge of the mat:** The competitors may enter the passive zone, while wrestling on the ground. If standing then the referee may call the wrestler zone (red or blue) and may order them to come to the centre.

Prohibitions

Illegal Holds:

(a) Throat hold

(b) Twisting of arms more than 90 deg

(c) Two hands applying pressure to head or neck

(d) Arm bar applied to the fore arm

(e) Force bridge into head or neck

(f) Three quarter nelson with both hands

(g) A chancery hold in any sense (exclusive twisting of the neck)

Special Prohibitions

Greco-Roman Wrestling: In this style it is forbidden to grasp the opponent below the hips or to squeeze him with the legs. Pushing, pressing or lifting by means of contact with the legs on any part of the body of the opponent is also prohibited.

Freestyle: A scissor lock with the feet is forbidden on the head, neck or niques should not have any added downward force.

Pairing Rules

Each weight class is divided into two groups–A and B–as two preliminary groups and paired off for each round. This is performed according to the numerical order allocated to each of them by drawing of lots held before the beginning of the competition during the weigh-in. Drawing of lots will be done on the weighing machine and by the contestant himself.

Wrestlers who are assigned odd numbers form group A and those who have even numbers form group B.

In the first round, each wrestler will be paired with the immediate next one. The one who is left without pair would receive a "Bye". In the second round and onwards, the eligible wrestlers will be paired in the same manner but with the immediate next with whom he has not wrestled before. "Bye" will always be placed on top in the next round. For instance and so on.

GROUP A			GROUP B	
Round 1	*Round 2*	*Round 3...*	*Round 1*	*Round 2...*
1	9	7	2	2
3	1	9	4	4
5	3	1	6	6
7	5	3	8	8
9 BYE	7 BYE	5 BYE		

Scoring

1 Point: A wrestler who brings down his opponent to the ground while passing behind and is in a position to hold him down in this position.

2 Points: Application of correct hold and placing the opponent in danger or the opponent touches the floor with both shoulders in ground wrestling.

3 Points: (a) A correct hold by a lift from "par terre" position bringing the opponent in a danger position.

(*b*) Lifted the opponent completely off the mat to a danger position.

(*c*) A correct hold from a standing position that brings an opponent into a danger position.

5 *Points:* For executing a throw of great height that results in an immediate danger position. The attacking wrestler employs major technical hold.

In the case of a draw the sudden death rule is applied, i.e., whosoever scores the first point is the winner.

Game Officials

Referee: The referee should be in white trousers, white shirt with the emblem of his country, white socks and white athletic shoes to be worn only on the mat. He should have a red sleeve or band on his left arm and a blue sleeve or band on his right arm.

The referee is responsible for the orderly conduct of the bout which he must direct according to the rules. He contributes to the allocation of points, which he indicates, with his fingers after a hold is executed. He indicates the points with the hold of his fingers to the judge and Mat Chairman by raising his right or left hand depending upon the points scored by the red or blue wrestler.

Judge: The judge follows the referee's indication closely and records them in a score sheet. At the same time he will declare the score to the public by raising the number-bat of the colour attributed to the concerned wrestler. In case of the electronic score board, the points must be made known to all either by the judge if he is controlling it or by the special operator. The score board must be visible to the referee as well as to the wrestlers.

Mat Chairman: The Mat Chairman coordinates the work of the referee and the judge. In case of disagreement between the judge and the referee, he settles the issue to determine the results, the number of points, the falls, the cautions, disqualification, etc.

If there is any difference in the decision of the referee and the judge, the Mat Chairman's decision will be final.

Controller: Whenever the third caution is to be given the controller is the consultant.

Wrestling Weight Categories

Wrestling is carried out in different weight categories. They are as follows:

Weight Category	Freestyle	Greco-Roman
1. Light-flyweight	45-48 kg	—
2. Flyweight	Upto 52 kg	Same
3. Bantamweight	Upto 57 kg	Same
4. Featherweight	Upto 62 kg	Same
5. Lightweight	Upto 68 kg	—
6. Welterweight	Upto 74 kg	—
7. Middleweight	Upto 82 kg	Same
8. Light-heavyweight	Upto 90 kg	Same
9. Middle-heavyweight	Upto 100 kg	Same
10. Super-heavy weight	100 - 130 kg	Same

Other Wrestling Styles

The various types of wrestling in different countries are given below:

1. **Cumberland and Westmoreland:** This style is popular in Britain.
2. **Davon and Cornwall:** Practised in Britain.
3. **Glima:** Popular in Iceland for over 900 years.
4. **Kushti:** It is the national style of wrestling practised in India.
5. **Sambo:** A style of wrestling popular in Russia, Japan and Bulgaria.
6. **Schwingen:** This style has been practised in Switzerland for hundreds of years.

7. **Sumo:** It is Japan's spectacular national sport.

8. **Yagli:** This type of wrestling is a national sport in Turkey.

Names to Remember

Aleksander Medved (Russia, 1937-): A skilful Russian wrestler with 103.5 kg weight. Between 1962 and 1972 he lost the Olympic or world title, on only one occasion during the 1965 world championship. He is the gold medal winner in the 1964, 1968 and 1972 Olympics, in light-heavyweight, heavyweight and heavyweight plus category.

Hamit Kaplan (Turkey): Turkish heavyweight wrestler who was successful in both freestyle and Greco-Roman style. He won Olympic gold in 1956, silver in 1960 and bronze in 1964. In world championships he got gold in 1955, bronze in 1958 and silver in 1961.

Ivar Johansson (Sweden) : He is one of the two men to win three Olympic golds. Greco-Roman wrestler who competed in middleweight and welterweight class.

Ved Prakash (India): Participated in the 1970 Commonwealth Games at the age of 18 in light-flyweight class and won the championship.

Free Style

Mavlet Batirov (born December 12, 1983 in Khasavyurt, Dagestan) is a Russian wrestler who competed in the men's freestyle 55 kg category at the 2004 Summer Olympics and won the gold medal. In April 2006, in Moscow, he became the 60 kg European champion.

Buvaysa Saytiev is a Russian wrestler who is five-time world champion and who won gold medals at the 1996 Summer Olympics and 2004 Summer Olympics.

Cael Norman Sanderson (born June 20, 1979 in Salt Lake City, Utah), (pronounced "kale") is an American wrestler and current head wrestling coach at Iowa State. A 2004 Olympic champion, he also went undefeated in four years of college wrestling (159-0), including four consecutive NCAA titles (1999-2002) and was the first NCAA wrestler to go undefeated with more than 100 wins. Sports Illustrated named his college career as the No. 2 most outstanding achievement in college history. He was also the 2003 World Championship silver medalist, and a three-time national freestyle champion (2001-03).

Artur Taymazov (born July 20, 1979 in Vladikavkaz, Russia) is an Uzbek wrestler who competed in the Men's Freestyle 120 kg at the 2004 Summer Olympics and won the gold medal. He won the silver medal in Sydney 2000.

Greco Roman

Karam Ibrahim Gaber (born September 1, 1979 in Alexandria) is an Egyptian wrestler who competed in the Men's Greco-Roman 96 kg at the 2004 Summer Olympics and won the gold medal. He had already won the silver medal at the 2003 World Championships. Karam Gaber may be considered the best wrestler in Egyptian history. His win at the 2004 Olympics Greco-Roman Finals Match was utterly stupendous. Defeating his opponent in a matter of minutes, Karam won with a gap of 10 points (10-0). Also, his skills can back this up. He is very fast for his size. Using his speed and pure power, Gaber can throw around his opponent like a rag-doll. His physique is that of which a glorious competitor should be.

Khasan Baroev (born December 1, 1982 in Dushanbe, Tajikistan) is a Russian wrestler of Ossetian origin who competed in the Men's Greco-Roman 120 kg at the 2004 Summer Olympics and won the gold medal. He is also the 2003 world champion.

Wang Xu (born 27 September 1985) is a woman freestyle wrestler who competed at the 2004 Summer Olympics in Athens, winning a gold medal in the 72 kg weight class.

■

Notes

ADVENTURE SPORTS

ADVICE

All adventure sports are inherently dangerous. The author / publisher of this book cannot be held responsible for any accidents. Even the correct use of equipment and techniques may result in serious consequences. Any person using techniques described in each chapter of the book assumes all risks and full responsibility for all damages or injury mentally or physically which may result from the use of them. There is no substitute for instructions by a trained and competent person. Therefore get your self properly equipped and trained before participating in adventure sports.

BUNGEE JUMPING

Chapter - 58

Bungee jumping (or bungy jumping) is the sport of leaping from a tall structure while connected to a large rubber band. The tall structure is usually a bridge, crane or hot-air-balloon. The intense thrill comes as much from the free-falls as from the rebounds.

When the person jumps, the cord stretches to absorb the energy of the fall, then the jumper flies upwards again as the cord snaps back. The jumper oscillates up and down until all the energy is dissipated.

Bungee Jump in Normandy, France (Souleuvre Viaduct)

History

The word bungee (pronounced bunjie) first appeared around 1930 and was the name for rubber eraser. The word bungy, as used by A J Hackett, is said to be "Kiwi slang for Elastic Strap".

In the 1950s David Attenborough and a BBC film crew had brought back footage of the "land divers" of Pentecost Island in Vanuatu, young men who jumped from tall wooden platforms with vines tied to their ankles as a test of courage. This film inspired Chris Baker of Bristol, England to use elastic rope in a kind of urban vine jumping. The first modern bungee jump was made on 1 April 1979 from the 250ft Clifton Suspension Bridge in Bristol, and was made by four members of the Dangerous Sports Club. The jumpers, led by David Kirke, were arrested shortly after, but continued with jumps in the US from the Golden Gate and Royal Gorge bridges, (this last jump sponsored by and televised on the American program—"That's Incredible"*—spreading the concept worldwide. By 1982 they were jumping from mobile cranes and hot air balloons, and putting on commercial displays.*

The first operator of a commercial bungee jumping concern was New Zealander, A J Hackett, who made his first jump from Auckland's Greenhithe Bridge in 1986. During the following years Hackett performed a number of jumps from bridges and other structures (including the Eiffel Tower), buildings of public interest in the sport. Hackett remains one of the largest commercial operators, with concerns in several countries.

View from the top of AJ Hackett Bungy Tower, Cairns, Queensland

Despite the inherent danger of jumping from a great height, several million successful jumps have taken place since 1980. This is attributable to bungee operators rigorously conforming to standards and guidelines governing jumps, such as double checking calculations and fittings for every jump. As with any sport, injuries can still occur, but there have been few fatalities. A relatively common mistake in fatality cases is to use too long a cord. The cord should be substantially shorter than the height of the jumping platform to allow it room to stretch. To illustrate how easy it is to overestimate the permissible length of cord, consider the following question:

When the cord reaches its natural length, does the jumper: ·

(a) stop?

(b) start to slow?

(c) keep getting faster?

The answer, perhaps surprisingly, is (c). One does not even start to slow until the cord has already stretched somewhat, because the cord's resistance to distortion is zero at the natural length, and increases only gradually after, taking some time to even equal the jumper's weight.

Equipment

The elastic rope first used in bungee jumping, and still used by many commercial operators, is factory-produced braided shock cord. This consists of many latex strands enclosed in a tough outer cover. The outer cover may be applied when the latex is pre-stressed, so that the cord's resistance to extension is already significant at the cord's natural length. This gives a harder, sharper bounce. The braided cover also provides significant durability benefits. Other operators, including A J Hackett and most southern-hemisphere operators, use unbraided cords in which the latex strands are exposed. These give a softer, longer bounce and can be home-produced.

View of the bungee tower atop the Verzasca Dam, Lucarno, Switzerland

Although there is a certain elegance in using only a simple ankle attachment, accidents in which participants became detached led many commercial operators to use a body harness, if only as a backup for an ankle attachment. Body harnesses are generally derived from climbing equipment rather than parachute equipment.

Retrieval methods vary according to the site used. Mobile cranes provide the greatest recovery speed and flexibility, the jumper being lowered rapidly to ground level and detached. Many other mechanisms have been devised according to the nature of the jump platform and the need for a rapid turnaround.

The Guinness Book of World Records states the highest commercial bungee jump is off of the Bloukrans River Bridge, 40km east of Plettenberg Bay in South Africa. This jump takes place from a platform below the roadway of the bridge, and the height from the platform to the valley floor is 216m (709 feet). There is another commercial bungee jump currently in operation which claims to be slightly higher, at 220m (722 feet). This jump is located near Locarno, Switzerland, and takes place from the top of the Verzasca Dam. This jump was prominently featured in the opening scene of the James Bond film *Golden Eye*. In December 2006, AJ Hackett added bungee jumping to his Macau Tower facility in Macau S.A.R. China, making it the world's highest commercial bungee jump at 233m (764 feet).

One commercial jump higher than either took place from Colorado's Royal Gorge Bridge, in conjunction with the 2005 Go Fast Games. The height of the platform was 321m (1053 feet). However, this opportunity lasted for only three days, and it is unclear whether it will be repeated in future games.

Competition

For the many participants who make jumps as a one-off thrill, the idea of competing is irrelevant, but regular jumpers have gone to great lengths to devise criteria for competition, mostly based on acrobatics. Bungee jumping was featured in the early days of the ESPN X Games but the lack of an objective measure of skill detracted from the event compared to other extreme sports.

Bungee jumping in the mass media

Several major movies have featured bungee jumps, most famously the opening sequence of the 1995 James Bond film *Golden Eye* in which Bond makes a jump over the edge of a dam in Russia in reality the dam is in Switzerland: Verzasca Dam, and the jump was genuine, not an animated special effect.

In the television program The Fresh Prince of Bel-Air, the secondary character Trevor was killed while proposing to Hilary Banks during a bungee jump aired live on his television news program.

In 1986, the BBC TV programme The Late, Late Breakfast Show, presented by Noel Edmonds, was taken off the air after a volunteer for its 'Whirly Wheel' live stunt section, Michael Lush, was killed while rehearsing a bungee jump.

In the second season of the television program Scrubs, episode 207 "My First Step," the character JD is a medical resident, comfortable in what he calls his "wait-and-see" approach to treating his patients. When his fellow resident and friend Elliot Reid takes a chance in diagnosing a patient and the patient dies, he taunts her because his tactic was "fail proof." Eventually, she is commended and praised for giving the patient surgery, saying without it the patient had "a popsicle's chance in hell" (according to Dr. Kelso), and subsequently teaches JD the value of taking a chance on things. The episode ends with her encouraging him to bungee jump and the two leap from a bridge in a tandem style.

In 1997, Laura Patterson, one of a 16-member professional bungee jumping team, died of massive cranial trauma when she jumped from the top level of the Louisiana Superdome with improperly handled bungee cords and smashed head-first into the concrete-based playing field. She was practicing for an exhibition intended to be performed during the halftime show of Super Bowl XXXI. The bungee jumping portion of the show was removed from the program and a commemoration of Patterson was added.

Variations

In "Catapult" (Reverse Bungee or Bungee Rocket) the 'jumper' starts on the ground. The jumper is secured and the cord stretched, he/she is then released and shoots up into the air. This is often achieved using either a crane or a hoist attached to a (semi-)perma structure. This simplifies the action of stretching the cord and later lowering the participant to the ground.

"Twin Tower" is similar with two oblique cords.

Bungy Trampoline uses, as its name suggests, elements from bungy and trampolining. The participant begins on a trampoline and is fitted into a body harness, which is attached via bungy cords to two high poles on either side of trampoline. As they begin to jump, the bungy cords are tightened, allowing a higher jump than could normally be made from a trampoline alone.

Bungee Running involves no jumping as such. It merely consists of, as the name suggests, running along a track which is usually inflatable with a bungee cord attached. One often has a velcro-backed marker which is used to mark how far the runner got before the bungee cord pulled back. There is always a competitor alongside.

Safety and possible injury

There is a wide spectrum of possible injuries during a jump. One can be injured during a jump if the safety harness fails, the cord elasticity is miscalculated, or the cord is not properly connected to the jump platform. In most cases this is a result of human error in the form of mishandled harness preparation. Another major injury is if the jumper experiences cord entanglement with his/her own body. Other injuries include eye trauma , rope burn, uterine prolapse, dislocations, bruises, pinched fingers and back injury.

Age, equipment, experience, location and weight are some of the factors that matter, and nervousness can exacerbate eye traumas.

■

HANG GLIDING

Chapter - 59

History

Hang gliding is one of the simplest forms of human flight. A hang glider is a non-motorized, foot-launched wing. A hang glider has a rigid frame maintaining the shape of the wing, with the pilot usually flying in a prone position. The hang glider wing is constructed of rip-stop nylon or mylar over an aluminum frame.

Model of Jan Wnek's glider

In 1893 some of the first attempts of flight used hang gliders, pilots such as Otto Lilienthal, Octave Chanute and the Wright brothers. Hang gliding reemerged in the 1970's. The design has significantly improved since the 70s. Today's gliders are equipped with flight instruments, radios, and emergency parachutes. The early models were called kites. Today, they look like wings. The earliest models were constructed of plastic on bamboo frames. They have been redesigned with high tech fabrics and aluminum frames. With the improved designs better glide to sink ratios could be maintained, which meant longer flights. The flight records today are over 300 miles.

Otto Lilienthal, first documented controlled flights, early 1890s.

Many early glider designs copied from birds failed, the problem was that early flight pioneers often copied bird wings without understanding the underlying principles that made them work. The American historian Lynn White found two accounts indicating that a successful glider flight was made in the year 875 by a Moorish chemist and inventor named Abbas Ibn Firnas near Cordoba, Spain (Ibn Firnas crater on the Moon is named in his honor). It's possible that word of

Dry lake towing tests of NASA's Parasev glider

Ibn Firnas' flight was brought to England by returning Crusaders and to a monk called Eilmer of Malmesbury[2] who studied mathematics and astrology. A fellow monk and historian—William of Malmesbury—reported years later that Eilmer flew off the roof of an Abbey in Malmsbury, England, sometime between the years 1000 and 1010 gliding about 200 m (220 yards) and crashed breaking a leg.

Barry Palmer

A legend from the area of Slovakia tells of a Cyprian monk called Kamadul, a generally educated remedial worker and botanist. He put together a hang glider and went to the highest peak in the region known as Tri Koruny, located just behind the Dunajec river on the Polish side. Legend has several versions though, one is that he was burned as a heretic, another said only the glider was burned and he was locked in the monastery for the rest of his days.

An exception probably was an illiterate Polish sculptor and carpenter Jan Wnek, who built several wing models and, although he did not understand the aerodynamics of lift, he mimicked a bird's wing. He tested his weighted models by throwing them by hand. In 1866, he completed construction of an ash wood frame which he covered with linen impregnated with varnish. Jan Wnek was firmly strapped to the glider by the chest and hips and controlled his glider by twisting the wing's trailing edge via strings attached to stirrups at his feet. Wnek managed his first short controlled flights in June of that same year from a small hill. After several short flights, Wnek felt confident enough to ask for authorization from the village church priest to build a special ramp on top of the church tower to launch from. The tower stood 45m high and was located on top of a 50 m high hill, making a 95 m (311 ft) high launch above the valley. Church records indicate that Jan Wnek made several public flights between 1866–1869 especially during religious festivals, carnivals and New Year celebrations. His flying activities spanned about four years in time but Wnek left no known written records or drawings, thus having no impact on aviation progress.

Otto Lilienthal of Germany duplicated some of his contemporaries' work and greatly expanded on it from 1874, publishing all of his research in 1889. He also produced a series of ever-better gliders, and in 1891 was able to make flights of 25 meters or more routinely. He rigorously documented his work, influencing later designers; for this reason he is one of the best known of the early aviation pioneers. His type of aircraft is now known as a hang glider. By the time of his death in 1896, he had made about 2500 flights on a number of designs, when he crashed from a height of roughly 17 m (56 ft) fracturing his spine. Lilienthal had been working on small engines suitable for powering his designs at the time of his death.

Picking up where Lilienthal left off, Octave Chanute (North American) took up aircraft design after an early retirement, and funded the development of several gliders. It was mostly Wenham's wind tunnel and the documented work done by Otto Lilienthal and Octave Chanute that gave the Wright brothers the concepts needed to create their gliders and a number of sophisticated devices to measure lift and drag on the 200 wing designs they tested. As a result, the Wrights corrected earlier mistakes in calculations regarding drag and lift. On December 17, 1903, the Wright brothers flew a rudimentary airplane based on the design of their successful 1902 glider.

Hang Gliding Operation

Hang gliders are controlled by shifting the pilot's weight with respect to the glider. Pilots are suspended from a strap connected to the glider's frame (hence the name "hang" glider). By moving forward and backward and side to side at the end of this strap, the pilot alters the center of gravity of the glider. This then causes the glider to pitch or roll in the direction of the pilot's motion and thus allows both speed control and turning.

Hang gliding is an exciting way to fulfill your dream of free flight! You run down a slope and glide away from the mountain. You do not free-fall or jump from a cliff. Your launches and landings are deliberate and, once in the air, you will probably be surprised by how peaceful the experience is.

Even if you have a fear of heights, it will rarely be a factor, since there is no sensation of falling. Your solo lesson will require more effort (physical and mental) than your tandem lesson, but it lays the basic groundwork necessary to becoming your own pilot.

With a hang glider, you can fly like a bird, soaring upwards on currents of air. Hang gliders routinely stay aloft for 3 hours or more, climb to elevations of 15,000', and go cross-country for vast distances. If you would like to watch the sunset from the air, supported by the buoyant evening air, with perhaps an eagle or hawk joining you off your wing tip, then hang gliding is for you.

Difference between Hang Gliding and Parasailing or Parachuting

It is not the same as parasailing. Parasailing in India is done at limited places. Indian Air force adventure cell holds the parasailing camp on the Air Force runways, where you get a long strip of runway to pull the para-sailor up in the air. In the USA this is done on a beach. You are in a modified parachute tied to a boat. The boat drags you around the harbor. You get lifted up in the air on that parachute and remain there as long as the boat runs. It is not possible to pilot or guide a parasail.

Parasailing

It is not the same as parachuting either. Parachutes are designed to be deployed during free-fall from an airplane and to then descend to the ground. On the other hand , the hang glider is designed to be launched from a gentle hillside. Hang gliders are designed to go up rather than down. Because they can generate lift and have much more aerodynamic characteristics.

Difference between Paragliding and Hang Gliding

Difference between a hang glider and paraglider is that a hang glider has a rigid frame maintaining the shape of the wing, with the pilot usually flying in a prone position. Whereas, the paraglider canopy shape is maintained only by air pressure and the pilot is suspended in a sitting or supine position. The hang glider has a "cleaner" aerodynamic profile and generally is capable of flying at much higher speeds than a paraglider.

The paraglider folds up into a 14 to 15 kg backpack in about five minutes and can be easily transported. People commonly carry their paragliders to the top of peaks in the Cascades, Alps, Andes. It may be mentioned here that this sport is fairly young to our country. The hang glider, due to its weight and rigid frame, is transported on a vehicle with a roof rack and requires about 30 minutes to set up and again to take down.

Because hang gliders fly faster, they can cover greater distances more easily. But paragliders, which have advanced rapidly over the last few years, can now cover distances almost as great and, due to their tighter turning radius, can often stay aloft in light lift when hang gliders can't.

It's somewhat easier to learn to fly a paraglider. Paragliding has a faster learning curve than hang gliding due to the paraglider's slower forward speed and more forgiving design. Your launches are not "committed" with a paraglider; if you want to stop your launch, you just stop running and the canopy floats down behind you. By contrast, once you start your launch in a hang glider, which weighs anywhere from 30 to 45 kgs, you are committed.

Don't be Afraid

Do not forget that hang gliding is an outdoor sport and weather plays the most important role. The primary safety factors are personal judgment and attitude. You must be willing to learn gradually and use good judgment and have a proper attitude. If you don't, then you may get injured., But if you are careful and ready to learn then you could carry on with the hang gliding for a long time well into the old age.

You can learn hang gliding, like most adventure sports, as safe or dangerous as you want. The best way to make it absolutely safe is to receive proper training under professional hang gliders. Use safe equipment and have good respect for the weather.

Flying School

Similar to flying school for the aeroplanes there are ground schools for hang gliders and that is your classroom work where you learn about safety, the weather and wind, and the fundamentals of aerodynamics. You will learn about your equipment, how to rig and de-rig, how to launch, control and land the glider.

Ground handling is where you practice how to correctly hold, balance, and run with the glider. You will also practice the in-flight control movements while suspended in a harness. Such facilities are yet to be built in India.

You're now prepared for the training hill. Here you will try your hand (or feet) at launching. You will learn to launch, fly and land.

This is really the hardest part of learning to hang glide, is to carry the 25 kg. training glider up the hill. This could be the most frustrating and exhausting point. But once you have taken off once, you'll be looking forward for the next.

Similar to a regular aeroplane, the glider should move at a certain speed before it lifts off. An aeroplane will run on the runway. Hang glider pilots will run the glider down hill. You don't actually need winds to fly. As the glider moves through the air it creates it's own wind.

It won't take long before you start liking it and learning to fly. Your first few flights will be at an elevation of a few feet. As you progress, the altitude will increase to heights of around 75 feet.

It's important to go slowly. The worst thing you can do is to move ahead of your competence and confidence levels. You run the risk of hurting yourself, but also of becoming scared of the sport.

Rating Hang 1: To pass this student stage and move on to a Hang 1 rating, you will need to demonstrate your knowledge of wind and weather conditions and its effects on the glider. You will also need to show your ability to fly your glider independently. This includes preflight checks, proper launch, control while flying, and landing. It should take about six days of classes to get to this stage. But it is advised that do not be in a hurry and take your time. The

Hang 1 rating allows you to fly at an altitude of 150 feet in winds up to 15 mph. Next you must try to achieve Hang 2 rating.

First solo: The Hang 2 rating should take approximately 15 additional hours of instruction. At this stage you'll work on greatly improving your glider handling skills. You'll also be able to begin applying your knowledge of the wind to your flying.

In the USA, in order to get a Hang 2 rating, you'll have to pass a written and practical test. At this level you'll be allowed to fly at an elevation of 300 feet in winds up to 18 mph.

Hang 3 rating: This usually takes a long time, even up to a year requiring lots of flying time. A Hang 3 pilot is a very experienced pilot. It takes a minimum of 90 flights and 30 flying days. It also requires a complete understanding of all elements of flying, including stalling, thermals, spins and turns. Additionally the pilot must demonstrate proficiency in landing. You'll need to prove this by landing within 50 feet of a chosen spot. With this rating the pilot is allowed to fly in winds up to 25 mph.

Micrometerology is the study of weather in a small localized area, usually around hills or valleys. Controlling your glider is your first level of training. To become a proficient pilot you must now become an expert in the weather. You must learn the nature and behavior of winds as they relate to the mountains, valley and other types of landscapes. You'll learn to find lifts and thermals and avoid areas of turbulence.

Never Come Down

The goal of the **Hang 4** (Advanced) and **Hang 5** (Master) pilots is to literally never come down. Their flights consist of always looking for the next lift. Reading and mastering the wind to fly like birds.

There are stories of hawks joining gliders in their flight pattern, soaring wing to wing. The beauty of gliding is the ability to fly without noise and soar like a bird. You feel the freedom of a bird.

As an expert hang glider pilot your control moves become second nature. You feel one with your equipment.

Some Essential Points

- Like in most sports, stay cool, calm and collected in the face of all issues.

- You'll go through lots of temperature changes during your flight. It's important to dress appropriately and be in good physical condition.
- Don't wear polarized sunglasses. They make reading your controls difficult and can make it difficult to see horizontal powerlines.

Safety

- Make conservative decisions. Think with your head, not your ego.
- Make sure your reserve parachute is packed correctly and in good shape. Check it often.
- Your glider should be equipment with a para swivel. This will ensure that a spinning broken glider doesn't foul your reserve parachute.
- Certain medicines and health conditions maybe effected by the altitude. Consult your doctor before you take any medication and fly.

Donts

- Don't just follow someone's lead, educate yourself on every aspect of hang gliding and paragliding, the correct procedures, equipment, etc. This is a solo sport. You'll only have yourself to count on.
- Don't be afraid to ask questions.
- Don't buy any equipment without assessing it.

Launch

Launch techniques include foot-launching from a hill, tow-launching from a ground-based tow system, aerotowing (behind a powered aircraft), and powered harnesses. Other, more exotic launch techniques have also been used successfully, such as hot air balloon drops for very high altitude. Flights in non-soarable conditions are referred to as "sled runs".

Hang glider launching from Mount Tamalpais

Soaring Flight

Good gliding weather. Well formed cumulus clouds, with darker bases, suggests active thermals and light winds.

Good gliding weather. Cumulus clouds with dark flat base.

Glider pilots can stay airborne for hours. This is possible because they seek out rising air masses (lift) from the following sources:

Soaring Flight

Thermals

The most commonly used source of lift is created by the sun's energy heating the ground which in turn heats the air above it. This warm air rises in columns known as thermals. Soaring pilots quickly become aware of visual indications of thermals such as: cumulus clouds, cloud streets, dust devils and haze domes. Also, nearly every glider contains an instrument known as a variometer (a very sensitive vertical speed indicator) which shows visually (and often audibly) the presence of lift and sink. Having located a thermal, a glider pilot will circle within the area of rising air to gain height. In the case of a cloud street thermals can line up with the wind creating rows of thermals and sinking air. A pilot can use a cloud street to fly long straightline distances by remaining in the row of rising air.

Ridge Lift

Another form of lift occurs when the wind meets a mountain, cliff or hill. The air is deflected up the windward face of the mountain forming lift. Gliders can climb in this rising air by flying along the feature. Another name for flying with ridge lift is slope soaring.

Mountain Wave

The third main type of lift used by glider pilots are the lee waves that occur near mountains. The obstruction to the airflow can generate standing waves with alternating areas of lift and sink. The top of each wave peak is often marked by lenticular cloud formations.

Convergence

Another form of lift results from the convergence of air masses, as with a sea-breeze front.

More exotic forms of lift are the polar vortexes which the Perlan Project hopes to use to soar to great altitudes. A rare phenomenon known as Morning Glory has also been used by glider pilots in Australia.

Performance (2006)

With each generation of materials and with the improvements in aerodynamics, the performance of hang gliders has increased. One measure of performance is the glide ratio. For example, a ratio of 12:1 means that in smooth air a glider can travel forward 12 meters while only losing 1 meter of altitude.

- Topless gliders: glide ratio ~17:1, speed range ~30 to >145 km/h, best glide at ~45 to 60 km/h
- Rigid wings: glide ratio ~20:1, speed range ~ 35 to > 130 km/h, best glide at ~50 to 60 km/h

Note: Glide ratio is typically not provided by the manufacturers as it is nearly impossible to measure reliably and because the pilot is in the airstream (unlike in a sailplane) depends on many factors like pilot weight, pilot position, harness design, helmet, placement of instruments and so on.

Balast: The extra weight provided by ballast is advantageous if the lift is likely to be strong. Although heavier gliders have a slight disadvantage when climbing in rising air, they achieve a higher speed at any given glide angle. This is an advantage in strong conditions when the gliders spend only little time climbing in thermals.

Costs (2003)

- Rigid wings: ~10000 Euro
- Topless gliders: 5-6000 Euro
- Intermediates: ~4000 Euro
- Beginner gliders: < 3000 Euro
- Harness: 500 - 1500 Euro
- Parachute: ~ 500 Euro
- Instruments: 200 - 1000 Euro
- School: 2-3 lessons (introductory package) 3-400 Euro
- School: 10 lessons (full course) 800-1000 Euro

Instruments

In order to maximise a pilot's understanding of how the hang glider is flying, most pilots carry a series of instruments. The most basic being a variometer and altimeter—often combined. Some more advanced pilots also carry airspeed indicators and radios. When flying in competition or "Cross country" pilots often also carry maps and/or GPS units. Hang gliders do not have instrument panels as such, so all the instruments are mounted to the control frame of the glider.

Vario

People can sense the acceleration when they first hit a thermal, but they cannot detect the difference between constant rising air and constant sinking air, so they turn to technology for help. A variometer is a very sensitive vertical speed indicator; in other words, indicates climb or sink rate with audio signals (beeps) and/or a visual display. These units are generally electronic, vary in sophistication and often include, an altimeter and airspeed indicator. More advanced units often incorporate a barograph for recording flight data and/or a built in GPS. The main purpose of a variometer is in helping a pilot find and stay in the 'core' of a thermal to maximise height gain, and conversely indicating when he or she is in sinking air, and needs to find rising air. Variometers are sometimes capable of electronic calculations based on the 'MacCready Ring' to indicate the optimal speed to fly for given conditions. The MacCready theory solves the problem of how fast a pilot should cruise between thermals, given both the average lift the pilot expects in the next thermal climb, as well as the amount of lift or sink he encounters in cruise mode. Some electronic variometers make the calculations automatically, after allowing for factors such as the glider's theoretical performance (glide ratio), altitude, hook in weight and wind direction.

Vario

Radio

Pilots use radio for training purposes, and for communicating with other pilots in the air — particularly when travelling together on cross-country flights.

Radios used are PTT (push-to-talk) transceivers, normally operating in or around the FM VHF 2-metre band (144–148 MHz). Usually a microphone is incorporated in the helmet, and the PTT switch is either fixed to the outside of the helmet, or strapped to a finger.

2m Band Radio

GPS

GPS (global positioning system) is a necessary accessory in flying competitions, where it has to be demonstrated that way-points have been correctly passed.

It can also be interesting to view a GPS track of a flight when back on the ground, to analyse flying technique. Computer software is available which allows various different analyses of GPS tracks (e.g. CompeGPS).

Other uses include being able to determine drift due to the prevailing wind when flying at altitude, providing position information to allow restricted airspace to be avoided, and identifying one's location for retrieval teams after landing-out in unfamiliar territory.

More recently, the use of GPS data, linked to a computer, has enabled pilots to share 3D tracks of their flights on Google Earth. This fascinating insight allows comparisons between competing pilots to be made in a detailed 'post-flight' analysis.

Records

Records fall into nearly the same categories as those for sailplanes and are sanctioned by the FAI. The current world record(s) (as of 2005) for "free distance" is held by Manfred Ruhmer with 700.6 km (435.3 miles) in 2001, but Mike Barber has flown an uncertified distance of 704 km (437 miles) on June 19, 2002, in Zapata Texas.

Competitions

Competitions started with "flying as long as possible" and spot landings. With increasing performance cross-country flying replaced them. Usually two to four waypoints have to be passed with a landing at a goal. In the late 90s low-power GPS units were introduced and have completely replaced photographs of the goal. Every two years there is a world championship. The Rigid and Women's World Championship in 2006 was hosted by Quest Air in Florida. Big Spring, Texas is hosting the 2007 World Championship. Hang gliding is also one of the competition categories in World Air Games organized by Fédération Aéronautique Internationale (World Air Sports Federation—FAI). The FAI also has a chronology of the FAI World Hang Gliding Championships.

■

(from Wikipidia free Encyclopedia)

HOT AIR BALLOONING Chapter - 60

History

Unmanned hot air balloons are mentioned in Chinese history. Zhuge Liang in the Three Kingdoms era, Shu Kingdom, used airborne lanterns for military signaling. These lanterns are known as Kongming lanterns .

There is also some speculation that hot air balloons were used by the Nazca Indians of Peru some 1500 years ago as a tool for designing vast drawings on the Nazca plain.

Hot air balloons are the oldest successful human flight technology, dating back to the Montgolfier brothers' invention in Annonay, France in 1783. The first flight carrying humans was made on November 21, 1783, in Paris by Pilâtre de Rozier and the Marquis d'Arlandes. Hot air balloons that can be propelled through the air rather than just being carried along by the wind are known as airships or, more specifically, thermal airships.

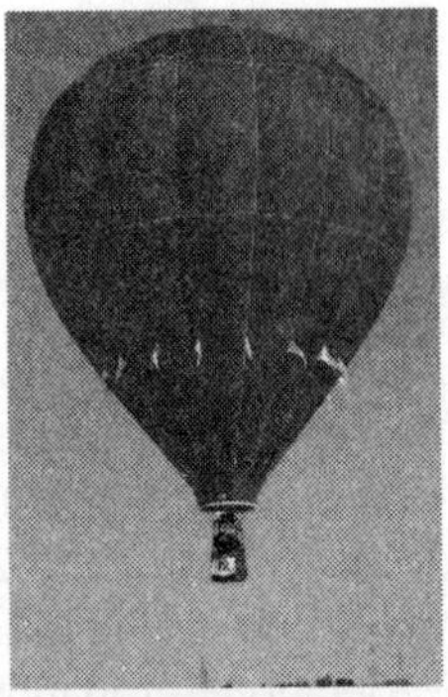

Hot air balloon in flight

A hot air balloon consists of a bag called the envelope that is capable of containing hot air. Suspended beneath is the gondola or wicker basket (in certain, long distance or high altitude balloons, a capsule) which carries a source of heat capable of producing a sufficient temperature gradient between the air inside the envelope and the surrounding air mass to give enough lift to keep the balloon and its passengers aloft. Unlike gas balloons, the envelope does not have to be sealed at the bottom since the rising hot air only exerts pressure on the upper hemisphere of the balloon to provide lift.

In today's sports balloons the envelope is generally made from nylon fabric and the mouth of the balloon (closest to the burner flame) is made from fire resistant material such as Nomex.

Recently, balloon envelopes have been made in fantastic shapes, such as hot dogs, rocket ships, and the shapes of commercial products.

First recorded flight

The first clearly recorded instances of balloons capable of carrying passengers used hot air to obtain buoyancy and were built by the brothers Josef and Etienne Montgolfier in Annonay, France. They were from a family of paper manufacturers who had noticed the ash rising in fires. After experimenting with unmanned balloons and flights with animals, the first balloon flight with humans on board took place on October 19, 1783 with the physician Pilâtre de Rozier, the manufacture manager, Jean-Baptiste Réveillon and Giroud de Villette, at the Folie Titon in actual Paris. Officially, the first flight was 1 month later, 21 November 1783. King Louis XVI had originally decreed that condemned criminals would be the first pilots, but a young physicist named Pilâtre de Rozier and the Marquis Francois d'Arlandes successfully petitioned for the honor. The first hot air balloons were basically cloth bags (sometimes lined with paper) with a smoky fire built on a grill attached to the bottom. They had a tendency to catch fire and be destroyed upon landing.

A model of the Montgolfier brothers' balloon at the London Science Museum

Military use

The first military use of aircraft took place during the French Revolutionary Wars, when the French used a tethered hydrogen balloon to observe the movements of the Austrian army during the Battle of Fleurus (1794). Hot air balloons were employed during the American Civil War. Though the military balloons used by the Union Army Balloon Corps under the command of Prof. Thaddeus S. C. Lowe were limp silk envelopes inflated with coke gas or hydrogen, the Confederate Army did attempt to counter with a rigid Montgolfier style hot air, or "hot smoke balloon." Captain John R. Bryant inflated his rigid cotton balloon with a fire of oil-soaked pine cones. The balloon was soon captured by Union forces as the Confederate's techniques of balloon handling were not competent.

Modern revival

The first modern hot air balloon was designed and built in 1960 by Ed Yost. He made the first free flight of such an aircraft in Bruning, Nebraska, on 22 October 1960. Initially equipped with a plastic envelope and kerosene fuel, Yost's designs rapidly moved onto using a modified propane powered "weed burner" to heat the air and lightweight nylon fabric for the envelope material.

The Virgin Pacific Flyer collapsed on a frozen lake in the Canadian tundra after the first and only crossing of the Pacific in a hot air balloon. Most of the giant jettisonable propane fuel tanks are no longer attached. One still hangs in front of the two-man sealed pressurized capsule. The flight holds the distance record for a hot air balloon.

Today

Today, hot air balloons are used primarily for recreation. There are some 7,500 hot air balloons operating in the United States.

Hot air balloons are able to fly to extremely high altitudes. On November 26, 2005, Vijaypat Singhania set the world altitude record for highest hot air balloon flight, reaching 21,290 meters (69,852 feet). He took off from downtown Bombay, India, and landed 240 km (150 miles) south in Panchale. The previous record of 19,811 meters (64,980 ft) had been set by Per Lindstrand on June 6, 1988 in Plano, Texas. However, like all registered aircraft, oxygen is needed for all crew and passengers for any flight that reaches and exceeds an altitude of 12,500 feet.

The furthest that a hot air balloon has ever been flown is 7,671.91 km. On January 15, 1991, the Virgin Pacific Flyer balloon completed the longest flight in a hot air balloon when Per Lindstrand (born in Sweden, but resident in the UK) and Richard Branson of the UK flew from Japan to Northern Canada.

With a volume of 74,000 m^3 (2,600,000 ft^3), the balloon envelope was the largest ever built for a hot air craft. Designed to fly in the trans-oceanic jetstreams the Pacific Flyer recorded the highest ground speed for a manned balloon at 245 mph (394 km/h).

The longest duration hot air balloon flight ever made is 50 hours and 38 minutes made by Michio Kanda and Hirosuke Tekezawa of Japan on January 2, 1997.

Construction

A hot air balloon is partially inflated with cold air from a petrol-driven fan, before the propane burners are used for final inflation.

A hot air balloon for manned flight uses a single-layered, fabric gas bag (lifting "envelope"), with an opening at the bottom called the mouth or throat. Attached to the envelope is a basket, or gondola, for carrying the passengers. The basket is usually made of wicker and ratan, but can be made of aluminum. Mounted above the basket and centered in the mouth is the "burner" which injects a flame into the envelope, heating the air within. The heater or burner is fueled by propane, a liquefied gas stored in pressure vessels, similar to high pressure forklift cylinders.

Envelope

Modern hot air balloons are usually made of light-weight and strong synthetic fabrics such as ripstop nylon, or dacron (a polyester).

During the manufacturing process, the material is cut into panels and sewn together, along with structural load tapes (webbing) that carry the weight of the gondola or basket. Vertical rows of panels are referred to as gores due to their triangular shape. Envelopes can have as few as 4 gores or as many as 24 or more. The use of more gores usually means a smoother shape.

Envelopes often have a crown ring at their very top. This is a hoop of smooth metal, usually aluminum and approximately 1 foot in diameter, to which vertical load tapes attach.

Fabric coatings

The fabric (or at least part of it, the top 1/3 for example) may be coated with a sealer, such as silicone or polyurethane, to make it impermeable to air. It is often the degradation of this coating and the corresponding loss of impermiability that ends the effective life of an envelope, not weakening of the fabric itself. Heat, moisture, and mechanical wear-and-tear during set up and pack up are the primary causes of degradation. Once an envelope becomes too porous to fly, it may be retired and used as a 'rag bag': cold inflated and opened for children to run through. Products for recoating the fabric are becoming commercially available.

Envelope sizes

A range of envelope sizes is available. The smallest, one-person, basket-less balloons (called "Hoppers" or "Cloudhoppers") have less than 1,000 cubic meters (35,000 ft^3) of envelope volume. At the other end of the scale are the balloons used by large commercial sightseeing operations that carry well over two dozen people and have envelope volumes of up to 15,000 cubic meters (600,000 ft^3). However, most balloons are roughly 2,500 cubic meters (100,000 ft^3) and carry three to sometimes four people.

Vents

The top of the balloon usually has a vent of some sort. The most common type of vent is a disk-shaped flap of fabric called a parachute vent. The fabric is connected around its edge to a set of "vent lines" that converge in the center. (The arrangement of fabric and lines looks roughly like a parachute — thus the name.) These "vent lines" are themselves connected to a control line that runs to the basket. A parachute vent is opened by pulling on the control line. Once the control line is released, the pressure of the remaining hot air pushes the vent fabric back into place. A parachute vent can be opened briefly while in flight to initiate a rapid descent. (Slower descents are initiated by allowing the air in the balloon to cool naturally.) The vent is pulled completely open to collapse the balloon after landing.

The inside of a hot air balloon's envelope, seen from the gondola.

An older, and today less commonly used, style of vent is called a "Velcro-style" vent. This too is a disk of fabric at the top of the balloon. However, rather than having a set of "vent lines" that can repeatedly open and close the vent, the vent is secured by "hook and loop" fasteners (such as Velcro) and is only opened at the end of the flight. Balloons equipped with a "Velcro-style" vent typically have a second "maneuvering vent" built into the side (as opposed to the top) of the balloon.

Some hot air balloons have turning vents which are side vents which, when opened, cause the balloon to rotate. Such vents are particularly useful for balloons with rectangular baskets in order to align the wider side of the basket for landing.

Burner

The burner unit gasifies liquid propane, mixes it with air, ignites the mixture, and directs the flame and exhaust into the mouth of the envelope. The unit may consist of one or more individual burners of which the pilot may use one or more at a time to generate the desired heat. Each burner is characterized by a metal coil of propane tubing through which the flame shoots in order to preheat the incoming liquid propane.

The burner unit may be suspended from the mouth of the envelope, or rigidly supported over the basket. The burner unit may be mounted on a gimbal to enable the pilot to aim the flame and avoid overheating the envelope fabric.

The pilot actuates a burner by opening a propane valve, called a blast valve. The valve may be spring loaded so that it closes automatically, or it may stay open until closed by the pilot. The burner has a pilot light to ignite the propane and air mixture. The pilot light may be lit by the pilot with an external device, such as a flint striker or a lighter, or with a built-in piezo electic spark.

A burner may have a secondary propane valve that releases propane more slowly and thereby generates a different sound. This is called a whisper burner and is used for flight over livestock to lessen the chance of spooking them. It also generates a more yellow flame and is used for night glows because it lights up the inside of the envelope better than the primary valve.

Burners can generate heat on the order of 30 million BTUs.

Fuel Tanks

Propane fuel tanks are usually cylindrical pressure vessels made from aluminum, stainless steel, or titanium with a valve at one end to feed the burner and to refuel. They may have a fuel gauge and a pressure gauge. The pressure necessary to force the fuel through the line to the burner may be supplied by the vapor pressure of the propane itself, if warm enough, or by the introduction of an inert gas such as nitrogen. Common sizes are 10, 15, and 20 gallons.

Instrumentation

A balloon may be outfitted with a variety of instruments to aid the pilot. These commonly include an altimeter, a rate of climb (vertical speed) indicator, envelope (air) temperature, and ambient (air) temperature. A GPS receiver can be useful to indicate ground speed (traditional aircraft air speed indicators would be useless) and direction.

Combined mass

The combined mass of an average system can be calculated as follows:

- the envelope: 250 lbs, 113 kg
- basket: 140 lbs, 63.5 kg
- burner: 50 lbs, 22.7 kg
- 3 fuel tanks with fuel: 3x135 lbs = 405 lbs, 184 kg
- 5 passengers: 5 x150 lbs each = 750 lbs, 340 kg
- the air in the envelope (100,000 ft³ at 0.062 lb/ft³ = 3.1 tons, 2812 kg) For a total of 3538 kg or 3.9 tons

Theory of operation

Generating lift

A pair of Hopper balloons

Raising the air temperature inside the envelope makes it lighter than the surrounding (ambient) air. This causes the balloon and its payload to rise. The amount of lift (or buoyancy) provided by a hot air balloon depends primarily upon the difference between the temperature of the air inside the envelope and the temperature of the air outside the envelope. For most envelopes made of nylon fabric, the maximum internal temperature is limited to approximately 120 °C (250 °F). It should be noted that the melting point of nylon is significantly higher than these maximum operating temperature — about 230 °C (450 °F). However the lower temperatures are generally used because the higher the temperature, the more quickly the strength of the nylon fabric degrades over time. With a maximum operating temperature of 120 °C, balloon envelopes can generally be flown for between 400 and 500 hours before the fabric needs to be replaced. Many balloon pilots operate their envelopes at temperatures significantly below the maximum in order to extend the longevity of their envelope fabric.

For typical atmospheric conditions, a hot air balloon requires about 3 cubic meters of envelope volume in order to lift 1 kilogram (50 ft^3/lb). The precise amount of lift provided depends not only upon the internal temperature mentioned above, but the external temperature, altitude above sea level, and humidity of the surrounding air. On a hot day, the balloon cannot be loaded as much as on a cool day, because the temperature required for launch will exceed the maximum sustainable for nylon envelope fabric.

In the lower atmosphere, the lift provided by a hot air balloon decreases about 3% for each 1,000 meters (1% per 1,000 ft) of altitude gained.

Hybrids

The Rozier type of hybrid balloon, called after its creator, Jean-François Pilâtre de Rozier, has separate cell for helium as well as a cone below for hot air (as is used in a hot air balloon) to heat the helium at night.

Control

The direction of flight depends on the wind, but the altitude of the balloon can be controlled by changing the temperature of the air inside the envelope. The pilot may open one or more burner blast valves to increase the temperature inside the envelope, thereby increasing lift, and thus ascend or slow or stop a descent. The pilot may also open a vent, if the envelope is so equipped, to let hot air escape, decreasing the temperature inside the envelope, thereby decreasing lift, and thus descend or slow or stop an ascent. Absence of any action by the pilot and the air inside the envelope will slowly cool, by seepage or by contact with cooler outside air, and slowly provide less lift.

Delayed response

One of the tricks involved in flying a balloon is learning to deal with the delayed response. To slow or stop a descent requires the pilot to open a burner blast valve. This sends hot combustion exhaust through the mouth into the envelope where it expands and forces some cooler air out of the mouth. This lightens the total weight of the system and increases its buoyancy, but not immediately. From the time that the burner is lit until the balloon slows or stops its descent can take 30 seconds or more, depending on its rate of decent, how cold it has become, and how powerful the burner. This delay requires a great deal of anticipation on the part of the pilot.

Safety equipment

To help ensure the safety of pilot and passengers, a hot air balloon may carry several pieces of safety equipment.

In the basket

In order to relight the burner, in case the pilot light goes out and the optional piezo ignition fails, the pilot should have ready access to a flint spark lighter.

Many systems, especially those that carry passengers have completely redundant fuel and burner systems: two fuel tanks, connected to two separate hoses, which feed two distinct burners. This enables a safe landing in the case of a clog somewhere in one system or if a system might be disabled because of a fuel leak.

On the occupants

At least the pilot should wear flame resistant gloves. These can be made of leather or some more sophisticated material, such as nomex. These will enable the pilot to shut off a gas valve in the case of a leak even if there is a flame present. Quick action on the pilot's part to stop the flow of gas can turn a potential disaster into an inconvenience.

At least the pilot should wear clothes made of natural fibers. These will singe and not burn readily if brought into contact with an open flame. Many synthetic fibers unless especially formulated for use near flame or high temperatures, such as nomex, will melt onto the wearer and can cause severe burning.

Some balloon systems, especially those that hang the burner from the envelope instead of supporting it rigidly from the basket, require the use of helmets by the pilot and passengers.

On the ground crew

The ground crew should wear gloves on their hands whenever the possibility of handling ropes or lines exists. The mass and exposed surface to air movement of a medium sized balloon is sufficient to cause rope burns to the hands of anyone trying to stop or prevent movement.

The ground crew should also wear sturdy shoes and at least long pants in case of the need to access a landing or landed balloon in rough or overgrown terrain.

Maintenance and repair

As aircraft, hot air balloons require regular maintenance in order to remain airworthy. As aircraft made of fabric and that lack direct horizontal control, hot air balloons may occasionally require repairs to rips or snags.

While some operations, such as cleaning and drying, may be performed by the owner or pilot, other operations, such as sewing, must be performed by a qualified repair technician and recorded in the balloon's maintenance log book.

Maintenance

To ensure long life and safe operation, the envelope should be kept clean and dry. This prevents mold and mildew from forming on the fabric and abrasion from occurring during packing, transport, and unpacking due to contact with foreign particles. In the event of a landing in a wet (because of precipitation or early morning or late evening dew) or muddy location (farmer's field), the envelope should be cleaned and laid out or hung to dry.

The burner and fuel system must also be kept clean to ensure safe operation on demand. Damaged fuel hoses need to be replaced. Stuck or leaky valves must be repaired or replaced.

The wicker basket may require occasional refinishing or repair. The skids on its bottom may require occasional replacement.

Repair

In the case of a snag, burn, or rip in the envelope fabric, a patch may be applied or the effected panel completely replaced. Patches may be held in place with glue, tape, stitching, or a combination of these techniques. Replacing an entire panel requires the stitching around the old panel to be removed, and a new panel to be sewn in with the appropriate technique, thread, and stitch pattern.

Licensing

Depending on the size of the balloon, location, and intended use, hot air balloons and their pilots need to comply with a variety of regulations.

Balloons

In the USA, balloons below a certain size (empty weight of less than 254 pounds or 115 kg) can be used as ultralights and cannot carry passengers, except for pilot training. Anything larger than that must be registered (have an N-number), have an airworthiness certificate, and pass annual inspections.

Pilots

In the United States, a pilot does not need a license to fly an ultralight aircraft, but training is highly advised. However, a pilot of a hot air balloon that does not meet the requirements of the ultralight category must have a pilot certificate from the FAA and it must carry the rating of "hot air balloons with airborne heater".

In order to carry paying passengers for hire (and attend many balloon festivals), a pilot must have a commercial pilot certificate. Commercial hot air balloon pilots may also act as hot air balloon flight instructors.

Manufacturers

The largest manufacturer of hot air balloons in the world is Cameron Balloons of Bristol and part owned subsidiary company, Lindstrand Balloons of Oswestry, England. Aerostar International, Inc. of Sioux Falls, South Dakota was North America's largest balloon manufacturer and a close second in world manufacturing before ceasing to build balloons in January 2007. Firefly Balloons, formerly known as The Balloon Works, is another popular manufacturer of hot-air balloons located in

Statesville, North Carolina. Another long time producer of hot air balloons is Head Balloons, Inc., located in Helen, Georgia. One manufacturer in Canada is Fantasy Sky Promotions.

Cameron Balloons, and another English balloon manufacturing company, Thunder and Colt (since acquired by Cameron), have been the main innovators and developers of special shaped balloons. These hot air balloons use the same principle of lift as conventional inverted teardrop shaped balloons but often sections of the special balloon envelope shape make no contribution to the balloon's ability to stay afloat.

■

(from Wikipidia free Encyclopedia)

MOUNTAIN BIKING

Chapter - 61

History

Bicycles have been ridden off-road since their invention. However, the modern sport of mountain biking primarily originated in the 1970s. There were several groups of riders in different areas of the USA who can make valid claims to playing a part in the birth of the sport. Riders in Crested Butte, Colorado, and Cupertino, California, tinkered with bikes and adapted them to the rigors of off-road riding. Other riders around the country were probably copying their friends with motorcycles and riding their bikes on trails and fire roads. However, a group in Marin County, California, is recognized by the Mountain Bike Hall of Fame to have played a central role in the birth of the sport as we know it today. They began racing down Mount Tamalpais (Mt Tam) on old 1930s and '40s Schwinn bicycles retrofitted with better brakes and fat tires. This group included Joe Breeze, Otis Guy, Gary Fisher and Keith Bontrager, among others. It was Joe Breeze, who built the first new, purpose-maae mountain bike in 1977. Tom Ritchey built the first regularly available mountain bike frame, which was accessorized by Gary Fisher and Charlie Kelly and sold by their company called MountainBikes (later changed to Fisher Mountain Bikes then bought by Trek, still under the name Gary Fisher). The first two mass produced mountain bikes were sold in 1982—the Specialized Stumpjumper and Univega Alpina Pro.

In 1988, the Mountain Bike Hall of Fame was founded to chronicle the history of mountain biking, and to recognize the individuals and groups that have contributed significantly to this sport.

Beginning

Mountain Biking is a typical adventure sports well liked by the western society. They take the adventure to its true spirits and enjoy at the same time. Mountain biking can take on many forms, from the sleek and thin lined racing bikes, touring bikes, fat tired beach cruisers, hybrid cross designs, trickster bikes, to your stout mountain bikes equipped with shocks. In India the sport has not developed because of many constraints. But considering the terrain in Himalayas, Western and Eastern Ghats the sports can be easily developed. The thousands of kilometers of the Himalayas can throw a genuine challenge to mountain bikers.

There is a feeling with biking that it is unlike any other sport. Wind rushing through your hair, zipping around the neighborhood.

The beauty of the sport, as one rider put it, was that your whole body is riding. Your mind is alert ready for sudden changes in the trial requiring quick adjustments. Mountain biking is more aggressive than riding a bike on the plain roads. which is compared to a stroll in the woods.

Mountain biking is also a sport that will leave you totally tired. It is a great work out. You must eat a good meal before you venture out for this sports. Also carry out lot of water and continue drinking as you go along, Do not forget about your eye and head protection. The bikes are specially built for riding in the mountains with different speeds and gears.

To Begin With

At the very beginning you must procure a proper mountain capable bike. These may not be easily available in a country like India. But in the USA or in other advanced nations these are easily available but are fairly costly.

However, if you have a bike, then you must have your helmet and eye protection. Gloves are also very useful. Put on regular tennis shoes and if need be carry change of clothes. Sweating is a part of this game.

Going uphill

Five kilometers is considered a short ride and around 32 kilometers is a long ride. The intensity of the terrain will have a big impact on how far you actually ride. If it is steep and difficult terrain even a 5 km ride can be "long". Mountain biking takes an incredible amount of physical strength and endurance. If you take on this sport then build up your stamina slowly.

Going downhill

Before you venture out prepare yourself in every respect. That means food, water, first aid kit, and equipment to make repairs enroute. If you happen to get a flat tire, you should know how to change it. Carry a spare tube, tools, and a pump on your bike.

Even in the advanced countries this is still a young sport. The advances to equipment and material are many. Rear suspension systems, disc brakes, and space age materials are now being used. And do not forget to keep your equipment in the best possible condition before you ride out into the mountain like the Himalayas.

Certain Things to Remember

- Don't ride alone. You can get hurt, lost, or just have an equipment break down. If you're unable to ride or walk back, you'll need your partner to go for help.
- Be careful of your front brake going down hill. After the front tire leaves the ground, if you have the front brake on when you touch down, the stopped tire will cause the back of the bike to lift off the ground and flip the bike.
- There is such a thing as path or trail etiquette for mountain bikers all over the world. Don't ride full speed past anyone. Pull over when you see someone coming. Practicing trial etiquette will ensure that mountain bikers can share trails.
- When riding keep your arms shoulder length apart so that your chest area is open and breathing isn't constricted.
- Mix your water with some fruit juice like apple, nothing too acidic. The sugar will help maintain your energy level.
- Carry some chocolate bars.
- Make sure you drink and eat before you feel thirsty or tired. If you start to feel thirsty, your body may already be dehydrated.

Safety Measures

- Your helmet must fit well and not slide around.
- Wear non-shattering eye protection.
- Bring a first aid kit.

Mountain Biking Equipment

Eye Protection : The equipment for eye protection is the bug like wrap around frames. It looks little strange but it helps to keep wind, dirt, and insects out of your eyes. Whatever style you choose, they should provide Ultra Violet protection and be made with a non-shattering material.

Mountain Bike

Gloves

Gloves are basic mountain biking gear which protect your hands from chaffing and blisters caused by constant contact with the handlebars. They are usually lightweight nylon with a thicker padding for the palm.

Helmet

Get a good light helmet. If your helmet doesn't fit correctly, it will bounce around while riding and won't protect you if you fall. Some of the fancier models come in aerodynamic shapes. They look very smart and will reduce the level of wind resistance or "drag". Most helmets also come with small openings for vents. These help to keep your head cool. If you're riding in the winter and need to keep your head warm, helmet liners also can be used.

Shoes

You need to make sure your cycling shoes are compatible with the clipless pedal system you're using. One of the features that you should look for in a cycling shoe is a hard toe. This will protect your feet from any branches or rocks you might hit.

Seats

A recent development in mountain biking equipment is bike seat designed for women. They offer better support, which helps your posture and your back. Also available is "gel" padding instead of foam. Because gel is denser than foam, it absorbs shocks and bumps better.

Clothing

It would be better if you could get hold of padded bike shorts. They will be very useful on a long ride. When riding during the cooler months, it's important to wear clothing that wicks away perspiration. Cotton is not advisable since it traps moisture close to your skin. Nylon, or silk blends, material will be good.

Bikes

These are costly. That is why to begin with try to get a slightly used mountain bike. As it stands mountain biking has many forms and styles. Biking styles range from off-road, to cross-country, and down hilling. Off-road is generally considered riding on dirt paths with limited vertical climbs and descents. Cross-country is both steep climbs and bumpy descents. Downhilling is long, fast difficult descent.

Downhilling in advanced nations is relatively new and being offered during the summer at ski resorts. A chair-lift type service takes you up to the top of the mountain and you take the long wild ride down. Weight is less a factor in descending as it is in climbing. The downhilling bike is made with the best suspension systems, disc braking system, an indestructible frame, and with only eight speeds.

Cross-country bikes are the most popular. An intermediate level bike will be light weight, with 24 speeds and a front shock. The more advanced equipment includes a rear suspension and v-brakes, which offer more stopping power. It's important to equip your bike with a quick gear shifting system. If the shifting system holds up even a little, you'll loose valuable momentum on an assent.

Names to Remember

Julien Absalon (born August 16, 1980 in Remiremont) is a French mountain biker. In 2004 he won a gold medal at the Summer Olympics. He currently rides for the professional trade mountain bike team Orbea.

Absalon has won three consecutive Mountain Bike World Championships (2004, 2005, 2006).

Gunn-Rita Dahle Flesjå (born February 10, 1973) is a Norwegian cross-country mountain biker. She won the women's cross country gold medal at the 2004 Olympic Games and is a multiple world champion. She has won 6 World championships and 6 European championships. Dahle has also won 4 UCI World Cup XC in a row.

Major Achievements

2006 – 1st overall UCI World Cup in cross country
1st (Gold) UCI Mountain Bike World Championships in cross country
1st (Gold) UCI Mountain Bike Marathon World Championships
1st European Championship in cross country
1st European Championship in marathon.

■

MOUNTAINEERING

Chapter - 62

Beginning

One widespread fallacy that constitutes an obstacle to the growth of climbing is the general impression that it is a very dangerous sport. It is true that climbing carriers with it certain risks and it is a fact that lives can be lost and have been lost in the mountains. Nevertheless, it is equally true that for an experienced climber who takes the normal precautions, the margin of risk is very much less than what popular imagination would seem to accord it.

Many climbing accidents occur because of inexperience people taking insufficient precautions. The potential for the advancement of Indian mountaineering in the future is great. As roads penetrate the Himalayas and bring the peaks ever closer to the plains, as the enthusiasm of the pioneers spreads to more and more people, it is difficult to believe that at least some part of the potential will not be realised.

While the equipment of a climber is of great importance, the individual equipment—both mental and physical fitness of the mountaineer, is of even greater importance. One slip or thoughtless action may turn the joy of the heights into the sorrow of the depths. Good judgment, constant care and teamwork are indispensable items in the climber's outfit.

The first rule of mountaineering is simple. You must understand what are you going to start. So start by reading few books on mountaineering before you begin. *Freedom of the Hills,* published by The Mountaineers, is widely considered the beginner's bible. Next, learn the fundamentals from an experienced mountaineer or certified guiding service. In India it would be advisable to ask the guidance

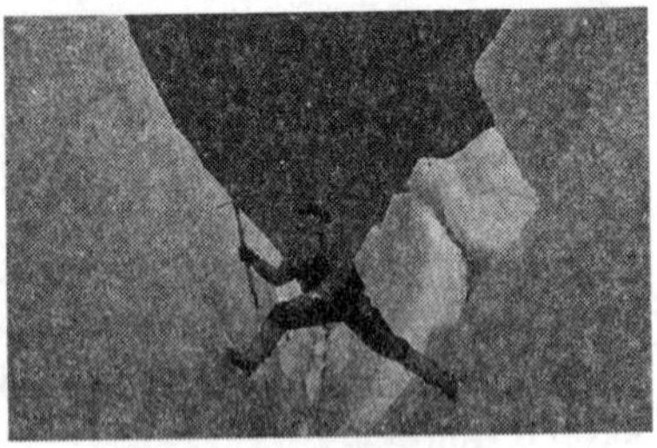

from the mountaineering institutes. Before making your first ascent, learn basic climbing techniques (including rappelling, belaying, anchor systems, and climbing protection), basic rope management, useful climbing knots, and most important, basic wilderness survival.

Your physical condition is directly related to the amount of fun you'll have while climbing. Prior to a challenging climb, workout routines should be frequent and rigorous. For cardiovascular conditioning, which will keep you going, try walking with a weighted backpack, running, biking, swimming, cross-country skiing, and stair climbing. For upper-body strength, try push-ups, pull-ups, sit-ups, and indoor climbing. This may be reason that our foot soldiers of the Mountain Divisions are good mountaineers and have established many records so far.

Equipment

The equipment list should include a seat harness, climbing rope, ice axe, stiff-soled over-the-ankle boots, warm clothing, energy food and drinks, survival gear, and at least one partner. Depending on the mountain and its conditions, you also might need crampons for traction; a helmet; slings; protection that can be used on rock, ice, or snow; carabineers; an avalanche beacon; and a chest harness.

The cost of a mountaineer's basic tool kit--ice axe, crampons and harness is not very heavy. But you should be ready to spend the money. More difficult peaks require double-plastic mountaineering boots and extreme winter clothing that can cost into the thousands. Camping equipment and oxygen, if necessary, are typically supplied by the outfitter.

Learn the Language

Anchor or **Protection:** A fixed item on the climbing terrain that holds the weight of a climber when falling or descending. Includes bolts drilled and hammered into rock, natural features such as boulders or trees, pitons, camping devices, ice screws, and snow pickets.

Belay: Various techniques used by a roped climber to produce a controlled descent. Usually requires a partner to create drag on the rope.

Carabiner: A metal snap-link used for attaching the rope to an anchor or sling.

Crampons: Metal boot attachments with multiple spikes that provide traction on slippery snow and ice.

Rappel: A controlled slide down an anchored rope to descend steep terrain.

Sling: Nylon tubular webbing with its ends either tied or professionally sewn together forming a loop. Used to attach to anchors. The rope is threaded through the loop to prevent excessive drag or abrasion of the rope.

Technical Part of Climbing

Rope and the Knots

A rope is the most essential of all the mountaineering equipments. To use it you may have to learn to tie the knots given here. Every knot has its use in different places. One must understand these knots and their use. Names of the knots are as such.

- Overhand knot
- Clove hitch
- Munter hitch
- Autoblocking knots
- Water knot
- Double fisherman's knot
- Alpine butterfly
- Slip knot
- Garda hitch

Avoiding friction

When you are leading a climb you should try to minimize friction on the rope, not out as a safety issue, simply to keep things practical. You can do this by lengthening your quick draws by using a runner; when you do this you should keep in mind that doing so means you will fall further down, so try to find a compromise between both issues.

For double rope

When using a double rope you can clip in each strand separately, keeping both strands as straight as possible. Notice that as you do so you can no longer use a single carabiner with the Münter hitch, you need two separate carabiners with two separate hitches.

Distress Signals

Alpine distress signal: A white circle on a red plane is an internationally recognized signal of distress.

Ground signals: The following signals are signals you make on the ground so they can be spotted from the air. Make them as big as possible and in a color that stands out against the surface. When you are making the signal try to imagine how it looks from above. Make lines as straight as you can and angles as close to 90° as possible; this will make your signals easier to spot.

Other signals

- SOS (Save Our Souls) is probably the best known distress signal.
- A signal that is often used in the mountains is a series of 6 short signals evenly spaced apart (about 10 sec.), repeat this after a pause of 1 minute . The answer is given by continuous short signals (about 20 sec. apart).

Both these signals can be send by light flashes and sound.

Equalization of anchors

When you have two (or more) anchors you will probably want to tie into all of them at the same time. You could tie into them separately, using one as backup for the other, but this isn't the safest option. Often it is better to connect the anchors and divide the force on the anchors.

This is probably the first option you think of, but this isn't a safe situation at all; imagine what would happen if one of the anchors fails, right, the carabiner would slide over the loose end and fall into the direction of the force. So don't use it. There are basically two sorts of equalization: static equalization and self equalization.

Static equalization

Static equalization means that the forces are only distributed over all the anchors when the system is loaded in one specific direction. When it is loaded in another direction all the force is put on one of the anchors.

Self equalization

This system provides equalization over a larger amount of angles. When belaying a second climber who will go on and lead on the following pitch, use self equalization; if you use static equalization you will have to change your belay when the second climber reaches the belay.

Hoists

These are some rescue techniques which enable you to pull up a person who has fallen and is possibly injured. They can be applied both in snow and ice, and in rock.

Assisted hoist

Now take a second carabiner(2), put it on your reserve end of the rope and lower it to the victim which then clicks it into the harness. You can and an extra prusik on the reserve end, in rock you can take a new carabiner for this. Now pull; the victim can help by pulling the middle piece of rope.

This hoist can only be applied if there is enough reserve rope and the victim is still conscious.

Simple unassisted hoist

Put a second prusik on the rope leading towards the victim, attach a carabiner to it and put the rescuer's end of the rope through that carabiner. Now slide down the lower prusik as far as you can and start pulling. When the lower prusik reaches the upper one, slide down the upper one a bit until it holds all the force. Now you can slide down the lower prusik again and start pulling again.

This hoist works well if you only have to pull up the victim a few meters but it is too tiring for larger distances since it only divides the force needed by 2.

Rappelling

Rappelling is essentially sliding down the rope in a controlled manner. When you want to descent there are basically two options: you can walk or climb down, or you can rappel. When the terrain is easy walking or climbing down is the best choice. But when the terrain becomes too difficult rappelling is the faster, easier and safer solution.

Rappelling without equipment

This technique should only be used on gentle slopes. It is often used for short rappels when it would take too long to take out your harness and other equipment. It can also be used in case of an emergency when there is no other option.

Walking on steep terrain

When you are walking on steep terrain you should always try to get the most grip with the surface as possible, with normal shoes this means getting the biggest possible contact surface, with crampons this means getting the most possible points in the snow or ice. The only way to do is by tilting your ankles so that your feet are flat on the surface.

Using your axe

The simplest and most common way to use an axe is to use it as a cane; this works fine providing the terrain isn't too steep.

A second way to use your axe is to put it in the sloop sideways, with one hand push it in the sloop and with the other hand lean on the axe as close to slope as possible. This technique is very good for traversing slopes.

When descending a steep slope you can use your axe in a third way: put in the axehead as far down as possible, now you can use the axe as a handle by pulling it. As you go down slide down your hand.

Protection in rock (basics)

Always make sure the protection holds the force in the direction of the fall.

For protection with stifi wires (steal wire) always use a quickdraw or else the movement of the rope could wiggle it out of place; for protection with a cord or webbing you can click a carabiner directly into it.

Always try to place the nut so that it has the most contact with the rock as possible.

Placing Camalots and Friends

The angle between the cams should never be greater than 120°. All the cams should always be touching the rock. Camalots and Friends are about seven times as expensive as nuts, so it is advised that you first buy a good set of nuts instead of one Camalot.

Hexentrix

An hexentrix is a type of nut with an eccentric hexagonal shape. It can be used in much the same way as an ordinary nut. For the larger ones don't buy those with steal wire but use a piece of cord and try to tie it so that you can put the knot inside the hex.

Other things you can use as nuts

A rock can serve as a nut, the placement is pretty much the same as an ordinary nut.

A overhand loop can also serve as a nut; place the knot flat into the crack, this way the knot will block when pulled.

Protection in rock (advanced)

Stacking nuts: Stacking nuts is a technique which enables you to make a large nut out of two smaller ones.

Protection in Snow and Ice

Foot belay: The belaying technique can be used for a quick belay on a snow slope when your partner jumps over a crevasse.

Placing ice screws: When you want to place an ice screw you should first remove the rotten ice until you reach the good ice. Don't put the ice screw perpendicular to the surface but tilt it slightly so that the angle becomes about 80°. An ice screw that isn't completely inserted into the ice should be tied of with a runner; this is necessary to avoid a lever-effect.

T-anchor : This is an anchor you can use in snow. Simply dig a T-shaped hole attach a piece of cord to your ice-axe and put in your ice-axe.

Snow or ice bollard: A snow or ice bollard is a good anchor for rappelling if you don't want to leave any of your expensive equipment. The size of the bollard depends on the quality of the snow or ice; for snow the diameter of the bollard should be between 1 and 3 meters, for good ice about 40 centimeters, the height should be about 15-20 cm. It is better to make it a bit too big than a bit too small.

Abalakov: The Abalakov is a good anchor in ice; you can use it for rappelling without leaving behind any ice screws, you only have to leave behind a piece of cord.

Recoverable rappelling anchors

This is an anchor you can use for rappelling on a snow slope without leaving behind any equipment but it requires two ice-axes.

Roping up for glacier travel

When you want to cross a glacier, you should always rope up to avoid serious accidents when someone falls down a crevasse; although it might look safe almost all glaciers have hidden crevasses. You can use a single rope or one part of a double with a length of about 45 to 50 meters. On the ascent the most experienced person should lead and the strongest or heaviest person should come last; on the descent the strong and heavy members of the party walk at the back of the group and the most experienced person comes last.

Two persons

Although this is a common size for a party, it is not really a safe one, so avoid glaciers as much as you can in this case. You should make sure the distance between the both of you is great enough. For extra protection you can put 3to5 knots (small overhand loops or figure-8 loops) in the middle of the rope, these will cut into the side of the crevasse if someone falls in and thereby help the other to hold the fall.

Three persons

This is a safer party-size. You should still use the knots for extra protection. Although this is a good party-size for glacier travel, it is not for rock climbing; remember this if you want to do a mixed route.

More persons

Four is probably the best number of people in a group because this gives a saving party-size for glacier travel and the team can be split up into two groups of two for rock climbing.

It is important to always keep the rope tight between all members of the group; if there is too much slack and someone falls down a crevasse the others will most likely be dragged down too.

Roping up for other terrain

When you are on a moderate snow-slope, you should consider not roping up because when you are roped up and somebody falls, he (or she) will drag the whole party down. By the time the first person manages to stop by using self-arrest technique, the others will have picked up momentum, pulling the first down again, and so on.

On an arrest the middle person(s) should tie in using the technique with the double figure-8 knot (not with an autoblocking knot) and for the persons at the ends of the rope it is best to tie in with a figure-8 loop and a carabiner at the correct distance off the others and put the rest of the rope in the backpack (or coil it around your body). The distances between the members of the group should be much smaller than the distances used for glacier travel, a distance of a couple of meters is ideal. This to insure that when someone starts sliding he can be stopped immediately, before he picks up speed.

Self-arrest

This technique is used to stop yourself when you are sliding downhill after a fall or slip. Don't rely on it, this is just your last resort. When you are sliding there are four possible ways to do it:

—facing down with your head uphill; this is the only position in which you can apply the technique immediately. All the others are merely techniques to get into this position.

Webbing (slings)

When you buy webbing you should always look for the narrow type. Carabiners have their maximum strength when they are loaded exactly in the vertical direction; with narrow webbing you can do this but with the broader type the carabiner will also be loaded along the horizontal axis. Another thing to look out for is the stiffness of the webbing; tests have shown that the stiffer webbing (Petzl slings) breaks much faster than flexibel webbing when it is tied in a knot.

Mountaineering Sites in the Himalayas

Mountaineering in Ladakh, J&K

The Suru and Zanskar valleys provide some of the more spectacular and difficult climbing in Ladakh. The Nun Kun Massif is one of the most frequent climbing areas of the region and is booked out for months ahead, sometimes years, by climbing expeditions. The approach to the twin peaks is from the Kargil-Padum Road, about 70-km south of Kargil. The main approach is either from Tangole or Gulmadong. Some expeditions have also approached from Parkutse along the Kangri Glacier. To reach the base camp for Kun it is for the climbers necessary to cross the Suru River.

Pir Panjal mountaineering range is situated south of the Himalayas. The vale of Kashmir is sandwiched between the Pir Panjals and the Himalayas. Similarly the Lahaul valley, north of Manali and south of Ladakh, is sandwiched between the two ranges.

Mountaineering in Manali, the Himachal Pradesh

The area around Manali presently forms the core of mountaineering in the Himachal. The Beas Kund region and lower reaches of the Hanuman Tibba (5,930m), the Manali and Shitidhar peaks around the source of the river Beas, and the Deo Tibba (6,001m) area, are suggested for beginners with some experience.

Mountaineering in the Garhwal & the Kumaon Himalayas, Uttarakhand

The Garhwal and Kumon region in the state of Uttarakhand not only constitutes a large part of the Himalayas, but also contains some of the most challenging peaks — Nanda Devi, Trisul, Dunagiri, Kamet, Chaukhamba, Nilkanth, Bandarpoonch.

Mounatineering in the Sikkim Himalayas

The Sikkim Himalayas, the epitome of the world's mountains, encompass a wonderland, which for sheer beauty and magnificence remain unbeaten elsewhere in the globe. In the southwestern part of Sikkim, in the main Himalayan range, lies the majestic Kanchendzonga or Kanchenjunga, rising to a staggering height of 8,585 m (28,169 ft) above sea level. Beside this third largest peaks, other famous mountaineering peaks in Sikkim include — Kabru, Kirat Chulior Tent Peak (7,365 m) and Sinolchu (6,887 m).

Mountaineering in Nepal

The Everest or Khumbu region is justifiably the most famous of all trekking and mountaineering regions of Nepal. Populated by Sherpas, the attractions of this area are the majestic mountains, the high mountain villages, the isolated monasteries, and the local peoples. This area includes the highest mountain in the world, Everest at 8,848m, and many of the world's 8,000m peaks such as Lhotse, Cho Oyu, and Makal.

Mounatineering in Tibet

Even if Tibet is new to the mountaineering and adventure sport circuit, still if you like to explore the unexplored visit this cold desert land. Tibetan mountaineering associations have been issuing permits to foreign climbers for mount Everest and twenty other summits. The majority of these mountains are part of the high Himalayas between Everest and Shishapangma, though several other interesting 7,000m and 6,000 peaks have been opened in other regions of Tibet.

Mountaineering in Bhutan

Just like Tibet, mountaineering in the Bhutanese Himalayas is a recent development. Bhutan is one of the most exclusive and rare destinations for any tourist. The unique culture, architecture, lofty snowcapped peaks, fortress like "Dzongs", Lamaist Buddhist traditions and its friendly people leave an everlasting impression on the visitor. Almost all the trekking and mountaineering expeditions in Bhutan range above 3,000m.

■

SCUBA DIVING

Chapter - 63

Beginning

Scuba is an acronym for 'self-contained underwater breathing apparatus'. There are several ways one can go under water (breath-hold, helmet diving, submarine, etc.)."Diving with scuba" signifies using apparatus that is completely carried by the diver and not connected to the surface, hence self-contained.

If you like the water and snorkeling, you'll love this sport. Scuba diving gives you more freedom of movement than snorkeling, and lets you stay underwater for extended periods. Once you get comfortable with all the equipment and settle down with the water, you'll start to feel just like one of the fishes.

Scuba Diver Patting Dolphin

There are several options to finding out if this sport is for you. Snorkeling is the easiest introduction to the oceans and seas. For many, snorkeling is just a tease. The desire to go underwater and stay awhile is just too great.

Another type of introduction to the water is called SNUBA. Similar to scuba, Snuba allows you to remain underwater for an extended period. In Snuba, you don't carry compressed air in tanks on your back; instead air is pumped down from the surface through a hose, which you breathe through. You have limited amount of freedom, about 30 feet of hose. It's quite safe and because it requires little equipment, it's easy to do.

The next level is through a resort course. Resorts offer a one-day scuba diving package for people who have never had any dive training. The package includes a 30-minute class, diving equipment and two dives in 30 to 40 feet of water. You are not certified or properly trained after this, but you may have a wonderful experience and are motivated to get certified. However, most certified divers will warn you against the resort dive experience. It can be very dangerous. If you aren't 100% confident and comfortable in the ocean, don't take a resort course. Get properly trained first. The course is too short to build your confidence, and panicking underwater can be very hazardous.

Scuba originally began with military and commercial applications, where it is still employed. However, by far its widest use, in terms of number of participants, is recreational. Recreational scuba today is like any other sport that requires specialized equipment and training, such as snow skiing, sailing, mountain climbing and horseback riding.

In the early days of scuba diving (roughly 1950-1970), participants were predominately young men. Today the sport is enjoyed by people in all age groups and both sexes. Any teenager or adult who enjoys the water and can swim, and who does not have heart or lung impairment, can learn to scuba dive. It does not take great physical strength or unusual exercise tolerance. All it takes is the desire, plus some basic classroom and in-water training. An estimated 2.5–3.5 million Americans participate in recreational scuba diving. Another 500 thousand become certified each year in the United States.

SCUBA Equipment

Please refer to the picture below showing scuba divers equipped ready to jump into the water. They are carrying compressed air tank, and is wearing buoyancy compensator (BC), mask with snorkel, and fins. Her Mouthpiece is attached to the second stage regulator, and it in turn is attached by hose to the first stage regulator on top of the tank. The alternate second stage regulator is also shown. The equipment includes.

- a tank of compressed air carried by the diver on his or her back;
- a first stage regulator attached to the tank that serves to lower air pressure delivered to the diver;
- a second stage demand regulator and mouthpiece, that delivers air on inhalation and closes on exhalation;
- a face mask that covers the diver's eyes and nose, to allow

Scuba Gear

for both underwater vision and equalization of air pressure within the mask;

- an extra second stage regulator and mouthpiece, carried by the diver in case of emergency (when attached to a long hose, this extra second stage is called an octopus);

Scuba Gear underwater

- two submersible gauges, one to display an accurate depth and the other to show how much air remains in the tank (or, alternatively, a single gauge that combines both functions, e.g., as part of a dive computer);
- an inflatable vest (buoyancy compensator, BC) worn to provide a means of establishing positive buoyancy when needed;
- a weight belt and weights (or some other type of weight system), worn to compensate for the positive buoyancy of the diver and scuba apparatus;
- fins to facilitate self-propulsion in the water; and
- a wet suit or other type of body protection to prevent hypothermia (and secondarily to prevent cuts and abrasions under water); in cold water gloves and a hood may be worn for hypothermia protection also.

Optional equipment for scuba diving are, snorkel, dive knife, small tank of extra air, dive computer, compass, dive lights, writing slate, whistle, and inflatable signaling device. Depending on the circumstances (e.g.,lights for night diving, a snorkel for surface swimming) some of these items may at times be essential, but they are not part of basic scuba equipment.

With the basic scuba equipment a qualified diver can safely remain underwater for anywhere from a few minutes to over two hours; the time limit for any given dive will depend on the depth of that dive, the rate of air consumption, and the profile of any dives made within the previous 6-12 hours.

First Descent

The first dive experience should either be in a pool or through a resort diving course. Resort courses are less safe because you are not

Scuba Diver jumping into water

properly trained. Even if you're only diving in 30 feet of water, there are hazards when you're using compress air.

If you're going to do a short course, make sure it's a good course. They should provide at the least a ½ hour lecture, any less time means you're not getting the basic information you need. In a resort course, a dive instructor will go with you underwater. It's important that there aren't too many students. three or four students to an instructor should be the maximum. Any more and the instructor will have a hard time making sure everyone is safe. When you're diving, stay close to the instructor. That way, if you get into trouble, you will be able to get help quickly.

Once you've decided to get trained, its time to find a scuba class. There are three main organizations providing certification. For the first level of certification, the general opinion is that all three are equal. PADI and NAUI are the most familiar organizations within the dive community in the USA. Additionally, the YMCA is the oldest scuba instruction organization in the U.S. They are considered to have the highest training standards.

The standard equipment from your first day in the water is a mask, snorkel, fins, BC (buoyancy compensator), weight belt, regulator, and tank. During the course, the BC, weight belt, regulator and tanks will be provided. It is better for one to buy one's mask, snorkel and fins. Real scuba diving equipment should be purchased by oneself and not swim or beach equipment. Buy good equipment that fits properly. At 60 feet under you don't want to be worried about a mask that leaks. Your dive course provider will be able to help you to find the correct equipment.

Don'ts

- Don't touch or stand on the reef, ever. Don't let your equipment touch or drag across the reef. This is really important, because one touch is all it takes to kill the coral. And it takes hundreds of years to rebuild the damage. The world is rapidly losing its dive sights because of ignorant divers.

- Don't take anything. You may hear of some divers taking shells, but it is not an acceptable practice among the diving community. A good scuba diver strives to leave the underwater environment totally unchanged by the visit.
- Don't leave your dive buddy. You've agreed to stay together, so stay near.
- Don't just follow your dive buddy's lead, leaving your safety in someone else's hands. Play a role in the dive. Don't rely on someone else to watch the time, your depth, etc. If you don't feel right about going somewhere or doing something, say so.

Some Essential Points

- In order to keep your equipment from dragging, use Velcro strips to keep your gauges close to your BC jacket.
- Always wear some kind of wetsuit or dive skin, no matter how warm the water is. Even if the water is 85°, you'll get cold after an hour.
- Bring your own wetsuit. Rentals are kind of nasty.
- Bring a flash light.
- It can be difficult, but finding a regular dive partner can really enhance your diving.

Safety

- Number one rule for safety is stay calm. Panicking underwater just magnifies any situation making things worse.
- If it's been over 12 months since your last dive , a refresher course would be better.
- Plan your dive, before you dive.

Certification in SCUBA

Potential hazards that every scuba diver must be aware of include de-compression sickness, air embolism, hypothermia, physical exhaustion, injuries from marine life, boating accidents, sunburn, and out-of-air catastrophes. Despite the list of potential problems, recreational diving is actually a safe sport if the diver is healthy and trained properly, each dive is carefully planned and dive limits are followed. The most serious problems, and how to avoid them, are covered in the entry level scuba course.

The entry level course, also known as 'basic open water' or 'basic certification,' takes about 30 hours. About 10 hours is spent in classroom instruction and the remainder in supervised pool and open water diving. 'Open water' means a natural body of water open to the sky. Upon completion, a certification or 'C' card is issued. The C card contains the new diver's picture, date of course completion and signature of the instructor. The basic open water course is fairly standard and is given under the auspices of one of several national training agencies.

Many people are first exposed to scuba through the "resort course." This is an introductory lesson offered at a resort or on a cruise, and is always taught by an instructor (i.e., one who is also qualified to teach the standard open water course). The resort course is highly variable; it may include only a brief lecture on a crowded bus on the way to the dive site, or a leisurely morning pool session before the afternoon open water dive. Because the resort course contains no textbook and very little in the way of theory or skills testing, it does not certify for independent diving. It is also good only for that resort and for the time you are a guest there. If you return six months or a year later to the same resort you would have to start all over with another resort course.

Resort courses are fine for introduction to scuba, but anyone who has enjoyed the experience is encouraged to take a standard certification course and learn the necessary skills and theory. Standard certification is also more practical. The C card allows one to rent or buy scuba equipment anywhere in the world, and to engage in recreational diving without supervision by an instructor.

The certification process distinguishes recreational scuba diving from most other sports that use specialized equipment (e.g., snow skiing, mountain climbing). Without a C card (i.e., without certification) one should not go scuba diving (unless accompanied by a professional scuba instructor).

Scuba Instructor

In college the lowest academic rank is the "instructor," usually someone in graduate school who is assigned to teach and work under a "professor." In the world of scuba the instructor is the highest level. A scuba instructor is the only person trained and qualified to teach scuba diving. The scuba instructor can be assisted by other scuba professionals who are in training to become a scuba instructor; they may have the title of dive master (the entry level position for a scuba professional) or assistant instructor. However, only someone with instructor status can teach the basic open water course.

Differences of Scuba Diving from Other Forms of Diving

Diving was revolutionized by the development of a workable demand regulator, co-invented in 1943 by Jacques Cousteau and Emil Gagnan. The "sport" of scuba diving did not catch on for another 10 years. Today the greatest use of scuba equipment is for recreational diving. Recreational scuba diving, as taught by national certifying agencies, is defined as :

- Uses only compressed air as the breathing mixture.
- It is never done solo.
- Does not exceed a depth of 130 feet.
- It has a depth-time profile not requiring a decompression stop; if necessary one can ascend to the surface without stopping.
- It does not require specialized training beyond the basic open water course.

  Scuba equipment is also widely employed by two other types of divers, loosely categorized as "professional" and "technical".
- Professional diving is done for military, governmental, commercial, or scientific purposes. Professional divers are paid to dive. They have a specific mission for each dive, e.g., lay a mine or recover a bomb (military), look for a body or a weapon (law enforcement agency), explore for oil (commercial), map an ancient wreck or examine a new species of fish (scientific).
- Technical diving is the term for all diving that exceeds recreational limits but is not engaged in for profit. Although many, if not most, technical divers consider themselves involved in a recreational activity, the nature of their diving and type of equipment used exceed the boundaries of Recreatronial Scuba Diving (RSD). The forms of Technical divings are:
- cave diving
- ice diving
- very deep diving (to greater than 130 feet)
- mixed gas diving (using gas mixtures other than air, such as nitrox or trimix)
- deep-penetration wreck diving
- diving with specialized life-support equipment (e.g., breathers)

Much of technical diving is taught by agencies other than the national open water certification agencies. No matter how diving activities are classified, no one should engage in any diving activity unless certified in that activity or else supervised by a qualified instructor.

The Buddy System

It is required that each diver be accompanied under water by a buddy who can share air or provide other assistance. Scuba apparatus is designed to carry an extra demand regulator. This is required in case one diver runs out of air and has to share a single tank with his or her buddy. Ideally, the buddies should have similar training and skill levels; it does no good to have a buddy who dives deeper or stays down longer than you do. Buddies should stay close together and always be aware of each other's location.

130 Feet Limit

The 130-foot limit is an arbitrary depth originally adopted by the U.S. Navy because it gave navy divers about 10 minutes of bottom time on compressed air; going any deeper on air made no sense to the Navy because the time available to do useful work was simply too short. As with many diving issues in the early days of scuba (e.g., the 'no decompression' limits), the Navy standard was also adopted by the recreational training agencies.

Some experienced recreational divers do go deeper than 130 feet, and yet still stay within no decompression limits. However, since the risks of the bends, running out of air, and nitrogen narcosis increase as you go deeper, the training agencies feel that some arbitrary limit must be set and have stayed with 130 feet. Thus, although one can dive deeper and stay within no decompression limits, diving deeper than 130 feet is not taught by the recreational training agencies, and must be undertaken with great care and an understanding of the increased risks.

What is Mandatory Decompression and why is it not part of Recreational Scuba Diving?

"Decompression" always occurs when we go from a higher to a lower ambient pressure. Thus all compressed gas diving is decompression diving. When recreational diving is referred to as "no decompression diving" it really means "no mandatory decompression stop diving." A decompression stop should never be necessary within the guidelines of RSD.

A decompression stop is often necessary in dives deeper or longer than allowed in RSD; it provides time for some of the excess nitrogen that entered the tissues to "gas off" (diffuse into the blood stream and then be ventilated out by the lungs), thereby minimizing risk of decompression sickness (DCS). Based on experiments, plus much trial and error experience, the amount of excess nitrogen remaining in the tissues after a planned, mandatory decompression stop should not cause DCS.

Since professional and technical divers often spend longer periods under water and/or dive deeper than recreational divers, they must know when to stop on ascent and how long to wait before surfacing. By contrast, each recreational dive is planned so that the diver can ascend continuously to the surface without encountering decompression sickness; the diver is still decompressing on the way up, but doesn't have to stop to allow further decompression. The basic assumption is that diving is inherently made safer by avoiding dives that require decompression stops. This is both the philosophy and practice of recreational diving today.

The "no decompression stop" limits in RSD are based on maximum depth, time under water, and extent of any preceding dives, all factors which directly affect tissue nitrogen uptake. The limits are set in dive tables known to every certified diver, and are incorporated into all dive computers.

Excess nitrogen, which enters tissues due to the increased ambient pressure under water, determines the "no-decompression stop" limits. A non-repetitive dive (no previous dive within a specified time period, typically 6-12 hours) to 130 feet has an allowable "actual bottom time" (measured from the time dive commences to start of ascent) of only about 5-10 minutes for a dive to 130 feet. Beyond this brief time span the diver risks developing decompression sickness from a continuous ascent. In contrast, at 35 feet, on a non-repetitive dive, the 'no decompression' bottom time is about 205 minutes.

Although RSD is always planned for no decompression stop required, it is routine practice to make a 3-to 5-minute "safety stop" at 15 feet before surfacing from any dive deeper than about 40 feet. This is a decompression stop but it is not mandatory, just added for extra safety to the dive; hence the term safety stop. In theory, when adhering to the recreational diving tables one should not experience DCS if a safety stop is not made. Nonetheless, all dives deeper than about 40 feet should incorporate a safety stop, and it is universally practised. If any dive requires a decompression stop for any reason, it has exceeded the limits of recreational diving.

Different Levels of Recreational Diving

Within the universe of recreational diving there are many levels, based on extent of training, experience, or both. The following paragraphs pertain to the certified diver.

Training: One can take several courses beyond basic open water, and they can be divided into two "tracks." The first kind is for people who want more training but have no intention of ever teaching scuba. With such courses as advanced diving, stress and rescue, underwater photography, ice diving, and deeper diving (60-130 feet), one can gain additional knowledge and skills, all under the purview of recreational diving.

Scuba Diver playing with dolphin

The second kind is for people who plan to turn professional and teach scuba. They will take courses leading up to the instructor level (advanced diving, stress and rescue, divemaster, assistant instructor, instructor). Once an individual achieves instructor level he or she is a full-fledged professional within recreational scuba and can teach the basic certification course.

Unless they have taken special training, scuba instructors are not trained to exceed the recreational limits. Thus they are not technical divers and would need further training to do mixed gas diving, for example. Of course many scuba instructors do obtain training in these and other technical diving skills.

Most recreational divers never take more than the basic open water course. However, after making many dives over the years they become highly experienced and adept in all the important skills. In recent years scuba agencies have developed a way to recognize the more experienced divers, by creating "dive cards" showing the number of dives obtained, in round numbers. Thus, with proper documentation you can get a card that shows you have done anywhere from 50 to 5000 lifetime dives. The utility of this type of card is that it can quickly show your level of experience, such as when you go to rent equipment or sign on for a boat dive. Experience counts for much in scuba diving (as with any activity), and the cards are a way of acknowledging this.

Sport Surface-Supplied Compressed Air Diving vs Scuba Diving

As its name indicates, sport surface-supplied compressed air diving (sometimes shortened to 'sport surface-supplied air,' SSSA) separates the compressed air source from the diver. For this reason it is not "scuba,"which is self-contained (the scuba diver always carries his/her own air source). SSSA uses a small gasoline- or electric-powered air compressor that can sit on a boat, dock or a floating inner tube, so it can literally go to any dive site and remain over the heads of the divers .The compressor can provide air to more than one diver at the same time.

Scuba Divers surfacing on a line

Each SSSA diver is tethered to the compressed air source by a long hose. The entire apparatus is sometimes called a hookah, after the Egyptian term for a pipe that cools water, but "surface-supplied compressed air" is the more correct term. At the end of each hose is a second stage regulator and mouth-piece, just like in scuba diving; exhaled air is expelled into the water.

SSSA diving is limited by the strength of the air compressor, the length of the hose and, as in scuba, the level of diver training. As sold by Brownies, each unit serves at least two divers; some can serve three or four divers at 30 feet. Other units allow deeper diving, up to 90 feet for two divers. In principle SSSA diving is the same as professional helmet diving, except that the depths are generally less, no helmet is worn by the diver, only compressed air is used (professionals may use mixed gases), and the amount of surface support (i.e., other people on the surface) may be minimal to none. The box below lists advantages and disadvantages of SSSA compared to scuba.

SSSA vs. Scuba

Principal advantages of SSSA diving

- Can provide unlimited supply of compressed air.

- Allows diving to full limit of dive tables without running out of air; only small amount of gasoline required for dives that would otherwise require several tank refills.
- Eliminates need to carry a heavy tank into the water.
- Eliminates need for first stage regulator.
- Each system is designed to be used by at least two divers, fostering buddy system; buddy is always close by and connected.
- Since there is no tank and therefore no changing tank pressure, diver's buoyancy tends to stay constant throughout dive.

Dive Safety

- Spread of hyperbaric chambers to all popular dive sites; development of affordable, portable hyperbaric chambers that can be carried on a dive boat.
- Universal use of dive computers air integrated to the scuba tank, eliminating the high pressure hose connection.
- Use of full face masks that remain on the diver's face if there is any panic or loss of consciousness (absence of a mouthpiece reduces the risk of drowning in these situations).
- Implementation of underwater voice communication technology.
- Development of "heads up" displays for dive data; instead of data displayed on a wrist device or on a dangling console, all data will appear inside the diver's mask, available for reading with only a turn of the eye. Critical information may flash, assuring the diver's attention.
- Implementation of diver-specific algorithms (adjusted for the diver's age, weight, and perhaps other characteristics) for dive computers. Such algorithms may become available from studies that correlate dive accident experience with a wide range of dive profiles in a diverse group of divers.

Extension of bottom time or distance traveled under water

- Use of nitrox, perhaps with a depth limiter to prevent diving too deep and incurring risk of oxygen toxicity.
- Use of stronger tanks (carbon fiber) that can hold higher pressures and thus more cubic feet of gas.

- Underwater scooters that allow the diver to range further on a given dive with the same amount of air.
- Use of re-breathing "closed circuit" scuba technology.

Much of this technology and equipment are available now, if not for the recreational diver than in technical circles. Just as other once-new technology gradually became accepted (e.g., dive computers), it seems likely that much of today's "cutting-edge" technology will be adopted by recreational divers in the coming years. Cost and complexity will certainly be a limiting factor, however. Many recreational divers may not want to be burdened with more equipment or ever more complicated and expensive technology.

■

SEA KAYAKING

Chapter - 64

A Sea kayak or touring kayak is a kayak developed for the sport of paddling on open waters of lakes, bays, and the ocean. Sea kayaks are seaworthy small boats with a covered deck and the ability to incorporate a spraydeck. They trade off the extreme maneuverability of whitewater kayaks for cargo capacity, ease of straight-line paddling, and comfort for long journeys.

Sea kayaks are now used around the world for marine journeys from a few hours to many weeks, as they can accommodate one or two (occasionally three) paddlers together with room for camping gear, food, water, and other supplies. The sport of sea kayaking (sometimes called ocean kayaking) combines much of the appeal of hill-walking with a maritime aspect, few access issues and an almost infinite area to enjoy.

History

Contemporary sea kayaks trace their origins primarily to the native boats of Alaska, northern Canada, and Southwest Greenland. Wooden kayaks and fabric kayaks on wooden frames (such as the Klepper) were dominating the market up until 1950s, when fiberglass boats were first introduced. Rotomolded plastic kayaks first appeared in 1984.

Design

Modern sea kayaks come in a wide array of materials, designs, and sizes to suit a variety of intended uses. The primary distinction is between rigid kayaks and folding kayaks. While many modern kayaks carry the design features of traditional craft, recent design innovation includes:

Kayaking in a double on Lake Union in Seattle, USA

- Recreational kayaks, shorter sea kayaks with wide beams and large cockpits;
- Sit-on-top kayaks, rotomolded boats without an enclosed cockpit, but with some other sea kayak features;
- Inflatable kayaks, sometimes employing a rigid frame with inflatable sponsons; and
- Surf skis, long, narrow boats intended for open ocean racing.

Size

Most production sea kayaks are between 12–24 feet in length, the larger kayaks often built for two (or in rare cases, three) paddlers. The width (beam) of typical kayaks varies from 18 to 28 inches, though specialized boats such as surf skis may be narrower. The length of a kayak affects not only its cargo capacity (for both gear and paddlers) but may also affect its "tracking" ability—the ease with which the boat travels in a straight line. While other design features also impact tracking, very long kayaks are easier to paddle straight (and harder to turn). The width of a kayak affects the cargo capacity, the maximum size of the cockpit (and thus the size of the paddler in that cockpit), and (to a degree that depends on the design of the hull) the stability.

Material

Most rigid production kayaks are now made from fiberglass, rotomolded polyethylene, or carbon-kevlar, though there are more exotic materials, such as carbon fiber and foam core, and hand-built systems from as plywood or wood strip covered with fiberglass. Skin-on-frame kayaks are built on wood or aluminum frames covered in canvas, dacron or other fabrics, and may include inflatable tubes called sponsons.

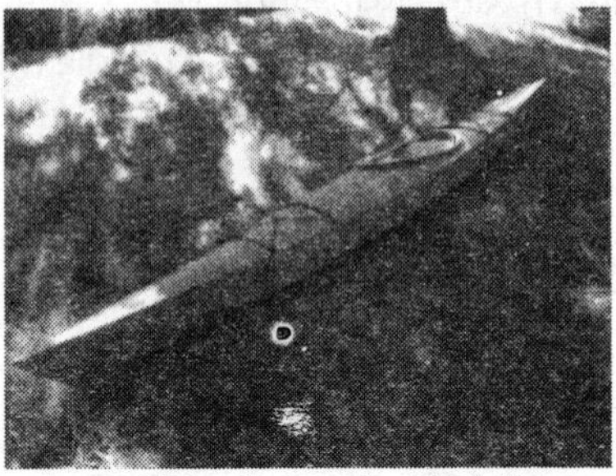

A sea kayak constructed from plywood, epoxy and fibreglass

Bow, stern, and deck

There are many design approaches for the bow, stern, and deck of kayaks. Some kayaks have upturned bows, with the intention of better performance into wave and better wave-shedding ability, while others aim to achieve this through increased buoyancy in the bow. Kayaks with unobstructed stern decks may ease certain types of self-rescue. Waterproof bulkheads in modern kayaks provide flotation in the event of capasize, and sea kayak decks typically include one or more hatches for easy access to the interior storage space inside. Kayak decks often include attachment points for deck lines of various kinds, which are aids in self-rescue and attachment points for above-deck equipment.

Other

Many sea kayaks have steering gear or tracking aids in the form of rudders or skegs. In most cases rudders are attached at the stern and operated, via wires, from foot peddles in the cockpit. Rudders are typically retractable for beach landings. Skegs are straight blades that drop from a well in the stern of the boat. Both devices assist in paddling when a strong wind is coming from a direction other than directly in front.

Paddles

Sea-kayak paddles, and the associated paddling styles, fall into two basic classifications:

- **European:** It is a paddle with two roughly spoon-shaped blades at either end of a cylindrical shaft. This paddle style was developed for fast acceleration and sudden maneuvering in whitewater kayaking, and then back-ported to sea-kayaking. Euro paddles can be made of aluminum, plastic or even wood,

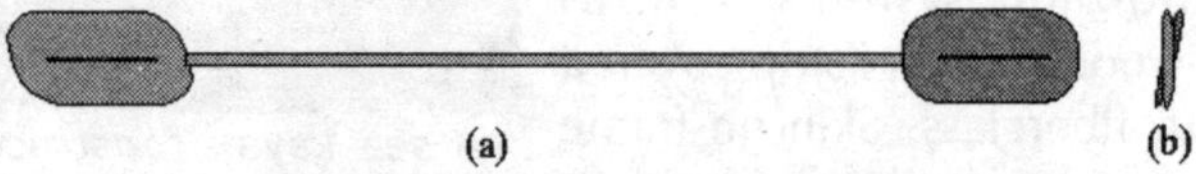

A European style kayak paddle, (a) top view, (b) axial view

  but the best are usually formed of more expensive materials like carbon-fiber for lightness. Often the two blades are feathered, or set at an angle relative to each other (both for ergonomic efficiency, and so that as one blade moves backwards through the water, the opposite blade moving forward through the air presents its edge, rather than its face).

- **Greenland:** Relatively narrow blades which are rounded and full near the loom and blade roots, and becoming oval near the blade tips. Some paddles feature a "shoulder", or abrupt transition between the loom and blade roots. Greenland paddle blades are most often not feathered. Short Greenland paddles (generally one arm-span in length), called storm paddles, are used with a sliding stroke, where the hands are shifted along the blades for each stroke. Storm paddles are often used as spares and in very windy locations, as there is very little outboard blade to catch the wind.
- **Wing:** The blade of the paddle is shaped with a profile like a wing. When used with a special stroke, the blade actually produces lift as it moves through the water, enabling the kayaker to produce more forward motion than with any other kind of paddle. The paddling technique is different from both European style paddles and Greenland style. It is most often used in racing, but also seen in some limited use in recreational paddling such as touring.

Dimensions

Sea kayaks come in many different designs resulting in different dimensions. The length of a typcal Solo sea kayak can range anywhere from 12'-18' long, and Tandem kayaks can range from 15'-20' long. Sea kayaks can range from 22.5" wide to 30" wide. Wider Touring kayaks 26-30" are better for bigger paddlers, or small/average size paddlers looking for more initiall satbility and manueverbality. narrower beams 22"-25" are good for small-medium paddlers that want more speed and less manueverability. And lastly, kayak depth (or the height from the hull to the highest area of the deck) can range from 13"-15.8" high.

Sea Kayaking at Wilsons Promontory in Victoria, Australia

Trips

Weekend trips with overnight camping are popular amongst recreational kayakers, and many people combine kayaking with watching wildlife. Modern sea kayaks are designed to carry large amounts of equipment, and unsupported expeditions of two weeks or more are conducted in environments from the tropics to the arctic. Expedition kayaks are designed to handle best when loaded, so it may be necessary to ballast them on shorter trips.

Notable Expeditions

- In November 2005 the first kayak circumnavigation of South Georgia in the Southern Atlantic was completed in 18 days, a distance of 600 km.
- In 1977, Paul Caffyn was the first person to circumnavigate the South Island of New Zealand. He describes it in his book *Obscured by Waves.* He then went on to complete the first circumnavigation of Australia in 1986 covering a distance of 9,420 miles.
- Paul Caffryn and Nigel Dennis were the first sea kayakers to circumnavigate of Britain in 1980, a distance of 2,200 miles in 85 days.
- Harry Whelan, Barry Shaw and Phil Clegg are considered to have been the fastest around Britain in 2005, completing the circumnavigation in 80 days.
- In his book *Cold Oceans* (1999), Jon Turk describes his solo circumnavigation of Cape Horn.
- Adventurer Chris Duff has circumnavigated both Ireland in 1996 and New Zealand's South Island in 2000.
- Eric Stiller and Tony Brown attempted circumnavigation of Australia, described in the book *Keep Australia* .
- Trys Morris, Gemma Rawlings and Justine Curgenven succesfully circumnavigated Tasmania in 2004. This journey is featured in *This Is The Sea.*

Safety

A sea kayak's primary safety device is its paddler. Some modern kayakers consider a well-practised self-righting move called an Eskimo roll to be essential to safe open-water kayaking, though this move can be difficult in a heavily-laden boat. While there are a number of techniques for unassisted righting and re-entry of a kayak after a capsize, most paddlers consider it the safest to paddle with one or more others, as assisted rescues are more likely to succeed. Nonetheless, experienced paddlers do attempt open water crossings unaccompanied, and several major long-distance kayak expeditions have been carried out "solo". There is a strong culture of self-sufficiency amongst sea kayakers and extensive safety equipment such as towing lines, repair kits and survival gear is routinely carried.

■

(from Wikipidia free Encyclopedia)

SKY DIVING

Chapter - 65

Beginning

Sky Diving as sport is fairly popular like many other sports in USA. It is not so popular in India because of many restrictions. Except for the Indian Air Force team of sky divers there is no organization that has taken up the challenges. In the USA one can contact the local parachuting operation—normally referred to as a "drop zone" (DZ). They will generally provide you with enough information to make arrangements to attend the First Jump Course. One may contact also the United States Parachute Association to get the name of an affiliated drop zone in an area of interest.

Most DZs will offer the First Jump Course (FJC) at least once each weekend. Some will offer it during the week or several times during the weekend. The FJC consists of about 4-6 hours of ground school followed by the jump.

There are several different types of training you can take:

- Static Line,
- Accelerated Freefall, or
- Tandem .

Age

Most dropzones will require one to be 18 years of age to make a skydive. In the USA, some dropzones in some states will allow 16-year olds to jump with parental consent. So, if you are under 16, you will just have to wait. On the other side, there is no maximum age.

Physical Requirements

In general, the prospective student should be in reasonably good physical shape, this is a sport after all. You will be required to wear around 20 kgs of equipment, endure opening shock, maneuver the canopy, land, and possibly trudge great distances on foot. You will experience 30 degree changes in temperature, atmospheric pressure changes, and four hours of lecture.

Training for Sky Diving

The instructors teach the students every thing they need to know to safely make their first jump. There are several different programs available for first jumpers; the one you choose will depend on your personal preferences and circumstances. The differences of each are summarized below.

Static Line (SL)

This method has evolved over the last ~30 years from its military origins into a successful method for training sport parachutists. The student gets 4-5 hours of ground training and is then taken to an altitude of about 3000 feet for the jump. The jump itself consists of a simple "poised" exit from the strut of a small single engine Cessna aircraft. As the student falls away from the plane, the main canopy is deployed by a "static line" attached to the aircraft. The student will experience about two to three seconds of falling as the parachute opens.

The first freefall is a "clear & pull", where the student initiates the pull sequence immediately upon leaving the aircraft. Next is a 10-second delay jump. Subsequent jumps go to progressively higher altitudes with longer delays. After 20 freefalls, and meeting certain other basic requirements, the students receive their A license and are cleared off student status.

Accelerated Free Fall (AFF)

The AFF program was instituted in 1982 as an "accelerated" learning process as compared to the traditional static line progression. The AFF program will give you a true taste of modern sport skydiving.

The ground training is a bit more extensive than SL (~5 hours) because the student will be doing a 50-second freefall on his/her very first jump. The student will exit the aircraft at 10,000-12,000 feet along with two AFF Jumpmasters (JM) who will assist the student during freefall. The jumpmasters maintain grips on the student from the moment they leave the aircraft until opening, assisting the student as necessary to fall stable, perform practice ripcord pulls, monitor altitude, etc. The student then pulls his/her own ripcord at about 4000 ft.

Each AFF level is designed to take one jump, and requires about 45 minutes of training. After successfully performing the objectives of each level, the student moves on to the next level.

After graduating Level 7, the student enters a more free format stage called "Level 8" where they practise and hone their skills by themselves.

Tandem Jumps

Tandem jumps are meant to offer an introduction to the sport. They allow the neophyte to "take a ride" with an experienced jumper. A tandem jump requires from 15 to 45 minutes of ground preparation (it is not a First Jump Course).

If the Parachute Doesn't Open

This is the most Frequently-Asked-Question from the prospective jumpers. By law (FAA regulations), all intentional parachute jumps must be made with a single harness, dual parachute system with both a main canopy and a reserve canopy. In other words, you have a second (or spare) canopy in case the first one fails to open properly.

However, it must be noted that the technology utilized in today's sport parachuting equipment is light years ahead of the old military equipment used in the '60s and '70s. The canopies are drastically different from the classic military parachutes. The materials are stronger, lighter and last longer, the packing procedures are simpler, the deployment sequence is much more refined, etc.

The reserve canopies are even more carefully designed and packed. The reserve parachute must be inspected and repacked every 120 days by an FAA in the USA rated parachute Rigger — even if it has not been used during that time.

The student's main canopy is always packed either by a rigger or under a rigger's direct supervision by experienced packers.

There are also additional safety features employed to ensure canopy deployment such as Automatic Activation Devices (AAD) and Reserve Static Lines (RSL) which add still more layers of safety.

Rate of Fall

When you leave the aircraft, you are moving horizontally at the same speed as the aircraft, typically 90-110MPH. During the first 10 seconds, a skydiver accelerates up to about 115-130MPH straight down. (A tandem pair uses a drouge chute to keep them from falling much faster than this). It is possible to change your body position to vary your rate of fall. In a standard face-to-earth position, you can change your fall rate up or down a few (10-20) miles per hour. However, by diving or "standing up" in freefall, any experienced skydiver can learn to reach speeds of over 160-180MPH. Speeds of over 200MPH require significant practice to achieve. The record freefall speed, done without any special equipment, is 321MPH. Obviously, it is desirable to slow back down to 110MPH before parachute opening. Once under parachute, decent rates of 1000ft/min are typical. A lighter student with a bigger canopy may come down much more slowly, and, obviously, a heavier person may have a somewhat faster decent. Experienced jumper's canopies descend (in normal glide) at up to 1500ft/min. During radical turns, the decent rate can go well over 2000ft/min.

Landing

The canopies used today bear little resemblance to the classic round canopies of years gone by. Today, nearly all jumpers and jump schools use "square" canopies for parachuting. These canopies are actually rectangular in shape, and when open, act like an airplane wing (or an airfoil). They are more like gliders than umbrellas.

The aerodynamics of the square canopy provide it with exceptional maneuverability, allowing the jumpers to land almost anywhere they wish. This wing shape also provides tippy-toe soft landings for even the novice jumper. The days of landing like a sack of flour are history. Most students land standing up on their first jump.

Cost in USA

Cost vary from DZ to DZ. Typically, the S/L course runs ~$120-$150, AFF from $250-$300, and the tandem from $140-$200. Some

DZs can provide a freefall videoman to tape your skydive for an additional $50-75. These prices include the ground school and the first jump.

Equipment can run from $1000 to $3500 depending on what you want to spend. There is a used equipment market (much like the used car market) which can save you lot of money, or you can custom order everything brand-spanking-new with your own personalized colors and sizes, which will cost a lot.

Breathing During the Freefall

One can breathe in freefall—if it were necessary. However, due to the high speed of terminal freefall (and much higher speeds in vertical freefall dives), the jumper's body is exposed to O2 molecules at a much higher rate than someone walking around on the ground. The body is able to absorb the necessary O2 through the skin. This is why jumpers flap their cheeks in freefall, it presents a larger surface area to the airstream for oxygen osmosis. Once under canopy, the jumper resumes breathing normally.

Flying Your Body

The principles of freefall flight are quite simple; after all, you are dealing with just two things: your airfoil (body) and the wind. In a perfect, relaxed arch, or box man, you will fall straight down at a constant rate. To an observer falling along side, you appear stationary. You only seem to be falling relative to someone not in freefall, such as an observer in the airplane or on the ground.

The basic moves are well understood. The most commonly used maneuvers are turns, forward and backward movement, and faster or slower falling. All are accomplished by changing the flow of air around your body. If you think of your box man as being balanced on his center in a neutral position, all he has to do to turn left is deflect more air off his right arm than his left. This is done by simply banking like an airplane—left arm down slightly, right arm up in proportion. The turn will continue until he resumes the neutral position. Lowering one knee relative to the other accomplishes the same thing. That's why an unintentional turn can often be stopped by assuming a neutral position and then giving a little "legs out" to increase awareness and balance the legs.

Turns are also based on deflection of air. In the neutral position, equal amounts of air spill off both sides of the body. To turn right, our box man banks his arms, just as an airplane does in a turn. More air flows off the left side, creating a right turn. Note that the position of the arms relative to each other does not change; both arms tilt as a unit. The rest of the body remains neutral. To stop the turn, simply return to neutral.

Forward motion works on the same principle of deflection. To deflect more air to the rear, resulting in forward now think about how to go up and down. Everyone knows that given the same power, a streamlined vehicle can go faster than one that isn't. It slips through the air easier, just as a canoe knifes through the water more easily than a barge. So to speed up, you simply arch more, letting air slip off easily. Flatten out, or lower your knees and elbows, and you will fall slower. Incidentally, the faster you fall the more stable you are because your center of gravity is further below your control surfaces (arms and legs).

Exits

There is nothing particularly complicated about exits and the techniques you use on your first freefall will be the same as those used by skydivers with thousands of jumps. Your exit makes or breaks the skydive, so we spend a lot of time practising this part of the jump. A weak exit consumes valuable freefall time and puts you in a mental position of having to catch up, adding unwanted stress to your skydive. With a good exit you can get on with your learning and enjoyment at once, finishing the freefall tasks with plenty of time to spare. The two essentials of an exit are presentation and timing. Presentation refers to how you relate to the relative wind. Timing refers to your relationship with the other skydivers.

Until your parachute opens, your last contact with the world of solid objects is the airplane. If you jump in a hurry, you will have some momentum that will tend to make you go over on your back, just as if you stood with your back to a pool and pushed off of something solid. Just arch and face the wind.

As you leave the aircraft, the relative wind (arrow) is parallel to the ground. In a good arch with your head up, you should see only the airplane and sky rather than the ground during the first second or two of freefall.

Losing forward speed and accelerating downward, the relative wind gradually shifts from parallel to the ground to perpendicular. This transition takes several seconds. You will not be facing the ground until about eight seconds after the exit.

At no time do you look directly down at the ground. Even after the transition is over and you are falling straight down, in a good arch your head is up and your eyes are on the horizon.

The aircraft's speed is about 100 miles an hour. When you leave, you lose some of that horizontal speed and actually slow down for the first few seconds. Then gravity takes over and you gradually accelerate to 110 miles per hour. That's why there is no sensation of sudden acceleration — you only gain ten miles per hour in ten seconds!

Relax, arch, and face the wind is all you really need to do to achieve a stable exit. But remember that you are jumping with other people. For everyone to have a good exit, you also need group timing. Just as a band starts playing to a count, we'll start skydiving to a count. That count, used all over the country, is "ready, set, go!" It should be done with a smooth, even cadence. Because it's noisy outside an airplane, the count should be loud. Finally (think of a conductor with his baton giving a visual count to the orchestra) you, the conductor, need to give the other jumpers a visible count. We have you bring up your left knee on "set" and turn into the wind on go.

In the Aircraft

Every skydive starts before you board the airplane. Before you get on the airplane, you should be totally prepared for the jump ahead. This means that you know exactly what you are going to do on the jump and have had your equipment inspected. Make sure you have your helmet and goggles, remove jewelry and take sharp objects out of your pockets, tie your shoes tightly, and so on. Each jumper is responsible for their personal equipment, and you should always check to be sure you have everything necessary for the skydive.

Another part of the ground preparation is being ready to board the aircraft on time. Jump planes are just like airliners: they can't hold up twenty people because one wasn't ready. At the start of your skydiving progression, your jumpmaster will usually take care of reserving your slot on an airplane after you are completely trained and outfitted with the necessary equipment. It is then your responsibility to stay in the area and join up at the appropriate time with your jumpmasters.

Before you Board

- It's too late to ask questions once you are in the airplane, so before you board know exactly what you will do on the skydive and review your emergency procedures. On the ride to altitude you should review the dive mentally, imagining a perfect performance. Keep in mind, however, that you are not compelled to jump from the airplane just because you happen to be on it. If you realize on the aircraft that you are not ready to jump, you may comeback.

- ❖ Check your equipment. Your jumpmasters will help you to be sure everything is correctly routed. Be sure your altimeter is set to zero, your goggles are clean, etc. If you will be boarding an airplane when its engines are running, keep a good grip on your goggles and gloves!
- ❖ Stay close to your jumpmaster and away from the propellers, other aircraft, and any other hazardous objects. Remember that the pilot may not be able to see you when he is taxiing the airplane; he always has the right of way.
- ❖ Once you are in the airplane, sit where instructed. Be sure to wear your seat belt until you are high enough for an emergency exit. It is also a good idea to put your helmet on for the take off. Your two responsibilities in the airplane are to minimize movement and to protect your deployment handles. Avoid snagging not only your equipment but that of other jumpers. Until we are on jump run you should stay seated. Then, at the jumpmaster's command you can get to your feet and move carefully to the door. As you move about in the airplane, watch out for door handles, emergency exit releases, seat belt buckles, etc. While inside the airplane your job is to protect your parachute!

Landings

There are two goals when landing your parachute: the first is to land safely and the second is to land where you want to. Clearly, the first goal is much more important than the second one, yet a surprising number of skydivers have had the opportunity to consider their values at leisure while recuperating from landing injuries. A parachute is only as safe as the person operating it.

As soon as you have determined that your parachute is functioning properly, it is time to start thinking about the landing. Look for potential landing sites — any level area free of obstacles will do but we try to land at an established point, our student landing area, if we can. Usually you can get back over this landing area with at least a thousand feet of altitude left. If this is not the case check the area below you and between you and your target for possible hazards; if you are not positive you can make it safely to the planned landing area, you must select an alternate site. Do not go below the thousand foot mark without making a firm decision about where you will land.

As you hold into the wind you can make a rough guess as to how far you could fly in, say, 250 feet of vertical descent. Take that estimated distance and lay out an imaginary line of that length from the target to a point downwind. Now just work your way to that point and stay near it until you are about three hundred feet up. Turn towards the target. If your original guess was good, you would slightly overshoot the target. A small "S" turn—ninety degrees one way, then 180 back to the approach, and ninety degrees back into the wind—will line you up on a good final approach. As long as you start your final approach a little high, you can continue these "S" turns to adjust until you are on approach at the right altitude.

Three most important points for a safe landing

- First, always pick a safe place. Be sure of your landing site before you reach 1,000 feet.
- Second, never land in a turn. We know that a parachute's descent rate increases dramatically in a turn, and that speed remains for a few seconds after the turn is stopped. Landing in turns is by far the biggest cause of skydiving injuries. No low turns!
- Third, land into the wind. This one is too obvious to need elaboration; the slower you are going, the softer you land. However, landing down wind or cross wind is less likely to cause injury than landing in a turn or on obstacles! On a breezy day, turn towards your parachute after you touch down and pull in one line to collapse the canopy. You may need to run around down wind of the canopy.

In India sky diving is not popular because of many reasons. The public access to the facilities to fly an aircraft to learn sky diving is a pipe dream. The Indian Air Force Adventure cell has a well equipped team of sky divers in the name of "Akash Ganga". They only perform sky diving displays at important national festivals.

■

SNORKELING

Chapter - 66

Snorkeling is swimming with fins, a mask, and a tube called a snorkel that allows you to have your face down in the water and still breathe. The difference between Snorkeling and Scuba diving is that snorkeling doesn't require tanks and other expensive equipment like regulators. Scuba diving allows you to breathe under water, while snorkeling allows you to breathe while you are on the surface with your face down. Snorkeling doesn't require any certification, while scuba diving requires certification.

One of the wonderful things about snorkeling is that people of all ages can participate. And one of the great things about Maui and the other Hawaiian Islands is that there are many great places for beginners to try out.

You need not be a good swimmer to carryout snorkeling. Because there are many places all over the world where the snorkeling is possible in a very shallow water. It is recommended that you do have some comfort and experience when you are in water though. A few things to consider is that your fins help you a great deal in terms of movement, and they float. As well, the mask that you wear will have air trapped in it will help you float as well. If you don't feel safe enough, you can also rent floatation devices, as well as boogie boards that you can lay on top of.

Many of the snorkeling spots on Maui on right off shore and are in water less than 5 feet deep. It just depends which sites that you go to, and your comfort level with water and your equipment.

Snorkeling Equipment

Mask: This is what you put on your face. This allows you to see under water without getting your eyes and nose wet. It's important that the mask is a good fit when renting or buying a mask. If the mask doesn't fit well, you will experience some leakage of water in the mask.

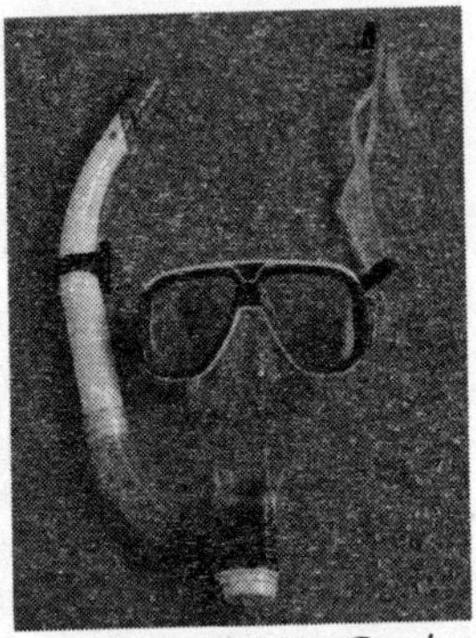

Snorkel and Swim Goggles

It is recommended that while using a mask it should be ensured that the mask has a "silicon skirt". The skirt is the soft substance that is molded to fit your face, and prevents water from entering the mask. You can also rent or buy masks that use rubber ask the skirt, but the seal is not nearly as good as the silicon, and is quite simply an outdated technology. Ask your local snorkel or dive shop about choosing a mask that fits well. They will help with the same.

Snorkel

Well, this is what makes you a snorkeler. A snorkel is a hollow curved tube that is placed in the mouth that allows you to breathe while you are face down in the water. So basically, while you looking down into the water, the snorkel is sticking out of the water on one end while the other end is in your mouth. When looking for a snorkel, I would recommend asking for what is called a "purge" snorkel.

Fins

This is what makes life a lot of fun. Fins allow you to swim like a fish. Yeeeha! There are two kinds of fins, but for snorkeling in warm water, most people will do just fine with the close heeled kind. The open heeled kind is more for scuba divers which requires a special boot (bootie), or for colder waters. Any ways, make sure that the fins are a good fit, or else you will either be cutting off circulation to your feet, or they will easily come off. Make sure that they are a snug fit, but you should be able to wiggle your toes.

How to Begin Snorkeling?

Well, it's a good idea to get comfortable with your equipment before you go out to the reef. Try out the equipment at your hotel pool. The first step is getting used to the mask. One thing about masks is that they have a tendency to fog up. You can either apply anti-fog goop (available at all snorkel shops) to the inside of the mask, or you can use your own spit. It sounds gross, but spit works quite well for preventing the fogging up of your mask. Make sure that the spit/anti-fog goop is spread across the full surface of the glass on the inside of the mask. Now wash it out in the water. This should prevent, or at least greatly reduce any fogging up of the mask. When putting on the mask, make sure there are no hairs stuck it between the silicon part of the mask. Hair will break the seal that keeps the water from entering the mask. Also keep the strap in the middle of the back of your head, and don't have the strap too tight. Now, put on your mask and look under water while you're standing up. You're looking under water. No fish yet, but soon you will see them.

Next, attach the snorkel to your mask strap with the clip that's on the snorkel. Put the snorkel in your mouth and breathe. Don't try to breathe with your nose or else the mask will quickly fog up. Breathe through your mouth in relaxed, normal breaths. Now try breathing with your face in the water. Nothing to it, right? Take as long as you want to get used to breathing underwater. That's the biggest mental hurdle for first time snorkelers. Are you comfortable yet?

If so, put on your flippers and give it a try. With your face down and body stretched out, start kicking with your fins. Remember to keep your legs straight while you lightly kick. You don't have to thrash around to swim well. Stay relaxed, and swim around the pool, getting used to breathing, kicking, and looking around.

Best Climatic condition for Snorkeling

The best times to go are when the waves are minimal, and it's sunny outside. Not only do large waves make things more challenging

to get around and potentially dangerous, but a disturbance such as big waves also make the water murky, greatly decreasing visibility. A good rule of thumb is if there are surfers in the area, it's probably a bad day or place to go snorkeling. Bays often offer more protection from a surge (big waves). The ideal snorkeling conditions are waves at 0-1 feet.

It's also best to go snorkeling when the sun is out. Sunlight increases visibility, and brings out the true colors of fish and coral. It brings out the 'wow' factor for fish and overall experience. But the sun also brings out the 'sun burn' factor. If you're not wearing some sort of wet suit, shorty, or other coverings, make sure that you've got your back, neck, shoulders, butt, and thighs covered in sun block. To make things a bit easier, just wear an old shirt.

Diving Underwater can be Risky

Although many snorkelers dive under water. But try to avoid. If you see a fish several feet below you though, and you want to get a closer look, you'll have to dive down. By doing this, your snorkel will fill up with water, and you will not be able to breathe until you clear the passage of your snorkel of water once you have resurfaced. It sounds a bit scary, but it's a common thing for more experienced snorkelers to dive down and fill their snorkel with water.

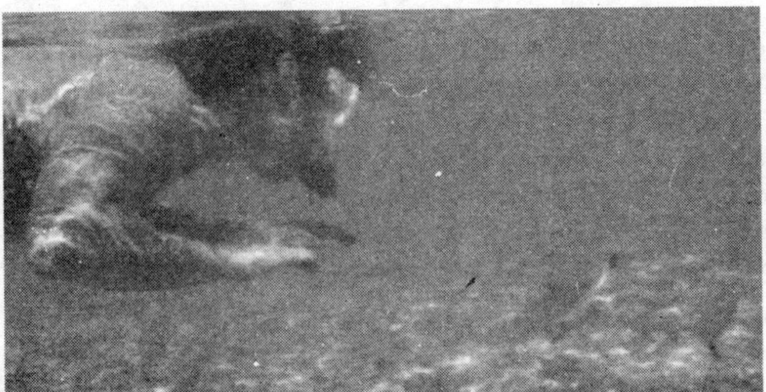

To clear the snorkel of water, you must resurface, give a good strong blow of the snorkel as your head reaches the surface once again, and the top of the snorkel has penetrated the surface of the water. This should clear most if not all of the water that has filled the snorkel, and allow you to breathe normally through the snorkel once again. If you use what is called a "purge" snorkel, you will rarely get water back in your mouth. It is recommended that this may be first tried in a pool.

Once you get comfortable doing this as well as the other techniques mentioned, you will feel more confident, and will have a more positive relaxed experience out on the reef.

Snorkeling is a popular recreational activity, particularly at tropical resort destinations and many places recreational scuba divers venture. Snorkeling is also employed by scuba divers when near the surface, and search and rescue teams may snorkel as part of a water-based search.

The primary attraction of snorkeling is the opportunity to observe underwater life in a natural setting. This may include coral reefs and their denizens, such as fish, octopuses, starfish, sea urchins, and mollusks. Snorkeling in sandy areas may allow sighting of rays and various flatfish. Other organisms that can be seen while snorkeling include various forms of seaweed, jellyfish, sea turtles, and occasionally anything else which may be found in the ocean. Many of the organisms found in reef locations are vibrantly colored and very abundant, making for an engrossing experience.

WATER SKIING

Chapter - 67

History

Over a period of time Water Skiing as a water sport became popular in many countries where the ideal water conditions prevail. It is presumed that the sport made its beginning in Lake City, Minnesota, in 1922. For water skiing what you need is an expanse of water unaffected by wave motion. Rivers, lakes, and sheltered bays etc also are the place where the sprot can be undertaken by the water sports enthusiasts.

Before the introduction of fibreglass based composites the water skis used to be made from wood . These are of similar length to downhill snow skis but are somewhat wider. Instead of a rigid binding, they have rubber mouldings in which the feet are placed. Skiers are pulled along by a rope with a handle fitted at one end and attached to a powerboat at the other.

It is actually easier to travel faster than at slower speeds because of the greater lift and stability. Beginners on two skis are usually pulled along at around 25-35 kilometres per hour, whereas more advanced social skiers travel at between 40 and 55 kilometres per hour. Within the confines of being pulled along by the boat, skiers can control their direction by balancing their weight on different sides of their ski. This is used to zip back and forth behind the boat.

Recreational skiers usually learn to ski with a ski on each foot, but as they improve usually progress to using a single ski, placing the other foot into another binding behind the main one. There are several forms of competition performed on waterskis.

Slalom: Slalom most resembles recreational water skiing. In it, a set of buoys are set up. The boat drives through the middle of the buoys, and the skiier must pass to the outside of each buoy. The winner of the contest is the individual who can complete going round the buoys with the shortest rope. Elite skiers can perform this feat with a rope shorter than the distance between the boat center (the origin of the rope) and each buoy.

Trick Skiing: Trick skiing is performed using two very short skis rather than the conventional equipment. Here, skiiers try to perform tricks somewhat similar to those of gymnasts while being pulled along by the boat. Trick skiing is judged by the difficulty of the tricks performed and the accuracy of execution.

Ski Jump: The ski jump is performed on two long skis similar to those a beginner uses (but with no tail fin). Skiers towed behind a boat at fixed speed manoeuver to achieve maximum speed when hitting a ramp floating in the water, launching themselves into the air with the goal of travelling as far as possible before touching the water. Good ski jumpers can travel up to 60 metres.

Ski Race: Ski races simply involve a powerboat race with a skier attached. These events are usually conducted on rivers to make the course more interesting. One such event held at Echuca on the Murray River, Australia. Skiers and boats typically average 160 km/h over the 80 kilometre course.

Barefoot Skiing: A variation of the sport, barefoot skiing, as the name suggests involves water skiing without the aid of skis. Several new sports have been invented that involve being towed behind a boat. They include wakeboarding.

Personal Equipment

Ability to swim would be advisable for potential skiers, but swimming ability is no substitute for a well-fitting Personal Flotation

Device (PFD). Wearing a PFD is essential when water skiing, even for expert swimmers, and is required by law in almost every country where the water skiing is in vogue.

Signals

It is a must for the skier and the boat driver to know and understand the signals given here, because as the sport progresses there could be no communication between the boat driver and the skier.

1. Speed up the boat: Thumb up.
2. Slow down the boat: Thumb down.
3. Cut Motor/Stop (also used by driver or observer): Slashing motion over the neck.
4. Turn the boat (also used by driver): Circle motion with arms over-head then point in desired direction.
5. Return to dock: Pat on the head.
6. Speed and boat path OK or signals understood: OK signal with hand.
7. Skier OK after falling: Hands clasped over head.

Some signals in preparation for takeoff are vocal. When the skier is comfortable in the water with skis in position, he informs the driver that he is ready by shouting, "In gear!". The boat then moves slowly forward to take up slack in the line. When the line becomes taut, the skier shouts, "hit it!", which is the signal for the driver to open the throttle for takeoff.

Once on plane, the skier signals with one hand. A thumb-down motion requests slower speed, while a thumb-up movement signals the driver for more speed. An acceptable alternate to these signals is a palm-down or palm-up motion. When the speed is all right, the skier gives the familiar thumb and forefinger "OK" sign.

When the skier desires to turn, he makes a curving motion with palm horizontal, either the right or left, depending on the desired direction change. When the skier wishes to stop, he can make the palm-up, fingers extended, policeman-type signal, or he can draw a finger across his throat to signal the driver to cut the throttle. Of course, if he wishes to stop in a hurry, the skier can just release the handle.

Once a skier is down, one of the most important signals is to let the driver know immediately that the skier is all right. This is done by the simple gesture of clasping both hands over the head. In the absence of this signal, the driver can only assume the skier is injured and he must come about immediately to help.

Another important signal on the part of the skier is to hold up a ski so his position will be more visible to his own driver and operators of other boats in the vicinity. This signal is especially important in areas where other boats and skiers are in action.

Choosing Where To Ski

This size of the area needed for water skiing safely will vary with the configuration of the body of water. However, some guidelines apply under most conditions. Each boat using a waterway for skiing should operate in a corridor about 200 feet wide, giving a safety area of 100 feet on either side of the boat. A corridor length of 2000 to 3000 feet is desirable.

The skier and driver should agree in advance on the general path of the boat. A skier who inadvertently turns in the same direction that the boat driver is about to manoeuver the boat will get line slack that could result in a fall or entanglement of the line. If the skier moves in a direction opposite to that of an unanticipated boat turn, a crack-the-whip reaction could follow, creating the potential for a high-speed spill.

If a waterway is heavily used by skiers, a traffic pattern might be established. Such patterns usually are anti clockwise. The skier and driver should determine in advance whether it has been established and, if so, strictly adhere to it.

Water skiing should never be attempted in swimming areas, low-speed mooring lanes and marina channels. Boats towing skiers should give a wide berth to fishermen, either in boats or on shore, and to slow-moving craft such as canoes and sailboats.

The Boat Driver

A boat driver must remember that the skier at the end of the tow rope is the extension of the boat, and the driver must continually be aware of the skier's presence and safety The responsibility is on the driver for keeping the skier away from dangerous areas as well as giving him a good ride. Keep the boat a safe distance from the shore, docks and other objects in the water. Be on the look out for other boats about to enter the ski area. If this happens, shut down the boat and wait for the area to clear. The driver must be alert for downed skiers or stopped boats in his path. Before turning the boat, look to each side and behind to make sure there are no overtaking boats and that the turn will not endanger the skier. He must also understand that he must always pull novice skiers slowly. The new boat drivers should never pull any skier fast. Speed isn't essential to enjoyable water skiing.

Another important point is to understand that always approach a downed skier so he is on the driver's side of the boat and in full view of the driver. Turn off the engine when taking a skier aboard from the water. There are no exceptions to this rule.

Drinking beverages containing alcohol, taking prescription and over-the-counter medications, or use of illegal drugs can contribute to impaired judgment. Being on the water and fatigued, can increase the effects beyond your normal tolerance. Never drive or ski when your judgment is impaired.

Basic Techniques of Water Skiing

Entering the water

The first part of the water-skiing procedure is to get out of the boat and enter the water. It is useful to have the ski nearby, because otherwise you will have to swim for some distance to reach it. Observe the orientation in the water here, and in particular the feet. At no other stage in water-skiing, is this a suitable orientation of the feet. The soles of the feet always face downwards.

Pulling-out of the water

When the time comes to start, you need to lift out of the water so that you are skiing on the top. There are various ways of accomplishing this, but the one illustrated here is one of the more interesting.

The technique here is not perfect, with that angle of ski somewhat upright. At that angle, if sufficient care is not taken, there is a risk that the skier will get into trouble.

Catching the ski-rope

At the beginning, you need to take hold of the ski-rope which is towed behind the boat. Some people integrate this with the previous stage, but here we see an attempt to catch the rope as it trails behind the boat. Timing is critical here, and in this example the skier is too late to reach the rope and cannot catch it.

This shows a better example where the rope is caught in the hands of the skier. Note also the sharp turn to come into line with the direction of travel of the boat, and the slack in the rope which exists in the early stages. Don't be concerned about the slack, as it is normal.

Waves

On land we are quite familiar with the concept of steps. The equivalent on the water are waves. Waves come in many shapes and sizes. It is recommended that beginners start with small waves of a nondescript shape to gain familiarity. Large waves may aid in a subsequent follow-through to falling off.

In this photograph, the skier has raised one foot ready to step up onto a wave. Care must be taken to raise to the correct height. It is not necessary to look as awkward as this, but it may help.

When water-skiing, one should always be careful of the prevailing weather conditions, and watch the wind and wave behaviour.

Turning

There are laws of physics that make it hard to go in a different direction to the boat for sustained periods. Here we see the skier traveling at right angles to the boat, and the distinct lean shows that he is being pulled over towards the boat. At this point, it is necessary that either a turn be initiated, or you will fall off.

Falling off

The falling off step is most often executed when you lose balance, or as an artistic variation on one of the other maneoeuvers. Sometimes people will unpredictably add this into their routine. When used in a combination sequence, it is better to do it at the end.

Boat Driver Tasks:

- Find out how many RPMs (40 KPMH is on your particular boat).
- Remember where the throttle position should be for 40 KMPH.

- Idle out gently when taking up the slack allowing the skier to get in position.
- Line the boat up so the skier is going to go straight for a bit.
- If you're going to hit another boat's wake, try and quarter the wake or cross as close to parallel as possible.
- Understand the Hand signals from the skier: Thumbs up for more speed, Thumbs down for less speed.

Water Skier Tasks

- Adjust the ski bindings to that the skis are snug, but can come off in a fall.
- Make sure your life jacket (PFD) is the right size.
- Put your feet in the skis, bring your knees to your chest.
- Keep the skis at a 45 degree angle with 3-6 inches of the tip of the skis out of the water.
- Some people have better luck with the rope in front of their knees with their arms around their legs.
- Keep your legs together.
- Have the driver start pulling you when you are ready.
- Don't stand up too early. Squat until you are on plane, then stand up.
- Bend your knees quite a bit once you're up until you start to get the feel of it.
- Hand signals to the driver: Thumbs up for more speed, Thumbs down for less speed.
- Staying in the ski boat's wake will give you smoother water if there are other boat wakes around.

Do let go of the rope when you fall

- Do be patient and realize that it will take few tries to get up on the water.
- If you are continually being pulled over the tips of your skis on your starts, then ask the driver accelerate more slowly.

■

WHITEWATER KAYAKING

Chapter - 68

Whitewater Kayaking Basics

Whitewater kayaking offers plenty of excitement, thrills and challenges. Rivers are beautiful and relaxing places to spend your free time, but can also be challenging.

There are several options for enjoying rivers. Whitewater vessels range from rafts, canoes, and kayaks. And within each of these groups are a wide range of types and designs.

Whitewater kayaking is one of the best ways to build your whitewater skills. The boat is light and very reactive, so you'll begin to feel the river. This is important for eventually being able to read the river. Some people seem to have a natural ability to read water. It's subtle, but key to avoiding potentially hazards as well as finding good clean paths or lines.

Kayaking offers plenty of excitement and adrenaline. It's different from most sports in that a major part of the sport is in your head. You have to keep your fear in check. What most beginners forget, kayaking is about being upside down. It's about playing in the water: you paddle up the eddyline, drop into a wave, surf, get capsized, roll back up, get back on the wave, surf, drop your bow down and spin your boat in a pirouette.

Where to Begin

For many their first whitewater kayaking experience is in the pool with an instructor. A certified instructor is the key. The first thing you'll want to learn is what it feels like to be upside down and how to get out of your boat.

After learning to get out of your boat, one idea is to get onto the river to learn your boat handling skills and of course how to "swim".

Swimming refers to capsizing and coming out of your boat versus rolling the boat back up.

The beauty of most beginner river sections is that there are large pools at the bottom of the rapids, which allows a "swimmer" to regroup. This is a good place to practise your moves.

While in whitewater Kayaking you should learn the Eskimo roll, which entails learning to right yourself while remaining in the boat.

The only way for you to improve your Kayaking skills is to get on the water. If there is a long period between trips, you'll have to get your balance and the feel again. There are plenty of skills to practice, like ferrying across the river and catching eddies. All of these are important skills and are worth spending lots of time and energy on. Any and all paddling will be beneficial.

Almost immediately you'll learn your mandatory equipment—Boat, Paddle, Spray Skirt, Lifejacket (PFD), and Helmut. You can't paddle without these. It's a good idea to wear even the PFD and helmet during your flat water/pool sessions. This will help you get used to them.

Intermediate

There are a couple of ways to improve your whitewater skills. The first one is to find a wave with a nice pool behind it and get in there! You need to read the water and find a path so you can paddle up to it. Paddle hard to get in there. Feel the wave catch the boat. Manoeuver the boat to keep it in position. If you get flipped, roll back up and start over. You'll be working on all your skills at one time: reading the water, your stroke from a power stroke to fine adjustments, bracing, and rolling.

Another way to improve your skills is to paddle with kayakers that have better skills. You can learn a lot just by watching. They'll also be able to give you tips and critique your style.

It is highly recommended as you improve your skills and push your level of difficulty that you also improve your safety skills. Take a safety course. On class III rapids you'll begin to notice boaters standing ready on the rocks with a throw bag. They are there to throw you a line if you get into trouble. You owe it to yourself and your boating buddies to be able to offer help and rescue them if needed, as you will need to count on them to offer you help.

Extreme Kayaking

The more you kayak the better your boat handling skills will be, and advanced boating skills come with extensive experience. Advanced boaters don't think about what paddle strokes they use. This comes second nature and are usually a combination of the techniques and stokes you learn as a beginner and intermediate. However they do spend time scouting and mapping out their perfect line.

Even as an expert boater, you can have your good days and the bad ones. Listen to yourself. If you don't feel right about running a rapid, then don't. Run the river for yourself, not to prove something to someone else. Sooner or later you'll experience the phenomenon called "they did it so I should do it". It's got less to do with skill level, as it has to do with physical and mental state. If you're unfocused, tired, not as aggressive as usual, these are all signs that say "save it for another day".

As you become more involved in the kayaking community, you'll learn more about the environmental and political issues that surround the sport. It requires lots of energy to keep the rivers clean and open to boaters. Look into participating in organizations that are working to do this. Your membership dues are the first steps to supporting these causes.

Safety

- Use your common sense. Don't just follow someone else's lead.
- Know the difficulty level of the river first. If it's a step up in level, be prepared to walk or portage around the rapids.
- Plan your trip by confirming paddle buddies, checking release levels and weather conditions.
- Scout any questionable rapids.
- Always kayak with another paddler who is able to rescue you if you get into trouble.
- Dress for the weather and water temperature. Layers work well. Hypothermia is not uncommon.

- Don't drink and paddle. Drinking on the river is never done. Yet, a beer and some munchies at the take out are not uncommon.
- Paddlers often face more dangers on land than on the water. Be careful getting your boat to the river at the put-in and back to the car at the take-out. These are usually narrow rocky paths that can be treacherous.
- Poison ivy and poison oak are abundant on the riverbanks. Learn to distinguish and bring lotion if you're highly allergic.
- Always double check that your spray skirt release loop is out and free to pull.
- Your boat should have float bags in the stern and bow.

Whitewater Kayaking Equipment

Whitewater kayaking is an equipment intensive sport. A checklist and separate gear bag are a good way to keep it all organized. Just remember you must have your boat, paddle, lifejacket, sprayskirt, and helmet. Besides the mandatory whitewater kayaking gear, a nose clip, drinking water and a snack should be brought along. Another key item is a dry sack, available at most canoe and kayaking stores. They're perfect for packing lunch, a disposable camera, extra Polypropylene top, sunscreen, etc. It should be clipped into the boat, so it doesn't float away if you end up swimming.

Boats

There are a lot of boats on US market. When shopping for a boat you'll quickly become familiar with the basic boat design terminology. The length of a kayak effects its speed and manoeuverability. The longer it is the straighter it tracks. The more volume a boat has the more buoyant it is. The boat's rocker refers to the upward curve of the bottom of a boat. More rocker will help the boat to manoeuver and turn quickly. A flat bottom will help the boat to plane and surf. Beginner boats are usually high volume; longer with a rounded bottom compared to advanced play boats.

Clothing

Paddling when you're too hot or too cold will drain your energy. The right clothing makes all the difference. It can take time to find the right combination for you, especially when the water is cold and the air is hot. Layering your clothing will allow you to shed layers if you begin to overheat or add if you get cold. Some of the best technical fabrics are used for kayak clothing. Look for waterproof and breathable fabrics. It's also advisable to carry clothes that are quick drying and wicking, made of Polypropylene type materials. Cotton absorbs moister and can keep you chilled. Remember, even in summer the water temperature of most rivers in the mountains will be cool.

Drysuits

For extreme cold weather and water a drysuit will be safer than a wetsuit. Drysuits also come in handy for sea kayaking, sailing and windsurfing. They're expensive, so you should try to get one that meets all your needs. As the name suggests, a drysuit is a waterproof jumpsuit that will keep you dry if you go for a swim. The suit has rubber seals around the neck, wrists and ankles that prevent water from getting into your suit.

Safety Gear

The two most important safety items you'll wear are your lifejacket and your helmet. As stated before, never go out without them. They should be comfortable. There are also several other items that you should have. A whistle attached to your lifejacket is an easy device to signal for help. This should only be used when you are in an emergency, not just to get someone's attention.

Hypothermia is not uncommon in whitewater kayaking. It's important to dress wisely in order to avoid getting cold. As a beginner you should plan on bringing more clothes. You'll be spending more time in the water, which can quickly reduce body heat. The most common signs of mild hypothermia are shivering, exhaustion, and blue lips. Don't ignore it. Advanced kayakers who have safety training will also carry a throw bag and knife. Taking a class in proper rescue techniques is also recommended once your skill level has increased.

Sprayskirts

Finding the proper spray skirt isn't always easy. It must properly fit you and the boat. The skirt is designed to keep water out of the boat, so it needs to provide a solid seal. It is also important that it releases quickly when the pull strap is grabbed. Remember the pull straps must be easy to grab and not be caught inside the skirt. Double-check this before you launch and every time you re-secure your skirt.

Wetsuits

A wetsuit is helpful for staying warm in cold water. The water temperature and how often you end up swimming will determine if you should be wearing a wetsuit or a drysuit. The wetsuit vest also works well to insulate your core body, useful even in the summer. You may also use the dive skin. These originated for scuba diving in warm water. They are less restricting but offer the same insulation and warmth. A dive skin is good for cool days, but not the coldest of winter paddling.

■

WHITEWATER RAFTING

Chapter - 69

Whitewater rafting in the Himalayas is very challenging. The challenge of turbulent rivers is no less than that of the rugged mountains. The Himalayas are the source of some of India's mighty rivers. Fed by innumerable streams they race along tortuous boulder strewn beds, cutting deep gorges and breaking into silvery white rapids.

The Garhwal and Kumaon hills provide ideal locales for the perfect water adventure. Through these hills, an intricate network of mountain rivers flowing through a myriad of different colours of rocky gorges, forests, flowers and high mountain villages, offers exciting adventure for whitewater rafting.

The sport of whitewater river rafting calls for a triumph over the swift swirling river as it gushes past spectacular mountains. It is practised mainly in the upper reaches where the water is wild and white as it froths and foams, crashing against narrow gorges, rocky outcrops and falls at deep gradients.

Before one enters the hills one must enjoy the pleasure of a gentle canoe trip in a lightweight alloy-metal craft which holds two to three people. The gradient best suited for canoeing is the stage near the river's entry into the plains where the trip can be combined with moderate hiking and a naturalist holiday in the forest. For this, the suitable areas are Rishikesh, Dakpathar and the Ramganga in Corbett National Park. For the slightly more adventurous, kayaking is appealing as it is in tandem. The degree of difficulty would depend on the river gradient and its rapids.

The suitable period for whitewater rafting in this part of the world would be September-November and March-April-May, when the volume of water should be at appropriate level of this kind of sports. A detailed list of equipment is given towards the end of this article but if you are not venturing into too much into the rapids then an ordinary outdoor

gear, goggles, antiseptic cream and a liking for getting wet will take care. But never overlook the safety factor.

As with trekking, mountaineering and other sports, river rafting too has been classified and graded in terms of degrees of difficulty. According to Wikipedia (and based on the International Scale of River Difficulty), there are six types of rapids, classified according to navigational difficulty:

- **Class I – Easy:** Small waves in fast moving water. Few obstacles.
- **Class II – Novice:** Wide channels and rapids that are easy to navigate, without many turns or obstacles. Small waves less than two feet high.
- **Class III – Intermediate:** Strong currents require training and ability to manoeuver quickly and effectively. From this class on, rafters require a guide. Not suitable for young children.
- **Class IV – Advanced:** Powerful rapids for strong paddlers that can handle fierce turns and spins. Drops and waves are common.
- **Class V – Expert:** Violent, dangerous rapids, usually through obstructed channels, tight turns, and soaring falls. Requires professional equipment.

Types of Crafts

Kayaks – Kayaks designed for white water are usually shorter than sea kayaks and most are made of plastic (although fiberglass kayaks are popular among racers). Kayaks are prevalent because paddlers can easily roll them back upright when flipped (a manoeuver known as the "Eskimo Roll").

Rafts: The preferred type of craft for large groups, they are made of inflatable plastic, and can handle almost any type of current.

Catarafts: Similar to rafts but easier to manoeuver, they consist of two inflatable tubes held together by a frame.

Canoes: Made of fiberglass or plastic, they can handle an Eskimo roll the same way kayaks do. They are either decked (closed) or open, as a typical canoe.

Whitewater Rafting Equipment

In India the kit suggested below may not be required fully. But it would be better to check the list before you venture out into the rough water of the hills. Some places have very specific outfit rules, so it's always better to ask in advance. These are some basic needs:

- Wetsuit (in spring and fall), bathing suit or shorts (summer)
- Wetsuit booties or strapped sandals (no flip-flops)
- Pogies or special gloves to use when dealing with cold water
- Polypropylene t-shirt (avoid cotton, as it takes a long time to dry)
- Wool socks and a windbreaker if weather turns colder
- Waterproof sunscreen
- Bug spray
- Sunglasses (with neck strap)
- Disposable waterproof camera (do not bring any expensive equipment)
- First aid kit (if you're not going with a group)
- Fresh water
- Depending on the location, the water may be cold even in May, so make sure you ask beforehand so you can decide what to wear.

Safety First

You will not find much in your library therefore log on to Internet and learn as much as you can about the sport. Consider buying a video that shows the basic skills and manoeuvers and learn them by heart. There are also whitewater rafting classes that teach you the basic techniques before you even get into moving water. DO all these preparations because do not forget that safety is paramount.

Make sure your swimming skills are good. If not, the head for the nearest swimming pool and spend a lot of time before you head to the Himalayas. Do not go alone. Either hire a guide, join a group, or take a friend along.

Do upper body exercises (weight training is optimal) to ensure you have the strength to handle paddling in strong waters. If you're not in reasonably good physical condition, you shouldn't attempt rafting.

Do no⁺ raft in the dark. Allow plenty of time for the trip back, so you'll be safely on the ground when darkness falls.

Whitewater Rafters Paddling in the rapids

Check the local regulations. Some states do not allow rafters under the age of 12.

Do not drink alcohol before or during a trip. You will not only endanger yourself, you'll also be a risk to other rafters.

Choose a lifejacket you feel comfortable in. Avoid oversized vests. "Always, always wear personal floatation devices (lifejackets) on whitewater rivers," says Brown. "This is standard procedure for professionally guided trips and should also be practised by those paddling on their own."

Rafting in Garhwal

In Garhwal region the Ganga offers the professional as well as the amateur the exhilaration of whitewater rafting. The Alaknanda and Bhagirathi are the main tributaries of Ganga and meet at Devprayag, frothing from their racy descent. Their waters are of Grade IV to V, challenging the expert to savour the thrill.

Down river from Devprayag, the Ganga changes into a pool drop river. This stretch of almost 70 km is perfect for amateur and the novice, for here the river offers some fine Grade III rapids and two Grade IV 'GOLF COURSE', four kilometres below Shivpuri village; each followed by rapids, the 'WALL' at Byasi and the deep and placid pools.

Sandy beaches line the river at intervals, allowing river rafters to pull up alongside. The slopes on either side are covered with oak, pine, spruce and fur, with the occasional village and its terraced fields dotting the landscape. Wildlife is visible at a distance, comprising mainly of spotted deer, monkey, leopard, while multi-hued butterflies flit among flowering bushes. Spiritual retreats (*ashrams*) overlook the river and add to the spiritual experience.

Rafting Stretches in Himalayan Rivers

As per Garhwal tourism, they have identified following stretches of each river for safe whitewater rafting both for tourists and professionals.

River Yamuna

Barkot to Bernigad: Both professional and tourist stretch.
Damta to Yamuna Bridge: Both professional and tourist stretch.
Mori to Tuni: (Khoonigad) 30km tourist stretch.

River Alaknanda

Kaliasaur to Srinagar: 16km, tourist stretch.
Srinagar to Bagwan: 20km, tourist stretch.
Kaliasaur to Rishikesh.

River Bhagirathi

Matli to Dunda: 12km. Both professional and tourist stretch.

Harsil to Uttarkashi.

Dharasu to Chham: 12km. Both professional and tourist stretch.
Jangla to Jhala: 20km. Both professional and tourist stretch.
Bhaldyana to Tehri: Both professional and tourist stretch.

River Bhilangana

Ghansali to Gadolia: 32km. Professional stretch.

River Mandakani

Chandrapuri to Rudraprayag: 26km. Professional stretch.

■

WINDSURFING

Chapter - 70

A windsurfer with modern gear tilts the rig and carves the board to perform a planing gybe (downwind turn) close to shore in Maui, Hawaii, one of the popular destinations for windsurfing.

Windsurfing is a surface water sport using a windsurf board, also commonly called a sailboard, usually two to five meters long and powered by a single sail. The rig is connected to the board by a free-rotating flexible joint called the Universal Joint (U-Joint). Unlike a rudder-steered sailboat, a windsurfer is steered by the tilting and rotating of the mast and sail as well as tilting and carving the board.

The sport combines aspects of both sailing and surfing, along with certain athletic aspects shared with other board sports like skateboarding, snowboarding, waterskiing, and wakeboarding. Although it might be considered a minimalistic version of a sailboat, a windsurfer offers experiences that are outside the scope of any other sailing craft design. A windsurfer holds the world speed record for sailing craft and, windsurfers can perform jumps, inverted loops, spinning manoeuvers, and other "freestyle" moves that cannot be matched by any sailboat. Windsurfers were the first to ride the world's largest waves, such as Jaws on the island of Maui, and, with very few exceptions, it was not until the advent of tow-in surfing that waves of that size became accessible to surfers.

A windsurfer using short board to perform a small jump.

Windsurfing includes speed sailing, slalom, course racing, wave sailing, superX, and freestyle as distinct disciplines.

Though windsurfing is possible in winds from near 0 to 50 kts, the ideal conditions for planning are 15-25 kts, with lighter winds resulting in displacement mode sailing.

With coaching and favorable conditions, the basic skills of sailing, steering, and turning can be learned within a few hours. Competence in the sport and mastery of more advanced manoeuvers such as planing, gybing (turning downwind at speed), tacking (turning upwind), jumping, and more advanced moves can require lengthy practice.

Windsurfing, as a sport and recreational activity, did not emerge until the latter half of the twentieth century. Because of the financial stakes in the manufacture and sale of windsurfing equipment, there has been considerable dispute and litigation between parties claiming the rights to the invention.

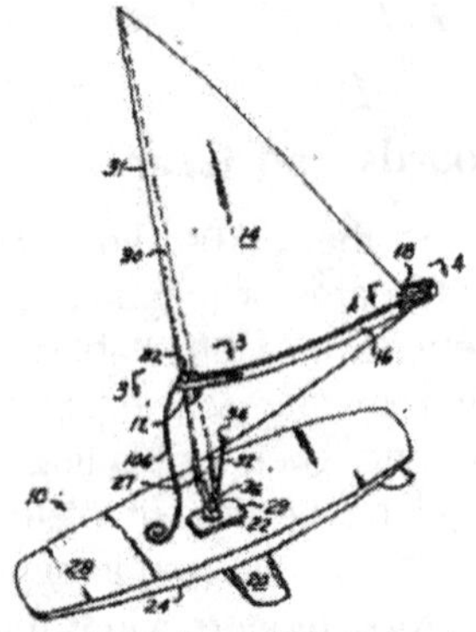

Illustration from US Patent 3,487,800, issued to inventors Jim Drake and Hoyle Schweitzer on January 6, 1970.

Different courts in different jurisdictions have recognized different inventors, clouding any possibility of clear attribution. However, what is clear from the historical record is that windsurfing, as it is known today, owes much if not all to the promotion and marketing activities of Hoyle and Diana Schweitzer. In 1968, in Southern California, they founded the company Windsurfing International to manufacture, promote and license a windsurfer design. Together with Jim Drake, an aerospace engineer at the RAND Corporation, they were the holders of the very first windsurfing patent ever, which was granted by the USPTO in 1970, after being filed in 1968. They also originated the term "Windsurfer," which was registered to them as a trademark by the USPTO in 1973.

Eventually US courts recognized the Schweitzer windsurfer as an obvious step from Darby's prior art. Schweitzer had to reapply for a patent under severely limited terms, and finally it expired in 1987. Shortly thereafter, having lost its license royalty income, Windsurfing International ceased operations.

For their part, Australian courts, in a 1983 patent case, reported in "Intellectual Property Reports" 3 IPR 449, attributed the first legally accepted use to an Australian boy, Richard Eastaugh. Between the ages of ten and thirteen, from 1946 to 1949, aided by his younger brothers, he built around 20 galavanised iron canoes and hill trolleys which he equipped with sails with spilt bamboo booms. He sailed these near his home on the Swan River in Perth. There is no evidence that any of the later "inventors" ever sighted the Eastaugh craft of a decade earlier on the other side of the world.

The boom of the 1980s led windsurfing to be recognized as an Olympic sport in 1984. However, windsurfing's popularity saw a sharp decline in the mid-1990s, as equipment became more specialized, requiring more expertise to sail. Now the sport is experiencing a modest revival, as new beginner-friendly designs are again becoming more readily available.

Boards and Gear

In the 1970s and 1980s, windsurfers were classified as either shortboards or longboards. Longboards were usually longer than 3 metres, with a retractable daggerboard, and were optimized for lighter winds or course racing. Shortboards were less than 3 metres long and were designed for planing conditions. However, this classification by length has become obsolete, as new techniques, designs, and materials have taken the sport in new directions.

Most modern windsurfers (1990s and later) are derived from the shortboard design, and are intended to be used primarily in planing mode, where the board is mostly skipping over the surface of the water, rather than cutting through, and displacing the water. Planing is faster and gives more manoeuverability, but requires a different technique from the displacement mode (which is also referred to as slogging or schlogging). Generally, smaller (i.e., lower volume, shorter length, narrower width) boards and smaller area sails are used as the wind increases.

Windsurfing and kitesurfing on the Columbia River at Hood River, Oregon

While windsurfing is possible under a wide range of wind conditions, most recreational windsurfers prefer to sail in conditions that allow for consistent planing with multi-purpose, not overly specialized, free-ride equipment. Larger (100 to 140 liters) free-ride boards are capable of planing at wind speeds as low as 12 knots if rigged with an adequate, well-tuned sail in the six to eight square meter range. The pursuit of planing in lower and lower winds has driven the development and spread of wider and shorter boards, with which planing is possible in wind speeds as low as 8 knots, if sails in the 10 to 12 square meter range are used.

Classification of modern windsurfing boards

- **Freeride:** Boards meant for comfortable recreational cruising (mostly straight-line sailing and occasional turning) at planing speed (aka blasting), mainly in flat waters or in light to moderate swell. They typically fall into the volume range of 90 to 170 liters. The so-called freeride sailing movement diverged from course racing as more recreational sailors chose to sail freely without being constrained to sailing on courses around buoys.
- **Formula Windsurfing Class:** Shorter boards up to one meter in width, for use in Formula Windsurfing races.
- **Wave boards:** Smaller, lighter, more manoeuverable boards for use in breaking waves. Characteristically, sailors on wave boards perform high jumps while sailing against waves, and they ride the face of a wave performing narrow linked turns (bottom turns, cutbacks, and top-turns) in a similar way to surfing. Wave boards usually have a volume between 65 and 90 liters, with a length between 230 and 260 centimeters, and 50 to 60 centimeters in width. A general rule is for a sailor to use a wave board whose volume in liters is about the same as the sailor's weight in kilograms — more volume providing additional flotation for sailing in light winds, and less for high winds, where less volume is needed to achieve planing. In recent years, the average width of wave boards has increased slightly, as the length has shrunk, while the range of volume has been maintained the same more or less — according to board designers this makes wave boards easier to use under a wider range of conditions by sailors of different abilities. The most common sizes of sails used with wave boards are in the range of 4.0 to 6.0 square meters, depending on the wind speed and the weight of the sailor.

- **Freestyle boards:** Related to wave boards in terms of manoeuverability, these are wider, higher volume boards geared specifically at performing acrobatic tricks (jumps, rotations, slides, flips and loops) on flat water. Usually 80 to 110 litres in volume, and about 240 to 250 centimeters in length, with widths frequently in excess of 60 centimeters. Freestyle boards began to diverge more noticeably in design from wave boards in the early part of the 2000 decade, as aerial tricks (the Vulcan, Spock, Grubby, Flaka, and related New School manoeuvers, almost all involving a jump-and-spin component) became the predominant part of the freestyle repertoire, superseding Old School moves, in which the board did not leave contact with the water.
- **Slalom boards:** Shortboards aimed at top speed, rather than manoeuverability or ease of use.
- **Beginner boards:** (sometimes called funboards) these often have a daggerboard, are almost as wide as Formula boards, and have plenty of volume, hence stability.
- **Racing longboards:** Mistral One Design, or the olympic RS:X class race boards.

There are many attempts to bridge a gap between two of these categories, such as freerace, freestyle-wave, freeformula, and so on.

Windsurfing in the late evening on a longboard

The original windsurfer board had a body made out of polyethylene filled with PVC foam. Later, hollow glass-reinforced epoxy designs were used. Most boards produced today have an expanded polystyrene foam core reinforced with a composite sandwich shell, that can include carbon fiber, kevlar, or fiberglass in a matrix of epoxy and sometimes plywood and thermoplastics. Racing and wave boards are usually very light (5 to 7 kg), and are made out of carbon sandwich. Such boards are very brittle, and veneer is sometimes used to make them more shock-resistant. Boards aimed at the beginners are heavier (8 to 15 kg) and more robust, contain more fiberglass, or even have an indestructible molded plastic shell.

Sails

A windsurfing sail is made of monofilm (clear polyester film), dacron (woven polyester) and mylar. Sensitive parts are reinforced with kevlar mesh.

Two designs of a sail are predominant: camber induced and rotational. Cambered sails have 1-5 camber inducers, plastic devices at the ends of battens which cup against the mast. They help to hold a rigid aerofoil shape in the sail, better for speed and stability, but at the cost of manoeuvrability and generally how light and easy to use the sail feels. The trend is that racier sails have camber inducers while wave sails and most recreational sails do not. The rigidity of the sail is also determined by a number of battens.

Beginners' sails often do not have battens, so they are lighter and easier to use in light winds. However, as the sailor improves, a battened sail will provide greater stability in stronger winds.

Rotational sails have battens which protrude beyond the back aspect of the mast. They have to flip to the other side of the mast when tacking or jibing, hence the rotation in the name. Rotational sails have aerofoil shape on the leeward side only when filled with wind. They can be absolutely flat and depowered when sheeted out.

In comparison with cambered sails, rotational designs offer less power and stability when sailing straight, but are easier to handle when manoeuvering. Also, rotational sails are much easier to rig.

The leading edge of a sail is called the luff. The mast is in the luff tube. The rear edge is called the leech. The front bottom corner of the sail, where the mast foot protrudes, is called the tack, and the rear corner, to which the boom is attached, is called the clew. The bottom edge, between the clew and the tack, is called the foot.

A windsurfing sail is tensioned at two points: at the tack (by downhaul), and at the clew (by outhaul). There is a set of pulleys for downhauling at the tack and there's a grommet at the clew. Most shape is given to the sail by a very strong downhaul, bending the mast in the luff tube. The outhaul tension is relatively weak, mostly to provide leverage for controlling the sail's angle of attack.

The sail is tuned by adjusting the downhaul and the outhaul. Generally, the sail has to be trimmed more for stronger winds. More downhaul tension loosens the upper part of the leech, "spilling" the wind at the gusts and shifting the center of effort of the sail down. Releasing the downhaul tension shifts the center of effort up. More outhaul lowers the camber/draft, making the sail flatter and easier to control, but less powerful, and less outhaul brings more overall depth to the sail, more low-end power, shifts the center of effort upward and to the front, and may limit speed by increasing aerodynamic resistance.

Different sails are used for various disciplines of windsurfing: wave, freestyle, freeride, race. Wave sails are reinforced to survive the surf, and are absolutely flat when depowered to allow riding the waves like surfers do. Freestyle sails are also flat when depowered, and have high low-end power to allow quick accelerations. Freeride sails are all-rounders that are comfortable to use and are meant for recreational windsurfing. Racing sails, obviously, provide speed at the expense of qualities like comfort or manoeuverability.

The size of the sail is measured in square metres and can be from $3m^2$ to $6.5m^2$ for wave sails and from $6m^2$ to $12.5m^2$ for racing sails, with ranges for freestyle and freeride sails spanning somewhere between these extremes. Learning sails for children can be as small as $1.7m^2$ and racing sails being up to $12.5m^2$ large.

Indoor windsurfing

Indoor windsurfing competitions are held, especially in the European winter.

A competition is held annually at the Schroders International Boat show, at London's Excel Centre in January. Each year a massive indoor pool is constructed and housed in a marquee. Powerful fans propel the boards along the pool. The competitions held include slalom style races, jumping competitions and more.

Permanent indoor windsurfing facilities are being constructed around the globe including Germany.

Additional equipment

- Harness
- Harness lines
- Joint
- Wet/dry suit
- Footwear
- Helmet
- Personal flotation device
- Fin/Skeg

Competitions

In windsurfing competitions, there are the following disciplines:

- Olympic Windsurfing Class
- Formula Windsurfing Class
- Slalom
- Super X
- Speed Racing
- Freestyle
- Wave

Slalom at the 2005 national championship at the Columbia River Gorge.

Freestyle and Wave are judged competitions, the sailor with best technique and diversity wins. Olympic Boardsailing, Formula windsurfing, Slalom and SuperX are races where many sailors compete on a course, and Speed Racing is a race where sailors compete on a straight 500m course in turns.

Olympic class

In Olympic Windsurfing 'One Design' boards are used. All sailors use the same boards, daggerboards, fins and sails. The equipment is chosen to allow racing in a wide range of sailing conditions. This is important for the Olympic Games, as events have to take place regardless of whether there is enough wind for planing.

The Neil Pryde RS:X is the current olympic class which is going to be used for the first time in the 2008 Summer Olympics.

Formula class

Formula windsurfing has developed in the recent years in order to facilitate high performance competition in light and moderate winds. Formula is now a class of windsurfing boards controlled by the International Sailing Federation that have the principal characteristic of a maximum 1m width. They have a single fin, with a maximum length of 70cm and carry sails up to 12.5m². Class rules allow sailors to choose boards of different designs, as long as they are certified as Formula boards, and use fins and sails of different sizes.

Formula racer in San Francisco Bay

Large sails in combination with the 'wide-style' design allow planing in very low wind conditions. However, if these requirements are not met, the boards cannot be used and events will not take place, as non-planing sailing is very difficult with this design. Formula boards are used on "flat water" as opposed to coastal surf; but racing is still held in windy conditions involving swell and chop.

Formula boards have excellent upwind and downwind ability, but are not very comfortable on a beam reach unless sail and fin sizes are reduced. This explains why the course is usually a box with longer upwind and downwind legs, or just a simple upwind-downwind loop.

- International Race Calendar Formula Windsurfing including results, equipment list, reports, photos and videos.

Slalom

Slalom is a high speed race in a course shaped like a figure of eight. Most of the course goes on a beam reach with floating marks that have to be jibed around. Slalom boards are small and narrow, and require high winds. Funboard class racing rules require the wind of 9-35 knots for the slalom event to take place.

Super X

This is a new discipline in windsurfing competitions, a cross between freestyle and slalom. The competing sailors are racing on a short downwind slalom course, have to use duck jibes on all turns, and are required to perform several tricks along the way, such as jump over an obstacle, spock or even front loop. The competitors are required to wear protective equipment.

Speed sailing

Speed sailing takes several forms. The ISA (International Speedsurfing Association) organizes (under the umbrella of the ISAF) competitions at various locations around the world known for conditions suitable for good speeds. The events are made up of heats sailed on a 500m course. The average of each sailors best 2 speeds on the 500m course which is typically open for 2 hrs/heat is their speed for that heat. As such it is possible for the sailor with the outright fastest time not to win the heat if his second best time pulls his average down. Points are given for the placings in the heats and overall event winner is the sailor with the best point score (again not necessarily the fastest sailor). Likewise points are given for places in the events and at the last event a World Speedsurfing Champion is crowned.

On record attempts controlled by the World Speed Sailing Record Council (WSSRC) competitors complete timed runs on a 500m or 1 nautical mile (1,852m) course. It is not a competition as such but a race against the clock. The current outright (500m course) sailing record is held by Finnian Maynard at 48.7 knots. Finian also held the nautical mile record which he took from Bjorn Dunkerbeck at Walvis Bay in Namibia in October 2005 in an epic contest with Dunkerbeck and another multiple world windsurfing champion Antoine Albeau. In October 2006, Dunkerbeck improved on Finian's speed of the previous year by over 1 knot. Currently his best nautical mile speed is 41.14 knots. A new record can not be publicly claimed until verified by the WSSRC who has an observer at the event.

With the advent of cheap and small GPS units sailors have been able to organise impromptu competitions amongst themselves as well as more formal competitions such as the European Speed Meetings and Speedweeks/fortnights in Australia. See www.gps-speedsurfing.com for more information. With over 1200 sailors registered it is possible for windsurfers all over the world to compare speeds. In Namibia,

Hennie Bedenkamp was the first sailor over 40 knots for the nautical mile, on Oct 31 2006. Later that day Dunkerbeck did improve this to 41.14 knots. The next day in Holland, Martin van Meurs achieved a peak gps speed of 46.9 knots. On 11 November, Bob Cunningham achieved a peak of 45.2 knots at West Kirby in the UK while in the southern hemisphere Chris Torkler made 44.6 knots in Auckland, New Zealand, on the 9th and Chris Lockwood achieved 48.9 knots 2 second peak speed at Sandy Point in Australia on the 13th November 2006 with a 500m average of 46.1knots. On 18th January 2007, Dutch sailor, Martin van Meurs went on to increase his (max 2 sec) speed to an incredible 49.4 knots at West Kirby, UK.

Freestyle

Freestyle is a timed event which is judged. The competitor who has the greatest repertoire, or manages to complete most stunts, wins. Freestyle is about show and competitors are judged on their creativity. Both the difficulty and the number of tricks make up the final score. Sailors who perform tricks on both tacks (port and starboard) score higher marks. High scoring moves include; Double Forward Loops, the Funnell (invented by freestyle champion Ricardo Campello in memory of Andy Funnell), the Chachoo and the Clew First Puneta (switch stance Spock). For novice windsurfers, low wind freestyle tricks are an appropriate start; such as sailing backwards with the skeg out of the water, or transitioning from a sailing stance to sitting on the board while continuing to sail.

Wave

Similar to freestyle (though wavesailing preceded freestyle) except that the stunts are generally performed in surf and points are awarded for how well the waves are ridden. A typical wave contest will score two jumps and two waves. A good heat would consist of a clean forward rotating jump, a backward rotating jump, a long slashy wave ride and a trick on the face of the waves such as a goiter or wave 360.

International stars

- Robby Naish: One of the first windsurfing champions to gain long-lasting international fame, he dominated the early years of competition in the 1970s and 1980s. Pre-PWA World Champion from 1976 to 1979, PWA Overall World Champion from 1983 to 1987, and PWA Wave World Champion in 1988, 1989, and 1991.

- Bjorn Dunkerbeck: the successor to Naish, he dominated competition for many years in the late 1980s and 1990s. Twelve time PWA Overall World Champion.
- Stephan van den Berg, world champion 1980-1983, winner first Olympic windsurfing contest in 1984.
- Ricardo Campello: A freestyle innovator, he created many new difficult moves, PWA Freestyle World Champion in 2003, 2004, and 2005.
- Kauli Seadi: Pioneered freestyle manoeuvers in wave competition. Ranked first in PWA Wave competition in 2005.
- Karin Jaggi: Multiple PWA World Champion in freestyle, wave, speed competition, 1990s and 2000s.
- Natalie Lelievre: Overall World Champion, 1984, 1985.
- Daida Moreno: PWA Wave World Champion, 2000-2005, Freestyle World Champion 2003-2006.
- Iballa Moreno: PWA Wave World Champion, 2006. Twin sister of Daida Moreno.
- Jason Polakow: PWA Wave World Champion, 1997, 1998.
- Kevin Pritchard: PWA Wave World Champion, 2006, PWA 1st overall ranking, 2000.
- Nik Baker: Three-time PWA Wave World Vice-Champion, six-time Indoor World Champion.

■

(from Wikipidia free Encyclopedia)

Index